Social Comput

Principles, Netwo

and Applicati

Social Computing: Principles, Networks and Applications

Edited by
Melva Sawyer

STATES
ACADEMIC PRESS
www.statesacademicpress.com

Published by States Academic Press,
109 South 5th Street,
Brooklyn, NY 11249, USA

ISBN: 978-1-63989-486-4

Cataloging-in-Publication Data

Social computing : principles, networks and applications / edited by Melva Sawyer.
    p. cm.
Includes bibliographical references and index.
ISBN 978-1-63989-486-4
1. Computer systems--Social aspects. 2. Online social networks.
3. Information technology--Social aspects. 4. Internet--Social aspects. I. Sawyer, Melva.
QA76 .S63 2022
004--dc23

For information on all States Academic Press publications
visit our website at www.statesacademicpress.com

Contents

Preface

The systems that support the accumulation, processing and distribution of information across social collectives, fall under the umbrella of social computing. It is a branch of computer science that lies at the intersection of computational systems and social behavior. Social computing involves the recreation of social conventions and social contexts by using software and technology. There are several technologically and socially oriented principles of social computing such as collective intelligence, network effects, lightweight models, unbounded collaboration, etc. The computational systems which support social interactions among groups of people are known as social software. Some of the examples of social software are social media, blogs and online gaming. Groups of people can interact with each other via these computing systems in a variety of ways. The ever growing need of advanced technology is the reason that has fueled the research in the field of social computing in recent times. This book brings forth some of the most innovative concepts and elucidates the unexplored aspects of social computing. It is a resource guide for experts as well as students.

The information contained in this book is the result of intensive hard work done by researchers in this field. All due efforts have been made to make this book serve as a complete guiding source for students and researchers. The topics in this book have been comprehensively explained to help readers understand the growing trends in the field.

I would like to thank the entire group of writers who made sincere efforts in this book and my family who supported me in my efforts of working on this book. I take this opportunity to thank all those who have been a guiding force throughout my life.

Editor

A strategic model for network formation

Omid Atabati[1][†][*] and Babak Farzad[2][†]

*Correspondence:
oatabati@ucalgary.ca
[†]Equal contributor
[1] Department of Economics,
University of Calgary, 2500
University Drive NW, Calgary, AB
T2N 1N4, Canada
Full list of author information is
available at the end of the article

Abstract

We study the dynamics of a game-theoretic network formation model that yields large-scale small-world networks. So far, mostly stochastic frameworks have been utilized to explain the emergence of these networks. On the other hand, it is natural to seek for game-theoretic network formation models in which links are formed due to strategic behaviors of individuals rather than based on probabilities. Inspired by Even-Dar and Kearns' model (NIPS 19: 385-392, 2007), we consider a more realistic framework in which the cost of establishing each link is dynamically determined during the course of the game. Moreover, players are allowed to put transfer payments on the formation and maintenance of links. Also, they must pay a maintenance cost to sustain their direct links during the game. We show that there is a small diameter of at most four in the general set of equilibrium networks in our model. We achieved an economic mechanism and its dynamic process for individuals which firstly, unlike the earlier model, the outcomes of players' interactions or the equilibrium networks are guaranteed to exist. Furthermore, these networks coincide with the outcome of pairwise Nash equilibrium in network formation. Secondly, it generates large-scale networks that have a rational and strategic microfoundation and demonstrate the main characterization of small degree of separation in real-life social networks. Moreover, we provide a network formation simulation that generates small-world networks.

Keywords: Network formation; Linking game with transfer payments; Pairwise stability; Pairwise Nash equilibrium; Small-world phenomenon

Introduction

In recent years, networks have been extensively studied mostly in terms of their structure but also their formation and dynamics. Structural characteristics of various networks, which emerge from disciplines, such as economics, computer science, sociology, biology, and physics, have been investigated. Many of these networks, in spite of their different origins, indicate large commonalities among their key structural properties, such as small diameter, high clustering coefficient, and heavy-tailed degree distribution which are often quantified by power-law probability distributions. Hence, it is an exciting challenge to study network formation models capable of explaining how and why these structural commonalities both occur and evolve. The series of experiments by Milgram in the 1960s [2] were among the pioneering works that quantified the *small-world phenomenon*[a] and introduced the 'six degree of separation'. Recent experiments [3] showed that today's online social networks such as Facebook indicate that the degree of separation (for almost any two individuals in a given database) must be even smaller than 4.

The *small-world model* by Watts and Strogatz [4] was one of the first models that generates networks with small diameter. This work was followed by Kleinberg's stochastic model [5] that was located in a grid graph. It introduced a process that adds links with distance d to the grid with a probability proportional to $1/d^\alpha$. These models, however, can not be applicable when there is a strategical purpose in players' making or losing their connections. In these cases, players, which are represented by vertices, strategically establish and sever their connections to obtain an advantageous position in their social network. Hence, we refer to a class of *game-theoretic network formation*, also known as strategic network formation (see [6,7] for comprehensive surveys). Models in this class are in their early efforts. They generally assume that players make connections based on a utility maximization and treat the network as the equilibrium result of the strategic interactions among players.

Our contribution

Our game-theoretic network formation model is mainly inspired by Even-Dar and Kearns (EK model) [1]. In their model, players (i.e., vertices) seek to minimize their collective distances to all other players. The network formation starts from a seed grid. Also, the cost of establishing each link in this model is considered to be the grid distance between the endpoint players of that link and the power of α, which is the parameter of the model. Hence, their model uses a *fixed link-pricing* for each link. Both link creation and link severance are considered unilateral by players. In addition, the equilibrium is defined in terms of *link stability*: no players benefit from altering a single link in their link decisions. The EK model achieves small diameter link stable networks within the threshold of $\alpha = 2$. However, they faced an unbounded diameter that grows with the number of players, when $\alpha > 2$.

We define three types of costs for links: (i) the link-price, (ii) the maintenance cost, and (iii) the transfer payment. The link-price p_{ij} is the price of establishing link ij. Only the initiator of the connection would bear its payment. It is a one-time charge when establishing the link. We introduce a new viewpoint to this game that better echoes with reality by constructing a *dynamic link-pricing*. When characterizing the formation of a network, the involved dynamics is a crucial and determining element. We aim to effectuate the impact of this dynamics in our model with the revised link-pricing. We update the used distances of each pair of players in the related link-prices from the current network rather than sticking with the initial grid distances.

In addition, we introduce maintenance costs to make the model more real where a player can give up her payment and sever her connection, if she will be better off by doing so. Also, it is reasonable to assume that refunding the link-prices may not be possible in lots of real-world scenarios. Hence, maintenance costs make the link severance scenario well-defined. In our model, player i is charged for all of its incident links by considering recurring maintenance costs c_{ij}. In other words, for each decision made in the game, players should take the maintenance cost of their incident links into their consideration. Lastly, we allow individuals to put transfer or side payments on their links. Transfers are a sort of communication between players for their connections. In fact, without transfer payments, many agreements on these connections would simply never exist.

We use the myopic notion of pairwise stability with direct and indirect transfers (PS^t)[b] as our equilibrium notion. This notion has the advantage of being compatible with the cooperative and bilateral nature of link formation. Moreover, the pairwise stability has the desirable simplicity required for analyzing players' behaviors under this notion[c].

On the other hand, due to the bilateral agreement for any link formation, the typical notion of Nash equilibria have some drawbacks in terms of coordination failures, e.g., an empty network is always a Nash equilibrium. In other words, Nash equilibria networks can contain some mutually beneficial link(s) that are left aside. To solve this coordination problem when employing Nash equilibria, the notion of pairwise Nash stability[d] was introduced. Pairwise Nash stable (PNS^t) networks are at the intersection of the set of Nash equilibrium networks and the set of pairwise stable networks.

In this paper, we not only guarantee the existence of pairwise stable networks but also demonstrate that, in our model, the set of pairwise stable networks coincide with the set of pairwise Nash stable networks. Finally, we show that the general set of equilibrium networks exhibits a short diameter of at most 4. The rest of this paper is organized as follows. In the 'Preliminaries' section, we explain the required preliminaries and provide the setup of our model. 'Fixed link-pricing model' section contains an analysis and extension to the EK model. We then provide the main results for our grid-based model with the dynamic link-pricing and transfer payments in the 'Dynamic link-pricing model with transfer payments' section. In the 'Simulations' section, we present the outcome of a network formation simulation that we carried out.

Preliminaries

The network and players. Let $N = \{1, \ldots, n\}$ be the set of n players forming a network G. Network G is undirected and includes a list of pairs of players who are linked to each other. Link $ij \in G$ indicates that player i and player j are linked in G. Let G^N denote the complete network. The set $\mathcal{G} = \{G \subseteq G^N\}$ consists of all possible networks on N. We define network G_0 to be the starting network of the game, which is also called the *seed network*. The set of player i's neighbors in G is $\mathcal{N}_i(G) = \{j | ij \in G\}$. Similarly, $\mathcal{L}_i(G) = \{ij \in G \mid j \in \mathcal{N}_i(G)\}$ denotes the set of links, which are incident with player i in G. If l is a subset of $\mathcal{L}_i(G)$, then $G - l$ is the network resulted by removing the existing links in the set l from G. Similarly, if $l = \{ij \mid j \notin \mathcal{N}_i(G), j \neq i\}$, then the network $G + l$ is obtained by adding the links in set l to G.

The *utility* of network G for player i is given by a function $u_i : G \to \mathbb{R}^+$. Let $\mathbf{u}$ denote the vector of utility functions $\mathbf{u} = (u_1, \ldots, u_n)$. So, $\mathbf{u} : \mathcal{G} \to \mathbb{R}^N$. Also, the value of a network, $v(G)$, is the summation of all players' utilities in the network G, i.e., $v(G) = \sum_{i=1}^{n} u_i(G)$. For any network G and any subset $l_i(G) \subseteq \mathcal{L}_i(G)$, the marginal utility for a player i and a set of links $l_i(G)$ is denoted by $mu_i(G, l_i(G)) = u_i(G) - u_i(G - l_i(G))$.

Strategies, transfer payments. Each player $i \in N$ announces an action vector of transfer payment $\mathbf{t}^i \in \mathbb{R}^{n(n-1)/2}$. The entries in this vector indicate the transfer payment that player i offers (to pay) or demands (to gain) on the link jk. If $i \in \{j, k\}$, then we call it a *direct* transfer payment. Otherwise, it is called an *indirect* transfer payment. Typically, individuals can make demands (negative transfers) or offers (non-negative transfers) on their direct connections. However, they can only make offers (and not demands) on the indirect transfer payments[e]. In addition, a link jk is formed if and only if $\sum_{i \in N} t^i_{jk} \geq 0$. Thus, the profile of strategies or the announced vectors of transfer payments for all players is defined: $\mathbf{t} = (\mathbf{t}^1, \ldots, \mathbf{t}^n)$. Consequently, the network G, which is formed by this profile of strategies $\mathbf{t}$, can be denoted as follows: $G(\mathbf{t}) = \left\{ jk \mid \sum_{i \in N} t^i_{jk} \geq 0, \text{where } j, k \in N \right\}$.

The payoff function. The *distance* between a pair of players i and j in G, denoted by $d_G(i, j)$, is defined as the length of a shortest path between i and j in G. Similar to the EK model, players seek to minimize their total distances to all players. This benefit would be considered for each player with respect to the network G and links benefit both endpoints[f]. The link-price is defined to be $p_{ij} = d_G(i,j)^\alpha$ for $\alpha > 0$. The link-price function is non-decreasing and follows Kleinberg's stochastic model. Also, function c_{ij} denotes the maintenance cost for the link ij. The *utility function* of player i is the negative of her total distances and links expenses and is defined as follows:

$$u_i(G(\mathbf{t})) = -\sum_{j \in N} d_{G(\mathbf{t})}(i,j) - \sum_{j \in \mathcal{N}_i} (p_{ij} + c_{ij}) - \sum_{jk \in G(\mathbf{t})} t^i_{jk}. \tag{1}$$

The dynamic process. The following notion is stated from [15] that motivates the desired dynamics for our analysis.

Definition 1. An improving path represents a sequence of changes from one network to another. The changes can emerge when individuals create or sever a single link based on the improvement in the resulting network relative to the current network.

In each round of the game, one player adapts her strategy with respect to the current state of the network. We assume a random meeting mechanism for vertices (randomly choosing a pair of players), but we start with a seed network instead of an empty network [16,17]. If two networks G and G' differ in exactly one link, they are said to be *adjacent* networks. Also, if there exists an improving path from G to G', then G' *defeats* G.

The equilibrium strategies. In every equilibrium profile of strategies $\mathbf{t}^*$, there is no excess in the offer of transfer payments. A transfer payment t^{*i}_{ij} is negative if and only if maintaining the existing link ij is not beneficial for i. In other words, i's utility from network G is smaller that her utility from network $G - ij$. We refer to this difference as a utility gap. Player i can only use a transfer payment equal to her utility gap. Hence, for an equilibrium profile of strategies t^{*i}_{jk} that forms equilibrium network G, $G(\mathbf{t}^*) = \left\{ jk \mid \sum_{i \in N} t^{*i}_{jk} = 0, j, k \in N \right\}$.

We would like to indicate that other generalization of transfers' distribution among players are not among the main focuses of this paper[g].

The Definitions of equilibrium notions are as follows:

Definition 2. A network G is pairwise stable with transfers (PS^t) with respect to a profile of utility functions $\mathbf{u}$ and a profile of strategies $\mathbf{t}$ that creates network G if

(a) $ij \in G \implies u_i(G) \geq u_i(G - ij)$ as well as $u_j(G) \geq u_j(G - ij)$,

(b) $ij \notin G \implies u_i(G) \geq u_i(G + ij)$ as well as $u_j(G) \geq u_j(G + ij)$.

Also, $\mathrm{PS}^t(u)$ denotes the family of pairwise stable networks with transfers.

A pure strategy profile $\mathbf{t}^* = (\mathbf{t}^{*1}, \ldots, \mathbf{t}^{*n})$ forms a *Nash equilibrium* in the linking game with transfers if $u_i\left(G\left(\mathbf{t}^i, \mathbf{t}^{*-i}\right)\right) \leq u_i\left(G\left(\mathbf{t}^*\right)\right)$ holds for all $i \in N$ and all $t_i \in T_i$, where

$\mathbf{t}^*_{-i}$ is the equilibrium strategy for all players other than i, and T_i is the set of all available strategies for i. We can also indicate that in the context of network formation, a network G is Nash stable if $\forall i \in N$ and $\forall l_i(G) \subseteq \mathcal{L}_i(G)$: $u_i(G) \geq u_i(G - l_i(G))$.

Definition 3. A pure strategy profile $\mathbf{t}^* = (\mathbf{t}^{*1}, \ldots, \mathbf{t}^{*n})$ forms a *pairwise Nash equilibrium* in the linking game with transfers if

1. It is a Nash equilibrium, and
2. There does not exist any $ij \notin G(\mathbf{t}^*)$, and $t \in T$ such that

    (a) $u_i\left(G\left(\mathbf{t}^i_{ij}, \mathbf{t}^j_{ij}, \mathbf{t}^*_{-ij}\right)\right) \geq u_i(G(\mathbf{t}^*))$,
    (b) $u_j\left(G\left(\mathbf{t}^i_{ij}, \mathbf{t}^j_{ij}, \mathbf{t}^*_{-ij}\right)\right) \geq u_j(G(\mathbf{t}^*))$, and
    (c) at least one of (1) or (2) holds strictly,

where $\mathbf{t}^*_{-ij}$ includes all players' strategies in $\mathbf{t}^*$ except player i.

A tutorial example. Suppose that Figure 1 shows a sub-network of a network G that is obtained through an improving path. Also, assume that player i considers establishing a link to player j in the next random meeting. For this example, let us assume $\alpha = 2$ and $c_{ij} = 10$ for all i and j. Furthermore, $B_i(G+ij, ij) = -\sum_{k \neq i}\left(d_{G+ij}(i,k) - d_G(i,k)\right)$ defines the benefit of reduced distances in the whole network G that player i is received after adding link ij to G. We assume that $B_i(G+ij, ij) = 30$ and $B_j(G+ij, ij) = 5$ in this example.

According to the dynamic link-pricing, $p_{ij} = 3^2 = 9$. First, we can verify that player i has an incentive to buy link ij, as $B_i(G + ij, ij) = 30 \geq 9 + 10 = 19$. However, there is no advantage for player j in this linking, as $B_j(G + ij, ij) = 5 < 10$. Therefore, player j must demand the transfer payment $t^j_{ij} = -5$ that makes her indifferent regarding this linkage. Player i can offer the transfer payment $t^i_{ij} = 10 - 5 = 5$ to player j, since creating ij is still beneficial for i, as $30 \geq 5 + 19 = 24$. Consequently, link ij can be added to G and network G' is achieved along the improving path of game. The network formation continues until a pairwise stable network with transfers is reached. Note that we can also

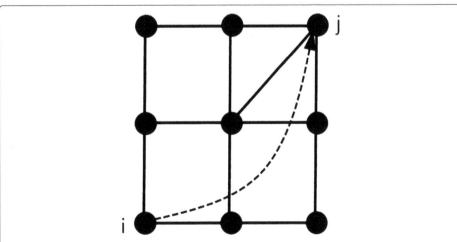

Figure 1 An example of a sub-network from network G during the dynamic process.

consider the indirect transfers that other players may offer for this linkage, which is not stated in this example for simplicity.

Fixed link-pricing model

In this section, we study the EK model [1] and consider an extension to this model. This also helps us to provide some insights regarding our results in the 'Dynamic link-pricing model with transfer payments' section.

The presence of cycles

The EK model takes a $\sqrt{n} \times \sqrt{n}$ grid as its seed network. It defines the link-price $p_{ij} = d_{G_0}(i,j)^\alpha$ for $\alpha > 0$ and defines $d_{G_0}(i,j)$ to be the grid distance of i and j. Consequently, the link prices are fixed during the course of the game. Furthermore, this model defines the set $\mathbf{s}_i \in \{0,1\}^{n-1}$ to be the action set of player i such that s_{ij} is one when player i creates a link to player j. Also, each link benefits both endpoints and $s_{ij} = 1$ if $s_{ji} = 1$. The utility function for player $i \in N$ is $u_i(G(\mathbf{s})) = -\sum_{j \neq i} d_{G_0}(i,j) - \sum_{j \in \mathcal{N}_i} p_{ij}$.

In the EK model, link creation is unilateral. Moreover, creation of a link only requires the agreement of at least one of the endpoint players of the link. This is in contrast to our model in which the presence of each link needs the consent of both players. Also, there is no transfer payment and maintenance cost in this model. Players can receive a refund of the link-prices given the severance of links. This model uses the notion of link stability, where link stable networks are immune against unilateral creation or severance of a single link by each player.

A problem that can arise in this model concerns the fact that the network formation may not converge to a link stable network. In other words, there exists the possibility for the formation of cycles in the evolving networks during this network formation model, as it is defined in the following.

Definition 4. A cycle C is a set of networks $(G_1, \ldots, G_k)$ such that for any pair of networks $G_i, G_j \in C$, there exists an improving path connecting G_i to G_j. In addition, a cycle C is a *closed cycle*, if for all networks $G \in C$, there does not exist an improving path leading to a network $G' \notin C$.

Generally, the presence of negative externalities can be seen as one of the potential reasons in the formation of cycles in linking games. Consider the following grid-based example shown in Figure 2. In this example, we can observe the formation of a cycle in the game.

Assume that $48 < 3^\alpha < 49$. First, it is easy to verify that player s has an incentive to create link st. Now, a cycle of strategical updates may be formed as follows. Player u saves 57 in $\sum_{i=1}^n d_{G(s)}(u, v_i)$ as it can be verified that the distance to u of nine players in area i is reduced by 1 and the distance to u of 24 players in area ii is reduced by 2. So, (I) player u has an incentive to buy link uv, as $p_{uv} = d_{G_0}(u,v)^\alpha = 3^\alpha < 9 + 48 = 57$. Then, with similar observations, it can be seen that the following strategical changes will be made in this order. (II) Player w buys link wu as $p_{wu} = d_{G_0}(w,u)^\alpha = 3^\alpha < 49$. (III) Player u is no longer willing to maintain link uv, as with existing link wu, it has a benefit of only 48. Therefore, u returns the link uv. (IV) Player w has no incentive to retain link wu, as with the removal of link uv, it has a benefit of only 34. So, w returns the

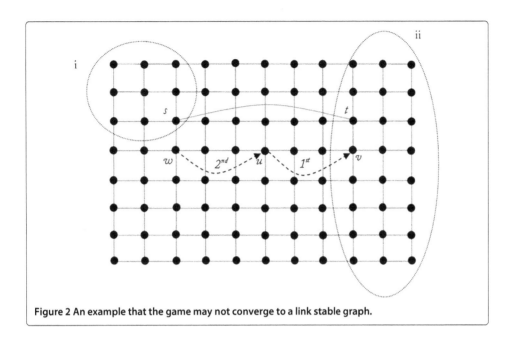

Figure 2 An example that the game may not converge to a link stable graph.

link wu. Thus, a cycle of steps (I) to (IV) may be formed and the game does not converge to stability. The example can be expanded to a large-scale grid as well. We note that player w, by establishing wu, creates a negative externality for u. Since it causes a reduction in player u's utility, u decides to sever uv that in overall leads to the formation of a cycle.

Forbidding link severance

In this model, players should be allowed to sever only those links that they themselves have purchased. However, this issue is not clear in the notion of link stability[h]. Let assume an extension of the EK model with forbidding severing links. Forbidding players to sever their links, although limits the applicability of model, makes the convergence of equilibrium networks possible for the network formation.

   Proposition 1. *Under the assumption of forbidding link severance in the EK model, the convergence of network formation to link stability is guaranteed.*

   Proof. When there is no link severance, the existence of negative externalities for players is ruled out. In other words, there is no player whose utility can be hurt during the game. Thus, the total value of the network is increased by each change during the dynamic process. This points to the *exact pairwise monotonicity*, introduced by Jackson and Watts [15], which guarantees the existence of stable networks. The proof of Theorem 1 can be adapted to imply Proposition 1.   □

Dynamic link-pricing model with transfer payments

Existence of pairwise stable network with transfers

In all game-theoretic problems, one of the primary questions concerns the existence of equilibria or stable states. This question in the framework of network formation is translated to the existence of pairwise stable networks and have been first addressed by Jackson and Watts [15]. We show that their arguments can be extended and adapted in our model. As a result, we guarantee the existence of pairwise stable network with transfers in our model.

While improving paths that start from a seed network may end in an equilibrium network, it is also possible to find the formation of cycles as the result of an improving path. Jackson and Watts showed that in any network formation model there exists either a pairwise stable network or a closed cycle. Their argument is based on the fact that a network is pairwise stable if and only if it does not lie on an improving path to any other network. We provide the following lemma and refer to the work of Jackson and Watts [15] for its proof, where the exact arguments can be applied for the notion of PS^t in our model.

Lemma 1. *In the network formation model with transfer payments, there exists either an equilibrium network from* $\text{PS}^t(u)$ *or a closed cycle of networks.*

Theorem 1. *In the linking game with direct and indirect transfers given the utility function in* (1),

(a)   *There are no cycles,*

(b)   *There exists at least one pairwise stable network* $(\text{PS}^t(u))$.

Proof. We can rule out the existence of cycles in a network formation model if we show that the following holds: for any two networks G and G', G' defeats G if and only if $v(G') > v(G)$ and G and G' are adjacent[i]. We can briefly argue that our linking game satisfies this condition. Since the direct and indirect transfer payments between players prevent the situations, where a player's utility can get hurt by actions (link addition or deletion) of others. In fact, this is one of the main function of transfers. Therefore, the value of networks through each improving path must be increased. Conversely, if G and G' are adjacent in an improving path such that $v(G') > v(G)$, G' must defeat G, where G is a network in the cycle.

Now, since there are finitely many networks that can be reached through the dynamic process, if there is a cycle, then the exact pairwise monotonicity of our linking game implies $v(G) > v(G)$; contradiction. Ruling out the existence of cycles along with Lemma 1 guarantees the existence of at least one pairwise stable network with transfer payments. □

Strictly pairwise stability

Now, we show that given the utility function $u(.)$ in (1), the family of networks in $\text{PS}^t(u)$ satisfies the notion of strictly pairwise stability. It is first described by Chakrabarti and Gilles [20], which is a variation of pairwise stability.

Definition 5. A network G is *strictly pairwise stable* for **u** if

(a) $\forall i \in N$ and $\forall l_i(G) \subseteq \mathcal{L}_i(G), u_i(G) \geq u_i(G - l_i(G))$,

(a) $\forall i \in N, ij \notin G$ implies $u_i(G + ij) < u_i(G)$ as well as $u_j(G + ij) < u_j(G)$.

In order to progress our argument, we need to provide the following definition and lemma.

Definition 6. Let $\alpha \geq 0$. A utility function $u(.)$ is α-*submodular in own current links* on $\mathcal{A} \subseteq \mathcal{G}$ if $\forall i \in N, G \in \mathcal{A}$, and $l_i(G) \subseteq \mathcal{L}_i(G)$, it holds that $mu_i(G, l_i(G)) \geq \alpha \sum_{ij \in l_i(G)} mu_i(G, ij)$.

The case $\alpha = 1$ corresponds to submodularity, also called superadditivity in [9].

Lemma 2. *The utility defined in* (1) *is submodular in own current links.*

Proof. The proof is inspired by the arguments in [18]. First, we show the related inequality in Definition 6 holds for the case when the subset $l_i(G)$ consists of two distinct links ij and ik, which is indicated in the below inequality:

$$mu_i(G, ij + ik) \geq mu_i(G, ij) + mu_i(G, ik) \tag{2}$$

If we consider any player such as m in network G, the distance between i and m ($d_G(i, m)$) contributes to the distance expenses in i's utility. It is important to note that removing any link such as ij or ik from the network G cannot decrease this distance; however, if the removed link belongs to the shortest path between i and m in G, then the distance would be increased. This argument can be extended to the severance of two links such as ij and ik from G.

$$d_G(i, m) \leq d_{G-ij}(i, m) \leq d_{G-ij-ik}(i, m) \tag{3}$$

$$d_G(i, m) \leq d_{G-ik}(i, m) \leq d_{G-ij-ik}(i, m) \tag{4}$$

In computing the marginal utilities of networks $G - ik$, $G - ij$, and $G - ij - ik$, we should note that the link-prices of removed links cannot be refunded for player i:

$$mu_i(G, ij) = -\sum_{m \neq i} \left(d_G(i, m) - d_{G-ij}(i, m) \right) - c_{ij} - t_{ij}^i \tag{5}$$

$$mu_i(G, ik) = -\sum_{m \neq i} \left(d_G(i, m) - d_{G-ik}(i, m) \right) - c_{ik} - t_{ik}^i \tag{6}$$

$$mu_i(G, ij + ik) = -\sum_{m \neq i} \left(d_G(i, m) - d_{G-ij-ik}(i, m) \right) - c_{ij} - c_{ik} - t_{ij}^i - t_{ik}^i \tag{7}$$

According to Inequalities (3) and (4), we can simply imply the Inequality (2). Finally, we can easily extend this argument for any subset of links $l_i(G)$.   □

Proposition 2. *Given the utility functions $u(.)$ defined in* (1), $\mathrm{PS}^t(u) = P^\star(u)$.

Proof. According to the definitions, it can be derived that $P^\star(u) \subseteq \mathrm{PS}^t(u)$. We further prove that $\mathrm{PS}^t(u) \subseteq P^\star(u)$.

Let $G \in \mathrm{PS}^t(u)$, then for any link $ij \notin G$, neither player i nor j can benefit from creating link ij. This is one of the impact of allowing players to put transfer payments on the links. Thus, pairwise stable networks with transfers satisfy the second condition in the Definition 5. Further, we know that $\forall i \in N$ and $\forall j \in l_i(G)$, $u_i(G - ij) \leq u_i(G)$. Let assume there are k links in the subset $l_i(G)$. Hence, $\sum_{ij \in l_i(G)} u_i(G - ij) \leq (k)u_i(G)$. On the other hand, based on Lemma 2, $\sum_{ij \in l_i(G)} mu_i(G, ij) \leq mu_i(G, l_i(G))$. This implies:

$$(k)u_i(G) - \sum_{ij \in l_i(G)} u_i(G - ij) \leq u_i(G) - u_i(G - l_i(G)). \tag{8}$$

Since the left-hand side of Inequality (8) is positive, the expression in the right-hand side must be positive too. So, this proves the first condition in the Definition 5 for the networks in $PS^t(G)$. □

Convergence to pairwise Nash stability

Calvó-Armengol and Ilkiliç [13] show the equivalency of pairwise stable networks and pairwise Nash stable networks, given a utility function that is α-submodular. It targets the simple observation that given a α-submodular utility function, if a player does not benefit from severing any single link, then she does not benefit from cutting any subset of links simultaneously as well. A similar argument can be adapted to our linking game with transfers as well. So, we provide the following proposition without proof.

Proposition 3. *Given a profile of utility functions $\mathbf{u}$ in (1) in a linking game with transfers, $PS^t(u) = PNS^t(u)$.*

Small diameter in equilibrium networks

We take a large-scale $\sqrt{n} \times \sqrt{n}$ grid as the seed network in this model. In order to prove the main result for the diameter of the equilibrium networks, we provide the following lemmas.

Let $T_{G(t)}(i, j)$ be the set of players that use link ij in their unique shortest paths to i in the network $G(t)$: $T_{G(t)}(i, j) = \{k \in N \mid d_{G'(t)}(i, k) > d_{G(t)}(i, k)\}$, where $G' = G - ij$.

Lemma 3. *Let $G(t)$ be an equilibrium network and $i, j \in N$ be an arbitrary pair of players in this network. If $ij \notin G(t)$, then $|T_{G(t)}(i, j)| < \dfrac{d_{G(t)}(i, j)^\alpha + c_{ij} + t_{ij}^i}{d_{G(t)}(i, j) - 1}$.*

Proof. Since i and j are not linked in the equilibrium network, the benefit of establishing ij has to be less than its linking costs for i and j. On the other hand, $T_{G(t)}(i, j)$ represents the set of players that creates a part of this benefit by reducing the distance $d_{G(t)}(i, j)$ between i and j to 1. Hence, we can state that paying $d_{G(t)}(i, j)^\alpha + c_{ij} + t_{ij}^i$, which is necessary for establishing ij, cannot be beneficial for player i. As a result, $|T_{G(t)}(i, j)| \left(d_{G(t)}(i, j)-\right) < d_{G(t)}(i, j)^\alpha + c_{ij} + t_{ij}^i$. □

Remark 1. For any $i, j \in N$, c_{ji} can be noted as an upper bound for the transfer payment t_{ij}^i. Hence, if $c = \max_{\forall i, j \in N}(c_{jk})$, it is an upper bound for any direct transfer payment in the network.

Lemma 4. *In any equilibrium network $G(t)$, for any player $i \in N$, let $S_i^d = \{k \in N \mid d_{G(t)}(i, k) \leq d\}$. Then, $|S_i^d| \left(1 + \dfrac{d^\alpha + 2c}{d - 1}\right) \geq n$, where $c = \max_{\forall i, j \in N}(c_{ij})$.*

Proof. The set S_i^d consists of players in the neighborhood of i within a distance at most d. Furthermore, for each of these players such as k in the set S_i^d, according to Lemma 3, we consider the set $T_{G(\mathbf{t})}(i,k)$. All players outside of this set should use one of players such as k in their shortest path to i. As a result, we can cover all players outside the set S_i^d by allocating a set $T_{G(\mathbf{t})}(i,k)$ to i for all players in set S_i^d. By doing so, an upper bound of $|T_{G(\mathbf{t})}(i,k)||S_i^d| + |S_i^d|$ for the number players in network (n) is achieved.

In order to obtain an upper bound for the set $T_{G(\mathbf{t})}(i,k)$ in wide range of different possible choices for i and k, we define c to be the maximum maintenance cost for all possible links in network. According to Remark 1, this is an upper bound for all the possible direct transfer payments as well. Hence, $|T_{G(\mathbf{t})}(i,k)| \leq \dfrac{d^\alpha + 2c}{d-1}$. By substituting the upper bounds of $T_{G(\mathbf{t})}(i,k)$ and S_i^d in $|T_{G(\mathbf{t})}(i,k)||S_i^d| + |S_i^d| \geq n$, the desired inequality can be achieved.   □

Lemma 5 shows an upper bound for the set $|S_i^2|$.

Lemma 5. $|S_i^2| \leq \Delta^\alpha + 2c/k\left(\Delta - \left(h_1 + h_2(g_1 + 2) + h_3(2f_1 + f_2 + 3)\right)\right)$, where Δ is the diameter of any equilibrium network $G(\mathbf{t})$, and $0 \leq k, f_i, g_i, h_i \leq 1$ denote some fractions of players in the set S_i^2 based on their reduced distances to player i when forming the link ij. Also, $f_1 + f_2 + f_3 = g_1 + g_2 = h_1 + h_2 + h_3 = 1$.

Proof. Let G be an arbitrary instance from the set of equilibrium networks in our model, which are the set of pairwise stable networks with transfer ($G \in \mathrm{PS}^t(u)$), given the utility function $u(.)$ in (1). Also, let $\mathbf{t}$ be the the profile of strategies for players that forms G. Further, assume that the largest distance between any two players (or diameter) in network G exists between two players i and j. We denote Δ to be the size this distance. Note that the pair of i and j is not necessarily unique.

Based on the stable state, we can imply that creation ij is not beneficial for neither i nor j. If j wants to establish a link to i, $|S_i^2|$ is a lower bound for the j's benefit that comes from the reduced distances to players in S_i^2. This set includes i itself and two subsets of players that are in distance 1 (type 1) and 2 (type 2) from i. First, let k represents players in S_i^2 such that their distances to j can be reduced by adding ij, as a fraction with respect to all players in $|S_i^2|$. Moreover, let h_1 represents player i itself as a fraction with respect to all players in $|S_i^2|$. By establishing ij, j's distance to i reduced by $\Delta - 1$.

Furthermore, let h_2 and h_3 represent the fractions of the number of type 1 players and type 2 players, respectively, in S_i^2. Their reduced distances for j is computed according to the initial distances of these two types of players in S_i^2 from j. Among the type 1 players, there are two subsets of players that g_1 and g_2 are their fractions with distance of $\Delta - 1$ and Δ from j, respectively. Furthermore, in type 2 players, there are three subsets of players in terms of their distance from j with fractions of f_1, f_2, and f_3 that are in distance of $\Delta - 2, \Delta - 1$, and Δ from j, respectively.   □

Theorem 2. *For a sufficiently large network, there is a small diameter of at most 4 for any equilibrium network in the dynamic link-pricing model with transfer payments.*

Proof. Based on our arguments in Lemma 4 and Lemma 5, we can state that

$$n \leq (1 + 2^\alpha + 2c)(\Delta^\alpha + 2c)/k\left(\Delta - \left(h_1 + h_2(g_1 + 2) + h_3(2f_1 + f_2 + 3)\right)\right). \qquad (9)$$

For sufficiently large network, when the diameter is greater than $\lfloor h_1 + h_2(g_1 + 2) + h_3(2f_1 + f_2 + 3) \rfloor$, it contradicts Inequality (9). Clearly, we can specify that $3 \leq 2f_1 + f_2 + 3 \leq 5$ and $2 \leq g_1 + 2 \leq 3$. Thus in this case, the upper bound for the diameter is the weighted average of 1, $2f_1 + f_2 + 3$, and $g_1 + 2$, and it is surely smaller than 5. Therefore, the diameter cannot be bigger than 4 for any choice of parameters. However, we cannot have the same claim for smaller diameter and rule out their possibility. □

Simulations

We carried out a set of simulations that improves the EK model by implementing the dynamic link-pricing and a fixed maintenance cost c. These simulations generate networks that show (*i*) a small diameter of at most 4, (*ii*) a high clustering coefficient (with respect to edge density), and (*iii*) a power-law degree distribution. The dynamical simulations are implemented on a grid with $n \approx 1,000$. At each iteration of the dynamic process, two players i and j are chosen uniformly at random. Then, with probability $1/2$ player i considers establishing a link to j (if $ij \notin G$) and with probability $1/2$, she considers severing her link to j (if $ij \in G$). Note that these considerations are such that in each random meeting, the decision for adding (or removing) a link is implemented based on the corresponded benefit and cost to that link with respect to the current state of the evolved network. We used the notion of link stability. In this set of simulations, we aim to indicate our improvements and extension on the EK model in order to generate small-world networks. Note that by using the dynamic link-prices, the emergence of a small diameter of at most 4 in link stable networks are directly implied similarly by our argument in the 'Small diameter in equilibrium networks' section[j].

In many instances of our simulations, it can be seen as in Figure 3 that the degree distribution is a good estimation for the power-law degree distributions in the real-life social networks. Figure 3 shows the impact of parameters c and α on the degree distributions of resulting networks. The larger plots are the distributions where their vertical axis is the probability for degrees and their horizontal axis determines different values for the degree of nodes. The smaller plots are the log-log plots of these distributions. Their vertical axis are the logarithm of the number or the frequency for nodes with different values

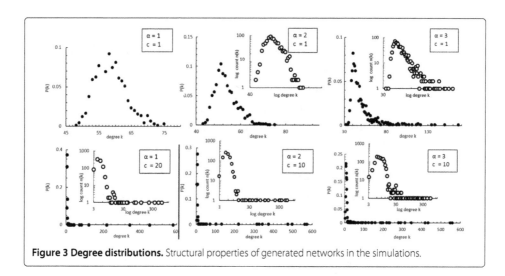

Figure 3 Degree distributions. Structural properties of generated networks in the simulations.

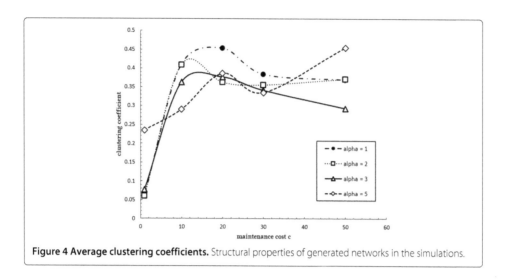

Figure 4 Average clustering coefficients. Structural properties of generated networks in the simulations.

for their degree. Moreover, the appearance of few high degree nodes represents the few hubs in these networks.

Figure 4 demonstrates the clustered structure of the link stable networks: a high average clustering coefficient is present in all instances after increasing the maintenance cost from $c = 1$. The high clustering in these networks can be highlighted by pointing out their small edge-density in the range from 0.007 for the network with $c = 50, \alpha = 5$ to 0.069 for the network with $c = 1$ and $\alpha = 1$. The diameter in all instances was either 3 or 4 as expected.

Endnotes
[a] The principle that individuals are all linked by short chains of connections and acquaintances.

[b] The pairwise stability is the major notion of stability that assumes myopic players and has been studied in related literature. In a linking game with transfers, it was first introduced as an extension in [8] and then developed in [9,10].

[c] Computing the best responses of players in Nash equilibria within some similar models [11,12] are proved to be NP-hard.

[d] See [9,10,13,14].

[e] This assumption is reasonable in our framework, since the formation of other links cannot hurt the utility of non-involved players with respect to the distance-based structure of our utility function in (1).

[f] See e.g. [8,10,12] for some application instances of distance-based payoff structures.

[g] See [18,19] for some instances of study in the case of bargaining between players on network. In fact, despite the rich literature in general for bargaining between players, bargaining on networks is in its early attempts.

[h] Adding a charging scheme for the maintenance of existing links is a reasonable extension that can resolve this issue, and it is studied in our model.

[i] This condition is denoted as exact pairwise monotonicity by Jackson and Watts.

[j] Note that although the existence of stable networks and convergence to the Nash outcomes would not be guaranteed in this assumption, we achieved a set of link stable networks by implementing many trials for different sets of α and c.

Competing interests
The authors declare that they have no competing interests.

Authors' contributions

OA contributed to the characterization of the model and theoretical arguments, and implemented the simulation. BF contributed to the formulation of the problem and the theoretical arguments. Both authors participated in the organization of this research, and read and approved the final manuscript.

Author details

[1]Department of Economics, University of Calgary, 2500 University Drive NW, Calgary, AB T2N 1N4, Canada. [2]Department of Mathematics, Brock University, 500 Glenridge Ave., St. Catharines, ON L2S 3A1, Canada.

References

1. Even-Dar E, Kearns M. A small world threshold for economic network formation. In: Advances in Neural Information Processing Systems 19. Cambridge, MA: MIT Press; 2007. p. 385–392.
2. Milgram S. The small world problem. Psychol. Today 1967;1:61–67.
3. Daraghmi EY, Yuan S. We are so close, less than 4 degrees separating you and me! Comput. Hum. Behav 2014;30: 273–285.
4. Watts D, Strogatz S. Collective dynamics of small-world networks. Nature 1998;393:440–442.
5. Kleinberg J. The small-world phenomenon: an algorithmic perspective. Symposium on the Theory of Computing. New York: Association of Computing Machinery; 2000, pp. 163–170.
6. De Martí J, Zenou Y. Social networks. Handbook of Philosophy of Social Science. London: SAGE Publications; 2011, pp. 339–361.
7. Jackson MO. Social and Economic Networks. Princeton, NJ: Princeton University Press; 2008.
8. Jackson MO, Wolinsky A. A strategic model of social and economic networks. J. Econ. Theory 1996;71:44–74.
9. Bloch F, Jackson MO. Definitions of equilibrium in network formation games. Int. J. Game Theory 2006;34(3):305–318.
10. Bloch F, Jackson MO. The formation of networks with transfers among players. J. Econ. Theory 2007;133(1):83–110.
11. Myerson R. Game Theory: Analysis of Conflict. Cambridge, MA: Harvard University Press; 1991.
12. Fabrikant A, Luthra A, Maneva EN, Papadimitriou C. H, Shenker S. On a network creation game. In: 22nd Annual ACM Symposium on Principles of Distributed Computing. New York: ACM Press; 2003. p. 347–351.
13. Calvó-Armengol A, Ilkiliç R. Pairwise-stability and Nash equilibria in network formation. Int. J. Game Theory 2009;38(1):51–79.
14. Hellman T. On the existence and uniqueness of pairwise stable networks. Int. J. Game Theory 2012;42:211–237.
15. Jackson MO, Watts A. The existence of pairwise stable networks. Seoul J. Econ 2001;14(3):299–321.
16. Watts A. A dynamic model of network formation. Games Econ. Behav 2001;34:331–341.
17. Jackson MO, Watts A. The evolution of social and economic networks. J. Econ. Theory 2002;106:265–295.
18. Gallo E. Essays in the economics of networks. PhD thesis, University of Oxford: Department of Economics; 2011.
19. Bayati M, Borgs C, Chayes J, Kanoria Y, Montanari A. Bargaining dynamics in exchange networks. Working Paper 2011.
20. Chakrabarti S, Gilles R. Network potentials. Rev. Econom. Des 2007;11(1):13–52.

2

Text normalization for named entity recognition in Vietnamese tweets

Vu H. Nguyen[1], Hien T. Nguyen[1*] and Vaclav Snasel[2]

*Correspondence:
hien@tdt.edu.vn
[1] Faculty of Information
Technology, Ton Duc Thang
University, Ho Chi Minh City,
Vietnam
Full list of author information
is available at the end of the
article

Abstract

Background: Named entity recognition (NER) is a task of detecting named entities in documents and categorizing them to predefined classes, such as person, location, and organization. This paper focuses on tweets posted on Twitter. Since tweets are noisy, irregular, brief, and include acronyms and spelling errors, NER in those tweets is a challenging task. Many approaches have been proposed to deal with this problem in tweets written in English, Germany, Chinese, etc., but none for Vietnamese tweets.

Methods: We propose a method that normalizes a tweet before taking as an input of a learning model for NER in Vietnamese tweets. The normalization step detects spelling errors in a tweet and corrects them using an improved Dice's coefficient or n-grams. A Support Vector Machine learning algorithm is employed to learn a classifier using six different types of features.

Results and Conclusion: We train our method on a training set consisting of more than 40,000 named entities and evaluate it on a testing set consisting of 3,186 named entities. The experimental results showed that our system achieves state-of-the-art performance with F1 score of 82.13%.

Keywords: Text normalization, Named entity recognition, Spelling error detection and correction

Background

In recent years, social networks have become very popular. It is easy for users to share their data using online social networks. Currently, Twitter is one of the most popular social networks. According to statistics from 2011, the number of tweets was up to 140 million per day.[1] With such a huge number of tweets being posted every day, effective extraction and processing of those data will be very beneficial, especially to information extraction applications.

Twitter provides an interactive environment that allows the users to create their own content through tweets. Since each tweet consists of only 140 characters, users tend to use acronyms, non-standard words, and social tokens. Therefore, the tweets contain many spelling errors, and this creates a significant challenge for named entity recognition (NER). Several recognition methods for named entities have been proposed for tweets in English and other languages [2, 17, 27, 31, 44]. Although there have been many

---

[1] https://blog.twitter.com/2011/numbers.

approaches proposed in formal texts for NER in the Vietnamese language, none is available for Vietnamese tweets. Thus, in this paper, we propose a method for NER in Vietnamese tweets to fill the gap. The system consists of three steps, i.e., (1) normalization of tweets by detecting and correcting spelling errors; (2) capitalization classifier; and (3) recognition of named entities. Table 1 shows an example of NER according to these three steps.

In this paper, we present the first attempt to provide NER capability in Vietnamese tweets, and this contribution has three components, i.e., (1) a method for the normalization of Vietnamese tweets based on dictionaries and Vietnamese vocabulary structures in combination with a language model; (2) a learning model for NER in Vietnamese tweets with six different types of features; and (3) a training set of more than 40,000 named entities and a testing set of 3186 named entities to evaluate the NER system of Vietnamese tweets.

The rest of this paper is organized as follows. The second section presents earlier work related to this effort. Our proposed method is presented in third section; fourth section is the experiments and their results. Our conclusions are presented in fifth section.

Related work

NER

Named entity recognition has been studied extensively on formal texts, such as news and authorized web content. Several approaches have been proposed using different learning models, such as condition random fields (CRF), maximum entropy model (MEM), hidden markov model (HMM), and support vector machines (SVM). In particular, Mayfield et al. [34] used SVM to estimate lattice transition probabilities for NER. McCallum and Li [35] applied a feature induction method for CRF to recognize named entities. A combination of a CRF model and latent semantics to recognize named entities was proposed in [18]. A method using soft-constrained inference for NER was proposed in [11]. In [8] and [54], the authors proposed a maximum entropy tagger and an HMM-based chunk tagger to recognize named entities. Unfortunately, those methods gave poor performance on tweets, as pointed out in [31].

Vietnamese NER

In the domain of Vietnamese texts, various approaches have been proposed using various learning models, such as SVM [49], classifier voting [48] and CRF [19, 52]. Some other authors have proposed other methods for NER, such as a rule-based method [36, 38], labeled propagation [21], the use of a bootstrapping algorithm and a rule-based model [51], and combined linguistically motivated and ontological features [39]. Pham et al. [41] proposed an online learning algorithm, i.e., MIRA [7] in combination with

Table 1 An example of named entity recognition

Original tweet	xe đón hồ ngọc hà gây tai nạn **kinhh** hoàng: sẽ khởi tố tài xế http://fb.me/2MwvznBbj
Step 1: Normalization	xe đón hồ ngọc hà gây tai nạn **kinh** hoàng: sẽ khởi tố tài xế
Step 2: Capitalization	**X**e đón **H**ồ **N**gọc **H**à gây tai nạn kinh hoàng: sẽ khởi tố tài xế
Step 3: NEs recognition	Xe đón <**PER**> Hồ Ngọc Hà </**PER**> gây tai nạn kinh hoàng: sẽ khởi tố tài xế

CRF and bootstrapping. Sam et al. [46] used the idea of Liao and Veeramachaneni in [28] based on CRF and expanded it by combining proper name co-references and named ambiguity heuristics with a powerful sequential learning model. Nguyen and Pham [22] proposed a feature selection approach for named entity recognition using a genetic algorithm. To calculate the accuracy of the recognition of the named entity, this paper used KNN and CRF. Nguyen and Pham [37] proposed a systematic approach to avoid the conflict between rules when a new rule was added to the set of rules for NER. Le and Tran [23] proposed some strategies to reduce the running time of genetic algorithms used in a feature selection task for NER. These strategies included reducing the size of the population during the evolution process of the genetic algorithm, reducing the fitness computation time of individuals in the genetic algorithm using progressive sampling for finding the (near) optimal sample size of the training data, and parallelization of individual fitness computation in each generation.

However, there have been no approaches that focused on NER in Vietnamese tweets or (short) informal Vietnamese texts.

To better collocate our results with other existing Vietnamese NER systems that used other techniques, we report the performances of other Vietnamese NER systems in Table 2.

NER in tweets

Regarding microblog texts written in English and other languages, several approaches have been proposed for NER. Among them, Ritter et al. [44] proposed an NER system for tweets, called T-NER, which employed a CRF model for training and Labeled-LDA. Ramage et al. [43] proposed an external knowledge base, i.e., Freebase[2] for NER. A hybrid approach to NER on tweets was presented in [31] in which a KNN-based classifier and a CRF model were used. A combination of heuristics and MEM was proposed in [17]. In [50], a semi-supervised learning approach that combined the CRF model with a classifier based on the co-occurrence coefficient of the feature words surrounding the proper noun was proposed for NER on Twitter. Li and Liu [26] proposed non-standard word (NSW) detection and decided a word is out of vocabulary (OOV) based on the dictionary, and then applied the normalization system of [25] to normalize OOV words. The results from NSW detection was used for NER based on the pipeline strategy or the joint decoding fashion method. In [32], a named entity was recognized using three steps, i.e., (1) each tweet is pre-labeled using a sequential labeler based on the linear conditional random fields (CRFs) model; (2) tweets are clustered to put those that have similar content into the same group; and (3) each cluster refines the labels of each tweet using an enhanced CRF model that incorporates the cluster-level information. Liu et al. [33] proposed jointly conducting NER and named entity normalization (NEN) for multiple tweets using a factor graph, which leverages redundancy in tweets to make up for the dearth of information in a single tweet and allows these two tasks to inform each other. Liu et al. [30] proposed a novel method for NER consisting of three core elements, i.e., normalization of tweets, combination of a KNN classifier with a linear CRF model, and a semi-supervised learning framework. Nguyen and Moschitti [40] presented a method for incorporating global

---

[2] http://www.freebase.com.

Table 2 Results of several previous works in Vietnamese NER

System	Entity types	Precision (%)	Recall (%)	F1 (%)
[19]	PER	84	82.56	83.39
[36]	PER, ORG, LOC, NA, FA, RE	92	76	83
[38]	PER, ORG, LOC	86.05	81.11	83.51
[46]	PER, ORG, LOC	93.13	88.15	79.35
[48]	PER, ORG, LOC, CUR, NUM, PERC, TIME	86.44	85.86	89.12
[49]	PER, ORG, LOC, CUR, NUM, PERC, TIME	89.05	86.49	87.75
[52]	PER, ORG, LOC, CUR, NUM, PERC, TIME, MISC	83.69	87.41	85.51

PER person, *ORG* organization, *LOC* location, *CUR* currency, *NUM* number, *PERC* percent, *TIME* time, *NA* nationality, *FA* facility, *RE* region, *MISC* miscellaneous

features in NER using re-ranking techniques that used two kinds of features, i.e., flat and structured features and a combination of CRF and SVM. In [55], a CRF model without being focused on Gazetteers was used for NER for Arabic social media.

Recently, [1] presented the results of Shared Tasks of the 2015 Workshop on Noisy User-generated Text: Twitter Lexical Normalization and Named Entity Recognition. According to this paper, most of researchers used CRF. However, several researchers in this workshop described new methods, such as [13], which used absolutely no hand-engineered features and relied entirely on embedded words and a feed-forward, neural-network (FFNN) architecture; Cherry et al. [3] developed a semi-Markov MIRA trained tagger; Yamada et al. [53] used entity-linking-based features, and other researchers used CRFs.

Since some of the specific features of Vietnamese were presented in [49], one cannot apply those methods directly to Vietnamese tweets.

In this paper, we propose a method for NER in Vietnamese tweets to fill the gap. Our method includes three main tasks, i.e., (1) a method for normalization of Vietnamese tweets based on dictionaries and Vietnamese vocabulary structures in combination with a language model; (2) a method for detecting and correcting suitable capital letters; and (3) a model for training and recognizing named entities in Vietnamese tweets. We also conducted experiments to evaluate our NER method focused on three entity types, i.e., PERSON, LOCATION, and ORGANIZATION.

Normalization

When we approached NER in Vietnamese tweets, we found that, on Twitter, they are noisy, irregular, brief, and consist of acronyms and spelling errors. Processing those tweets is more challenging than processing news or formal texts. To deal with this issue, several researchers have focused on other languages than Vietnamese. For example, Han et al. [14, 15] proposed a method to detect and handle errors based on the morpho-phonemic similarity. Choi et al. [4] detected and handled many non-standard words in online social networks using a diverse coefficient method, such as Dice, Jaccard, and Ochiai. Hassan and Menezes [16] used random walks on a contextual similarity bipartite graph constructed from n-gram sequences on large unlabeled text corpus to normalize social text. Sproat et al. [47] developed a novel method for normalizing and morpho-logically analyzing Japanese noisy text by generating both character-level and word-level normalization candidates and using discriminative methods to formulate a cost function. An approach to normalize Twitter messages in Malay based on corpus-driven analysis was proposed in [45]. Cotelo et al. [6] proposed a modular approach for lexical normalization applied to Spanish tweets. This system is proposed by including the detection of modules and candidate for correction for each out-of-vocabulary word and ranking the candidates to select the best one. Liu et al. [29] proposed a normalization system for short message service (SMS) and Twitter data based on a broad-coverage normalization system by integrating three human perspectives, i.e., enhanced letter transformation, visual priming, and string/phonetic similarity.

Recently, in the Shared Tasks of the 2015 Workshop on Noisy User-generated Text: Twitter Lexical Normalization and Named Entity Recognition, several methods were proposed for the normalization of Twitter lexical usages. According to the summary of results in [1], the common approaches were lexicon-based methods, CRF, and neural network-based methods. Among the constrained systems, neural networks achieved strong results even without off-the-shelf tools. In contrast, CRF and lexicon-based approaches were shown to be effective in the unconstrained category. Considering the Vietnamese language, we have not found any research work that has undertaken this task.

Proposed method

In this section, we present our method for NER in Vietnamese tweets. This model has two main parts, i.e., one for training and another for recognizing. Figure 1 describes our model. In our model, the gazetteers are used for both training and recognizing. We will provide more detail in the following subsections.

The theoretical background

Currently, there are several viewpoints on what is a Vietnamese word. However, to meet the goals of automatic error detection, normalization and classification, we followed the viewpoint in [48], i.e., "A Vietnamese word is composed of special linguistic units called Vietnamese morphosyllables." A morphosyllable may be a morpheme, a word, or something else [49]. And according to the syllable dictionary of Hoang Phe [42], we split a morphosyllable into two basic parts, consonants and syllables, as follows:

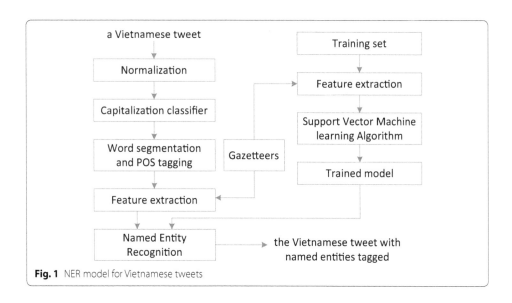

Fig. 1 NER model for Vietnamese tweets

- Consonants: The Vietnamese language has 27 consonants, i.e., "b," "ch," "c," "d," "đ," "gi," "gh," "g," "h," "kh," "k," "l," "m," "ngh," "ng," "nh," "n," "ph," "q," "r," "s," "th," "tr," "t," "v," "x," "p." In those consonants, there are eight tail consonants, i.e., "c," "ch," "n," "nh," "ng," "m," "p," and "t."
- Syllables: A syllable may be a vowel, a combination of vowels, or a combination of vowels and tail consonants. According to the syllable dictionary of Hoang Phe, the Vietnamese language has 158 syllables, and the vowels in these syllables do not occur consecutively more than once, except for the syllables "ooc" and "oong."

Vowels: The Vietnamese language has 12 vowels, i.e., "a," "ă," "â," "e," "ê," "i," "o," "ô," "ơ," "u," "ư," and "y."

Normalization

Because Vietnamese tweets on Twitter are noisy, irregular, and brief and consist of acronyms and spelling errors. Therefore, we propose a method to normalize them before performing NER. Our normalization method has two steps, i.e., error detection and error correction.

Error detection

Before performing this step, the noisy contents of tweets must be removed, such as emotion symbols (e.g., ❤❤), hashtag symbols, link url @username and others. To detect errors, we synthesized and built a dictionary for all Vietnamese morphosyllables, and it contains more than 7300 morphosyllables. A morphosyllable in a tweet will be identified as an error if it does not appear in the morphosyllable dictionary. Normally, Vietnamese tweets include two kinds of errors, i.e., typing errors and spelling errors.

Typing errors

Two popular typing methods are used to compose Vietnamese tweets, i.e., Telex typing and VNI typing. Each method combines letters to form Vietnamese tweets. Vietnamese characters have some extra vowels that do not exist in Latin characters, i.e., â, ă, ê, ô, ơ, one more consonant, đ; Vietnamese has five types of marks, i.e., acute accent ("á"), grave accent ("à"), hook accent ("ả"), tilde ("ã"), and heavy accent ("ạ"). The combination of vowels and marks forms the Vietnamese language its own identity.

Example:

- When using Telex typing, we have the combination of characters to form Vietnamese vowels, such as aa for â, aw for ă, ee for ê, oo for ô, ow for ơ, and uw for ư. Also we have one consonant, dd, for đ. For forming marks, we have s for acute accent, f for grave accent, r for hook accent, x for tilde, and j for heavy accent.
- Similar to Telex typing, we have the combination of characters in VNI typing, such as: a6 for â, a8 for ă, e6 for ê, o6 for ô, o7 for ơ, u7 for ư, and d9 for đ. To form marks, we have 1 for accent, 2 for grave accent, 3 for hook accent, 4 for tilde, and 5 for heavy accent.

Tweets are very short and prepared quickly, so the typing speed can cause errors. For example:

- With the word, "Nguyễn," we could have typing errors such as "nguyeenx," "nguyênx," or "nguyeenxx" with Telex typing, and "nguye6n4," "nguyên4," or "nguye6n44" with VNI typing.
- With the word, "người," we could type the following incorrect words: "ngườif," "ngườfi," "nguowfi," "nguowif," "nguofwi," "nguofiw," "nguoifw," "nguoiwf," or "nguowff" with Telex typing, and "nguwowi2," "nguơ2i," "nguo72i," "nguo7i2," "nguo27i," "nguo2i7," "nguoi27," or "nguoi72" with VNI typing.

To handle this issue, we built a set of syllable rules with their tone-marks and a set of rules to map these syllables to their errors, as shown in the following examples:

- "án": "asn," "ans," "a1n," or "an1"
- "àn": "afn," "anf," "a2n," or "an2"
- "ản": "arn," "anr," "a3n," or "an3"
- "ãn": "axn," "anx," "a4n," or "an4"
- "ạn": "ajn," "anj," "a5n," or "an5"

Spelling errors

Spelling errors occur frequently in Vietnamese tweets. Normally, they occur due to mistakes in pronunciation. Some examples of spelling errors are as follows:

- Error due to using the wrong mark: "quyển sách" (book) to "quyễn sách"
- Initial consonant error: "bóng chuyền" (volleyball) to "bóng truyền"
- End consonant error: "bài hát" (song) to "bài hác"
- Region error: "tìm kiếm" (find) to "tìm kím"

Error correction

For the detected typing and spelling errors, first, the system uses vocabulary structures and the set of syllable rules to normalize them. Then, the system uses *n*-gram to normalize these results based on the degree of similarity between them.

a. Similarity of two morphosyllables

To measure the similarity of two morphosyllables, we used the results in the research of Dice [9] with some improvements we made. To use Dice's research, we split all of the characters of the morphosyllables to bigrams. Assuming that we have two morphosyllables, i.e., "nguyen" and "nguye," the bigrams of these morphosyllables can be represented as follows: $\text{bigram}_{\text{nguyn}} = \{\text{ng, gu, uy, yn}\}$, and $\text{bigram}_{\text{nguyen}} = \{\text{ng, gu, uy, ye, en}\}$.

Dice coefficient

The Dice coefficient, developed by Lee Raymond Dice [9], is a statistical approach for comparing the similarity of two samples. The Dice coefficient of the two morphosyllables, w_i and w_j, according to bigram can be calculated using Eq. 1:

$$\mathrm{Dice}(w_i, w_j) = \frac{2\times \mid \mathrm{bigram}_{w_i} \bigcap \mathrm{bigram}_{w_j} \mid}{\mid \mathrm{bigram}_{w_i} \mid + \mid \mathrm{bigram}_{w_j} \mid} \tag{1}$$

where

- $\mid \mathrm{bigram}_{w_i} \mid$ and $\mid \mathrm{bigram}_{w_j} \mid$ are the total bigrams of w_i and w_j
- $\mid \mathrm{bigram}_{w_i} \mid \bigcap \mid \mathrm{bigram}_{w_j} \mid$ are the number of bigrams which appear in w_i and w_j at the same time.

If two morphosyllables are the same, the Dice coefficient is 1. The higher the Dice coefficient, the higher the degree of similarity and vice versa.

Proposed method to improve the Dice coefficient

As observing from the experimental data using the Dice coefficient, we found that the above method will be accurate with misspelled morphosyllables which is having the misspelled character at the end. When misspelled characters occur close to the last character, at least we will lose the similarity of the last two grams. For a morphosyllable that has three characters, the degree of similarity is 0. For example: Dice("rất", "rát") = 0; Dice("gân", "gần") = 0;

From the above problem, we proposed a method to improve the Dice coefficient. The improvement of coefficient was performed by combining the first character with the last character of the two morphosyllables to form a new pair of bigrams. If the two members of this pair are different, the system will use the coefficients as shown in Eq. (1). In contrast, we use Eq. (2) as follows:

$$i\mathrm{Dice}(w_i, w_j) = \frac{2 \times \left(\mid \mathrm{bigram}_{w_i} \bigcap \mathrm{bigram}_{w_j} \mid + 1 \right)}{\mid \mathrm{bigram}_{w_i} \mid + \mid \mathrm{bigram}_{w_j} \mid + 2} \tag{2}$$

Let $\mathrm{fbigram}_w$ be an additional bigram of w. Each fbigram is the pair of the first and the last character of w. We can express the formula for improving the Dice coefficient as Eq. (3):

$$f\mathrm{Dice}(w_i, w_j) = \begin{cases} \mathrm{Dice}(w_i, w_j) : \text{if } \mathrm{fbigram}_{w_i} \text{ is different from } \mathrm{fbigram}_{w_j} \\ i\mathrm{Dice}(w_i, w_j) : \text{otherwise} \end{cases} \tag{3}$$

To illustrate the improvement of the Dice coefficient, we assumed that we have two morphosyllables to measure the degree of similarity, i.e., "nguyen" and "nguyn," as presented in the previous section, thus we have $\mid \mathrm{bigram}_{w_i} \bigcap \mathrm{bigram}_{w_j} \mid = 3$. Combining the first and the last characters of the two morphosyllables we have the new pair of bigram, which has the same result, i.e., "nn." So, using the improvement of the Dice coefficient, we have fDice("nguyen," "nguyn") = 0.727. If we use the normal coefficient of Dice, we have Dice("nguyen," "nguyn") = 0.667. Table 3 shows the results of measuring the similarity of two morphosyllables with the Dice coefficient and the improved Dice coefficient methods. With the improved method, the similarities are obviously improved.

Table 3 The results of measuring the similarity of two morphosyllables with the Dice coefficient and the improved of Dice coefficient methods

Error morphosyllable	Correct morphosyllable	Dice	fDice
rat	rất	0	0.333
rat	rác	0	0
Nguễn	Nguyễn	0.667	0.727
Nguễn	Nguy	0.571	0.571
tượg	Tượng	0.571	0.667
tượg	Tương	0.286	0.444

b. Similarity of two sentences

Assume that we need to measure the similarity of two sentences, i.e., $S_1 = w_1 w_2 \ldots w_n$ and $S_2 = w'_1 w'_2 \ldots w'_{n'}$. We compare the similarity of each pair of morphosyllables according to the improved Dice coefficient. Then, we compute the similarity of the two sentences by Eq. (4):

$$\text{Sim}(S_1, S_2) = \frac{\Sigma_{i=1}^{n} fDice\left(w_i, w'_i\right)}{n} \tag{4}$$

where w_i and w'_i are the corresponding morphosyllables of S_1 and S_2. n is the number of morphosyllables.

If two sentences are the same, their degree of similarity (Sim) is 1. The higher the Sim coefficent, the higher the degree of similarity becomes, and vice versa. Table 4 shows the results of the normalization of Vietnamese tweets that have spelling errors.

Capitalization classifier

Capitalization is a key orthographic feature for recognizing named entities [10, 12]. Unfortunately, in tweets, capitalization is much less reliable than edited texts. Users usually compose and reply to messages quickly, and they do not care much about capitalization. According to [5], a letter is capitalized in the following cases:

1. Capitalize the first letter of the first syllable of a complete sentence, after punctuation (.), question mark (?), exclamation point (!), ellipsis (· · ·) and new line.
2. Capitalize the name of people, locations, and organizations.
3. Other cases of capitalization include, e.g., medal name, position name, days of the week, months of the year, holidays, names of books, and names of magazines

Table 4 Tweets with spelling errors and their normalization

Spelling error tweets	Normalized tweets
xe đón hồ ngọc hà gây tai nạn **kinhh** hoàng: sẽ khởi tố tài xế http://fb.me/2MwvznBbj	xe đón hồ ngọc hà gây tai nạn **kinh** hoàng: sẽ khởi tố tài xế (the car picked up ho ngoc ha caused a terrible accident: the driver will be prosecuted)
hôm nay, **siinh** viên **ddaijj** học tôn **dduwcss** thắng được nghỉ học	hôm nay, **sinh** viên đại học tôn **đức** thắng được nghỉ học (today, students of ton duc thang university were allowed to absent)

Because our method focuses on three types of entities, i.e., person, organization, and location, in the capitalization classifier, we take the first and the second cases into account. For the first case, we detect the structure of the sentence and correct incorrect capitalization. In the second case, we use gazetteers of persons, locations, and organizations. Table 5 shows the results of the capitalization classifier of Vietnamese tweets.

Word segmentation and part of speech (POS) tagging
To perform word segmentation and POS tagging for normalized tweets, we used vnTo-kenizer[3] of [20] for word segmentation and VnTagger[4] of [24] for POS tagging.

Extraction of features
This phase aims to convert each word to a vector of feature values. Our system uses the IOB model to annotate data in the training and classification phases. IOB is expressed as follows:

- I: current morphosyllable is inside of a named entity (NE).
- O: current morphosyllable is outside of an NE.
- B: current morphosyllable is the beginning of an NE.

Table 6 shows the characteristic value of labels according to the IOB model with four classes, i.e., PER, LOC, ORG, and O. The selection of specific attributes from the training set has a key role in identifying the type of entity. Since the nature of the Vietnamese language is different from English, we used the most appropriate and reasonable features to achieve optimum accuracy for the system. Our system uses the following features:

- *Word position* The position of words in a sentence.
- *POS* POS tag of the current word.
- *Orthographic* Capitalization of first character, capitalization of all letters, lowercase, punctuation, numbers.
- *Gazetteer* We build several gazetteer lists, such as person, location, organization, and prefixes. These gazetteer lists consist of more than 50,000 names of people, nearly 12,000 names of locations, and 7000 names of organizations.
- *Prefix, Suffix* The first and the second character; the last and the next to the last character of the current word.
- *POS Prefix, POS Suffix* POS tags of two previous words and POS tags of two following words of the current word.

Evaluation
Data using for normalization
In this paper, to normalize for spelling errors that cannot be normalized by Vietnamese structure or a set of syllable rules, we used the tri-gram language model (tri-gram of

---

[3] http://mim.hus.vnu.edu.vn/phuonglh/softwares/vnTokenizer.

[4] http://mim.hus.vnu.edu.vn/phuonglh/softwares/vnTagger.

Table 5 Some results of capitalization classifier of Vietnamese tweets

Tweets before capitalization	Tweets after capitalization classifier
xe đón **h**ồ **n**gọc **h**à gây tai nạn kinh hoàng: sẽ khởi tố tài xế	xe đón **H**ồ **N**gọc **H**à gây tai nạn kinh hoàng: sẽ khởi tố tài xế(the car picked up Ho Ngoc Ha caused a terrible accident: the driver will be prosecuted)
hôm nay, sinh viên đại học **t**ôn đức **t**hắng được nghỉ học	hôm nay, sinh viên Đại học **T**ôn Đức **T**hắng được nghỉ học (today, students of Ton Duc Thang university were allowed to absent)

Table 6 The characteristic value of labels according to IOB model

Label	Value	Meaning
O	[1]	Outside a named entity
B-PER	[2]	Beginning morphosyllable of a NE belongs to a Person class
I-PER	[3]	Inside morphosyllable of a NE belongs to Person class
B-LOC	[4]	Beginning morphosyllable of a NE belongs to Location class
I-LOC	[5]	Inside morphosyllable of a NE belongs to Location class
B-ORG	[6]	Beginning morphosyllable of a NE belongs to Organization class
I-ORG	[7]	Inside morphosyllable of a NE belongs to Organization class

word). This model was built from SRILM[5] with a huge amount of data collected from online newspapers, e.g., http://www.vnexpress.net, http://nld.com.vn/, http://dantri.com.vn/, and others. The data were collected from many fields, such as current events, world, law, education, science, business, sports, and entertainment with over 429,310 articles. The total volume of collected data was about 1045 MB. The tri-gram model that was built from SRILM was about 1460 MB. To ensure the accuracy of results, we chose all of the tri-grams from the SRILM model in which the frequency of occurrences was greater than or equal five. The volume of selected tri-grams was around 81 MB, and the number of tri-grams was around 3.75 million.

NER training set

As seen in Fig. 1, before performing feature extraction, we perform word segmentation, POS tagging, and assigning labels in Table 6 for each word in the training set. Then, the system extracts features of the words and represents each of those words as a feature vector. A support vector machine learning algorithm was used to train the model using the training set.

In particular, we assigned labels for words in the training set using a semi-automatic program, meaning that we assigned labels to those words with a program we wrote and checked in hand. In our self-written program, we considered the noun phrase obtained after the tagging step with a list of dictionary of text files to label for those words. The text files of the dictionary contain:

---

[5] http://www.speech.sri.com/projects/srilm/.

Table 7 The results of assigning labels to words of two Vietnamese tweets

Tweets	Tweets after assigning labels
xe đón Hồ Ngọc Hà gây tai nạn kinh hoàng: sẽ khởi tố tài xế	xe đón <**PER**> Hồ Ngọc Hà </**PER**> gây tai nạn kinh hoàng: sẽ khởi tố tài xế (the car picked up Ho Ngoc Ha caused a terrible accident: the driver will be prosecuted)
hôm nay, sinh viên Đại học Tôn Đức Thắng được nghỉ học	hôm nay, sinh viên <**ORG**> Đại học Tôn Đức Thắng </**ORG**> được nghỉ học (today, students of Ton Duc Thang university were allowed to absent)

Table 8 Total number of named entities in the training set

Entity type	Number of named entities
PER	10,842
LOC	19,037
ORG	12,311

- The noun prefix for people such as you, sister, uncle, and president.
- The noun prefix for organizations such as company, firm, and corporation.
- The noun prefix for locations such as province, city, and district.
- List of dictionary for states, provinces of Vietnam, and others.

Table 7 shows the results of assigning labels to words of two Vietnamese tweets. The total number of entities to which we assigned labels in this phase is presented in Table 8.

After assigning the labels for words in Vietnamese tweets, we analyzed these tweets to build feature vectors for those words. The structure of a feature vector includes <label> <index1>:<value1> <index2>:<value2> <index3>:<value3> and other pairs, where

- **<label>**: value from 1 to 7 according to 7 labels (O, B-PER, I-PER, B-LOC, I-LOC, B-ORG, I-ORG).
- **<index>:<value>**: order of feature and value corresponding to feature of a word, respectively.

After representing words in the training set as feature vectors, we used libSVM[6] to train the model.

Experiments

We conducted experiments to evaluate our method using a test set including 2,271 Vietnamese tweets and 3,186 named entities. In order to show the performance of normalization, we also conduct experiments to evaluate the proposed normalization method.

To evaluate normalization method, we ran the test on the tri-gram model with the normal Dice coefficient (Dice) and the improved Dice coefficient (fDice) to measure the similarity of the two sentences. We used three metrics to evaluate our method, i.e., the precision, the recall, and the F-Measure methods.

---

[6] http://www.csie.ntu.edu.tw/cjlin/libsvm/#download.

Table 9 The results using fDice and Dice with tri-gram model

Method	Precision (%)	Recall (%)	F-Measure (%)
Dice	83.85	82.76	83.30
fDice	89.66	88.50	89.08

Table 10 Experimental results of case 1 and case 2

Case	# NEs in testing set	# recognized NEs	# correctly recognized NEs	# wrong recognized NEs	P (%)	R (%)	F1 (%)
1	3186	2593	2163	430	83.41	67.89	74.86
2	3186	2982	2533	449	84.94	79.50	82.13

Table 11 Comparison performance of our method with that of [49]

System	Precision (%)	Recall (%)	F1 (%)
Our system	84.94	79.50	82.13
System of [49]	83.10	77.62	80.27

- Precision (P): number of correctly fixed errors divided by the total number of errors detected.
- Recall (R): number of correctly fixed errors divided by the total error.
- Balance F-measure (F1): $F_1 = \frac{2*P*R}{p+R}$

Table 9 shows the experimental results of our normalization method. As seen in this table, the combination of our improved Dice coefficient and the tri-gram model achieved better performance than the normal Dice coefficient with the tri-gram model.

To evaluate the NER method and make a comparison of the impact of the normalization of the test set, we conducted two experiments, i.e., one without normalization and capitalization classifier of tweets (Case 1) and the other with normalization and capitalization classifier of tweets (Case 2). Table 10 shows our experimental results. In this case, we also used three metrics to evaluate our method, i.e., the precision, the recall, and the Balance F-Measure.

- Precision (P): the number of correctly recognized named entities divided by the total number of named entities recognized by the NER system.
- Recall (R): the number of correctly recognized named entities divided by the total number of named entities in the test set.
- Balance F-Measure (F1): $F_1 = \frac{2*P*R}{p+R}$

According to Table 10, when we applied the normalization to the test set, the precision, recall and balance F-Measure of this test were higher than the case of the test set without normalization.

We re-implemented the state-of-the-art method proposed in [49] and compared its performance with our method. The results of this comparison are shown in Table 11.

Conclusions

In this paper, we present the first attempt to NER in Vietnamese tweets on Twitter. We proposed a method for the normalization of Vietnamese tweets, based on the dictionaries and Vietnamese vocabulary structures in combination with a language model. We also proposed a learning model to recognize named entities using six different types of features. To evaluate for our normalization method, we built a tri-gram model that had a volume of about 81 MB and the number of tri-grams was around 3.75 million. The improvement in measuring the similarity of two words based on the modified Dice coefficient outperformed the original Dice coefficient, and our normalization method achieved a high performance with F1 score of 89.08%. To evaluate the NER method, we built a training set of more than 40,000 named entities and a testing set of 3186 named entities to evaluate our system. The experimental results showed that our system achieved encouraging performance, with 82.13% F1 score.

We plan to acquire a larger dataset to build and test the language model with bigram, trigram, and four-gram to improve our normalization performance. In addition, we also collected the data required to increase the number of named entities in the training set as well as to expand the Gazetteers so that we can increase the NER performance of our system.

Authors' contributions

All authors had contributed equally to this work, including problem definition, algorithms, experimental results, and the manuscript. VHN, as the first author, took the lead in composing the first draft of the manuscript, while HTN and VS edited it. All authors read and approved the final manuscript.

Author details

[1] Faculty of Information Technology, Ton Duc Thang University, Ho Chi Minh City, Vietnam. [2] Faculty of Electrical Engineering and Computer Science, VSB-Technical University of Ostrava, Ostrava, Czech Republic.

Competing interests

The authors declare that they have no competing interests.

References

1. Baldwin T, de Marneffe MC, Han B, et al. Shared tasks of the 2015 workshop on noisy user-generated text: Twitter lexical normalization and named entity recognition. ACL-IJCNLP. 2015;2015:126–35.
2. Bandyopadhyay A, Roy D, Mitra M, Saha S. Named entity recognition from tweets. In: Proceedings of the 16th LWA workshops: KDML, IR and FGWM, Aachen, Germany; 2014. p. 218–25.
3. Cherry C, Guo H, Dai C. Nrc: Infused phrase vectors for named entity recognition in twitter. ACL-IJCNLP. 2015;2015:54–60.
4. Choi D, Kim J, et al. A method for normalizing non-standard words in online social network services: A case study on twitter. Second International Conference Context-Aware Systems and Applications, ICCASA. 2014;2013:359–68.
5. Chu MN, Nghieu VD, Phien HT. Basis of linguistics and Vietnamese. Vietnam: Vietnam educational publisher; 2010.
6. Cotelo JM, et al. A modular approach for lexical normalization applied to spanish tweets. Expert Syst Appl. 2015;42(10):4743–54.
7. Crammer K, Singer Y. Ultraconservative online algorithms for multiclass problems. J Mach Learn Res. 2003;3:951–91.
8. Curran JR, Clark S. Language independent NER using a maximum entropy tagger. In: Proceedings of the seventh conference on natural language learning, CoNLL 2003, Held in cooperation with HLT-NAACL 2003, Edmonton, Canada; 2003. p. 164–7.
9. Dice LR. Measures of the amount of ecologic association between species. Ecology. 1945;26(3):297–302.
10. Downey D, Broadhead M, Etzioni O. Locating complex named entities in web text. In: IJCAI 2007, Proceedings of the 20th international joint conference on artificial intelligence, Hyderabad, India; 2007. p. 2733–9.
11. Fersini E, Messina E, Felici G, Roth D. Soft-constrained inference for named entity recognition. Inform Process Manag. 2014;50(5):807–19.
12. Florian R. Named entity recognition as a house of cards: classifier stacking. In: Proceedings of the 6th conference on natural language learning, CoNLL 2002, Held in cooperation with COLING 2002, Taipei; 2002
13. Godin F, Vandersmissen B, Neve WD, de Walle RV. Multimedia lab @ acl w-nut ner shared task: named entity recognition for twitter microposts using distributed word representations. ACL-IJCNLP. 2015;2015:146–53.

14. Han B, Baldwin T. Lexical normalisation of short text messages: Makn sens a# twitter. In: Proceedings of the 49th annual meeting of the association for computational linguistics: human language technologies, vol 1; 2011. p. 368–78.
15. Han B, et al. Lexical normalization for social media text. ACM Trans Intell Syst Technol. 2013;4(1):621–33.
16. Hassan H, Menezes A. Social text normalization using contextual graph random walks. In: Proceedings of the 51st annual meeting of the association for computational linguistics. Berlin: Association for Computational Linguistics; 2013. p. 1577–86.
17. Jung JJ. Online named entity recognition method for microtexts in social networking services: a case study of twitter. Expert Syst Appl. 2012;39(9):8066–70.
18. Konkol M, Brychcin T, Konopík M. Latent semantics in named entity recognition. Expert Syst Appl. 2015;42(7):3470–9.
19. Le H, Tran M, Bui N, Phan N, Ha Q. An integrated approach using conditional random fields for named entity recognition and person property extraction in Vietnamese text. In: International conference on Asian language processing, IALP 2011, Penang; 2011. p. 115–8.
20. Le HP, Huyên NTM, Roussanaly A, Vinh HT. A hybrid approach to word segmentation of Vietnamese texts. In: Second international conference on language and automata theory and applications, LATA 2008, Tarragona, Revised Papers; 2008. p. 240–9.
21. Le HT, Sam RC, Nguyen HC, Nguyen TT. Named entity recognition in Vietnamese text using label propagation. In: 2013 international conference on soft computing and pattern recognition, SoCPaR 2013, Hanoi; 2013. p. 366–70.
22. Le HT, Tran LV. Automatic feature selection for named entity recognition using genetic algorithm. In: 4th international symposium on information and communication technology, SoICT '13, Danang; 2013. p. 81–7.
23. Le HT, Tran LV, Nguyen XH, Nguyen TH. Optimizing genetic algorithm in feature selection for named entity recognition. In: Proceedings of the sixth international symposium on information and communication technology, Hue City; 2015. p. 5
24. Le-Hong P, Roussanaly A, et al. An empirical study of maximum entropy approach for part-of-speech tagging of Vietnamese texts. In: Traitement Automatique des Langues Naturelles-TALN 2010; 2010.
25. Li C, Liu Y. Improving text normalization via unsupervised model and discriminative reranking. In: Proceedings of the 52nd annual meeting of the association for computational linguistics, ACL 2014. Baltimore: Student Research Workshop; 2014. p. 86–93.
26. Li C, Liu, Y. Improving named entity recognition in tweets via detecting non-standard words. In: Proceedings of the 53rd annual meeting of the association for computational linguistics and the 7th international joint conference on natural language processing of the Asian federation of natural language processing, ACL 2015, Beijing, vol 1: Long Papers; 2015. p. 929–38.
27. Li C, Sun A, Weng J, He Q. Tweet segmentation and its application to named entity recognition. IEEE Trans Knowl Data Eng. 2015;27(2):558–70.
28. Liao W, Veeramachaneni S. A simple semi-supervised algorithm for named entity recognition. In: Proceedings of the NAACL HLT workshop on semisupervised learning for natural language processing; 2009. p. 28–36.
29. Liu F, Weng F, Jiang X. A broad-coverage normalization system for social media language. In: Proceedings of the conference on the 50th annual meeting of the association for computational linguistics 2012, Jeju Island, vol 1. Long Papers; 2012. p. 1035–44.
30. Liu X, Wei F, Zhang S, Zhou M. Named entity recognition for tweets. ACM TIST. 2013;4(1):3.
31. Liu X, Zhang S, Wei F, Zhou M. Recognizing named entities in tweets. In: Proceedings of the conference on the 49th annual meeting of the association for computational linguistics: human language technologies, Portland; 2011. pp. 359–67.
32. Liu X, Zhou M. Two-stage NER for tweets with clustering. Inform Process Manag. 2013;49(1):264–73.
33. Liu X, Zhou M, Zhou X, Fu Z, Wei F. Joint inference of named entity recognition and normalization for tweets. In: Proceedings of the conference on The 50th annual meeting of the association for computational linguistics, Jeju Island, Vol 1: Long Papers; 2012. p. 526–35.
34. Mayfield J, McNamee P, Piatko CD. Named entity recognition using hundreds of thousands of features. In: Proceedings of the seventh conference on natural language learning, CoNLL 2003, Held in cooperation with HLT-NAACL 2003, Edmonton; 2003. p. 184–7.
35. McCallum A, Li W. Early results for named entity recognition with conditional random fields, feature induction and web-enhanced lexicons. In: Proceedings of the seventh conference on natural language learning, CoNLL 2003, Held in cooperation with HLT-NAACL 2003, Edmonton; 2003. p. 188–91.
36. Nguyen DB, Hoang SH, Pham SB, Nguyen TP. Named entity recognition for Vietnamese. In: Second international conference on intelligent information and database systems, ACIIDS, Hue City. Proceedings, Part II; 2010. p. 205–14.
37. Nguyen DB, Pham SB. Ripple down rules for Vietnamese named entity recognition. In: Technologies and applications—4th International conference on computational collective intelligence, ICCCI 2012, Ho Chi Minh City, Proceedings, Part I; 2012. p. 354–63.
38. Nguyen TT, Cao TH. VN-KIM IE: automatic extraction of Vietnamese named-entities on the web. New Gener Comput. 2007;25(3):277–92.
39. Nguyen TT, Cao TH. Linguistically motivated and ontological features for Vietnamese named entity recognition. In: 2012 IEEE RIVF international conference on computing & communication technologies, research, innovation, and vision for the future (RIVF), Ho Chi Minh City; 2012. p. 1–6.
40. Nguyen TT, Moschitti A. Structural reranking models for named entity recognition. Intell Artif. 2012;6(2):177–90.
41. Pham QH, Nguyen ML, Nguyen BT, Cuong NV. Semi-supervised learning for Vietnamese named entity recognition using online conditional random fields. In: Proceedings of NEWS 2015 the fifth named entities workshop; 2015. p. 53–8.
42. Phe H. syllable Dictionary. Dictionary center. Hanoi: Encyclopedia Publishers; 2011.
43. Ramage D, Hall DLW, Nallapati R, Manning CD. Labeled LDA: a supervised topic model for credit attribution in multi-labeled corpora. In: Proceedings of the 2009 conference on empirical methods in natural language processing; 2009. p. 248–56.

44. Ritter A, Clark S, Mausam Etzioni O. Named entity recognition in tweets: an experimental study. In: Proceedings of the 2011 conference on empirical methods in natural language processing, EMNLP 2011, John McIntyre Conference Centre, Edinburgh, UK, A meeting of SIGDAT, a Special Interest Group of the ACL; 2011. p. 1524–34.
45. Saloot MA, et al. An architecture for malay tweet normalization. Inform Process Manag. 2014;50(5):621–33.
46. Sam RC, Le HT, Nguyen TT, Nguyen TH. Combining proper name-coreference with conditional random fields for semi-supervised named entity recognition in Vietnamese text. In: Advances in Knowledge Discovery and Data Mining—15th Pacific-Asia Conference, PAKDD 2011, Shenzhen, China, May 24–27, 2011, Proceedings, Part I; 2011. p. 512–24.
47. Sproat R, et al. Normalization of non-standard words. Comput Speech Lang. 2001;15(3):287–333.
48. Thao PTX, Tri TQ, Dien D, Collier N. Named entity recognition in Vietnamese using classifier voting. ACM Trans Asian Lang Inform Process. 2007;6(4):3.
49. Tran QT, et al. Named entity recognition in Vietnamese documents. Progress Inform. 2007;5:14.
50. Tran VC, Hwang D, Jung JJ. Semi-supervised approach based on co-occurrence coefficient for named entity recognition on twitter. In: 2015 2nd national foundation for science and technology development conference on information and computer science (NICS). New York: IEEE; 2015. p. 141–6.
51. Trung HL, Anh VL, Trung KL. Bootstrapping and rule-based model for recognizing Vietnamese named entity. In: 6th Asian conference on intelligent information and database systems, ACIIDS 2014, Bangkok, Proceedings, Part II; 2014. p. 167–76.
52. Tu NC, et al. Named entity recognition in Vietnamese free-text and web documents using conditional random fields. In: The 8th conference on some selection problems of information technology and telecommunication; 2005.
53. Yamada I, Takeda H, Takefuji Y. Enhancing named entity recognition in twitter messages using entity linking. ACL-IJCNLP. 2015;2015:136–40.
54. Zhou G, Su J. Named entity recognition using an hmm-based chunk tagger. In: Proceedings of the 40th annual meeting of the association for computational linguistics, Philadelphia; 2002. p. 473–80.
55. Zirikly A, Diab M. Named entity recognition for arabic social media. Proc NAACL-HLT. 2015;2015:176–85.

Hierarchical community detection via rank-2 symmetric non-negative matrix factorization

Rundong Du[1], Da Kuang[2], Barry Drake[3,4] and Haesun Park[3*]

*Correspondence:
hpark@cc.gatech.edu
[3] School of Computational
Science and Engineering,
Georgia Institute
of Technology, 266
Ferst Drive, Atlanta, GA
30332-0765, USA
Full list of author information
is available at the end of the
article

Abstract

Background: Community discovery is an important task for revealing structures in large networks. The massive size of contemporary social networks poses a tremendous challenge to the scalability of traditional graph clustering algorithms and the evaluation of discovered communities.

Methods: We propose a divide-and-conquer strategy to discover hierarchical community structure, nonoverlapping within each level. Our algorithm is based on the highly efficient rank-2 symmetric nonnegative matrix factorization. We solve several implementation challenges to boost its efficiency on modern computer architectures, specifically for very sparse adjacency matrices that represent a wide range of social networks.

Conclusions: Empirical results have shown that our algorithm has competitive overall efficiency and leading performance in minimizing the average normalized cut, and that the nonoverlapping communities found by our algorithm recover the ground-truth communities better than state-of-the-art algorithms for overlapping community detection. In addition, we present a new dataset of the DBLP computer science bibliography network with richer meta-data and verifiable ground-truth knowledge, which can foster future research in community finding and interpretation of communities in large networks.

Keywords: Community detection, Nonnegative matrix factorization, Constrained low rank approximation, Graph clustering

Background

Community detection is a key task in the study of large networks, which has recently become a very important area of research [1–3]. Although there are no generally accepted definitions of network communities, it is usually agreed that a community is defined as a group of nodes that have more intraconnections than interconnections. This high-level description defines community from a linkage point of view. In reality, a *functional* community in a network is usually based on some common affiliation, attribute, etc., which may not be directly related to linkage information. However, it has been shown that linkage-based communities usually have strong correlation with functional communities [4]. The purpose of community detection is to identify linkage-based communities or functional communities in a network.

Earlier work in this area mainly focused on finding linkage-based communities on small networks. Various measures have been defined and optimized for the difference between intraconnections and interconnections among network nodes, such as normalized cut, conductance, and others, using a variety of methods [4]. Manual examinations (such as visualization) of the results have typically been used in those studies, which may provide some valuable information and insights. Community detection on large networks is more challenging due to the following reasons: (1) many algorithms suitable for small networks are often not scalable; (2) there is a dearth of ground-truth communities defined for large networks and even for the datasets with ground truth, where the quality of the ground truth is often questionable; and (3) examining the results is nearly impossible. It has not been until recently [4] that ground-truth communities have been defined and studied in several real-world large-scale networks.

This paper introduces a scalable algorithm based on rank-2 symmetric nonnegative matrix factorization (rank-2 SymNMF) for large-scale hierarchical community detection. After summarizing some related works, we discuss the problem domain for our new results and our solutions for particular problems within that domain. Then, some highlights and speedup in our implementations are discussed, after which we present comprehensive experimental results to evaluate our new algorithm.

Related work

The study of network community detection dates back to the well-known Kernighan–Lin algorithm from the early 1970s [5]. At that time, the network community detection problem was often formulated as a graph-partitioning problem, which aims at "dividing the vertices" into a predefined number of nonoverlapping "groups of predefined size, such that the number of edges lying between the groups is minimal" [6]. Many methods that produce good-quality solutions were proposed, but they were based on combinatorial optimization algorithms and were not scalable. Later, when it was discovered that graph partitioning is an important problem for balanced distribution of work loads in parallel computing, computer scientists developed many algorithms, such as METIS [7], SCOTCH [8], and Chaco [9], for graph partitioning of parallel communication problems. These algorithms usually follow a multilevel strategy, where a large graph is first coarsened to a smaller graph by recursively contracting multiple vertices into one vertex, and then the small graph is partitioned applying a method like the Kernighan–Lin algorithm, and finally the partition is mapped back to the original graph with some refinement. Most of these algorithms (e.g., all three we mentioned above) scale well to very large networks containing millions of nodes.

A spectral clustering method that minimizes normalized cut was proposed as an image-segmentation algorithm [10], and it soon became popular in the area of graph clustering. However, due to the time-consuming eigenvector/singular vector computation in this algorithm, it is not scalable to the case when the number of communities is large. The Graclus algorithm [11] by Dhillon, Guan, and Kulis solved this issue by utilizing the mathematical equivalence between general cut or association objectives (including normalized cut and ratio association) and the weighted kernel k-means objective [12] and applying a multilevel framework. Kuang, Ding, and Park discovered that the SymNMF (symmetric nonnegative matrix factorization) objective function is also equivalent to normalized cut and ratio association objective functions with a relaxation different from that in spectral clustering [13, 14]. This algorithm has better interpretability like many other NMF-based methods.

Girvan and Newman [15] produced pioneering work developing graph-partitioning/clustering methods from a community detection viewpoint, which finds "groups of vertices which probably share common properties and/or play similar roles within the graph" [6]. Around that time period, many new algorithms were invented. Later, Newman and Girvan [16] proposed the modularity measurement for community detection, on which the biggest family of community detection algorithms is based [17]. A scalable example in this family of algorithms is the Louvain algorithm [18]. Several algorithms such as Walktrap [19] and Infomap [20] are based on random walk on graphs, with the idea that in a random walk, the probability of staying inside a community is higher than going to another community. The paper [6] provides a comprehensive review of the algorithms that appeared up to 2010.

The early overlapping community detection algorithms [21, 22] were not effective on large graphs. Lancichinetti et al. [23] proposed a scalable overlapping community detection algorithm—*order statistics local optimization method* (OSLOM), which was based on a measurement similar to modularity but was able to handle overlapping communities. Yang and Leskovec studied the properties of large-scale overlapping communities [4] and proposed the BigClam algorithm [1]. They provided some large-scale datasets with ground-truth communities available to researchers, which have become standard test datasets. The BigClam algorithm seeks to fit a probabilistic generative model that satisfies certain community properties discovered in their studies [1, 24]. Whang et al. [2] proposed another overlapping community detection algorithm called NISE, based on seed set expansion, which starts with a seed set generated by Graclus or other methods and uses random walk to obtain overlapping communities. These algorithms that are dedicated to community detection have demonstrated better performance in terms of discovering ground-truth communities compared with the traditional graph-partitioning algorithms.

Recently, [17] proposed a new nonoverlapping community detection algorithm, *scalable community detection* (SCD). Network communities of good quality should have stronger intraconnections than interconnections. Previous algorithms measure such strength of connectivity only through the number of edges. The uniqueness of SCD is that it is based on a triangular structure of edges. The goal is to identify communities where each node forms more triangles with nodes inside the community than those formed with nodes outside the community.

On the other hand, nonnegative matrix factorization (NMF)-based methods exhibit superior interpretability in many application areas such as text mining [25, 26] and image analysis [27, 28]. In this paper, we will show that our NMF-based algorithm has competitive performance and scalability for community detection. Although our algorithm currently only handles nonoverlapping community detection, it has achieved comparable or even better-quality than the state-of-the-art overlapping community detection algorithms (such as BigClam) in our extensive tests. Our algorithm is inspired by SymNMF [13, 14] for graph clustering and HierNMF2 [25] for fast document clustering.

Problem definition

As mentioned above, there is no universally accepted definition for network communities. Rather than defining community detection as optimizing some specific measurement criteria, we believe it would be more effective and flexible to understand the
problem by clearly defining what makes a community detection result good.

In this paper, we focus on link-based community detection, and use functional communities (if known) as ground truth. In general, to evaluate link-based community
detection results, we may ask several questions. The first is whether the result is coher-
ent from the point of view of network links (Q1). There are many measurement scores
defined based on the presumption that a community should have more intraconnections
than interconnections. These measures include normalized cut, ratio cut, conductance,
etc. The second question is whether the result agrees with prior knowledge, especially
the ground truth if it is known (Q2). There have been largely two approaches. One is
to manually analyze the results with some known meta-information (such as the entity
each node represents), which is not scalable to large networks. Another approach is to
compare the community detection result using some measures such as $F1$ score, which
assumes the existence of ground truth. Finally, we would like to know whether the result
reveals some new and useful information about the network (Q3). This is mostly relevant for the study of small networks [15]. For large networks, it is almost impossible to
manually check all communities discovered. However, the answers to Q2 may guide our
focus to more interesting parts of the network.

Ground-truth communities

Ground-truth communities of large networks were not available to researchers until
Yang and Leskovec [1] defined ground-truth communities (as found in SNAP[1]) for several real-world large networks, including several social networks, paper coauthorship
networks, and product copurchase networks. In their work, the ground-truth communities are defined using functional communities already present in the data. For example,
in social networks, user groups can be treated as communities; in paper coauthorship
networks, two authors publishing in the same venue can be seen to be in the same community; in product copurchase networks, product category can be naturally used as
communities. These functional communities are not necessarily directly related to network structures. For example, the product category is an inherent property of a product,
which can never be affected by copurchasing activities. Therefore, it is not reasonable to
expect that link-based community detection algorithms can fully recover functional
communities. On the other hand, many studies show that there are close relations
between link-based communities and functional communities. The paper [4] shows that
many linkage-based measurements (such as normalized cut, conductance, etc.) also have
good performance on functional communities. Also, the results of link-based community detection algorithms can sometimes recover functional communities.

Based on the above observations, we conclude that link-based community detection
algorithms have the ability to partially recover functional communities, but such ability

---

[1] https://snap.stanford.edu/data/.

is inherently limited by the essential differences between functional communities and link-based communities. This should be kept in mind when comparing link-based community detection results against ground-truth communities.

Overlapping vs nonoverlapping communities

Real-world network communities are usually overlapping. For example, it is common that one user joins a variety of groups in a social network. However, our current focus is on nonoverlapping community detection, since nonoverlapping community detection is also very useful for revealing the network structure, and our algorithm is designed to detect nonoverlapping communities efficiently. The results of a good-quality nonoverlapping community detection algorithm can be used as an effective starting point for overlapping community detection [2, 3].

Hierarchical rank-2 symmetric NMF

We present an algorithm called HierSymNMF2 for hierarchical community detection. HierSymNMF2 uses a fast SymNMF algorithm [14] with rank 2 (SymNMF2) for binary community detection and recursively apply SymNMF2 to further binary split one of the communities into two communities in each step. This process is repeated until a preset number of communities is discovered, or there are no more communities that are worthy of any further binary split. Our approach starts with a low rank approximation (LRA) of the data based on the nonnegative matrix factorization (NMF), which reduces the dimension of the data while keeping key information. In addition, the results of NMF-based methods directly provide information regarding the assignment of data to clusters/communities.

Given the vast amounts of nonnegative data available for extracting critical information, the NMF has found a wealth of applications in such domains as image, text, and chemical data processing. It can be shown that applying algorithms to such data without constraining the solution can result in uninterpretable results such as negative chemical concentrations and possibly false negative and/or false positive detections, which could lead to meaningless results [29]. For text analytics, a corpus of text documents can be represented by a nonnegative term-document matrix. Likewise, for graph analytics, the nonnegative adjacency matrix is used as an input to NMF algorithms. NMF seeks an approximation of such nonnegative matrices with a product of two nonnegative low rank matrices. With various constraints and regularization terms on the NMF objective function, there are many variants of NMF, which are appropriate for a large variety of problem domains. A common formulation of NMF is the following:

$$\min_{W \geq 0, H \geq 0} \|X - WH\|_F \qquad (1)$$

where $X \in \mathbb{R}_+^{m \times n}$, $W \in \mathbb{R}_+^{m \times k}$, $H \in \mathbb{R}_+^{k \times n}$ ($\mathbb{R}_+$ is the set of all real nonnegative numbers), and $k \ll \min(m, n)$. In this formulation, each data item is represented by a column of the matrix X, and each column in the matrix H can be seen as a low rank representation of the data item. Nonnegativity constraints allow such a low rank representation to be more interpretable than other low rank approximations such as SVD. This formulation can be applied to areas such as document clustering [26] and can be solved efficiently for very large m and n [30]. However, when k reaches a value on the order of thousands, NMF algorithms become slow. To solve this issue, [25] developed a divide-and-conquer method that relies on rank-2 NMF, where $k = 2$, which exhibits significant speedups. The framework of this divide-and-conquer method is shown in Algorithm 1. In this divide-and-conquer framework, the task of splitting one cluster into two clusters is performed by rank-2 NMF, which reduces the superlinear time complexity with respect to k to linear [25].

Algorithm 1 Divide-and-Conquer Framework for Divisive Hierarchical Clustering

1: **Initialization**: One cluster containing all nodes.
2: **repeat**
3:      Choose one of the clusters to split.
4:      Split the chosen cluster into two clusters.
5: **until** there are k clusters (or other stopping criteria)

A variant of NMF, SymNMF [13, 14], which is the symmetric version of NMF, can be used for graph clustering. The formulation of SymNMF is

$$\min_{H \geq 0} \|S - HH^T\|_F \tag{2}$$

where $S \in \mathbb{R}^{n \times n}$ is a symmetric similarity matrix of graph nodes: $H \in \mathbb{R}_+^{n \times k}$ and $k \ll n$. Some choices of the input matrix S for SymNMF are adjacency matrix $S^\mathcal{G}$ and normalized adjacency matrix $D^{-1/2} S^\mathcal{G} D^{-1/2}$, where $D = \mathrm{diag}(d_1, \ldots, d_n)$, and $d_i = \sum_{j=1}^n S_{ij}^\mathcal{G}$ is the degree of node i. When S is the adjacency matrix, (2) is a relaxation of maximizing the ratio association; when S is the normalized adjacency matrix, (2) is a relaxation of minimizing the normalized cut [13] (see Appendices A, B for a complete proof). SymNMF is an effective algorithm for graph clustering, but for large k, improvements in computational efficiency are necessary.

The algorithm we introduce in this paper uses the framework shown in Algorithm 1, where a cluster is a community, and the task of splitting a community is performed by our rank-2 version of SymNMF. The decision to choose the next node to split is based on a criterion discussed in the next section. In the following sections, we denote S as the similarity matrix representing a graph $\mathcal{G}$, and S_c as the matrix representation of a community, i.e., a subgraph of $\mathcal{G}$ (the corresponding submatrix of S).

Splitting a community using rank-2 SymNMF

Splitting a community is achieved by rank-2 SymNMF of $S_c \approx HH^T$ where $H \in \mathbb{R}_+^{n \times 2}$. The result H naturally induces a binary split of the community: suppose $H = (h_{ij})$, then

$$c_i = \begin{cases} 1, & h_{i1} > h_{i2}; \\ 0, & \text{otherwise.} \end{cases}$$

where c_i is the community assignment of the ith graph node.

A formal formulation of rank-2 SymNMF is the following optimization problem:

$$\min_{H \geq 0} \|S - HH^T\|_F^2 \tag{3}$$

where $H \in \mathbb{R}_+^{n \times 2}$. This is a special case of SymNMF when $k = 2$, which can be solved by a general SymNMF algorithm [13, 14]. However, by combining the *alternating nonnegative least squares* (ANLS) algorithm for SymNMF from [14] and the fast algorithm for rank-2 NMF from [25], we can obtain a fast algorithm for rank-2 SymNMF.

First, we rewrite (3) into asymmetric form plus a penalty term [31] as follows:

$$\min_{W,H \geq 0} \|S - WH^{\mathrm{T}}\|_F^2 + \alpha \|W - H\|_F^2, \tag{4}$$

where W and $H \in \mathbb{R}_+^{n \times 2}$, and $\alpha > 0$ is a scalar parameter for the tradeoff between the approximation error and the difference between W and H. Formulation (4) can be solved using a two-block coordinate descent framework, alternating between the optimizations for W and H. When we solve for W, (4) can be reformulated as

$$\min_{W \geq 0} \left\| \begin{bmatrix} H \\ \sqrt{\alpha}I_2 \end{bmatrix} W^{\mathrm{T}} - \begin{bmatrix} S \\ \sqrt{\alpha}H^{\mathrm{T}} \end{bmatrix} \right\|_F^2 \tag{5}$$

where I_2 is the 2×2 identity matrix. Similarly, when we solve for H, (4) can be reformulated as

$$\min_{H \geq 0} \left\| \begin{bmatrix} W \\ \sqrt{\alpha}I_2 \end{bmatrix} H^{\mathrm{T}} - \begin{bmatrix} S \\ \sqrt{\alpha}W^{\mathrm{T}} \end{bmatrix} \right\|_F^2. \tag{6}$$

We note that both (5) and (6) are in the following form:

$$\min_{Y \geq 0} \|FY - G\|_F^2, \tag{7}$$

where $F \in \mathbb{R}_+^{m \times 2}$, $G \in \mathbb{R}_+^{m \times n}$. This formulation can be efficiently solved by an improved active-set-type algorithm described in [25], which we call `rank2nnls-fast`. The idea behind `rank2nnls-fast` can be summarized as follows: the optimization problem (7) can be decomposed into n independent subproblems in the following form:

$$\min_{y \geq 0} \|Fy - g\|_2^2 \tag{8}$$

where y and $g \in \mathbb{R}_+^2$, where $Y = [y_1, \ldots, y_n]$, and $G = [g_1, \ldots, g_n]$. To solve (8) efficiently, we note that when $g \neq 0$, there will be only three possible cases for $y = [y_1, y_2]$, where only one of y_1 and y_2 is 0 or both are positive. These three cases can easily be solved by the usual least-squares algorithms, e.g., normal equations. Details can be found in Algorithm 2 in [25].

Choosing a node to split based on normalized cut

The "best" community to split further is chosen by computing and comparing *splitting scores* for all current communities corresponding to the leaf nodes in the hierarchy. The proposed splitting scores are based on normalized cut. We make this choice because (1) normalized cut determines whether a split is structurally effective since it measures the difference between intraconnections and interconnections among network nodes; and (2) for SymNMF, when S is the normalized adjacency matrix, the SymNMF objective function is equivalent to (a relaxation of) minimizing the normalized cut, which is the preferred choice in graph clustering [14].

Suppose we have a graph $\mathcal{G} = (V, E)$, where the weight of an edge (u, v) is $w(u, v)$. Note that for an unweighted graph, $w(u, v) = 1$ if edge $(u, v) \in E$; otherwise, $w(u, v) = 0$. Let $A_1, \ldots, A_k$ be k pairwise disjoint subsets of V, where $\bigcup_{i=1}^{k} A_i = V$; then, the normalized cut of the partition $(A_1, \ldots, A_k)$ is defined as

$$ncut(A_1, \ldots, A_k) = \sum_{i=1}^{k} \frac{out(A_i)}{within(A_i) + out(A_i)} \tag{9}$$

where

$$within(A_i) = \sum_{u,v \in A_i} w(u, v) \tag{10}$$

which measures the number of edges inside the subgraph induced by A_i (intraconnection); and

$$out(A_i) = \sum_{u \in A_i, v \in V \setminus A_i} w(u, v) \tag{11}$$

measures the number of edges between A_i and the remaining nodes in the graph (interconnection). Note that in the definition of $within(A_i)$ (10), each edge within A_i is counted twice. In the special case, $k = 2$, we have

$$out(A_1) = \sum_{u \in A_1, v \in A_2} w(u, v) = out(A_2) \overset{\text{def}}{=} cut(A_1, A_2) \tag{12}$$

From Eq. (9), it is evident that when each community has many more intraconnections than interconnections, there is a small normalized cut.

For example, the graph shown in Fig. 1 originally has three communities A_1, A_2 and A_3, and the corresponding normalized cut is

$$ncut(A_1, A_2, A_3) = \frac{out(A_1)}{within(A_1) + out(A_1)} + \frac{out(A_2)}{within(A_2) + out(A_2)} + \frac{out(A_3)}{within(A_3) + out(A_3)}$$

The community A_3 is now split into two smaller communities B_1 and B_2 and normalized cut can be used to measure the goodness of this split. We consider three possibilities: (1) isolate A_3 and compute normalized cut of the split as

$$ncut|_{A_3}(B_1, B_2) = \frac{out|_{A_3}(B_1)}{within(B_1) + out|_{A_3}(B_1)} + \frac{out|_{A_3}(B_2)}{within(B_2) + out|_{A_3}(B_2)}$$

where the subscript A_3 means only consider the edges inside A_3. We denote the above criterion by `ncut_local`. (2) A more global criterion is to also consider the edges that go across A_3:

$$ncut(B_1, B_2) = \frac{out(B_1)}{within(B_1) + out(B_1)} + \frac{out(B_2)}{within(B_2) + out(B_2)}$$

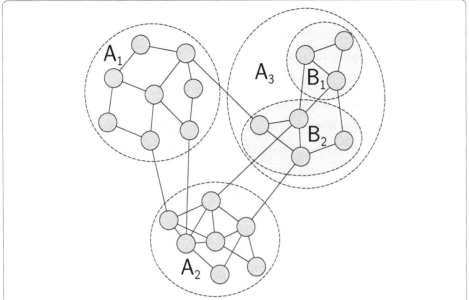

Fig. 1 A graph for illustrating normalized cut and our splitting criteria. The structure of the graph is inspired by Figure 1 from [15]

This criterion is denoted by `ncut_global`. (3) Minimize the global normalized cut using a greedy strategy. Specifically, choose the split that results in the minimal increase in the global normalized cut:

$$
\text{ncut}(A_1, A_2, B_1, B_2) - \text{ncut}(A_1, A_2, A_3)
$$
$$
= \frac{\text{out}(B_1)}{\text{within}(B_1) + \text{out}(B_1)} + \frac{\text{out}(B_2)}{\text{within}(B_2) + \text{out}(B_2)} - \frac{\text{out}(A_3)}{\text{within}(A_3) + \text{out}(A_3)}
$$

We denote this criterion by `ncut_global_diff` and will compare the performance of these three criteria in later sections.

Implementation

In the previous work on rank-2 NMF [32] that takes a term-document matrix as input in the context of text clustering, *sparse–dense matrix multiplication* (SpMM) was the main computational bottleneck for computing the solution. However, this is not the case with rank-2 SymNMF or HierSymNMF2 for community detection problems on typical large-scale networks. Suppose we have an $n \times n$ adjacency matrix with z nonzeros as an input to rank-2 SymNMF. In Algorithm 2, i.e., Nonnegative Least Squares (NLS) with two unknowns, SpMM costs $2z$ floating-point operations (flops), while searching for the optimal active set (abbreviated as `opt-act`) costs $12n$ flops. Of the $12n$ flops for `opt-act`, $8n$ flops are required for solving n linear systems each of size 2×2 corresponding to line 1 in Algorithm 2, and the remaining $4n$ flops are incurred by lines 4–5. Note that comparison operations and the memory I/O required by `opt-act` are ignored.

Algorithm 2 Algorithm for solving $\min_{\mathbf{g} \geq 0} \|B\mathbf{g} - \mathbf{y}\|_2^2$, where $B = [\mathbf{b}_1, \mathbf{b}_2] \in \mathbb{R}_+^{m \times 2}, \mathbf{y} \in \mathbb{R}_+^{m \times 1}$

1: Solve unconstrained least squares $\mathbf{g}^\emptyset \leftarrow \min \|B\mathbf{g} - \mathbf{y}\|_2^2$ by normal equation $B^T B \mathbf{g} = B^T \mathbf{y}$
2: **if** $\mathbf{g}^\emptyset \geq 0$ **then return** $\mathbf{g}^\emptyset$
3: **else**
4:     $g_1^* \leftarrow (\mathbf{y}^T \mathbf{b}_1)/(\mathbf{b}_1^T \mathbf{b}_1)$
5:     $g_2^* \leftarrow (\mathbf{y}^T \mathbf{b}_2)/(\mathbf{b}_2^T \mathbf{b}_2)$
6:     **if** $g_1^* \|\mathbf{b}_1\|_2 \geq g_2^* \|\mathbf{b}_2\|_2$ **then return** $[g_1^*, 0]^T$
7:        **else return** $[0, g_2^*]^T$
8:     **end if**
9: **end if**

The above rough estimation of computational complexity reveals that if $z \leq 6n$, or equivalently, if each row of the input adjacency matrix contains no more than 6 nonzeros on average, then SpMM will not be the major bottleneck of the rank-2 SymNMF algorithm. In other words, when the input adjacency matrix is extremely sparse, which is the typical case we have seen on various datasets (Table 1), then further acceleration of the algorithmic steps in `opt-act` will achieve higher efficiency.

Figure 2 (upper) shows the proportions of runtime corresponding to SpMM, `opt-act`, and other algorithmic steps implemented in Matlab, which demonstrate that both SpMM and `opt-act` are the targets for performance optimization.

Multithreaded SpMM

SpMM is a required routine in lines 1, 4, and 5 of Algorithm 2. The problem can be written as

$$Y \leftarrow A \cdot X, \tag{13}$$

where $A \in \mathbb{R}^{n \times n}$ is a sparse matrix and $X, Y \in \mathbb{R}^{n \times k}$ are dense matrices.[2]

Most open-source and commercial software packages for sparse matrix manipulation have a single-threaded implementation for SpMM, for example, Matlab[3], Eigen[4], and Armadillo[5] (the same is also true for SpMV, *sparse matrix–vector multiplication*). For the Intel Math Kernel Library[6], while we are not able to view the source, our simple tests have shown that it can exploit only one CPU core for computing SpMM. Part of the reason for the lack of parallel implementation of SpMM in generic software packages is that the best implementation for computing SpMM for a particular matrix A depends on the sparsity pattern of A.

In this paper, we present a simple yet effective implementation to compute SpMM for a matrix A that represents an undirected network. We exploit two important facts in order to reach high performance:

- Since the nodes of the network are arranged in an arbitrary order, the matrix A is not assumed to have any special sparsity pattern. Thus, we can store the matrix A in the commonly used generic storage, the *compressed sparse column* (CSC) format, as is

---

[2] The more general form of SpMM is $Y \leftarrow Y + A \cdot X$. Our algorithm only requires the more simplistic form $Y \leftarrow A \cdot X$, and thus, for this case, we wrote a specific routine saving n operations for addition.

[3] https://www.mathworks.com/.

[4] http://eigen.tuxfamily.org.

[5] http://arma.sourceforge.net/.

[6] https://software.intel.com/en-us/intel-mkl.

Table 1 Some statistics for ground-truth communities from SNAP

Dataset	#Nodes	#Edges	Nodes that belong to 0 Community		Nodes that belong to 1 Community		
			Count	%	Count	%	Rel %
DBLP06	317,080	1,049,866	56,082	17.69	150,192	47.37	57.55
Youtube	1,134,890	2,987,624	1,082,215	95.36	32,613	2.87	61.91
Amazon	334,863	925,872	14,915	4.45	10,604	3.17	3.31
LiveJournal	3,997,962	34,681,189	2,850,014	71.29	394,234	9.86	34.34
Friendster	65,608,366	1,806,067,135	57,663,417	87.89	3,546,017	5.40	44.63
Orkut	3,072,441	117,185,083	750,142	24.42	128,094	4.17	5.52

The last few columns show the number of nodes that do not belong to any communities and the number of nodes that belong to only one community. The "Rel %" is the number of nodes that belong to one community divided by the number of nodes that belong to at least one community

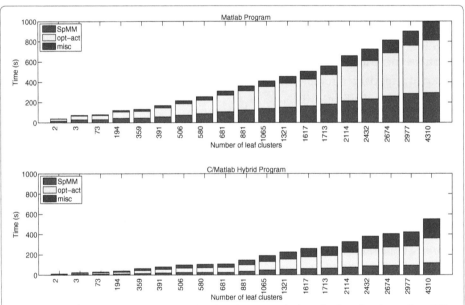

Fig. 2 Runtime for SpMM, opt-act, and other algorithmic steps (indicated as "misc") in the HierSymNMF2 algorithm. The experiments were performed on the *DBLP06* dataset. The plots show the runtime for generating various numbers of leaf nodes. *Upper* timing results for the Matlab program; *lower* timing results for the C/Matlab hybrid program

practiced in the built-in sparse matrix type in Matlab. As a result, nonzeros of A are stored column-by-column.

- The matrix A is symmetric. This property enables us to build an SpMM routine for A^TX to compute AX.

The second fact above is particularly important: When A is stored in the CSC format, computing AX with multiple threads would incur atomic operations or mutex locks to avoid race conditions between different threads. Implementing multithreaded A^TX is much easier, since A^T can be viewed as a matrix with nonzeros stored row-by-row, and we can divide the rows of A^T into several chunks and compute the product of each row chunk with X on one thread. Our customized SpMM implementation is described in Algorithm 3.

Algorithm 3 Sparse-dense matrix multiplication (SpMM) of a symmetric sparse matrix and a smaller dense matrix

---
Input: Sparse matrix $A \in \mathbb{R}^{n \times n}$, where $A = A^T$ with z nonzeros stored in the CSC format, dense matrices $X \in \mathbb{R}^{n \times k}$ and number of threads N_t.
Output: Dense matrix $Y \in \mathbb{R}^{n \times k} = AX$.
 1: Estimate number of nonzeros assigned to each thread: $z_t = \lfloor \frac{z-1}{N_t} \rfloor + 1$
 2: **for** $t = 1$ to N_t (in parallel)
 3:     **if** $t == 1$ **then** Start of row chunk $s = 0$
 4:     **else** Use binary search to determine s such that tz_t nonzeros appear before the s-th row
 5:     **end if**
 6:     **if** $t == N_t$ **then** End of row chunk $r = 0$
 7:     **else** Use binary search to determine r such that tz_t nonzeros appear before the $(r+1)$-th row
 8:     **end if**
 9:     Compute $Y(s:r,:) \leftarrow A(:,s:r)^T X$ using a sequential implementation
10: **end for**

In addition, the original adjacency matrix often has the value "1" as every nonzero entry, that is, all the edges in the network carry the same weight. Thus, multiplication operations are no longer needed in SpMM with such a sparse matrix. Therefore, we have developed a specialized routine for the case where the original adjacency matrix is provided as input to HierSymNMF2.

C/Matlab hybrid implementation of opt-act

The search for the optimal active set, opt-act, is the most time-consuming step in the algorithm for NLS with two columns (Fig. 2 (lower)) when the input matrix is extremely sparse. Our overall program was written in Matlab, and the performance of the opt-act portion was optimized with native C code. The optimization exploits multiple CPU cores using OpenMP, and the software vectorization is enabled by calling AVX (*advanced vector extensions*) intrinsics.

It turns out that a C/Matlab hybrid implementation is the preferred choice for achieving high performance with native C code. Intel CPUs are equipped with AVX vector registers, since the Sandy Bridge architecture and these vector registers are essential for applying the same instructions to multiple data entries (known as *instruction-level parallelism* or SIMD). For example, a 256-bit AVX register can process four double-precision floating point numbers (64-bit each) in one CPU cycle, which amounts to four times speed-up over a sequential program. AVX intrinsics are external libraries for exploiting AVX vector registers in native C code. These libraries are not part of the ANSI C standard but retain mostly the same interface on various operating systems (Windows, Linux, etc). However, to obtain the best performance from vector registers, functions in the AVX libraries often require the operands having aligned memory addresses (32-byte aligned for double precision numbers). The function calls for aligned memory allocation, which is completely platform dependent for native C code, means that our software would not be easily portable across various platforms if aligned memory allocation were managed in the C code. Therefore, in order to strike the right balance between computational efficiency and software portability, our strategy is to allocate memory within Matlab for the vectors involved in opt-act, since Matlab arrays are memory aligned in a cross-platform fashion.

Finally, note that the `opt-act` step in lines 1, 4, and 5 of Algorithm 2 contains several division operations, which cost more than 20 CPU cycles each and are much more expensive than multiplication operations (1 CPU cycle). This large discrepancy in time cost would be substantial for vector–scalar operations. Therefore, we replace vector–scalar division, in the form of $\mathbf{x}/\alpha$ where $\mathbf{x}$ is a vector and α is a scalar, by vector–scalar multiplication, in the form of $\mathbf{x} \cdot (1/\alpha)$.

Experiments

Methods for comparison

We compare our algorithm with some recent algorithms mentioned in the "Related work" section. We use eight threads for all methods that support multithreading. For NISE, we are only able to use one thread because its parallel version exits with errors in our experiments. For all the algorithms, default parameters are used if not specified. To better communicate the results, below are the labels that denote each algorithm, which will be used in the following tables:

- `h2-n(g)(d)-a(x)`: These labels represent several versions of our algorithm. Here `h2` stands for HierSymNMF2, `n` for the `ncut_local` criterion, `ng` for the `ncut_global` criterion, and `ngd` for the `ncut_global_diff` criterion (see previous sections for the definitions of these criteria); 'a' means that we compute the real normalized cut using the original adjacency matrix; and 'x' indicates that an approximated normalized cut is computed using the normalized adjacency matrix, which usually results in faster computations. We stop our algorithm after $k - 1$ binary splits where k is the number of communities to find. Theoretically, this will generate k communities. However, we remove fully disconnected communities, as outliers since they are often far from being significant because of their unusually small size and they correspond to all-zero submatrices in the graph adjacency matrix, which does not have a meaningful rank-2 representation. Therefore, the final number of communities are usually slightly smaller than k, as will be shown in "Experiment results" section.
- `SCD`: SCD algorithm [17].
- `BigClam`: BigClam algorithm [1].
- `Graclus`: Graclus algorithm [11].
- `NISE`: An improved version of NISE that is published in 2016 [3].

Evaluation measures

Internal measures: average normalized cut/conductance

Normalized cut (9) is a measurement of the extent that communities have more intra-connections than interconnections and is shown to be an effective score [4]. Since our algorithm implicitly minimizes the normalized cut, it is natural to use normalized cut as an internal measure of community/clustering quality. One drawback of normalized cut is that it tends to increase when the number of communities increases. In Appendix B, we prove that the normalized cut strictly increases when one community is split into two. In practice, we observed that the normalized cut increases almost linearly with respect to the number of communities. Some community detection algorithms automatically determine the number of communities; hence, it is not fair to compare normalized cut for such algorithms against others that detect a preassigned number of communities. Therefore, it makes more sense to use the average normalized cut, i.e., the normalized cut divided by the number of communities. In addition, since the average normalized cut can be treated as a per-community property, it also applies to overlapping communities. Given k communities $A_1, \ldots, A_k$ (which may be overlapping), we define the average normalized cut as

$$\mathrm{AvgNcut}(A_1, \ldots, A_k) = \frac{1}{k} \sum_{i=1}^{k} \frac{\mathrm{out}(A_i)}{\mathrm{within}(A_i) + \mathrm{out}(A_i)} \tag{14}$$

Conductance [33], which is shown to be an effective measure [4], is defined for a community as $\mathrm{Conductance}(A_i) = \frac{\mathrm{out}(A_i)}{\mathrm{within}(A_i) + \mathrm{out}(A_i)}$. Hence the average normalized cut is actually equal to the average conductance (per community).

External measures: precision, recall, and F-score

Alternatively, we can measure the qualities of detected communities by comparing them with ground truth. Suppose k communities $A_1, \ldots, A_k$ were detected, and the ground truth has k' communities $B_1, \ldots, B_{k'}$. We compute the confusion matrix $C = (c_{ij})_{k \times k'}$, where $c_{ij} = |A_i \cap B_j|$. Then, pairwise scores can be defined as

$$\mathrm{Precision}(A_i, B_j) = \mathrm{recall}(B_j, A_i) = \frac{c_{ij}}{|A_i|}$$

$$\mathrm{Recall}(A_i, B_j) = \mathrm{precision}(B_j, A_i) = \frac{c_{ij}}{|B_j|}$$

$$F_1(A_i, B_j) = F_1(B_j, A_i) = \frac{2c_{ij}}{|A_i| + |B_j|}$$

$$F_\beta(A_i, B_j) = F_{1/\beta}(B_j, A_i) = \frac{(1 + \beta^2)c_{ij}}{|A_i| + \beta^2 |B_j|}.$$

Although a global best match (i.e., finding a one-to-one mapping) between detected communities and ground-truth communities would be ideal, finding such a match is time consuming. We used per-community best match as a heuristic alternative. Specifically, we define the average F_1 score [1] as

$$F_1 = \frac{1}{2} \left(\frac{1}{k} \sum_{i=1}^{k} \max_j F_1(A_i, B_j) + \frac{1}{k'} \sum_{j=1}^{k'} \max_i F_1(B_j, A_i) \right).$$

The average precision and average recall can be defined in a similar way. When comparing detected communities against ground truth, we remove nodes without ground-truth labels from the detected communities to achieve meaningful comparisons.

Datasets

The data used for the experimental results of this paper are mostly from SNAP datasets [4, 34]. In our study, we found that the ground-truth information in SNAP is incomplete; for example, a large percentage of nodes do not belong to any ground-truth community.

Table 1 shows some statistics regarding the number of communities to which each node belongs.

Although all of these datasets can be conveniently accessed on the SNAP website as a graph with ground-truth communities, *DBLP06* is the only dataset with a complete raw dataset openly available to the public. The other five datasets (*Youtube, Amazon, Live-Journal, Friendster,* and *Orkut*) were obtained by crawling the web, and they are far from being complete. Crawling large complex graphs is challenging by itself that may need extensive and specialized research efforts. We do not aim to solve this issue in this paper. The *Orkut* and *Youtube* datasets can be acquired from [35]. Detailed descriptions are available explaining the crawling procedure and analysis of the completeness. It has been concluded that the *Orkut* and *Youtube* datasets are not complete. Such incompleteness in crawled datasets is expected due to intrinsic restrictions of web crawling such as rate limit and privacy protection. The *Friendster* data were crawled by the ArchiveTeam, and the *LiveJournal* data come from [36]. The *Amazon* data were crawled by the SNAP group [37]. However, information on how the data were collected and processed and the information on analysis of data completeness are not available.

Possible reasons that many nodes in these datasets do not belong to any communities are (1) SNAP removed communities with less than three nodes, which caused some nodes to "lose" their memberships; (2) the well-known incompleteness of crawled datasets; (3) for social networks (*Youtube, LiveJournal, Friendster,* and *Orkut*), it is common that a user does not join any user groups; (4) SNAP used the dataset from [36] to generate the *DBLP06* dataset, which was published in 2006. At that time, the DBLP database was not as mature and complete as it is today. Another issue of the above datasets is that all nodes are anonymized, which ensures protection of user privacy, but limits our ability to interpret community detection results.

The DBLP data are openly accessible, and are provided using a highly structured format—XML. We reconstructed the coauthorship network and ground-truth communities from a recent DBLP snapshot to obtain a more recent and complete DBLP dataset with all of the meta-information preserved (see the following subsection). Although the other datasets which we currently cannot improve are also valuable, our goal is to obtain new information from comparison of community detection results and ground-truth communities, rather than simply recovering the ground-truth communities.

Constructing the DBLP15 dataset

DBLP is an online reference for bibliographic information on major computer science publications [38]. As of June 17, 2015, DBLP has indexed 4316 conferences, 1417 journals, and 1,573,969 authors [39]. The whole DBLP dataset is provided in a well-formatted XML file. The snapshot/release version of the data we use can be accessed at http://dblp.dagstuhl.de/xml/release/dblp-2015-06-02.xml.gz. The structure of this XML file is illustrated in Fig. 3. The root element is the `dblp` element. We call the children of the root elements *Level 1 elements* and the children of Level 1 elements *Level 2 elements*, and so on. Level 1 elements represent the individual data records [40], such as `article` and `book`, etc. Since publication–venue relation makes more sense for the journal and conference papers, and these two types of publications occupy most of DBLP, we consider only `article` and `inproceedings` elements when constructing our dataset.

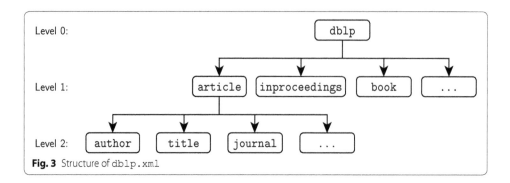

Fig. 3 Structure of dblp.xml

Level 2 elements contain the meta-information about the publications, such as title, authors, journal/proceeding names, etc.

Our goal is to obtain a coauthorship network and ground-truth information (venue–author relation) from the XML file. Although the XML file is highly structured, such a task is still not straightforward due to the ambiguity of entities, such as conflicts or changes of author names, various abbreviations, or even journal name change. DBLP resolves the author ambiguity issue by means of a unique number for each author. However, the venue ambiguity is still an issue in DBLP: there are no unique identifiers for venues. Fortunately, each record in DBLP has a unique key, and most paper keys contain the venue information as follows:

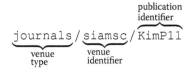

However, there are still a few exceptions. To examine the validity of venue identifiers efficiently, we manually examine the identifiers not listed in the journal and conference index provided by the DBLP website, since such indices seem to be maintained by humans and assumed to be reliable. Using this process, we found 5240 unique venues (journals or conferences).

Now unique identifiers for both authors and venues make extracting the network and community information very reasonable. The next step is to create a node for each author, and create a link between two authors if they have ever coauthored in the same publication. For community information, each venue is a community, and an author belongs to a community if he/she has published in the corresponding venue.

A few authors do not have any coauthor in the DBLP database, and become isolated nodes in the generated network. Thus, we remove these authors. However, after removing those authors, some venues/communities become empty because all of their authors are removed. Hence, we remove those empty communities. After this cleaning, we obtained 1,509,944 authors in 5147 communities (venues).

This cleaned network has 51,328 (weakly) connected components, where the largest connected component contains 1,357,781 nodes, which makes 89.9% of all nodes. The remaining 51,327 connected components are all small, the largest of which has only 37 nodes. We take the largest connected component as the network to study. By extracting the largest connected component, we obtain a network with 1,357,781 nodes, 6,369,212 edges and 5146 ground-truth communities. The ground-truth communities were divided into connected components, obtaining 93,824 communities. The divided ground-truth communities were used for comparison with detected communities.

The new *DBLP15* dataset is available at https://github.com/smallk/smallk_data/tree/master/dblp_ground_truth.

Experiment results

We run our experiments on a server with two Intel E5-2620 processors, each having six cores, and 377-GB memory. The results are listed in Tables 2, 3, 4, 5, 6, 7, 8, and 9.

In the "internal measures" table, "coverage" measures the percentage of nodes which are assigned to at least one community; "algorithm time" and "total time" provide the runtime information. We list two measures of runtime since our algorithm (and also NISE) implemented in MATLAB directly uses a processed matrix in memory as its input. Other algorithms must first read the graph stored as an edge list or an adjacency list and convert the graph to the appropriate internal representation. Therefore, we use "algorithm time" to measure the algorithm runtime without the time needed for reading and converting the graph, which is reported by the algorithms themselves. The "total time" is the wall clock time for running the algorithm, including the time for reading

Table 2 *DBLP06*: internal measures

Algorithm	Number of clusters	Coverage (%)	Algorithm time (s)	Total time (s)	Average Ncut
h2-n-a	4982	98.57	612.99	614.12	0.2089
h2-n-x	4981	98.55	587.98	589.10	0.2174
h2-ng-a	4984	98.48	921.99	923.14	0.1922
h2-ng-x	4982	98.50	872.48	873.64	0.1921
h2-ngd-a	4986	98.64	882.27	883.41	0.1767
h2-ngd-x	4984	98.66	908.31	909.46	0.1774
SCD	139,986	100.00	1.89	4.52	0.8091
BigClam	5000	90.57	N/A	230.59	0.6083
Graclus	5000	100.00	161.70	162.01	0.2228
NISE	5463	99.33	501.38	501.53	0.2026

Table 3 *DBLP06*: external measures

Algorithm	Number of clusters	F1	Precision	Recall	Reverse precision	Reverse recall
h2-n-a	3312	0.4355	0.8804	0.5242	0.9005	0.4030
h2-n-x	3298	0.4236	0.8855	0.5071	0.9007	0.3937
h2-ng-a	3211	0.4417	0.8708	0.5492	0.8490	0.3996
h2-ng-x	3118	0.4374	0.8742	0.5497	0.8574	0.3898
h2-ngd-a	3192	0.4577	0.8575	0.5800	0.8719	0.4091
h2-ngd-x	3138	0.4534	0.8541	0.5808	0.8768	0.4008
SCD	34,705	0.4644	0.9817	0.1268	0.7053	0.9755
BigClam	4952	0.3778	0.4857	0.6807	0.9269	0.3121
Graclus	4633	0.4765	0.6915	0.6006	0.8852	0.4517
NISE	4903	0.4118	0.5735	0.7942	0.9518	0.3552

Table 4 *Amazon*: **internal measures**

Algorithm	Number of clusters	Coverage (%)	Algorithm time (s)	Total time (s)	Average Ncut
h2-n-a	4989	98.84	466.99	468.09	0.1657
h2-n-x	4988	98.80	452.05	453.13	0.1711
h2-ng-a	4990	98.73	537.82	538.91	0.1617
h2-ng-x	4988	98.66	514.71	515.81	0.1709
h2-ngd-a	4990	98.82	573.64	574.73	0.1491
h2-ngd-x	4990	98.79	560.86	561.96	0.1545
SCD	141,405	100.00	1.86	4.37	0.8418
BigClam	5000	97.31	N/A	169.51	0.3198
Graclus	5000	100.00	119.25	119.45	0.1450
NISE	5182	99.63	990.84	990.86	0.1118

Table 5 *Amazon*: **external measures**

Algorithm	Number of clusters	F1	Precision	Recall	Reverse precision	Reverse recall
h2-n-a	1069	0.7883	0.9747	0.8179	0.9057	0.7593
h2-n-x	1038	0.7717	0.9787	0.8109	0.9070	0.7311
h2-ng-a	1209	0.7422	0.9657	0.7247	0.8748	0.7622
h2-ng-x	1185	0.7268	0.9655	0.7152	0.8743	0.7372
h2-ngd-a	1181	0.7813	0.9698	0.7741	0.8867	0.7922
h2-ngd-x	1168	0.7725	0.9702	0.7681	0.8869	0.7792
SCD	3841	0.6202	0.9998	0.3166	0.8186	0.9948
BigClam	1447	0.8389	0.9718	0.7824	0.9574	0.8744
Graclus	991	0.8555	0.9356	0.9471	0.9892	0.7525
NISE	2612	0.6673	0.6666	0.9733	0.9807	0.5390

Table 6 *Youtube*: **internal measures**

Algorithm	Number of clusters	Coverage (%)	Algorithm time (s)	Total time (s)	Average Ncut
h2-n-a	3782	98.10	1182.39	1185.94	0.1681
h2-n-x	3780	98.01	1189.09	1192.66	0.1634
h2-ng-a	3798	98.00	1885.15	1888.71	0.1520
h2-ng-x	3851	98.14	1816.98	1820.45	0.1491
h2-ngd-a	3886	98.27	1613.13	1616.57	0.1395
h2-ngd-x	3874	98.22	1621.04	1624.50	0.1428
SCD	998,722	100.00	12.03	20.39	0.9882
BigClam	5000	41.51	N/A	2379.84	0.7398
Graclus	5000	100.00	2160.11	2168.36	0.4919
NISE	5162	99.96	2598.25	2598.66	0.4313

and converting the graph, which is measured with an external timer. BigClam reports its algorithm time as the sum of time used in each core, and therefore, the results are not comparable. For completeness, we added the data-loading and data-preprocessing times, which are measured separately, to obtain a "total time" for the MATLAB algorithms (our algorithm and NISE).

Table 7 *Youtube*: external measures

Algorithm	Number of clusters	F1	Precision	Recall	Reverse precision	Reverse recall
h2-n-a	189	0.2907	0.9639	0.5247	0.9810	0.0403
h2-n-x	193	0.2972	0.9645	0.5411	0.9790	0.0412
h2-ng-a	241	0.2935	0.8684	0.5969	0.9315	0.0516
h2-ng-x	259	0.3027	0.8932	0.5915	0.9467	0.0551
h2-ngd-a	227	0.3030	0.9299	0.5694	0.9594	0.0484
h2-ngd-x	238	0.2978	0.9394	0.5476	0.9633	0.0507
SCD	27,864	0.3652	0.9709	0.1330	0.4453	0.9841
BigClam	3850	0.2354	0.3755	0.5187	0.4743	0.2370
Graclus	3802	0.3827	0.5761	0.5348	0.6532	0.4148
NISE	3778	0.2720	0.4762	0.7180	0.9912	0.2580

Table 8 *DBLP15*: internal measures

Algorithm	Number of clusters	Coverage (%)	Algorithm time (s)	Total time (s)	Average Ncut
h2-n-a	4982	99.66	1648.73	1654.71	0.1702
h2-n-x	4982	99.67	1666.13	1672.01	0.1743
h2-ng-a	4984	99.62	3262.76	3268.63	0.1606
h2-ng-x	4984	99.64	3220.70	3226.57	0.1568
h2-ngd-a	4987	99.69	2558.80	2564.60	0.1457
h2-ngd-x	4987	99.70	2503.58	2509.38	0.1463
SCD	565,235	100.00	16.89	33.22	0.8357
BigClam	5000	65.07	N/A	1352.57	0.6761
Graclus	5000	100.00	1980.38	1987.97	0.2732
NISE	5101	86.77	945.15	945.90	0.3482

Table 9 *DBLP15*: external measures

Algorithm	Number of clusters	F1	Precision	Recall	Reverse precision	Reverse recall
h2-n-a	4982	0.3028	0.7282	0.7000	0.9830	0.0445
h2-n-x	4982	0.2994	0.7229	0.6986	0.9833	0.0442
h2-ng-a	4984	0.3025	0.7188	0.7164	0.9066	0.0440
h2-ng-x	4984	0.2992	0.6978	0.7275	0.9095	0.0439
h2-ngd-a	4987	0.3036	0.6963	0.7455	0.9640	0.0446
h2-ngd-x	4987	0.3016	0.6839	0.7512	0.9658	0.0446
SCD	565,235	0.3477	0.8684	0.1050	0.5803	0.8218
BigClam	5000	0.0784	0.2357	0.9875	0.6806	0.0192
Graclus	5000	0.0861	0.2411	0.9874	0.7576	0.0275
NISE	5101	0.0955	0.3606	0.8307	0.7066	0.0253

The "number of clusters" in the "internal measures" table are different across different methods due to the following reasons. The SCD algorithm does not provide an interface for specifying the number of communities to detect, and instead detects the number of communities automatically. For other algorithms, we specify the number of communities to detect as 5000. The actual number of communities generated by HierSymNMF2 is usually less than 5000, as discussed in "Methods for comparison" section. Also, the number of communities generated by NISE are usually a little larger than 5000, which is also an expected behavior [3].

In the "external measures" table, the "reverse precision" and "reverse recall" refer to the scores computed as if the ground-truth communities are treated as detected communities and the detected communities are treated as the ground truth, respectively. Note that the number of clusters in "external measures" is less than the one in "internal measures" due to the removal of nodes that do not appear in the ground truth.

We have the following observations from the experimental results: (1) Our HierSym-NMF2 algorithm has significant advantages over other methods in average normalized cut on most datasets except the *Amazon* dataset. On the *Amazon* dataset, HierSym-NMF2 achieves much lower average normalized cut than SCD and BigClam, and the variant h2-ngd-a obtained comparable average normalized cut (0.1491) versus Graclus (0.1450), which is not as good as NISE (0.1118). (2) HierSymNMF2 runs slower than most other algorithms on *DBLP06* and *DBLP15*. On the *Youtube* dataset, HierSym-NMF2 runs faster than BigClam, Graclus and NISE. On the *Amazon* dataset, Hier-SymNMF2 runs faster than NISE, but slower than other methods. (3) HierSymNMF2 achieves better *F*1 score than BigClam and NISE on all the datasets we used. Graclus has better *F*1 score than HierSymNMF2 on *DBLP06*, *Amazon*, and *Youtube* datasets but obtained an unusually low *F*1 score on the *DBLP15* dataset. SCD achieves higher *F*1 scores than HierSymNMF2. However, SCD often discovers a significantly larger number of (nonoverlapping) communities than expected and has very unbalanced precision and recall scores compared with other algorithms. The SCD algorithm finds the number of communities as it finds the communities and the number of communities cannot be given to SCD as an input. The SCD algorithm starts by assigning an initial partitioning of the graph heuristically. In short, in the initial partitioning, each node and all its neighbors form a community, and special care is taken to ensure that no node belongs to more than one community. As a result, this initial step often creates many more communities than the optimal number, although later refining procedures may reduce the number of communities. As can be seen from the experimental results, when compared with Big-Clam, Graclus, NISE, and our proposed algorithms that take the number of communities as an input, a much larger number of communities that the SCD generates does not necessarily translate to a better overall community detection result in terms of either normalized cut or *F*1 scores.

Conclusions and discussion

Overall, HierSymNMF2 is an effective community detection method that optimizes the average normalized cut very well, although it is not the fastest method.

To address the quality issue of the ground-truth networks, we constructed a more complete and recent version of the DBLP dataset, where most nodes have at least one community membership and also the size of the data is significantly larger.

We partially answered the three questions we raised in "Problem definition" section. For Q1 and Q2, we used measurements that are commonly used in the current literature. One has to be careful when choosing community detection methods based on external measures such as *F*1 score because of the incompleteness of ground-truth communities and the difference between linkage-based communities (as detected) and functional communities (as in the ground truth). Therefore, it is important to use an internal measure such as the average normalized cut to evaluate an algorithm. In addition, we believe the current evaluation methods for large-scale community detection have certain limitations. These methods are mainly based on some quality scores, e.g., the $F1$ score. Such quality scores can be used to compare various algorithms. However, they do not provide much more information regarding the quality of results than the average performance. We assert that to better understand a community detection result, it is necessary to develop more comprehensive evaluation methods.

For Q3, we think that the large scale of the network and the large number of communities make the community detection results hard to interpret. One way to understand the community structure better would be to develop better methods for community visualization.

As a result of the growing popularity and utility of social media communications and other channels of communications between people and groups of people, there are vast amounts of data that contain latent community information. The amount of information is overwhelming and very demanding of our current technological capabilities, which may adversley impact the ability of stakeholders to make critical and timely decisions that are important in many domains such as natural disasters, local conflicts, healthcare, and law enforcement, to name a few. These domains typically involve groups of individuals with often hidden links. Thus, it is incumbent on the research community to develop fast and effective methods to first discover the communities formed by these links and then formulate useful summaries of the information provided by the algorithms and measures in order for decision makers to initiate appropriate actions as required.

Abbreviations
NMF: nonnegative matrix factorization; SymNMF: symmetric nonnegative matrix factorization; LRA: low rank approximation; NLS: nonnegative least squares; ANLS: alternating nonnegative least squares; SpMM: sparse–dense matrix multiplication; SpMV: sparse matrix–vector multiplication; CSC: compressed sparse column; AVX: advanced vector extensions; SIMD: single instruction, multiple data; `opt-act`: optimal active set.

Authors' contributions
DK, HP, and BD initiated the idea of the algorithm and problem formulation. RD proposed and implemented the splitting criteria, and constructed the DBLP15 dataset. DK designed and implemented the acceleration scheme and the algorithm framework. RD and DK conducted the experiments. RD wrote the initial draft of the paper and DK wrote the "Implementation" section. BD and HP rewrote and added revised and new content. All four authors iterated to finalize the manuscript. The work is supervised by HP. All authors read and approved the final manuscript.

Author details
[1] School of Mathematics, Georgia Institute of Technology, 686 Cherry Street, Atlanta, GA 30332-0160, USA. [2] Department of Mathematics, University of California, Los Angeles, 520 Portola Plaza, Los Angeles, CA 90095-1555, USA. [3] School of Computational Science and Engineering, Georgia Institute of Technology, 266 Ferst Drive, Atlanta, GA 30332-0765, USA. [4] Georgia Tech Research Institute, Georgia Institute of Technology, 250 14th Street, Atlanta, GA 30318, USA.

Competing interests
The authors declare that they have no competing interests.

Funding
The work of the authors was supported in part by the National Science Foundation (NSF) Grant IIS-1348152 and the Defense Advanced Research Projects Agency (DARPA) XDATA program Grant FA8750-12-2-0309. Any opinions, findings, and conclusions or recommendations expressed in this article are those of the authors and do not necessarily reflect the views of the NSF or DARPA.

Appendix A: Relations between SymNMF, ratio association and normalized cut

We mentioned that the SymNMF formulation

$$\min_{H \geq 0} \|S - HH^{\mathrm{T}}\|_F^2 \qquad \text{(2 revisited)}$$

is a relaxation of optimization problems related to graph partitioning. Specifically, let $S^{\mathcal{G}}$ be the adjacency matrix of graph $\mathcal{G}$. When $S = S^{\mathcal{G}}$, Eq. (2) is a relaxation of maximizing the ratio association. When $S = D^{-1/2}S^{\mathcal{G}}D^{-1/2}$, where $D = \text{diag}(d_1, \ldots, d_n)$ and $d_i = \sum_{j=1}^{n} S_{ij}^{\mathcal{G}}$ is the degree of node i, Eq. (2) is a relaxation of minimizing the normalized cut.

We defined normalized cut of a graph partition $(A_1, \ldots, A_k)$ as $\text{ncut}(A_1, \ldots, A_k)$ (Eq. (9)) using the concept of $\text{within}(A_i)$ (Eq. (10)), and $\text{out}(A_i)$ (Eq. (11)). With the same notations, the ratio association of a graph partition is defined as

$$\text{rassoc}(A_1, \ldots, A_k) = \sum_{i=1}^{k} \frac{\text{within}(A_i)}{|A_i|} \qquad (15)$$

where $|A_i|$ is the number of nodes in partition A_i.

In the following sections, we will use the convenient Iverson bracket [41]:

$$[P] = \begin{cases} 1 & \text{if } P \text{ is true;} \\ 0 & \text{otherwise.} \end{cases} \qquad (16)$$

where P is any statement. Also, $\mathcal{G} = (V, E)$ is the graph under study, where $V = \{v_1, \ldots, v_n\}$. The matrix $S = (w_{ij})$ is the adjacency matrix of graph $\mathcal{G}$, where $w_{ij} = w(v_i, v_j)$ is the weight of edge (v_i, v_j). The tuple $(A_1, \ldots, A_j)$ is a partition of graph $\mathcal{G}$.

Relation between SymNMF and ratio association

We rewrite Eq. (15) as

$$\text{rassoc}(A_1, \ldots, A_k) = \sum_{i=1}^{k} \frac{1}{|A_i|} \sum_{u,v \in A_i} w(u, v) \qquad (17)$$

Let $H = (h_{ij})_{n \times k}$ where n is the number of nodes in the graph, k is the number of partitions, and

$$h_{ij} = \frac{1}{\sqrt{|A_j|}}[v_i \in A_j]. \qquad (18)$$

Then, we have

$$\mathrm{tr}(H^{\mathrm{T}}SH) = \sum_{\substack{1 \le i \le k \\ 1 \le j,l \le n}} h_{ji} w_{jl} h_{li}$$

$$= \sum_{\substack{1 \le i \le k \\ 1 \le j,l \le n}} \frac{w_{jl}}{|A_i|} [v_j \in A_i][v_l \in A_i]$$

$$= \sum_{i=1}^{k} \frac{1}{|A_i|} \sum_{u,v \in A_i} w(u,v)$$

$$= \mathrm{rassoc}(A_1, \dots, A_k)$$

and

$$(H^{\mathrm{T}}H)_{ij} = \sum_{k} h_{ki} h_{kj}$$

$$= \sum_{k} \frac{1}{\sqrt{|A_i||A_j|}} [v_k \in A_i][v_k \in A_j]$$

$$= \frac{[i=j]}{|A_i|} \sum_{k} [v_k \in A_i]$$

$$= [i=j]$$

which means $H^{\mathrm{T}}H = I$. Therefore [42],

$$\max \mathrm{rassoc}(A_1, \dots, A_k) \Leftrightarrow \max \mathrm{tr}(H^{\mathrm{T}}SH)$$
$$\Leftrightarrow \min\{\mathrm{tr}(S^{\mathrm{T}}S) - 2\mathrm{tr}(H^{\mathrm{T}}SH) + \mathrm{tr}(I)\}$$
$$\Leftrightarrow \min \mathrm{tr}\left((S - HH^{\mathrm{T}})^{\mathrm{T}}(S - HH^{\mathrm{T}})\right) \tag{19}$$
$$\Leftrightarrow \min \|S - HH^{\mathrm{T}}\|_F^2$$

If the restriction (18) is relaxed using $H \ge 0$, i.e., nonnegative H, we will arrive at our SymNMF formulation.

Relation between SymNMF and normalized cut

Let $D = \mathrm{diag}(d_1, \dots, d_n)$, where $d_i = \sum_{j=1}^{n} w_{ij}$ is the degree of node i and let $H = (h_{ij})_{n \times k}$, where

$$h_{ij} = \frac{\sqrt{d_i}}{\sqrt{\mathrm{within}(A_j) + \mathrm{out}(A_j)}} [v_i \in A_j]. \tag{20}$$

Then, we have

$$\text{tr}(H^{\text{T}}D^{-1/2}SD^{-1/2}H) = \sum_{\substack{1 \le i \le k \\ 1 \le j,l \le n}} \frac{h_{ji}w_{jl}h_{li}}{\sqrt{d_j d_l}}$$

$$= \sum_{\substack{1 \le i \le k \\ 1 \le j,l \le n}} \frac{w_{jl}}{\text{within}(A_i) + \text{out}(A_i)}[v_j \in A_i][v_l \in A_i]$$

$$= \sum_{i=1}^{k} \frac{\text{within}(A_i)}{\text{within}(A_i) + \text{out}(A_i)}$$

$$= k - \text{ncut}(A_1, \ldots, A_k)$$

and

$$(H^{\text{T}}H)_{ij}$$

$$= \sum_k h_{ki}h_{kj}$$

$$= \sum_k \frac{d_k}{\sqrt{\text{within}(A_i) + \text{out}(A_i)}\sqrt{\text{within}(A_j) + \text{out}(A_j)}}[v_k \in A_i \cap A_j]$$

$$= \frac{[i = j]}{\text{within}(A_i) + \text{out}(A_i)}\sum_k d_k[v_k \in A_i]$$

$$= [i = j]$$

which means $H^{\text{T}}H = I$. Similar to (19), we have

$$\min \text{ncut}(A_1, \ldots, A_k) \Leftrightarrow \min\{k - \text{tr}(H^{\text{T}}D^{-1/2}SD^{-1/2}H)\}$$
$$\Leftrightarrow \max \text{tr}(H^{\text{T}}D^{-1/2}SD^{-1/2}H) \quad . \quad (21)$$
$$\Leftrightarrow \min \|D^{-1/2}SD^{-1/2} - HH^{\text{T}}\|_F^2$$

When the restriction (20) is relaxed to $H \ge 0$, our SymNMF formulation is obtained.

Appendix B: Normalized cut increases when a community is split into two communities

In Fig. 1, the community A_3 was split into B_1 and B_2, and the associated increase of normalized cut is

$$\Delta_{\text{ncut}} = \frac{\text{out}(B_1)}{\text{within}(B_1) + \text{out}(B_1)} + \frac{\text{out}(B_2)}{\text{within}(B_2) + \text{out}(B_2)}$$
$$- \frac{\text{out}(A_3)}{\text{within}(A_3) + \text{out}(A_3)} .$$

Denote $i_1 = \text{within}(B_1)$, $i_2 = \text{within}(B_2)$, $i_3 = \text{within}(A_3)$, $o_1 = \text{out}(B_1)$, $o_2 = \text{out}(B_2)$, $i_3 = \text{out}(A_3)$, and $c = \text{cut}(B_1, B_2)$, and note that $o_3 = o_1 + o_2 - 2c$ and $i_3 = i_1 + i_2 + 2c$. Then, we have

$$\Delta_{\text{ncut}} = \frac{2c(i_1 + o_1)(i_2 + o_2) + o_2(i_1 + o_1)^2 + o_1(i_2 + o_2)^2}{(i_1 + o_1)(i_2 + o_2)(i_1 + i_2 + o_1 + o_2)} > 0$$

Note that this proof does not say that more communities always correspond to larger normalized cut in general (i.e., when the communities are not obtained through recursive splitting).

References

1. Yang J, Leskovec J. Overlapping community detection at scale: a nonnegative matrix factorization approach. In: Proceedings of the sixth ACM international conference on web search and data mining. WSDM '13. New York: ACM; 2013. p. 587–96. doi:10.1145/2433396.2433471.
2. Whang JJ, Gleich DF, Dhillon IS. Overlapping community detection using seed set expansion. In: Proceedings of the 22nd ACM international conference on information & knowledge management. CIKM '13. New York: ACM; 2013. p. 2099–108. doi:10.1145/2505515.2505535.
3. Whang JJ, Gleich DF, Dhillon IS. Overlapping community detection using neighborhood-inflated seed expansion. IEEE Trans Knowl Data Eng. 2016;28(5):1272–84. doi:10.1109/TKDE.2016.2518687.
4. Yang J, Leskovec J. Defining and evaluating network communities based on ground-truth. Knowl Inf Syst. 2013;42(1):181–213. doi:10.1007/s10115-013-0693-z.
5. Kernighan BW, Lin S. An efficient heuristic procedure for partitioning graphs. Bell Syst Tech J. 1970;49(2):291–307. doi:10.1002/j.1538-7305.1970.tb01770.x.
6. Fortunato S. Community detection in graphs. Phys Rep. 2010;486(3–5):75–174. doi:10.1016/j.physrep.2009.11.002.
7. Karypis G, Kumar V. A fast and high quality multilevel scheme for partitioning irregular graphs. SIAM J Sci Comput. 1998;20(1):359–92. doi:10.1137/S1064827595287997.
8. Pellegrini F, Roman J. SCOTCH: a software package for static mapping by dual recursive bipartitioning of process and architecture graphs. In: Proceedings of the international conference and exhibition on high-performance computing and networking. HPCN Europe 1996. London: Springer; 1996. p. 493–8.
9. Hendrickson B, Leland R. An improved spectral graph partitioning algorithm for mapping parallel computations. SIAM J Sci Comput. 1995;16(2):452–69. doi:10.1137/0916028.
10. Shi J, Malik J. Normalized cuts and image segmentation. IEEE Trans Pattern Anal Mach Intell. 2000;22(8):888–905. doi:10.1109/34.868688.
11. Dhillon IS, Guan Y, Kulis B. Weighted graph cuts without eigenvectors a multilevel approach. IEEE Trans Pattern Anal Mach Intell. 2007;29(11):1944–57. doi:10.1109/TPAMI.2007.1115.
12. Dhillon IS, Guan Y, Kulis B. Kernel K-means: spectral clustering and normalized cuts. In: Proceedings of the tenth ACM SIGKDD international conference on knowledge discovery and data mining. KDD '04. New York: ACM; 2004. p. 551–6. doi:10.1145/1014052.1014118.
13. Kuang D, Ding C, Park H. Symmetric nonnegative matrix factorization for graph clustering. In: Proceedings of the 2012 SIAM international conference on data mining. Philadelphia: Society for Industrial and Applied Mathematics; 2012. p. 106–17.
14. Kuang D, Yun S, Park H. SymNMF: nonnegative low-rank approximation of a similarity matrix for graph clustering. J Glob Optim. 2014;62(3):545–74. doi:10.1007/s10898-014-0247-2.
15. Girvan M, Newman MEJ. Community structure in social and biological networks. Proc Natl Acad Sci. 2002;99(12):7821–6. doi:10.1073/pnas.122653799.
16. Newman MEJ, Girvan M. Finding and evaluating community structure in networks. Phys Rev E. 2004;69(2):026113. doi:10.1103/PhysRevE.69.026113.
17. Prat-Pérez A, Dominguez-Sal D, Larriba-Pey J-L. High quality, scalable and parallel community detection for large real graphs. In: Proceedings of the 23rd international conference on world wide web. WWW '14. New York: ACM; 2014. p. 225–36. doi:10.1145/2566486.2568010.
18. Blondel VD, Guillaume J-L, Lambiotte R, Lefebvre E. Fast unfolding of communities in large networks. J Stat Mech Theory Exp. 2008;2008(10):10008. doi:10.1088/1742-5468/2008/10/P10008.
19. Pons P, Latapy M. Computing communities in large networks using random walks. J Graph Algorithms Appl. 2006;10(2):191–218. doi:10.7155/jgaa.00124.
20. Rosvall M, Bergstrom CT. Maps of random walks on complex networks reveal community structure. Proc Natl Acad Sci. 2008;105(4):1118–23. doi:10.1073/pnas.0706851105.
21. Baumes J, Goldberg M, Krishnamoorty M, Magdon-Ismail M, Preston N. Finding communities by clustering a graph into overlapping subgraphs. In: Guimaraes N, Isaias P, editors. Proceedings of the IADIS international conference on applied computing. Applied computing, vol. 1. Lisbon: IADIS; 2005. p. 97–104.
22. Palla G, Derényi I, Farkas I, Vicsek T. Uncovering the overlapping community structure of complex networks in nature and society. Nature. 2005;435(7043):814–8. doi:10.1038/nature03607.
23. Lancichinetti A, Radicchi F, Ramasco JJ, Fortunato S. Finding statistically significant communities in networks. PLoS ONE. 2011;6(4):18961. doi:10.1371/journal.pone.0018961.
24. Yang J, Leskovec J. Structure and overlaps of ground-truth communities in networks. ACM Trans Intell Syst Technol. 2014;5(2):26–12635. doi:10.1145/2594454.
25. Kuang D, Park H. Fast rank-2 nonnegative matrix factorization for hierarchical document clustering. In: Proceedings of the 19th ACM SIGKDD international conference on knowledge discovery and data mining. KDD '13. New York: ACM; 2013. p. 739–47. doi:10.1145/2487575.2487606.
26. Xu W, Liu X, Gong Y. Document clustering based on non-negative matrix factorization. In: Proceedings of the 26th annual international ACM SIGIR conference on research and development in information retrieval. SIGIR '03. New York: ACM; 2003. p. 267–73. doi:10.1145/860435.860485.
27. Gillis N, Kuang D, Park H. Hierarchical clustering of hyperspectral images using rank-two nonnegative matrix factorization. IEEE Trans Geosci Remote Sens. 2015;53(4):2066–78. doi:10.1109/TGRS.2014.2352857.

28. Lee DD, Seung HS. Learning the parts of objects by non-negative matrix factorization. Nature. 1999;401(6755):788–91. doi:10.1038/44565.
29. Drake B, Kim J, Mallick M, Park H. Supervised Raman spectra estimation based on nonnegative rank deficient least squares. In: Proceedings 13th international conference on information fusion, Edinburgh, UK. 2010.
30. Kim J, Park H. Fast nonnegative matrix factorization: an active-set-like method and comparisons. SIAM J Sci Comput. 2011;33(6):3261–81. doi:10.1137/110821172.
31. Ho N-D. Nonnegative matrix factorization algorithms and applications. PhD thesis, ÉCOLE POLYTECHNIQUE. 2008.
32. Du R, Kuang D, Drake B, Park H. DC-NMF: nonnegative matrix factorization based on divide-and-conquer for fast clustering and topic modeling. J Glob Optim. 2017;68(4):777–98. doi:10.1007/s10898-017-0515-z.
33. Sinclair A, Jerrum M. Approximate counting, uniform generation and rapidly mixing Markov chains. Inf Comput. 1989;82(1):93–133. doi:10.1016/0890-5401(89)90067-9.
34. Leskovec J, Krevl A. SNAP datasets: Stanford large network dataset collection. 2014. http://snap.stanford.edu/data.
35. Mislove A, Marcon M, Gummadi KP, Druschel P, Bhattacharjee B. Measurement and analysis of online social networks. In: Proceedings of the 7th ACM SIGCOMM conference on internet measurement. IMC '07. New York: ACM; 2007. p. 29–42. doi:10.1145/1298306.1298311.
36. Backstrom L, Huttenlocher D, Kleinberg J, Lan X. Group formation in large social networks: membership, growth, and evolution. In: Proceedings of the 12th ACM SIGKDD international conference on knowledge discovery and data mining. KDD '06. New York: ACM; 2006. p. 44–54. doi:10.1145/1150402.1150412.
37. Leskovec J, Adamic LA, Huberman BA. The dynamics of viral marketing. ACM Trans Web. 2007;1(1):5. doi:10.1145/1232722.1232727.
38. dblp: What is dblp? 2015. http://dblp.uni-trier.de/faq/What+is+dblp.html. Accessed 29 June 2015.
39. dblp: dblp: computer science bibliography. 2015. http://dblp.uni-trier.de/. Accessed 17 June 2015.
40. dblp: What do I find in dblp.xml? 2015. http://dblp.uni-trier.de/faq/What+do+I+find+in+dblp+xml.html. Accessed 30 June 2015.
41. Graham RL, Knuth DE, Patashnik O. Concrete mathematics: a foundation for computer science, 2nd ed. Chap. 2.2: sums and recurrences. Boston: Addison-Wesley Longman Publishing Co., Inc.; 1994. p. 24.
42. Ding C, He X, Simon HD. On the equivalence of nonnegative matrix factorization and spectral clustering. In: SIAM international conference on data mining. 2005.

4

Coevolution of a multilayer node-aligned network whose layers represent different social relations

Ashwin Bahulkar[1*], Boleslaw K. Szymanski[1,2*], Kevin Chan[3] and Omar Lizardo[4]

*Correspondence:
bahula@rpi.edu;
szymab@rpi.edu
[1] Rensselaer Polytechnic
Institute, 110 8th St., Troy,
NY 12180, USA
Full list of author information
is available at the end of the
article

Abstract

Background: We examine the coevolution of three-layer node-aligned network of university students. The first layer is defined by nominations based on perceived prominence collected from repeated surveys during the first four semesters; the second is a behavioral layer representing actual students' interactions based on records of mobile calls and text messages; while the third is a behavioral layer representing potential face-to-face interactions suggested by bluetooth collocations.

Methods: We address four interrelated questions. First, we ask whether the formation or dissolution of a link in one of the layers precedes or succeeds the formation or dissolution of the corresponding link in another layer (temporal dependencies). Second, we explore the causes of observed temporal dependencies between the layers. For those temporal dependencies that are confirmed, we measure the predictive capability of such dependencies. Third, we observe the progress towards nominations and the stages that lead to them. Finally, we examine whether the differences in dissolution rates of symmetric (undirected) versus asymmetric (directed) links co-exist in all layers.

Results: We find strong patterns of reciprocal temporal dependencies between the layers. In particular, the creation of an edge in either behavioral layer generally precedes the formation of a corresponding edge in the nomination layer. Conversely, the decay of a link in the nomination layer generally precedes a decline in the intensity of communication and collocation. Finally, nodes connected by asymmetric nomination edges have lower overall communication and collocation volumes and more asymmetric communication flows than the nodes linked by symmetric edges.

Conclusion: We find that creation and dissolution of cognitively salient contacts have temporal dependencies with communication and collocation behavior.

Keywords: Coevolution of network layers, Machine learning for social network analysis, NetSense dataset

Background

In this paper we use a dataset containing longitudinal information on a group of individuals in a multilayer node-aligned network to examine dependencies across different types of relations (for details on data collection see [1]). We use this rich source of information, hereafter referred to as the *NetSense data*, to build three distinct network layers linking individuals over time. One is a *nomination* layer constructed from subjective reports of significant contacts, another is a *behavioral* layer constructed from electronic records of communications, and the third is a *behavioral* layer, constructed from blue-tooth records indicating spatial collocation of students.

In a previous version of this paper presented at the conference [2], we analyzed dependencies between the first two layers. Here, we aim to understand the relationship between all three layers to shed the light on the link between nominations, communication behavior, and spatial propinquity. This is important, since, as we note in the following section, the exact relationship between these forms of human connectivity is a long-standing, but understudied, problem in social network analysis [3, 4].

Motivating social science background for the research

Social scientists have traditionally distinguished various dimensions of human connectivity [5–9]. Perhaps the most well-studied dimension of this type in fields like anthropology and sociology is *cognitive saliency*. This can be defined as the subjective prominence of a given contact for an individual at a particular point in time [6, 10, 11]. Empirically, cognitive salience can be measured as the likelihood that an individual will "nominate" another individual as an important contact with regard to a given relation (e.g., friend, advisor, discussion partner, frequent interlocutor). The classical method used to study this dimension of connectivity among individuals is the network survey [6, 7, 12, 13], in which individuals are presented with a "name generator" (to elicit some predetermined number of salient nominees from memory) and a "name interpreter" (to collect relevant information on each nominee). This approach has generated a great deal of knowledge (usually at the level of "ego-networks"), about those contacts who are subjectively the most important to each individual. A key advantage of the NetSense data is the availability of such periodic network surveys recording each participant's most cognitively salient contacts.

A related dimension of human connectivity is *frequency of interaction* [7, 9, 14]. An important finding of network analysis in sociology is that, while frequency and cognitive salience usually go together [6], the correlation between the two factors is much weaker than would be expected if these two dimensions were two indicators of the same underlying construct such as "tie strength" [7, 9]. Instead, research has established that persons can have high rates of communicate interaction (e.g., established either via observational or self-report methods) with contacts who were not cognitive salient or considered particularly close [5, 7, 8]. In the same way, some non-negligible proportion of the most cognitively salient contacts may be characterized by relatively low rates of communicative frequency [15]. Overall, however, the question of whether frequency of interaction precedes, and therefore leads to, cognitive salience or whether salience leads to more interaction remains a highly debated issue [9, 14–16].

Finally, both classic and more recent work in social networks points to spatial contiguity or *propinquity* as an important indicator of social connectivity [9]. Just like with the relationship between cognitive salience and frequency of interaction, recent work shows that spatial contiguity is an independent dimension of human association, since it can vary independently of the other two factors mentioned. Persons may spent a lot of time (e.g., in workplaces, classrooms, and so on) in spatial proximity to people who are not particularly salient to them or with whom they seldom interact directly [15]. However, research also shows that strong social ties tend to emerge among people who spend time together in the same physical location [16], such that both cognitive salience and frequency of interaction may end up being the result of external factors that channel people into the same physical spaces. This is what [9] has referred to as "proximity" mechanisms governing the formation and maintenance of dyadic connections among individuals.

Research questions and hypotheses

Social network researchers have proposed studied dependencies between all three of the aforementioned dimensions of human association. Most of this work however, has looked at the connection between two of the aforementioned three dimensions at a time [14, 16], usually with an eye towards establishing the causal precedence of one factor (e.g., frequency of interaction or propinquity) over the other (e.g., the cognitive salience of a given contact). Seldom, however, has the mutual connection between these three factors been explored systematically. We use the rich set of data collected as part of the NetSense project to do just that.

In what follows, we begin by establishing the   validity of the cognitive salience and interaction frequency measures that were collected as part of the NetSense data. We thus begin by exploring the correlations between layers in a multilayer network having three types of links, one based on interaction frequency, another based on collocation frequency, while the third is based on cognitive salience. Social network theory leads us to conjecture that these two dimensions should be positively correlated, with cognitive salient ties displaying (on average) more frequent behavioral interaction than non-salient ties. In essence, we should expect that persons connected in the nomination layer, should have higher interaction frequencies [3, 5, 7, 9].

We then address the question of precedence between interaction frequency and cognitive salience. Drawing on models that see behavior as preceding cognition, we hypothesize that nodes linked by communication edges with large weights at a given point in time should be more likely to appear as cognitively salient contacts in the future. Following [9], we test the same hypothesis with regard to collocation behavior: We thus expect that the more an individual encounters another person in a proximate physical location at a given point in time, the more likely it is that person will appear as a cognitively salient contact in the future. A key issue is which behavioral mechanism, frequency of interaction or collocation, is more important in determining future salience in the nomination [9, 16]. This is an issue that has not been investigated in previous work but that we tackle here using state-of-the-art machine-learning methods.

While the hypothesis that behavior in large part determines cognitive salience is plausible, recent work on the culture-network link also proposes that the reverse arrow of causation is also equally plausible: That going from cognitive salience to behavioral interactions [17, 18]. We propose that a dissolution event in the nomination layer (e.g., being mentioned as a significant contact at time t but then not mentioning that contact at time $t + 1$) should be a accompanied by decreasing levels of behavioral interaction in terms of both communication and collocation events. Essentially, the disappearance of a nomination link should lead to a gradual decay of intensity of the communication and collocation layers.

We use the temporal features of the NetSense data to examine the question whether *variation* in cognitive salience determines the communication and collocation interactions. We take advantage of the differences in duration among cognitively salient ties (differentiating between newly salient and long-standing ties) hypothesizing that nodes connected by long-standing nomination ties should exhibit higher levels of communication and collocation than the ones linked by newly emerging ties.

In addition, we go beyond establishing differences in behavioral profiles of ties based on their levels of cognitive salience, and examine the question of whether the behavioral temporal signature of social ties differs depending on whether their nodes are linked in the nomination layer or not. We hypothesize that cognitive salient ties will also exhibit behavioral activity in days of the week and times of the day that are associated with informal sociability in this population (e.g., weekends and evenings), and that this feature differentiates them from ties whose nodes are disconnected in the nomination layer.

Finally, we aim to examine, for the first time, coupled asymmetries and non-reciprocities along the nomination and behavioral layers. In traditional networks built from subjective reports of cognitive salience, a common phenomenon is *asymmetry*. This refers to the situation where contact B is cognitively salient for person A, but not the reverse : A is not mentioned by B as a cognitive salient contact. Work in social network analysis shows that this situation is fairly common in human social networks, even for ties defined by friendship and intimacy [19]. Here we examine if asymmetries in nominations are connected to non-reciprocities in the two-way flow of communication in the behavioral layer. Recent work also shows that non-reciprocity is more common in human social interactions that would be expected from traditional social and anthropological theory pointing to the "norm" of reciprocity [20]. We hypothesize that these two phenomena are empirically linked: nodes connected by asymmetric nomination edges should be connected by behavioral edges characterized by non-reciprocity. We also connect the phenomenon of cognitive asymmetry with that of behavioral tie decay [21], and hypothesize that asymmetric cognitive ties should exhibit steeper rates of decay in the behavioral communication layer.

Related work on multilayer network dynamics

A model to generate two social networks synthetically, with both networks coevolving, capturing the properties of both networks is introduced in [22]. A rapidly evolving network based on games is studied in [23]. Nodes in this network have varying incentives to build links. We observe similar behavior in the NetSense data, where certain edges have incentive to develop into an edge in one of the networks, while others do not. A wide swath of previous work, impossible to fully review in this limited space, in social network analysis has investigated dependence and evolution of connections across multiple networks (for a review see [24]).

More generally, multilayer networks have been studied extensively in the Network Science literature. They have been formally defined in [25] which also includes a discussion of related topics such as multilayer networks, multilayer node-aligned networks, multiplex networks, and hypergraphs. The NetSense network can be classified as node-aligned multilayer network because it has one set of nodes and three types of edges connecting these nodes. This reference discusses several properties of multilayer networks and describes how link prediction is done across multilayer heterogeneous networks in [26, 27]. This reference defines also a "meta-path" approach, where sequences of different relations are used as features for link prediction. Novel community detection approaches for evolving multi-slice networks have been discussed in [28] and they will be useful for future work related to our paper.

A study similar in design to that of NetSense is discussed in [29]. The authors analyze a multilayer network of high school students, including a face-to-face interaction layer and a friendship survey layer. They study the difference in structural properties of three layers in their successive paper [30]. Smieszek et al. study a multilayer network between conference participants in [29] including a proximity sensor interaction layer, and the self-reported friendship layer. The authors study in what ways these two layers differ. In contrast to these two papers, our study focuses on the evolution of the edges in our multilayer network. The dataset that contains only records of communication between people is presented in [31]. The participants are high school students transitioning to college. The authors study the change of communication volume between pairs of students as they come into contact with new people, to discover the evolution of communication edges in response to external events. In our study, we focus on how changes of edges in one layer impact edges in other layers. Stopczynski et al. introduce in [32] the Copenhagen dataset defining a multilayer network that includes communication layer, a face-to-face interaction layer, and a Wi-Fi signal-based proximity layer. Several papers on the Copenhagen study describe how different social structures, like groups congregating at the same locations, are discovered using different layers of the network. Large-scale communication record datasets typically focus on basic features, such as call patterns, temporal features of communication records, and evolving communities in such network, as exemplified by [32, 33]. Miritello et al. [34] study how individuals adopt different tie formation strategies to activate and maintain ties. The Copenhagen dataset and the large-scale communication record dataset contain only behavioral edges, while an important element of our study is to investigate how behavioral edges impact changes in the nomination layer.

Additions to our previous work

The present research builds on, but moves beyond, our previous work, which explored how two-layered social network coevolves in time. This work was published in the *Proceedings of Fifth International Workshop on Complex Networks and their Application* [2]. Here, we introduce a second behavioral network layer, based on the bluetooth collocations of nodes. We demonstrate how the behavioral collocation layer coevolves with the nomination layer (based on nominations) as well as the first communication-based behavioral layer. We then look at the different behavioral stages in the evolution of the networks. In addition, we also included the analysis of temporal dependencies between the two behavioral layers and the nomination layers. Social ties and temporal features have been studied in [35]. However, here we study the temporal dependencies between different kinds of ties and the coevolution of these ties over time.

NetSense data and the networks

In this section, we introduce the NetSense data [1] and the networks derived from it. The data were collected at the University of Notre Dame. At the start the Fall semester in 2011, 200 incoming freshmen were enrolled in the NetSense study. Over 150 participated until their graduation in the Spring of 2015. Students participating in the study received free smartphones with unlimited voice and text plans as an incentive for participation. We obtained time-stamped logs of communication records for all study participants. These data contain information on the date, time, and duration (for calls) and character length (for text messages). Data for the first four semesters (lasting from the Fall of 2011 to the Spring of 2013) of the project were available for this study.

In addition to this, we have information about the bluetooth interactions between study participants. The bluetooth interactions are time-stamped. However, the bluetooth interaction data are available only from October 2011 to May 2012. From all the bluetooth interactions, we filter the interactions which are most likely to be face-to-face. Every bluetooth interaction has an associated signal strength value, which is referred to as the received signal strength indicator, or RSSI. The RSSI values vary between 0 and -120 dB, a value close to 0 implying high quality of the signal. RSSI values above -65 dB are generally inferred to be most likely face-to-face as mentioned in [36]. Therefore, we consider only the interactions where the RSSI values are above -65 dB.

Students participating in the NetSense study list up to twenty nominees at the beginning of each semester. Students were asked to list the names of those people with whom they thought they spent the most time communicating or interacting. Recent work has shown that this type of name generator is the most likely to produce an unbiased list of significant contacts [15]. Below, we refer to these cognitively salient contacts as nominees. For each student, nominees could be inside or outside the NetSense study. Because students were asked to also provide the primary phone number of each significant contact, we can link each of those mentioned in the survey to the time-stamped smartphone data.

Accordingly, we propose a model for analyzing the coevolution of multilayer networks whose layers represent different kinds of connections between nodes. We have two behavioral layers, the *communication* layer consists of the edges based on communication records of both telephone calls and text messages between individuals and the *collocation* layer consists of the edges based on bluetooth collocations between individuals. Weights on the edges in the behavioral layers change daily, depending on the volume of communication and the number and length of bluetooth collocations. The *nomination* layer includes edges based on (possibly non-reciprocal) nominations collected via surveys. Edges in the nomination layer may appear and disappear once per semester. Table 1 provides a summary of the three layers of the network.

Methodology and results
Dynamic coevolution of the nomination, collocation, and communication layers
In this paper, we are interested in understanding coevolving dynamics between the communication and collocation connectivity layers (indexing behavior) and the layer of nominations (indexing cognitive salience of contacts). We also seek initial validation of

Table 1 A summary of the NetSense layers

Layer	Nodes	Edges	Frequency of evolution
Cognitive salience	Students	Nominations in surveys	Every semester
Collocation behavior	Students	Bluetooth interactions	Evolves continuously
Communication behavior	Students	Calls and texts	Evolves continuously

these coevolution dynamics. Given that the period of time for which NetSense has gathered information covers the initial stages of a college cohort, we can expect that students will nominate others as significant contacts, communicate, and spend time in proximity of one another within a relatively closed environment. We postulate the existence of multiple relationships between the coevolving collocation, communication, and nomination layers.

We hypothesize that there is a delay between the onset of changing behavior, observed either in communication or collocation, and the nomination of another individual as a cognitively salient contact. Communication (mutual calls or texts) or collocation (i.e., spending time together, whether in a class or in a club or just casual meet-ups) would transition in a later time period to a contact appearing as significant enough to be nominated in the survey. We study how cognitive salience is affected by behavioral interaction whether in terms of communication or collocation. In this section we see how behavior can be used to predict the formation and persistence of cognitive salient relationships. We also expect to see the converse occur, where a decline in cognitive salience leads to a diminishing of communication and collocation.

Do nodes connected in the nomination layer have stronger edges in the behavioral layers?

We explore the differences in communication and collocation volumes between nodes who are and who are not connected in the nomination layer. Communication volume is measured by the number of calls and messages exchanged between dyads in a semester, while collocation intensity is measured by the number of bluetooth proximity detection events between the same dyads in a given semester.

As shown in Table 2, we find that nodes linked in the nomination layer (nominees) tend to have behavioral edges with significantly higher volumes of communication and collocations compared to those nodes that do not have a corresponding nomination link, non-nominees). Figure 1a, b illustrates how number of communication events and the number of collocations are distributed among students connected in the nomination layer (blue stars and green crosses) and those who are not mentioned as cognitively salient contacts (red circles). In all, not being mentioned as a cognitively salient contact is associated with lower volumes of communicative interaction and propinquity.

Do higher weight behavioral edges turn into new nomination edges?

We explore how dynamic changes in the cognitive salience of contacts, as indexed by the formation of new nomination links, correlate with the volume of interaction along the

Table 2 Difference between nodes connected and disconnected in the nomination layer in terms of weight of their communication and collocation edges

Semester	Nominees			Non-nominees		
	No. calls	No. messages	No. collocations	No. calls	No. messages	No. collocations
Semester 1	70	667	161.2	7	72	36.5
Semester 2	41	915	448.5	12	190	55.6
Semester 3	74	1063	–	5	51	–
Semester 4	34	729	–	4	37	–

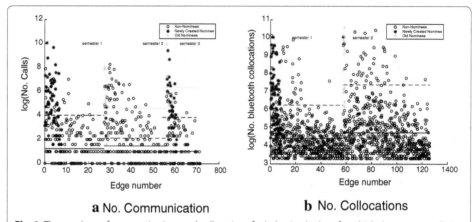

Fig. 1 The numbers of communications and collocations for behavioral edges for which the corresponding nomination edge is old (green plus signs), newly created (blue asterisk), and non-existent (red circles). The lines show the average value for the circles of the corresponding color in each semester, the blue dashed line shows the average for newly created edges, the green dotted line shows the average for old edges. The separation is significant between these lines. Generally, edges in which one node nominates the other have corresponding edges with a higher intensity of communication and collocation

corresponding link in the communication and collocation layer. We examine whether an increase in the cognitive salience of a given contact, is preceded by higher rates of behavioral communication and collocation. We also examine whether links that decline in cognitive salience, as indexed by a dissolution of the corresponding nomination edge, are characterized by lower volumes of communication and collocation the semester before.

We find that contacts that become more cognitively salient by forming a link in the nomination layer are characterized by higher volumes of communication and collocation. Table 3 lists the differences in communication and collocations. Figure 2a, b illustrates how the numbers of calls and collocations are distributed among the to-be-formed and not-to-be-formed nomination edges. In both the cases, we find that communication and collocation volume is higher among the existing and to-be-formed contacts in the nomination layer than among those individuals who do not share a nomination edge.

Predicting the formation of links in the nomination layer from the strength of edges in the behavioral layers

Here we examine whether formation and existence of edges in the nomination layer can be predicted from their respective edge weights in the communication and collocation layer. We take the weight of the behavioral edge, defined by the communication

Table 3 Difference in communication volume between pair of nodes who are to-be-nominees and the ones who are not-to-be-nominees

Semester	To-be-nominees			Not-to-be-nominees		
	No. calls	No. messages	No. collocations	No. calls	No. messages	No. collocations
Semester 1	40	407	191.8	5	58	35.7
Semester 2	52	782	195.6	6.5	105	46.7
Semester 3	18	248	–	4	41	–

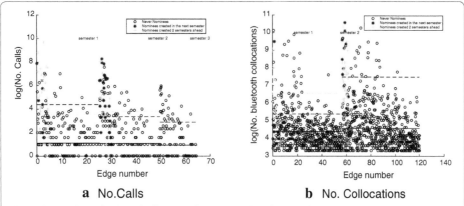

a No.Calls   **b** No. Collocations

Fig. 2 The numbers of calls and collocations between nodes who are to-be-nominees in one semester (blue asterisk), to-be-nominees in two semesters (green plus signs), and not-to-be-nominees (red circles). Generally, to-be-nominees have higher numbers of calls and collocations than not-to-be-nominees. The continuous lines show the average values for the circles of the same color. The separation is large between red and green dotted lines, red and blue lines, but small between dashed blue and dotted green lines. Most of the to-be-nominees edges appear in the first and second semester, since very few new nominations are formed in the fourth semester

or collocation volume, and consider whether behavioral edges above a threshold of the behavior volume can predict whether we observe a formation event in the nomination layer. We expect that edges below the threshold should be more likely not form an edge in the nomination layer in the future.

We measure the performance of this analysis in terms of recall and accuracy. Recall is defined as the ratio of the number of correct prediction to the number of true values in predicted dataset. Accuracy is defined as the ratio of correct predictions to the total number of predictions. We do not use precision as a measure, since the classification is very unbalanced, the number of positive examples is several times smaller than the number of negative examples. Table 4 lists the results for the prediction of existing edges.

Table 5 lists the results for prediction of future edges. We find that we are able to predict a significant proportion of nomination edges using information from the behavioral layers separately, about 70–80%, with a reasonable accuracy. We are also able to predict a significant proportion of future nomination edges using information from the behavioral layers; about 70–80% of edges are predicted with a reasonable accuracy.

In Fig. 3a, b we show how the performance of prediction changes with changing thresholds. This also reflects upon the differences between the distribution of behavioral weights of nominees and non-nominees and between the to-be-nominees and the not-to-be-nominees.

Table 4 Prediction of nominated contact based on the volume of communication in the communication behavioral layer

Semester	Calls		Messages		Collocations	
	Accuracy (%)	Recall (%)	Accuracy (%)	Recall (%)	Accuracy	Recall
Semester 2	69.3	68.5	73.4	63.1	–	–
Semester 3	73.8	70.5	70.5	81.5	82.1%	76.9%
Semester 4	77.8	75.5	77.9	83.6	–	–

Table 5 Prediction of future-nominated contact formation based on volume of communication between the corresponding nodes in the particular semester

Semester	Calls		Messages		Collocations	
	Accuracy (%)	Recall (%)	Accuracy (%)	Recall (%)	Accuracy	Recall
Semester 2	73.1	75.3	74.4	71.3	–	–
Semester 3	72.5	74.4	77.2	78.9	80.2%	75.1%

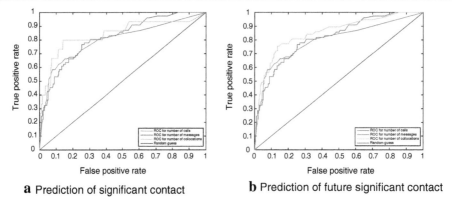

a Prediction of significant contact   **b** Prediction of future significant contact

Fig. 3 We plot the ROC curves for prediction based on different thresholds of number of calls, messages, and collocations. With a threshold of zero, the false positive rate is 100% and true positive rate (recall) is 100% as well. Moreover, with the threshold equal to the maximum value, the false positive rate is 0% and true positive rate (recall) is 0% as well. We observe that the predictability is significantly higher than random. We see that there is a sharp drop in the false positive rate (which means, increase in accuracy) accompanied by a sharp drop in the recall when the thresholds increase above a certain limit. Behavioral edges where the number of calls, messages, or collocations is above a certain threshold are classified as significant contacts. We observe that as the threshold increases, the false positive rate (FPR) and the true positive rate (TPR) decrease gradually. At a certain higher value of the threshold, the rate of change of both the FPR and TPR increases significantly. This reflects on the distribution of the values of behavioral weights (be it the number of calls, messages, or collocations) of nominees vs. non-nominees and to-be-nominees vs. not-to-be-nominees. Nominees and to-be-nominees are much more likely to have higher behavioral weights, non-nominees and not-to-be-nominees can have higher behavioral weights, but less often. Also, nominees and to-be-nominees are much less likely to have very low behavioral weights

We then investigate if using both behaviors, communication, and collocation, we can predict the formation of edges in the nomination layer. We use the following features in a machine-learning implementation: number of calls, number of messages, and number of collocations. We predict links in the nomination layer formed in the third semester from the second semester, training the machine-learning model on links formed in the second semester from the first semester. We tried Linear Regression, Support Vector Machines (SVM), SVM–Radial Basis Function (SVM–RBF), and classifiers using Random Forests and k-Nearest Neighbors to predict the evolution of nomination links, but it was Linear Regression that gave us the best results shown in Table 6 which also demonstrates that using both behavioral data types improves recall compared to using either one alone.

We also examine whether behavioral edges whose nodes are connected by nomination edges that persist into the next semester tend to have significantly higher weights, as compared to behavioral edges for the nodes with nomination edges that dissolve future. Table 7 lists the differences in communication, while Table 8 shows the differences in

Table 6 Difference in recall values when different combinations of behavior are used

Communication only	Collocation only	Collocation + communication
75.3	75.1	81

Table 7 Difference between persistent and dissolving nomination edges in terms of weights of the corresponding communication behavioral edges

Semester	Persistent edges		Dissolving edges	
	No. calls	No. messages	No. calls	No. messages
Semester 1	133.2	1373.1	40.8	492.8
Semester 2	92.1	2137.8	7.3	102.3
Semester 3	75.0	1148.6	8.2	205.9

Table 8 Difference between persistent and dissolving nomination edges in terms of the weights of their corresponding collocation behavioral edges

Semester	Persistent edges	Dissolving edges
Semester 1	346.4	116.6
Semester 2	665.8	100.7

the bluetooth collocations. We indeed find that persistent edges in the nomination layer have corresponding communication and collocation edges with significantly weights. The results also show that those nomination edges that are subject to decay tend to have smaller weights in the communication and collocation layers.

Do newly formed nomination edges differ from older nomination edges in terms of their communication and collocation volume?

Here we examine whether there are systematic differences between newly formed and older edges in the nomination layer, in terms of how strongly connected they are in the communication and collocation layers. To this end, we measure and compute the difference in the volume of communication and collocation between nodes joined by older (at least one semester old) and newly formed edges in the nomination layer.

As Table 9 shows, we find that nodes connected by older edges in the nomination layer have higher edge weights in the communication layer in comparison nodes connected by edges which have been just been formed in the nomination layer. We also observe that nodes connected by older edges in the nomination layer edges tend to find themselves in the same location more often than nodes connected by the newer edges in the nomination layer edges as shown in Table 10. Note we could calculate collocation results for only one semester due to the limited availability of the bluetooth data.

We also observe that as these newly formed nomination edges age, the nodes connected by them come to have communication volumes similar to, or perhaps slightly higher, than nodes connected by edges in the nomination layer that have existed for a longer time. To shed further light on this issue, we examine communication volumes between nodes connected by the nomination layer in the 3rd and the 4th semesters, and

Table 9 Difference in behavioral communication volumes between nodes connected by the old and new nomination edges

Semester	Newly observed nominations		Nomination contact older than one semester	
	No. calls	No. messages	No. calls	No. messages
Semester 2	6	57	61	1340
Semester 3	63	1026	172	2447
Semester 4	7	256	53	1067

Table 10 Difference in the numbers of behavioral collocations between nodes connected by the old and new nomination edges

Semester	Newly observed nominations	Nominations older than one semester
Semester 2	67.5	455.6

we divide them into edges which were created in the 2nd and the 3rd semesters, respectively, and edges which existed since the 1st semester. We call the former moderately old edges and the latter very old edges. We observe that the nodes connected by the moderately old edges carry on an average of 49 calls and 903 calls, while the nodes connected by the very old edges exchange 29 calls and 795 messages. We infer that communication between nodes that are connected in the nomination edge increases gradually, but then finally stabilizes over a period of time.

Is link decay in the nomination layer followed by a weakening of the corresponding edge in the behavioral layers?

In this section we examine the question of whether behavioral links tend to weaken and dissolve after the corresponding edges in the nomination layer decay. To that end, we measure the rate at which pairs of nodes that become disconnected in the nomination layer also become disconnected in the communication and collocation layers. Then we compare that with the rate at which behavioral links dissolve at random. We want to ascertain whether nodes that first experience a dissolution event in the nomination layer are more likely to dissolve edges in the behavioral layers than a random dyad does.

To do this, define the quantity BDND as the average link dissolution rate in the behavioral layers for persons who are not connected in the nomination layer, and BDNC as the average behavioral link dissolution rate for persons that are connected in the nomination layer. In the third and fourth semesters, BDND is significantly greater than BDNC, while the reverse is observed in the second semester. We observe values of 64, 55, and 50% for BDND for the three semesters, and 42, 74, and 62% for BDNC. We also measure the rate at which the nodes connected by edges in the nomination layer that persist into the following semester dissolve their behavioral edges, and denote it as BDNP. We find that BDNP is always 0, meaning that if the nomination link persists then so does the corresponding behavioral link. Yet, we rarely observe dissolution of collocation after the contact is no longer nominated to the list of significant contacts. This implies that people may continue to frequent the same places even after they are no longer cognitively salient contacts.

Are the temporal collocation signatures of nodes connected in the nomination layer different from those who are not connected?

In this section we examine the question of whether students who are connected in the nomination layer exhibit distinct patterns of temporal collocation behavior. In particular, we ask whether cognitive salient contacts are more likely to be in the same place during days of the week and times of the day more likely to be associated with sociability (such as weekends and evenings, respectively) than students who do not share a link in the nomination layer. We also look at whether temporal communication and collocation behavior differs for individuals who will become connected in the nomination layer in the future. A positive result here would indicate that we can use observed changes in temporal behavioral signatures among dyads to predict increases in the cognitive salience of a given contact over time.

To do this, we look at different temporal features of the collocation behavior and explore differences among four groups of dyads: nominees (dyads connected in the nomination layer), non-nominees (dyads disconnected in the nomination layer), to-be-nominees (dyads who will form a link in the nomination layer in the future), and not-to-be-nominees (dyads that will in the nomination layer). One key behavioral feature is the number of bluetooth collocations on weekdays versus the number of collocations on weekends. We include Friday evenings into the weekend count. Another is the number of collocations that happen during weekday days versus the number of collocations that happen on weekday evenings and nights. We define collocations that happen in the day, as the ones that happen between 8 a.m. and 6 p.m. and that evening collocations happen after 6 p.m. and before 8 a.m. We observe the behavior differences between nominees and non-nominees and between to-be-nominees and not-to-be-nominees and see if they are similar. Similar behaviors might indicate latent expression of nomination edges.

We observe a significant difference in the temporal patterns of collocation followed by nominees and non-nominees. Non-nominees have interactions largely only on weekdays, while nominees have significant interactions also on weekends. Table 11 lists these differences. On weekdays, non-nominees communicate more in the daytime, while nominees tend to communicate more in the evenings. Table 12 lists these differences.

We also looked at the differences between to-be-nominees and not-to-be-nominees. We observe a significant difference in the temporal patterns of collocation in the collocation behavioral layer followed by to-be-nominees and not-to-be-nominees. Individuals who remain disconnected in the nomination layer tend to be located in the same place largely on weekdays, while to-be-nominees tend to experience collocation on both weekdays and weekends. Table 13 lists these differences. On weekdays, not-to-be-nominees are more likely to be in the same place in the daytime, while to-be-nominees are more likely to be in the same place in the evenings. In addition, as shown in Table 14, to-be-nominees have temporal collocation behavior patterns that are very similar to current nominees.

Emergence of cognitively salient contacts through defined stages of interaction

In this section, we examine the dynamic coevolution of the two behavioral layers with respect to the nomination layer. We believe that while both behaviors, communication, and collocation are fairly interchangeable when it comes to prediction of contact

Table 11 Differences between nominees and non-nominees in numbers of collocations between weekdays and weekends

Semester	Nominees		Non-nominees	
	Weekday	Weekend	Weekday	Weekend
Semester 1	97	63	28	8
Semester 2	303	144	42	13

Table 12 Differences between nominees and non-nominees in numbers of collocations between evenings and daytimes

Semester	Nominees		Non-nominees	
	Evening	Day	Evening	Day
Semester 1	66	39	12	16
Semester 2	206	108	18	25

Table 13 Differences between to-be-nominees and not-to-be-nominees in the numbers of collocations between weekdays and weekends

Semester	To-be-nominees		Not-to-be-nominees	
	Weekday	Weekend	Weekday	Weekend
Semester 1	120	71	27	8
Semester 2	120	76	37	9

Table 14 Differences between to-be-nominees and not-to-be-nominees in the numbers of collocations between evenings and daytimes

Semester	To-be-nominees		Not-to-be-nominees	
	Evening	Day	Evening	Day
Semester 1	92	31	11	16
Semester 2	75	55	15	23

formation in the nomination layer, they are not necessarily synchronized and one might precede the other. First, we determine whether collocation is a predictor of future increases in communication, or whether communication predicts increases in future collocation. We then study whether the behavioral factor that follows the other is an intermediary mechanism linking the casually pre-eminent behavioral factor (e.g., collocation or communication) to edge formation in the nomination layer.

Emergence of cognitively salient contacts: from collocation to communication to cognitive salience

To look at the evolution of the two behavioral layers, we consider the paths from collocation to significant contact formation occurring through a communication relationship. We would like to know if the communication relationship is an intermediary variable between mere collocation and the formation of link in the nomination layer. We explore whether the formation of a communication edge is correlated with the weight of the corresponding collocation edge. We also examine whether forming or increasing the strength of an collocation edge precedes a corresponding edge creation in the communication layer.

For this purpose, we explore the differences in volume in the collocation layer between nodes that communicate and nodes that do not communicate, and between nodes that are going to become communicators and those that are not going to become communicators. Here, we look at communication edges without the corresponding nomination edges. We can then observe if the number of collocations associated with establishment of a communication relationship is significantly different, perhaps lower, than the number of collocations associated with the establishment of a link in the nomination layer. We also look at pairs of nodes that created communication edges in the second semester, and also became connected in the nomination layer in the third semester. We observe if there has been an increase in the number of collocations from the first to the second semester, and if the number of collocations between them in the second semester differs significantly from the number of collocations between nodes which did not become nominees in the third semester.

As shown in Table 15, we observe that dyads that communicate, but are not linked in the nomination layer, tend to experience more bluetooth collocations than dyads that do not communicate with each other. Note that while there is a difference, it is not as drastic as the difference in number of collocations between nominees and non-nominees. As the first column of Table 16 shows, we also find that people who are going to communicate in succeeding semesters, but are not going to be linked in the nomination layer, tend to have more bluetooth collocations than people who will not communicate in the succeeding semesters and also not going to be linked in the nomination layer. Note however, that the number of collocations associated with the establishment of a communication edge is significantly lower than the number of collocations associated with formation of a link in the nomination layer.

Step-wise evolution of significant contact formation

After confirming that increasing weight in the communication layer is very likely an intermediate stage preceding the formation of ties in the nomination, we can observe how some edges in the nomination layer emerge gradually over time, from mere

Table 15 Difference in the numbers of collocations between communicators and non-communicators

Semester	Communicators	Non-communicators
Semester 1	68.9	49.7
Semester 2	116.5	48.8

Table 16 Difference in the number of collocations between nodes to-be-communicators and not-to-be-communicators

Semester	To-be-communicators	Not-to-be-communicators
Semester 1	74.6	25.9
Semester 2	70.4	36.2

collocation to communication finally leading to nomination as cognitively salient contact. In the first semester, we find that students who start communicating in the second semester, but who do not achieve enough cognitive salience to nominate one another in the network survey, have on an average 74.6 collocations, while those who would not communicate have on an average 25.9 collocations. Now out of these communicators in the second semester, the ones who move on to become nominees in the third semester, have on an average 166.2 collocations, while those that do not become nominees have on an average 55.1 collocations in the second semester. So we observe how some of the emergence of nomination links progress from collocation to communication, gradually increasing the number of occasions in which they find themselves in the same place.

Are changes in collocation behavior more strongly affected by the dissolution of communication or nomination edges?

In this section, we examine the question of whether collocation behavior is affected more strongly by edge dissolution in the nomination layer or edge decay in the communication layer. To do this, we measure how many nodes with edges continue having collocation after the dissolution of communication, and if this behavior differs from collocation after the dissolution of links in the nomination layer. We observe that 42% of nodes initially connected by a communication link continue to have bluetooth collocations after this edge is dissolved. On the other hand, 93% of dyads continue to experience collocation after a contact is no longer nominated. This implies that communication behavior is more important in determining whether people spend time in the same place than cognitive salience. Conversely, this means that people spend time in the same place with persons that are not cognitively salient to them.

Analysis of asymmetric nomination edges in relation to the behavioral layers

As established in previous work in social network analysis [19], network links premised on cognitive salience, such as the edges in the NetSense nomination layer, have the property of potentially being *asymmetric*: one person may nominate the other as a cognitively salient contact but the other may fail to reciprocate (*A* nominates *B* but *B* does not nominate *A*). This is contrast to communication edges, which have continuous weights and in which relations can be more or less *reciprocal* but almost never completely asymmetric [20]. Behavioral collocations, by definition, have to be symmetric (if *A* is in the same place as *B*, then *B* is in the same place as *A*) [15].

Are there differences in communication and collocation volumes between nodes connected by the asymmetric and symmetric edges in the nomination layer?

We examine if nodes connected by asymmetric and symmetric nomination edges differ in communication and collocation volume. It is reasonable to expect that symmetric edges would have significantly higher levels of communication and collocation [15, 19, 20]. To this end, we examine if nodes connected by asymmetric and symmetric edges in the nomination layer differ in communication and collocation intensities. As shown in Table 17, we observe that, apart from the first semester, there is a significant difference in behaviors of nodes connected by asymmetric and symmetric edges in the nomination layer, with nodes connected by symmetric nominations communicating more frequently

Table 17 Difference in communication volumes between nodes connected by asymmetric and symmetric nomination edges

Semester	Asymmetric edges		Symmetric edges	
	No. calls	No. messages	No. calls	No. messages
Semester 1	69	472	58	842
Semester 2	25	638	39	636
Semester 3	40	351	112	2038
Semester 4	10	256	70	1406

than others. In the first semester, the same difference exists, but it is much smaller and visible only if the sum of calls and messages is taken into account. Table 18 shows the differences between the numbers of collocations for nodes connected by the symmetric and asymmetric edges in the nomination layer. As expected, we find that dyads connected by symmetric links in the nomination layer spend more time in the same location than dyads linked by asymmetric nomination links. These results provide strong support for the hypothesis that behavioral links are more intense among dyads connected by mutual nominations than they are for dyads in which one person is more cognitively salient to another than the reverse.

Are nodes with asymmetric edges in the nomination layer more likely to be connected by non-reciprocal communication edges?

Next, we examine whether nodes connected by non-reciprocal communication edges are also more likely to have asymmetric communication patterns. We define a non-reciprocal communication edge as one in which one node initiates communications with the other node more often than the reverse [20]. We compare communication imbalance between nodes connected by asymmetric and non-symmetric nomination links. To measure non-reciprocity in the communication layer, we first compute the ratio of the volume of communication in which the source node is the initiator to the volume of communication in which the destination node is the initiator: we call this quantity *One-Sided Communication Factor, OSCF*. We multiply the number of calls by 10, since messages are about 10 times more frequent than calls and add the product to the number of messages. Using this result, we measure the percentage of non-reciprocated communication for nodes connected by both asymmetric and symmetric in the nomination layer.

We find that nodes connected by symmetric nominations have high rates of reciprocal communications. In the first semester only 3% of nodes linked by symmetric nominations have corresponding behavioral edges that count as non-reciprocal according to the criterion defined in "Are nodes with asymmetric edges in the nomination layer more likely to connected by be non-reciprocal communication edges?" section. In comparison,

Table 18 Difference in the numbers of collocations between nodes connected by asymmetric and symmetric nomination edges

Semester	Asymmetric edges	Symmetric edges
Semester 1	108.9	28.6
Semester 2	145.6	37.5

asymmetric edges in the nomination layer are much more likely to be linked corresponding to non-reciprocal edges in the communication layer: In the first semester, the nodes connected by the asymmetric nomination edges were about ten times more likely (31%) to have imbalanced communication than the nodes connected by symmetric nomination edges. Table 19 summarizes these results.

Is behavioral edge dissolution faster for nodes linked by asymmetric edges in the nomination layer?

We examine if nodes connected by asymmetric nomination edges are more likely to experience behavioral edge decay than nodes connected by symmetric nominations. To do so, we measure the survival probabilities of behavioral edges between nodes connected by asymmetric and symmetric edges across all semesters. We find that nodes connected by asymmetric nominations are significantly more likely to experience decay and dissolution in the communication layer than the nodes connected by symmetric edges in the nomination layer in all three semesters.

Nodes joined by asymmetric edges in the nomination layer have dissolution probabilities of 90, 87.5, and 50% in the communication layer in each of the three semesters. In contrast, the corresponding probabilities for dyads joined by symmetric nomination links are 72, 66, and 16% in each of the three semesters. We also observe an overall downward trend in the dissolution probability in the communication layer. Initially, these are very high for the first semester, but they decline steadily over time. However, even in the third semester, nodes connected by asymmetric nomination edges are more than three times more likely to dissolve their behavioral edges than nodes joined by symmetric nominations.

Communication behavior profile: the "non-reciprocal sender" profile

We classify nodes that are more likely to be involved in non-reciprocal communication as *non-reciprocal senders*. We then examine the communication behavior profile of these nodes to see if the non-reciprocal sender profile differs from reciprocal sender profile. The goal is to verify if nodes with different communication profiles are more likely to experience their changes in the nomination layer, given the well-known psychological aversion to lack of reciprocity [3, 19, 37]. We find support for the hypothesis that non-reciprocal senders have a larger churn of nominees, in the observation that non-reciprocal senders retain 7, 16, and 38% of their links in the nomination layer, while reciprocal senders retain 25, 50, and 88% of their nomination links in the succeeding semesters.

Table 19 Difference between symmetric and asymmetric edges in the fractions of having non-reciprocal communication, OSCF

Semester	Asymmetric edges (%)	Symmetric edges (%)
Semester 1	31	3
Semester 2	30	1
Semester 3	39	10
Semester 4	31	6

Discussion

Implications of the results

A fundamental question in the analysis of social networks concerns itself with dependencies between links based on cognitive salience, such as those elicited from traditional network surveys, and behavioral linkages indicative of direct communicative exchange, or providing the potential for the formation of close relationships such frequenting the same physical location [3, 12, 37, 38]. Dependencies between cognitive salience, propinquity, and behavioral interactions have been difficult to study in the past, mainly due to lack of availability of dynamic, ecologically valid data in which the temporal dependencies of network ties across these different layers could be examined [9, 15].

In this paper, we have provided a unified empirical treatment of the temporal coevolution of network layers capturing these three key types of human connectivity. Our results provide confirmation for classical lines of network theory [6, 37, 38], while revealing novel insights about the linkage between cognition, communication, and behavior. First, we show that there are systematic dependencies between the cognitive salience of contacts and communication and collocation behavior. All else equal, persons tend to communicate and spend time in the same place as those contacts that are cognitively salient to them. This is particularly the case for those contacts whose cognitive salience persists over time. This is consistent with the idea that cognitive structure is a key determinant of behavioral structure [38], and that frequency of interaction and time-spent together are important components of the concept of tie strength [39]. However, our results also show that just in the same way that cognition is predictive of behavior, behavior is predictive of dynamic changes in the relative salience of contacts. Using state-of-the-art machine-learning techniques we showed that future changes in the cognitive salience of contacts can be predicted from pre-existing (and potential) interactions, both in terms of communication and propinquity behavior.

Previous work on the cognitive salience of social contacts using network surveys has shown that such ties are subject to what has been referred as *decay*; this is the phenomenon whereby a person may nominate another as a cognitively salient contact at time t but fail to do so at time $t + 1$. While the phenomenon of tie decay is well studied in social network analysis [40], it has not been previously linked to coevolution dynamics of behavioral ties. In this paper we showed that there are systematic links between tie-decay dynamics in terms of cognitive salience with respect to changes in dynamic behavioral layers. For ties that decline in cognitive salience over time, some changes in communication behavior and very minimal changes in collocation behavior occur. This implies that changes in cognitive salience are less predictive of behavioral changes than the reverse. Nevertheless, we do find that cognitive salientties exhibit systematic differences in terms of the *temporal profile* in which behaviors are enacted. Cognitively salient ties tend to be activated (either via communication or collocation) at days of the week or times of the day much more likely to be indicative of informal sociability. One implication of this novel result is that this behavioral temporal signature could be used to predict cognitive salience in the absence of subjective information of social ties.

In examining the linkage between these three different forms of human connectivity, an empirically validated model of the emergence of cognitive salient contacts suggests itself. According to our findings, collocation behavior emerges first, which leads to increases in communication behavior, which then leads to a contact rising up high enough in the cognitive salience hierarchy to be mentioned as a significant tie in a network survey. The process model suggested by our results is consistent with classic work on the evolution of social contacts from psychology and sociology [19, 37, 41]. We are able to provide systematic empirical evidence for the first time here.

Finally, our empirical work speaks to the fundamental role of asymmetry and non-reciprocity in human connectivity. Previous work has pointed to the fact that the cognitive salience relation can be asymmetric: A can be salient to B but B may not consider A salient [3]. In the same way, previous work has shown that communications can be either reciprocal or non-reciprocal [20]. Our empirical work connects these two lines of research for the time, showing that asymmetry at the level of cognitive salience is connected to non-reciprocity in communication behavior in systematic and intuitive ways. All else being equal, asymmetric nominations lead to non-reciprocities in communication. Not only that, asymmetry at the level of cognitive salience predicts tie decay in the communication layer, while also predicting the churning of ties at the level of the individual.

Limitations and suggestions for future research

The present work advances theory and research in social network analysis, especially with regard to the dynamic coevolution of social ties across multiple connectivity layers. However, our results also open up a variety of questions that cannot be answered given the limitations of the data, and which should be the subject of future work. In particular, moving our framework to a larger population beyond the college student setting, and ascertaining whether our results hold in other human interaction foci (such as work organizations) is important. Linking cognitive salience to other subjective features of social relations, such as emotional closeness, role-relations (e.g., friendship versus kin ties), the exchange of resources (e.g., advice, or emotional support), and looking at how these edge-level variables in the nomination layer interact with communication and collocation behavior also seems like a pertinent subject of future research. Finally, while only suggestive at this stage, expanding the work on asymmetries and non-reciprocities in both cognitive salience and behavioral interactions seems like a promising avenue of future research. This work could look at the individual, dyadic, and contextual correlates of reciprocities and non-reciprocities in interaction as these interact with subjective symmetries and asymmetries in cognitive salience. In all, the work reported here opens up multiple avenues for future work at the intersection of cognition, behavior, and human social networks.

Authors' contributions

This work is the result of a joint effort where all authors contributed equally to defining and shaping the problem definition, methodology, deciphering results, implementation, and manuscript. BA, as the first author, took the lead in composing the first draft of the manuscript, while everyone else edited it. All authors read and approved the final manuscript.

Author details

[1] Rensselaer Polytechnic Institute, 110 8th St., Troy, NY 12180, USA. [2] Społeczna Akademia Nauk, Lodz, Poland. [3] US Army Research Laboratory, Adelphi, MD 20783, USA. [4] University of Notre Dame, Notre Dame, IN 46556, USA.

Competing interests

The authors declare that they have no competing interests.

Acknowledgements and funding

This work was supported in part by the Army Research Laboratory under Cooperative Agreement Number W911NF-09-2-0053 (the Network Science CTA) and by the Office of Naval Research (ONR) Grant No. N00014-15-1-2640. The views and conclusions contained in this document are those of the authors.

References

1. Striegel A, Liu S, Meng L, Poellabauer C, Hachen D, Lizardo O. Lessons learned from the netsense smartphone study. In: Proceedings of the 5th ACM workshop on HotPlanet (HotPlanet '13). New York: ACM; 2013. p. 51–6.
2. Bahulkar A, Szymanski BK, Chan K, Lizardo O. Coevolution of two networks representing different social relations in NetSense. In: Proceedings of the international workshop on complex networks and their applications, studies in computational intelligence series 693. Berlin: Springer; 2016. p. 423–34.
3. Hammer M. Implications of behavioral and cognitive reciprocity in social network data. Soc Netw. 1985;7(2):189–201.
4. Lazer D. The co-evolution of individual and network. J Math Sociol. 2001;25: 69–108.
5. Campbell KE, Lee BA. Name generators in surveys of personal networks. Soc Netw. 1991;13(3):203–21.
6. Hammer M. Explorations into the meaning of social network interview data. Soc Netw. 1984;6(4):341–71.
7. Marsden PV, Campbell KE. Reflections on conceptualizing and measuring tie strength. Soc Forces. 2012;91(1):17–23.
8. Roberts SG, Dunbar RI. Communication in social networks: effects of kinship, network size, and emotional closeness. Pers Relationsh. 2011;18(3):439–52.
9. Rivera MT, Soderstrom SB, Uzzi B. Dynamics of dyads in social networks: assortative, relational, and proximity mechanisms. Ann Rev Sociol. 2010;36:91–115.
10. Brewer DD. Forgetting in the recall-based elicitation of personal and social networks. Soc Netw. 2000;22(1):29–43.
11. Marin A. Are respondents more likely to list alters with certain characteristics? Implications for name generator data. Soc Netw. 2004;26:289–307.
12. Feld SL, Carter WC. Detecting measurement bias in respondent reports of personal networks. Soc Netw. 2002;24(4):365–83.
13. Merluzzi J, Burt RS. How many names are enough? Identifying network effects with the least set of listed contacts. Soc Netw. 2013;35(3):331–7.
14. Grabowicz PA, Ramasco JJ, Gonçalves B, Eguíluz VM. Entangling mobility and interactions in social media. PLoS ONE. 2014;9(3):e92196.
15. Kitts JA. Beyond networks in structural theories of exchange: promises from computational social science. In: Advances in group processes. 2014. p. 263–98.
16. Wiese J, Kelley PG, Cranor LF, Dabbish L, Hong JI, Zimmerman J. Are you close with me? are you nearby? Investigating social groups, closeness, and willingness to share. In: Proceedings of the 13th international conference on Ubiquitous computing. New York: ACM; 2011. p. 197–206.
17. Fuhse JA. The meaning structure of social networks. Sociol Theory. 2009;27(1):51–73.
18. Vaisey S, Lizardo O. Can cultural worldviews influence network composition? Soc Forces. 2010;88(4):1595–618.
19. Carley KM, Krackhardt D. Cognitive inconsistencies and non-symmetric friendship. Soc Netw. 1996;18(1):1–27.
20. Wang C, Lizardo O, Hachen D, Strathman A, Toroczkai Z, Chawla NV. A dyadic reciprocity index for repeated interaction networks. Netw Sci. 2013;1(1):31–48.
21. Raeder T, Lizardo O, Hachen D, Chawla NV. Predictors of short-term decay of cell phone contacts in a large scale communication network. Soc Netw. 2011;33(4):245–57.
22. Zheleva E, Sharara H, Getoor L. Coevolution of social and affiliation networks. In: Proceedings of the 15th ACM SIGKDD international conference on knowledge discovery and data mining. New York: ACM; 2009. p. 1007–16.
23. Skyrms B, Pemantle R. A dynamic model of social network formation. In: Adaptive networks. 2009. p. 231–51.
24. Pattison P, Robins G, Wang P, Snijders TAB, Koskinen J. The co-evolution of multiple networks. In: Sunbelt XXVI international social networks conference vancouver. 2006.
25. Kivela M, Arenas A, Barthelemy M, Gleeson JP, Moreno Y, Porter MA. Multilayer networks. J Complex Netw. 2014;2(4):203–71. doi:10.1093/comnet/cnu016.
26. Zhang JKX, Yu PS. Transferring heterogeneous links across location-based social networks. In: Proceedings of the 7th ACM international conference on web search and data mining. New York: ACM; 2014. p. 303–12.
27. Zhang J, Yu PS, Zhou Z. Meta-path based multi-network collective link prediction. In: Proceedings of the 20th ACM SIGKDD international conference on knowledge discovery and data mining. New York: ACM; 2014. p. 1286–95.
28. Mucha PJ, Richardson T, Macon K, Porter MA, Onnela JP. Community structure in time-dependent, multiscale, and multiplex networks. Science. 2010;328(5980):876–8.
29. Smieszek T. Contact diaries versus wearable proximity sensors in measuring contact patterns at a conference: method comparison and participants' attitudes. BMC Infect Dis. 2016;16:341.
30. Mastrandrea R, Fournet J, Barrat A. Contact patterns in a high school: a comparison between data collected using wearable sensors, friend diaries and friendship surveys. PLoS ONE. 2015;10:e0136497.
31. Saramaki J, Leichtb E, Lopezb E, Robertsc S, Reed-Tsochasb F, Dunbare R. Persistence of social signatures in human communication. Proc Natl Acad Sci. 2014;111:942–7.
32. Stopczynski A, Sekara V, Sapiezynski P, Cuttone A, Madsen MM, Larsen J, Lehmann S. Measuring large-scale social networks with high resolution. PLoS ONE. 2014;9:e95978.

33. Saramaki J, Moro E. From seconds to months: multi-scale dynamics of mobile telephone calls. Eur Phys J. 2015;88:164. doi:10.1140/epjb/e2015-60106-6
34. Miritello G, Lara R, Cebrian M, Moro E. Limited communication capacity unveils strategies for human interaction. Sci Rep. 2013;3:1950.
35. Miritello G. Temporal patterns of communication in social networks. Berlin: Springer Theses. 2013. p. 294–6.
36. Liu S, Jiang Y, Striegel A. Face-to-face proximity estimation using bluetooth on smartphones. IEEE Trans Mob Comput. 2014;13(4):811–23.
37. Davis JA. Statistical analysis of pair relationships: symmetry, subjective consistency and reciprocity. Sociometry. 1968:102–19.
38. Carley K. Group stability: a socio-cognitive approach. Adv Group Process. 1990;7:1–44.
39. Marsden PV, Campbell KE. Measuring tie strength. Soc Forces. 1984;63(2):482–501.
40. Burt RS. Decay functions. Soc Netw. 2000;22(1):1–28.
41. Newcomb TM. An approach to the study of communicative acts. Psychol Rev. 1953;60(6):393.

5

Adding *ReputationRank* to member promotion using skyline operator in social networks

Jiping Zheng[1,2]* and Siman Zhang[1]

*Correspondence:
jzh@nuaa.edu.cn
[2] Collaborative Innovation
Center of Novel
Software Technology
and Industrialization, Nanjing,
China
Full list of author information
is available at the end of the
article

Abstract

Background: To identify potential stars in social networks, the idea of combining member promotion with skyline operator attracts people's attention. Some algorithms have been proposed to deal with this problem so far, such as skyline boundary algorithms in unequal-weighted social networks.

Methods: We propose an improved member promotion algorithm by presenting *ReputationRank* based on eigenvectors as well as *Influence* and *Activeness* and introduce the concept of skyline distance. Furthermore, we perform skyline operator over non-skyline set and choose the infra-skyline as our candidate set. The added *ReputationRank* helps a lot to describe the importance of a member while the skyline distance assists us to obtain the necessary condition for not being dominated so that some meaningless plans can be pruned.

Results: Experiments on the DBLP and WikiVote datasets verify the effectiveness and efficiency of our proposed algorithm.

Conclusions: Treating the infra-skyline set as candidate set reduces the number of candidates. The pruning strategies based on dominance and promotion cost decrease the searching space.

Keywords: Social networks, Member promotion, *ReputationRank*, Skyline distance, Infra-skyline

Background

Nowadays, more and more social activities take place in social networks (SNs for short) as the SNs become prevailing, such as sharing information, making friends or finishing some team work with others online. Human behaviours in SNs attract more attentions. We can conclude that different members play different roles, some members may be "leaders" [1], and others who seem ordinary for the moment but it may be outstanding in the future.

To specify who are about to be important in the future, making a standard of importance should be crucial. There are multiple disciplines to recognize an important one. For example, in an online community as "Sina Weibo", we consider the one who owns lots of followers as important or whose posts get many retweets as important [2]. In a word, different criteria make different "leaders", the one who does not match the criteria would fail to be important. Usually, a single attribute does not describe the importance of a member accurately. Thus, it is necessary for us to formulate a multi-criteria standard to measure importance. The skyline operator has thus been introduced to do this in SNs. It is well known that the skyline operator is a good tool for multi-criteria decision making. It can be used to query for those objects that are not worse than any other. When the skyline operator was first used to do promoting in SNs, Peng et al. [3] proposed the definition of member promotion and provided the brute-force algorithm to realize it. However, this algorithm was inadvisable for a waste of time and space. Thus the authors introduced the skyline operator and proposed the dominance-based pruning strategy to optimize the ways of result validation. Afterwards, they carried further research on it and put forward the concept of promotion boundary for limiting the promotion plans, thus led to the boundary-based pruning strategy [4]. At the same time, they also proposed a cost-based pruning strategy, which greatly improved the efficiency of member promotion. Nevertheless, the final result was unsatisfactory on account of the simple metric of importance.

In this paper, we mainly study directed social graphs with the knowledge of graph theory [4], taking *Influence*, *Activeness* and *ReputationRank* as metrics of member's importance. The attributes *Influence* and *Activeness* are easy to understand, and they are indegree and outdegree in a directed graph correspondingly. We consider that if a person owns lots of followers, s/he is influential and if a person follows lots of people, which indicates the ability to reach many other members, s/he is active. What is more, we learn from the idea of Google's *pagerank* algorithm, a way of measuring the importance of website pages, put forward *ReputationRank* to measure the importance of a member in SNs. Our goal is to find those members who can be "stars" in the future accurately and efficiently. To ensure accuracy, we assume that if a person is followed by some important persons, s/he is important too. Further, we assume that any two members in a specific direction can be connected only once and we employ edge addition as the promotion manner to simulate the process of relationship established. Usually, it will take cost to add new edges between two nodes. Therefore, the problem of member promotion in SNs is defined to excavate the most appropriate non-skyline member(s) which can be promoted to be skyline member(s) by adding new edges with the minimum cost. However, the calculation of added *ReputationRank* metric involves series of mathematical operations, it may need enormous computational cost.

To ensure efficiency and tackle the challenge of the computation cost, we mainly consider the changes of *Influence* and *Activeness* after adding edges, because we only need to add the number of directed edges involved. However, when calculating a point's *ReputationRank*, it involves some complicated matrix operations. We need to take the total number of the members as denominator. Apparently, for the great changes of the denominator (we assume the SN is dynamic), the subtle changes of numerator can be ignored. We conduct a skyline query on the dimensions of *Influence*, *Activeness* and *ReputationRank* to get the non-skyline set, then we carry out a second skyline query on the non-skyline set. We treat the skyline set in the second skyline query as our candidate set. It helps to reduce the number of candidates greatly. The contributions of this paper are summarized as follows.

- We learn from the *pagerank* algorithm and propose to add the *ReputationRank* to measure the importance of a member, which helps to improve the accuracy of the prediction.
- We carry a second skyline query over the non-skyline set which is obtained from the skyline query on the three-dimensional dataset and regard the infra-skyline as our candidates. It remarkably reduces the number of candidates. Then we introduce the skyline distance and the cost-based as well as dominance-based strategies to prune some meaningless promotion plans.
- Experiments on DBLP and WikiVote datasets are conducted to show the effectiveness and efficiency of our approach.

The rest of this paper is organized as follows. "Related work" section reviews related work. In "Preliminaries" section, we introduce several preliminary concepts. Then we bring forward the problem and propose the algorithm with analysis in "Prediction of promoting members in SNs" section. The results of the experiments are presented to show the effectiveness and efficiency of our algorithm in "Experimental analysis" section. Finally, we conclude our work in "Conclusions" section.

Related work

Skyline queries

The skyline operator was first introduced by Börzsöny et al. [5]. It was a tool for multi-criteria decision making. Then some representative algorithms for skyline computation were proposed, such as Block-Nested-Loops (BNL) and Divide-and-Conquer (D&C) [5], Bitmap and Index [6], Nearest Neighbor (NN) [7], and the Branch and Bound Skyline (BBS) algorithm [8]. Both BNL and D&C had to traverse the entire dataset before returning skyline points. The bitmap-based method transformed each data points to bit vectors. In each dimension, the value was represented by the same number '1'. However, it could not guarantee a good initial response time and the bitmaps would be very large for large values. Therefore, another method which transformed multiple dimensions into a single one space where objects were clustered and indexed using a B^+ tree was raised. It helped a lot to save processing time because skyline points could be determined without examining the rest of the objects not accessed yet. The NN algorithm was proposed by Kossmann et al. [7]. It could progressively report the skyline set in an order according to user's preferences. However, one data point may be accessed many times until being dominated. To find remedy for this drawback, Papadias et al. [8] proposed BBS, an R-tree based algorithm, which retrieved skyline points by traversing the R-tree by the Best-First strategy. There are also lots of studies on skyline variations for different applications such as subspace skylines [9], k-dominant skylines [10], probabilistic skyline computation on uncertain data [11], weighted attributes skylines [12], skyline queries over data streams [13], skyline analysis on time series data [14], spatial skyline queries [15], skyline computation in partially ordered domains [16] and using skylines to mine user preferences, making recommendations [17] and searching star scientists [18].

Member promotion

Peng et al. [3] first proposed the concept of member promotion in SNs and provided a brute-force algorithm to solve it. It stated that member promotion aimed at promoting the unimportant member which was most potential to be promoted and became important one. It considered "most potential" as the minimum promotion cost, which meant the member could be able to be promoted at minimum cost. And the brute-force algorithm tried out all the available added edges to find out the optimal promotion plans. However, some "meaningless" added edges would also be verified, it led to high time cost. Based on the characteristics of the promotion process, Peng et al. [3] proposed the IDP (Index-based Dynamic Pruning) algorithm, which could generate some prunable plans when met a failed promotion plan. Later, Peng et al. [4] conducted further research on the member promotion, which mainly focused on unequal SNs. They brought forward promotion boundary to limit promotion plans. At the same time, they proposed the cost-based and dominance-based pruning strategies to reduce the searching space. Furthermore, the authors expanded the algorithm, proposed an InfraSky algorithm based on equal-weighed SNs. They optimized the cost model and put forward a new concept named "Infra-Skyline" to remarkably prune the candidate space [4]. However, all the works of Peng et al. [3, 4] are limited for only metrics such as indegree and outdegree which could not describe a member's importance entirely, thus the prediction results of member promotion were not very satisfying.

A major distinction between our approach and Peng et al.'s works is that we add *ReputationRank* as a metric attribute, which is more suitable to describe a member's characteristic besides the two metrics. With an upgrade of the metrics, our work shows more efficiency.

Preliminaries

In this paper, SN is modeled as a weighted directed graph $G(V, E, W)$. The nodes in V represent the members in the SN. Those elements of E are the existing directed edges between the members. Each $w \in W$ denotes the cost for establishing the directed edge between any two different members.

Definition 1 (*Influence*) Given a node v in an SN $G(V, E, W)$, the *Influence* of v, marked as $I(v)$, is the indegree of v.

Definition 2 (*Activeness*) Given a node v in an SN $G(V, E, W)$, the *Activeness* of v, marked as $A(v)$, is the outdegree of v.

Definition 3 (*ReputationRank*) Given a node v in an SN $G(V, E, W)$, the *ReputationRank* of v, marked as $P(v)$, is the value of the corresponding component in the eigenvector of the normalized social relationship matrix whose eigenvalue is 1.

Example 1 Suppose that there are three nodes in an SN, let the nodes be v_1, v_2, v_3, if the SN's normalized social relationship matrix has an eigenvalue 1 and its corresponding eigenvector is $p = (p_1, p_2, p_3)$ (we can obtain these values by the method introduced in "ReputationRank" section), then we know that v_1, v_2, v_3's *ReputaionRank* is p_1, p_2 and p_3, respectively.

Definition 4 (*Social relationship matrix*) Given an SN $G(V, E, W)$, the social relationship matrix is an adjacency matrix which expresses the links between the members in the SN, denoted as M.

Definition 5 (*Normalization social matrix*) If a social relationship matrix is M, then its normalization social matrix is a matrix where the sum of the elements for each column is 1. We denote the normalization matrix as M'.

Definition 6 (*Dominance*) Given an SN $G(V, E, W)$, $\forall v_1, v_2 \in V$, we say v_1 dominates v_2 if and only if v_1 is not worse in *Influence* dimension, *Activeness* dimension and *ReputationRank* dimension, and is better in at least one dimension than v_2.

Definition 7 (*Dominator set*) Given an SN $G(V, E, W)$, if v_1 dominates v_2, we say v_1 is a dominator of v_2. Correspondingly, all dominators of a member v, marked as $\delta(v)$, are denoted as the dominator set of v.

Definition 8 (*Skyline*) Given an SN $G(V, E, W)$, the skyline of G, denoted as S_G, is the set of members which are not dominated by any other member.

Definition 9 (*Infra-skyline*) Given an SN $G(V, E, W)$, the infra-skyline of G is the skyline of the set of all non-skyline members of G, namely, if S_G is the skyline set of G, then the infra-skyline of G is S_{G-S_G}.

Example 2 Given an SN consists of seven members, namely $\{A, B, C, D, E, F, G\}$, suppose that the skyline set is $\{A, B, D\}$, what is more, E is dominated by F, then the infra-skyline in the SN is $\{C, F, G\}$.

Definition 10 (*Promotion cost*) Given an SN $G(V, E, W)$, the promotion cost of a candidate c, is the sum of all the weights corresponding to the edges being added at c, denoted as $cost(c, c') = \sum_{e \in E_a} \gamma(e)$, where c' is the point after the edges are added at point c, E_a is the set of added edges and $\gamma(e)$ is the cost of adding edge e.

Assume $I(v)$, $A(v)$ and $P(v)$ represent the *Influence*, *Activeness* and *ReputationRank* of node v in V, respectively. We consider the larger the values of $I(v)$, $A(v)$ and $P(v)$ are, the better they are.

ReputationRank

ReputationRank is obtained by counting the number and quality of followers to a person to determine a rough estimate of how important the person is. The *ReputationRank* of a member is defined recursively and depends on the number and *ReputationRank* metric of all followers. A member that is followed by many members with high *ReputationRank* receives a high rank itself.

From the point of mathematics, members' *ReputationRank* depends on the reputation of those members who follow them. The *ReputationRank* of the follower also depends on persons who follow her/him, and the subsequent process can be implemented in the same manner. Thus, for solving this kind of "infinite regression", we define $P(v_i)$ as the *ReputationRank* of member i, and we notice that the ith column of the social relationship matrix shows those members who follow her/him. Therefore, we can get v_i's *ReputationRank* by adding these products between the relation state and the *ReputationRank* of all other members, namely

$$P(v_i) = x_{1i}P(v_1) + x_{2i}P(v_2) + \cdots + x_{gi}P(v_g), \tag{1}$$

where the coefficient x_{ji} denotes the reciprocal of outdegree of member j, g is the number of the members.

Example 3 If there are seven members in an SN, as shown in Fig. 1, the member v_2 is followed by v_1, v_3 and v_4, then the rest entries of the second column in the social relationship matrix are all 0s. Furthermore, v_1's outdegree is 5, v_3's outdegree is 2 and v_4's outdegree is 4. Thus, we consider v_2's *ReputationRank* is $\frac{1}{5}p_{v_1} + \frac{1}{2}p(v_3) + \frac{1}{4}p(v_4)$.

From Example 3, we know that if the members v_1, v_3 and v_4 have a high *ReputationRank*, so does v_2.

Therefore, we have g formulas such as Eq. (1), and we have a system of g linear equations. If we compute the social relationship matrix M, put the value of the *ReputationRank* into the vector and adopt Katz's Suppose [19] to normalize the social relationship matrix, the whole formula system could be expressed as

$$P = M^{T'}P, \tag{2}$$

where P represents the vector consisting of the corresponding *ReputationRank* of each member in the limited state and $M^{T'}$ denotes the normalized transposed social matrix.

By reorganizing these formulas, we obtain the formula $(I - M^{T'})P = \mathbf{0}$, where I represents a g-dimensional unit matrix, and both P and $\mathbf{0}$ represent vectors with the length of g. The corresponding component of eigenvector P whose eigenvalue is 1 represents the *ReputationRank* of the members [12].

The property of ReputationRank

It should be noticed that a point's *ReputationRank* is partially consistent with its *Influence*. However, this property alone cannot show the difference between the top and the next. Actually, the *Activeness* also affects the *ReputationRank*.

Example 4 Given seven members in the SN, as shown in Fig. 1, its corresponding social relationship matrix M and its normalized transposed matrix $M^{T'}$ are as follows:

$$M = \begin{bmatrix} 0 & 1 & 1 & 1 & 1 & 0 & 1 \\ 1 & 0 & 0 & 0 & 0 & 0 & 0 \\ 1 & 1 & 0 & 0 & 0 & 0 & 0 \\ 1 & 1 & 1 & 0 & 1 & 0 & 0 \\ 1 & 0 & 1 & 1 & 0 & 1 & 0 \\ 1 & 0 & 0 & 0 & 1 & 0 & 0 \\ 0 & 0 & 0 & 0 & 1 & 0 & 0 \end{bmatrix}, M^{T'} = \begin{bmatrix} 0 & 1 & \frac{1}{2} & \frac{1}{4} & \frac{1}{4} & \frac{1}{2} & 0 \\ \frac{1}{5} & 0 & \frac{1}{2} & \frac{1}{4} & 0 & 0 & 0 \\ \frac{1}{5} & 0 & 0 & \frac{1}{4} & \frac{1}{4} & 0 & 0 \\ \frac{1}{5} & 0 & 0 & 0 & \frac{1}{4} & 0 & 0 \\ \frac{1}{5} & 0 & 0 & \frac{1}{4} & 0 & \frac{1}{2} & 1 \\ 0 & 0 & 0 & 0 & \frac{1}{4} & 0 & 0 \\ \frac{1}{5} & 0 & 0 & 0 & 0 & 0 & 0 \end{bmatrix}. \tag{3}$$

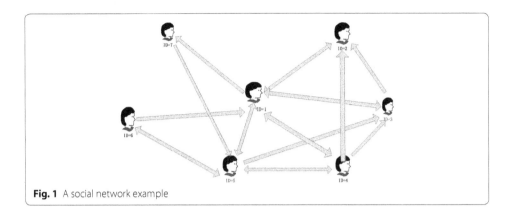

Fig. 1 A social network example

Then we obtain the eigenvector $\alpha = (0.304, 0.166, 0141, 0.105, 0.179, 0.045, 0.061)^{\mathrm{T}}$ of $M^{T'}$ when the eigenvalue is 1. We can conclude that the *ReputationRank* of each member is almost consistent with their value of *Influence*. It is obvious that the one whose ID is 1 has the highest *ReputationRank* almost for one third of all. We think it is because that Member 1 gains all the reputation from Member 2 who has high *ReputationRank*. What is more, Member 1 has the highest *Influence* and *Activeness*, thus we consider Member 1 is the most popular one in the SN. On the other hand, we find that although Member 2 and Member 3 have the same *Influence*, Member 2's *ReputationRank* is larger than that of Member 3. The reason is that Member 2 owns one second of Member 3's *Reputation-Rank* but Member 3 only owns one fourth of Member 5' *ReputationRank*. Therefore, we conclude that the *ReputationRank* of a member in an SN is not only related to the *Influence* but also to the *ReputationRank* of their followers and their followers' *Activeness*.

Prediction of promoting members in SNs

Problem statement

The problem we study in this paper is to locate the most "potential" member(s) for promotion by means of elevating it (them) into the skyline. Suppose we have two datasets D_1 and D_2. D_1 represents some data a few years ago and the D_2 represents that of the following years. If $S_1 = SKY(D_1)$, $S_1' = SKY(D_1 - S_1)$, $S_2 = SKY(D_2)$, where the $SKY()$ represents the skyline set of the dataset, then S_1' is the candidate set in our algorithm. After promoting towards each point in S_1', if there exist some points in S_1' appearing in S_2, the prediction is successful. Otherwise, it fails. Since the non-skyline members are candidates for promotion, if a non-skyline member is promoted, some edges are added to the network and the cost of this promotion is to sum up all the costs of the added edges. In addition, we know that added edges may have effects on the metrics of all members in the SN which may need to be recalculated frequently, thus the time cost to do promotion is extremely high. Therefore, finding the suitable non-skyline members promoted to be skyline members with minimum cost is the goal of member promotion in SNs.

The sort-projection operation

We project all the members into a two-dimensional Cartesian coordinate system in that we only consider the change of *Influence* and *Activeness*, where the *x*-axis represents the

Influence and the *y*-axis represents the *Activeness*. Taking the candidate *c* as an example, suppose that *c* is dominated by *t* skyline points, it is worth noting that the candidate *c* is dominated in three dimensions (the *Influence* dimension, *Activeness* dimension and *ReputationRank* dimension). But in the process of edge addition, we just consider the dominance on the *Influence* and *Activeness*. Because it is obvious that if a member is not strictly dominated on two dimensions, s/he will not be dominated on three dimensions either [10]. We simply sort the skyline points in ascending order on *x*-axis. What is more, we assume the weights to be arbitrary positive integer numbers from 1 to 10. Some terms mentioned above are defined as follows.

Definition 11 (*Strictly dominate*) Given an SN $G(V, E, W)$, if $p_1 \prec p_2$ and p_1 is larger than p_2 on each dimension, we say p_1 strictly dominates p_2, denoted by $p_1 \prec\prec p_2$.

Definition 12 (*Skyline distance*) Given a set DS of points in a two-dimensional space, a candidate *c*, and a path $Path(., .)$, the skyline distance of *c* is the minimum value of $Path(c, c')$, where c' is a position in the two-dimensional space such that $x.c' \geq x.c$, and $y.c' \geq y.c$, and c' is not strictly dominated by any point in DS. We denote the skyline distance as $SkyDist()$.

Suppose that *c* is strictly dominated by *t* skyline points in $SKY(DS)$. For any position c' which is not strictly dominated by any point in DS satisfies $x.c' \geq x.c$, and $y.c' \geq y.c$, the promotion from *c* to c' can be viewed as a path from *c* to c', which always goes up along axes. Since we use linear cost functions $cost(c, c')$ as the sum of the weighted length of the segments on the path. We aim to find a path with the minimum value so that the end point c' is not strictly dominated by any skyline point, and $x.c' \geq x.c, y.c' \geq y.c$.

Definition 13 (*Skyline boundary*) Given a set SKY of skyline points in DS, we say a point *p* is on the skyline boundary if there exists a point $u \in SKY$ such that $u \prec p$ and there does not exist a point $u' \in SKY$, such that $u' \prec\prec p$.

From the definition of skyline boundary, we conclude that the skyline distance of each point on the skyline boundary is 0 [20].

Given a candidate *c* and the *t* skyline points $s_1, s_2, \ldots, s_t$, we plot the lines $x = x_c$, $x = x_{s_i}$, $y = y_c$ and $y = y_{s_i}$, respectively, as shown in Fig. 2, we find there would be some intersections, we use triangles to represent these intersections. We call those intersections on the skyline boundary local optimal points. In Fig.2, p_1, p_2, p_3, and p_4 are the local optimal points.

Therefore, in the wo-dimensional space, for the candidate *c* and the *t* skyline points $s_1, s_2, \ldots, s_t$, if we have $x.s_1 < x.s_2 < \cdots < x.s_t$. Without loss of generality, we know $y.s_1 > y.s_2 > \cdots > y.s_t$. We can conclude that there are $t + 1$ local optimal points and the *i*th one p_i is given by the following formula:

$$P_i = \begin{cases} (x.c, y.s_1), & i = 1; \\ (x.s_{i-1}, y.s_i), & 2 \leq i \leq t; \\ (x.s_t, y.c), & i = t+1. \end{cases} \tag{4}$$

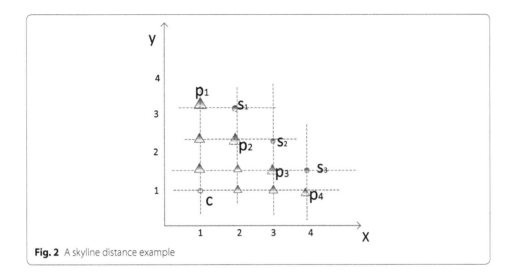

Fig. 2 A skyline distance example

Consider a candidate c dominated by t skyline points $s_1, s_2, \ldots, s_t$. Let $p_1, \ldots, p_r$ be the r local optimal points determined by c and $s_1, s_2, \ldots, s_t$, then the skyline distance of c is the minimum path from c to p_i.

Example 5   There is a candidate c and s_1, s_2, s_3 are skyline points which dominate c, as shown in Fig. 2, we can obtain the four local optimal points p_1, p_2, p_3 and p_4 by Eq. (4), by comparing the path between c and p_i, we can get the skyline distance of c. In Fig. 2, the path between c and p_1, p_2, p_3, and p_4 is 2, 2, 2.5 and 3, respectively. Therefore, the skyline distance of c is 2.

Algorithm 1 gives the pseudo-codes of the sort-projection operation. Assume that the number of input skyline points is m, it is easy to know that the cost of the sorting step is $O(m \log m)$. Then the time cost of remaining step for obtaining the skyline distance mainly depends on the number of local optimal points. From Eq. (4), we know that the time complexity of calculating the local optimal points is $O(1)$. Assume that the number of the local optimal points is k, then it is easy to know that the time complexity of obtaining the minimum path from candidate c to local optimal points is $O(k)$. Therefore, the time complexity of Algorithm 1 is $O(m \log m + 1 + k) = O(m \log m)$.

Algorithm 1: The sort-projection algorithm $SP(c, SKY)$

Input: $SKY()$
Output: $SkyDist(c)$

1 sort points in $SKY()$ in ascending order on x-axis;
2 $P = \{p_i \mid l\}$ where p_i is given by Equation (4);
3 return $\min\{Path(c, P) \mid P\}$.

Pruning by cost and dominance

Definition 14   (*Promotion plan*) Given an SN $G(V, E, W)$, for a candidate $c \in$ candidate set, the promotion plan of c includes all the added edges in the process of a promotion attempt.

After obtaining the skyline distance of a candidate, we get the necessary condition for the candidate not being dominated by skyline points. Taking the candidate c as an example, assume that c' is the end point after promotion with the skyline distance of c, then there exists three different solutions towards the different values of c':

1. If $x_{c'} = x_c$, then $x_{c''} = x_{c'}, y_{c''} = y_{c'} + 1$;
2. If $y_{c'} = y_c$, then $x_{c''} = x_{c'} + 1, y_{c''} = y_{c'}$;
3. If $x_{c'} \neq x_c$ and $y_{c'} \neq y_c$, then $x_{c''} = x_{c'} + 1, y_{c''} = y_{c'} + 1$.

We denote the transformed c' as c''. It is obvious that c'' could not be dominated by any point at all. If we call the position where a candidate will not be dominated as *GoodPosition()*, we say $c'' \in GoodPosition()$. Besides c'', all points in the skyline set will not be dominated either. Thus, the dominator set of c belongs to *GoodPosition(c)*.

In view of unequal costs for establishing different edges, it probably takes different costs to promote c by different plans. Therefore, we organize all the edges which can be added to the plans against each candidate c, respectively, denoted as E_c and sort the edges in ascending order of weights. Then we can locate the promotion plans which satisfy the constraints of *GoodPosition(c)* from the head of E_c and treat them as our original plans. These original plans will be put into a priority queue. When the plan is extracted from the priority queue to be verified, we first of all generate its successive plans and put the successive plans into the priority queue. The successive plans are generated by the Observation 1. Once the plan is verified to be successful to promote the candidates, the process of promotion will be ended. However, if a plan cannot successfully promote the candidates, we can generate some prunable plans based on the failed plan. The guidelines are shown in Observation 2. The idea is the same as the IDP algorithm [3].

Observation 1   The successive plans are generated by the following rules:

- If the current plan does not contain the minimum-cost edge e_0, add it to the current plan.
- If the current plan does not contain any successive edge of e_i, namely e_{i+1}, replace e_i with e_{i+1}.

Observation 2   The prunable plans are generated by the following rules:

Theorem 1   *If the added edge e connecting node v_i and the candidate node c still cannot promote c to the skyline set, all the attempts of adding an edge e' connecting the node v_j and c with the same direction as e cannot promote c to the skyline set either, where $v_j \in \delta(v_i)$.*

Proof   Assuming that after adding an edge e, $v_i(I(v), A(v))$ will change to $v_i(I'(v), A'(v))$, and $c(I(c), A(c))$ will change to $c(I'(c), A'(c))$. Assume there is a point p still dominates c, if we add an edge e' connecting node v_j and c with the same direction as e, and v_j should belong to $\delta(v)$, we consider there should be two situations for v_j:

1. $v_j \neq p$. If v_j is a dominator of v_i but not be p, after adding an edge from v_j to c, $(I(v_j), A(v_j))$ will change to $(I'(v_j), A'(v_j))$, and $(I(c), A(c))$ will change to $(I'(c), A'(c))$, then p will still dominate c;

2. $v_j = p$. If v_j is a dominator of v_i and dominates c when $(I(c), A(c))$ changes to $(I'(c), A'(c))$, after adding an edge from p to c, $(I(p), A(p))$ will change in $(I'(p), A'(p))$, and $(I(c), A(c))$ will change to $(I'(c), A'(c))$, it is obvious that the changed p will still dominate c because it dominates c before one of the two values corresponding to the metrics increases.

In summary, all the attempts of adding an edge e' connecting the node v_j and c with the same direction as e cannot promote c to the skyline set either, where $v_j \in \delta(v_i)$. □

Corollary 1 *If a promotion plan $p(e_1, \ldots, e_w)$ cannot successfully promote its target candidate c to the skyline set, all the plans with w edges which belong to $\prod_{i=1}^{w} l_i$ can be skipped in the subsequent verification process against c, where for each e_i connecting v_i and c, l_i is a list containing all the non-existing edges each of which links one member of $\delta(v_i)$ and c with the same direction as e_i ($i = 1, 2, \ldots, w$), $\prod_{i=1}^{w} l_i$ is the Cartesian product of l_i.*

Proof According to Theorem 1, if each edge in l_i cannot successfully promote c, it means l_i cannot do it either. Thus, all the plans with w edges belonging to the Cartesian product of l_i will fail to promote the candidate.

The steps for pruning some plans are shown in Algorithm 2. Note that e_{ic} denotes the edge which connects from v_i to c. In Algorithm 2, Lines 3–6 and 7–9 are based on Theorem 1 and Corollary 1, respectively. Thus, we obtain the prunable plans of a given candidate.

Assume that for the candidate c, the number of available edges is k. For the worst case that all edges belong to available edge set fail to make c successfully promoted, suppose that the number of nodes which dominate c is h, then the time complexity of generating some prunable edges against each failed point is $O(hk)$. Furthermore, the time complexity of generating the prunable plans is $O(1)$. Thus, the total time complexity in the worst case is $O(hk)$. □

Algorithm 2: GeneratePrunablePlans $GeneratePrunP(E_c)$

Input: E_c:available edge set against c
Output: prunable plans of c.

1   *initialize an empty edge set $PrunE = \{\}$*;
2   **for** *each edge $e \in E_c$* **do**
3   **if** *$e_{ic} \in E_c$ fails to make c promoted* **then**
4         $S = \delta(v_i)$;
5   **for** *each point $v_j \in S \&\& e_{jc} \in E_c$* **do**
6            $PrunE = PrunE \cup \{e_{jc}\}$;

7   **if** *a plan $pl(e_1, e_2, ..., e_w)$ fails to make c promoted* **then**
8      $l_i = PrunE_i$;
9      $PrunP = \prod_{i=1}^{w} l_i$;
10   return $PrunP$.

Verification of the result

After pruning some meaningless plans based on promotion cost and dominance, the remaining plans will be carried out for promotion. It is well known that the skyline set may change after a promotion attempt, thus the candidate may still be dominated by other members. Therefore, the final verification must be executed to examine the results of the promotions.

It is time-consuming if we recalculate the skyline set after each promotion. We notice that those points which do not dominate the candidate before promotion would not dominate it after promotion either. Thus we can ignore it in the verification process. Therefore, after pruning, we should just consider the following situations when verifying:

- The points which dominate the candidate before promotion.
- The points which are contained in the promotion plans.

The PromSky algorithm

The whole process of member promotion in an SN is presented in Algorithm 3. Line 2 represents the generation of candidate set. Line 4 represents a preprocessing phase by generating the sorted available edges. The skyline distance of each candidate is calculated in Line 5. Then *GoodPosition*() is generated in Lines 6–14. The point c' is the promoted point with the skyline distance of c. Line 16 shows that the corresponding promotion plans are generated and put into the priority queue Q. Once the queue is not empty, we fetch the plan with minimum cost for further verification. Line 18 shows that before verifying the plan, we first generate its children plans by Observation 1 so that we can verify all the possible plans in ascending order of cost. Lines 21–24 represent that after checking based on the result verification strategy the result will be output if the promotion succeeds. If not, some prunable plans will be generated. The generation of prunable plans are showed in Line 28. Lines 25–26 represent that if the plan is in the prunable list, there is no need of further verification. Lines 19–20 show that after a successful promotion, the process will halt once we encounter a plan with the higher cost.

We estimate the time complexity of our PromSky algorithm in the worst case. Assumed that the candidate set is M, it takes $O(|M|)$ time to build its available edge set and $O(|M| \log |M|)$ time to calculate the skyline distance. For the recursion on the basis of each plan, the worst time complexity of generating the children plans is $O(|M|)$. It will take $O(\log |M|)$ to build and search the min heap. The generation process of the prunable list will cost $O(|m|^2)$. We build an index such as B^+ tree for speeding up the search in the prunable list, whose time cost can maintain steady at around $O(|M| \log |M|)$. The result checking phase will take $O(|M|)$ at worst. Theoretically, the worst time complexity of Algorithm 3 is $O(|M|^3)$(However, the algorithm usually reaches the result at early time in experiments).

Algorithm 3: The promotion algorithm $PromSky(G)$

Input: social network $G(V, E, W)$.
Output: optimal members for promotion and corresponding plans.

1 *initialize a priority queue Q;*
2 $C = SKY(V - SKY(V))$;
3 **for** *each $c \in C$* **do**
4   E=genCandidateEdgeSet(c);
5      $SkyDist(c) = Path(c, SKY)$;
6   **if** $c.x == c'.x$ **then**
7          $good.x = SkyDist(c.x)$;
8          $good.y = SkyDist(c.y) + 1$;
9   **if** $c.y == c'.y$ **then**
10         $good.x = SkyDist(c.x) + 1$;
11         $good.y = SkyDist(c.y)$;
12   **else**
13         $good.x = SkyDist(c.x) + 1$;
14         $good.y = SkyDist(c.y) + 1$;
15   GetDominator(c);
16   P=getMinCostPlan(*good*, GetDominator(c), E) and add P into Q;
17   **while** *p=ExtractMin(Q)* **do**
18         $p_{child} = GenerateChildren(p, E)$ and add it into Q;
19   **if** $p_{succ} \neq NULL$ && $cost(c) > cost(p_{succ})$ **then**
20   break;
21   **if** *c is promoted by p* **then**
22   return c and p;
23   **if** $p_{succ} = \emptyset$ **then**
24                 $p_{succ} = p$;
25   **if** $p \in prunableList$ **then**
26   continue;
27   **else**
28   *genPrunablePlans(p, c)*.

Analysis

In the SkyBoundary algorithm, Peng et al. [4] only used the *Authoritativeness(indegree)* and *Hubness(outdegree)* as the metrics, and described the plan limitation for promotion by bringing forward a new concept called "promotion boundary", and then proposed an effective boundary-based pruning strategy to prune the searching space. In this paper, we propose the concept of *ReputationRank* based on the Google's *pagerank* algorithm and add it as a measure attribute to describe the importance of a member, which helps to improve the accuracy of the prediction to some degree. Then we present the definition of skyline distance to obtain the necessary condition for not being dominated. At the same time, it also helps a lot to cut down the number of promotion plans.

On the other hand, when making a comparison on the time, from the size of the candidate set, when experimenting on the real-world datasets, the candidate set is all the non-skyline set in the SkyBoundary algorithm [4]. However, we carry a skyline query over the non-skyline set under the consideration of three dimensions and take the infra-skyline as the candidates so that remarkably pruning the size of the candidates and controlling the result set in a reliable range. On the other hand, by calculating the skyline distance of the candidate, we obtain the minimum path from the candidate's position to where not being strictly dominated. Then after trying all the positions belong to *GoodPositions()*, we can get the promotion plans that succeed in promoting the candidate by verifying the plans one by one. However, in [4], the SkyBoundary algorithm although pruned some meaningless plans based on the promotion boundary and got the constraint of promotion plans. They merged all the possible good points with the skyline points which dominate the candidate, then verified it in sequence to get the minimum cost one. Apparently, their method needs more time compared to our proposed algorithm.

Experimental analysis

Setup

The experiments are implemented using C++ with Visual Studio 2010 and conducted on an Intel Core CPU i75500U@2.4GHZ machine with 8G RAM and 1 TBytes Hard disk running on Windows 7. We use two datasets for the experiments.

1. WikiVote dataset: Wikipedia is an encyclopedia that any volunteers all over the world are able to write on it collaboratively. The dataset[1] contains all administrator elections and vote history data from 2004 to 2008. 2794 elections with 103663 total votes and 7066 users participating in the elections are contained in the dataset. Users are those who cast votes or are voted on. Each record includes 5 parts such as E, T, U, N, V. They correspondingly represent whether the election is successful or not, the time election is closed, user id (and username) of editor that is being considered for promotion, user id (and username) of the nominator and each voter's voting results. Nodes in the network represent users and a directed edge from node p to node q represents that user p votes on user q. We set all the weights to be random integers between 1 and 10 for simplicity.

2. DBLP dataset: DBLP[2] is a computer science bibliography website. Each record of the DBLP dataset consists of authors' names, paper title and published year. We collect all the records from 1992 to 2016. For a paper that was accomplished by several authors, we think the first author generally makes major contributions and the others do minor contributions. Thus, we build a directed graph by the co-author network. Nodes in the graph represent the authors and the directed edges with the first author as the end node and the other authors, respectively, as the start nodes represent the relationships between authors. We set all the weights of edges to be random integers between 1 and 10 for simplicity.

Results

RanSky algorithm: we pick up a candidate from the candidate set, and we randomly choose some added edges from the available edges until this candidate being successfully promoted. We denote it as a RanSky algorithm which is an adaptive version of the random algorithm in [4].

Promotion cost comparisons

In this set of experiments, we make a comparison on promotion costs of our PromSky algorithm with the RanSky algorithm. We consider the sum of the added edges'

---

[1] http://snap.stanford.edu/data/wiki-Vote.html.

[2] http://dblp.org/.

weights as the promotion cost of the Random algorithm. Then we use the PromSky algorithm to find out the optimal promotion plans and calculate their promotion costs, respectively.

Figure 3 illustrates the promotion costs of the two algorithms on WikiVote and DBLP datasets, respectively. The promotion costs of the two algorithms both grow with the increase of the network scales. It is obvious that the promotion cost of RanSky algorithm is much more than the PromSky algorithm, which means that our PromSky algorithm always provides the optimal plans. What is more, the differences between the two promotion costs in both datasets basically grow along with the scale of the network. By the way, we think the promotion cost on the WikiVote dataset is much more than the cost on the DBLP dataset is due to the existing connected edges on the WikiVote are less than that on the DBLP dataset.

Successful rate comparisons

We make a comparison of our PromSky algorithm with the SkyBoundary algorithm and RanSky algorithm in various network scales. The target candidate is the one who can be successful promoted randomly selected from the result of our PromSky algorithm and its promotion cost is the optimal cost. We add e edges picked from the available edges against the candidate according to the PromSky and SkyBoundary algorithm, respectively, and add e edges randomly picked from the available edges, then we verify the result. We calculate the promotion successful rate by counting the number of successful promotions in ten times promotion attempts. We conduct the experiments on both WikiVote and DBLP. From Fig. 4, we find that the SkyBoundary algorithm and the RanSky algorithm cannot guarantee the promotion's success even though we picked the optimal candidate and achieved the minimal promotion cost, the RanSky algorithm works worse especially. On the contrary, our PromSky algorithm performs well in various network scales. This is because we add more attributes in our PromSky algorithm for a member that it should increase the number of skyline set. Thus our successful promotion rate is higher in various network scales.

Prediction on DBLP

In this section, we record the predicted potential stars and the skyline authors detected by our algorithm from 1992 to 2016. For each year's data, we consequently combine the current yearly data with its previous 4 years' data to generate a 5-year sub-network because publications too long ago will have little impact on the contributions made by the authors of the time and only one year's publications cannot accurately reflect the contributions of the authors [4]. Then we run our PromSky algorithm on each sub-network (from 1996 to 2016) to verify the corresponding yearly potential stars and those skyline authors in the following couple of years. The skyline authors are obtained by conducting a skyline query over the *Influence* dimension, *Activeness* dimension and *ReputationRank* dimension. The potential authors are the predicting results of our PromSky algorithm. We can get the successful rate using the number of potential stars promoted into skyline in the next few years divided by the size of the whole potential star set, namely

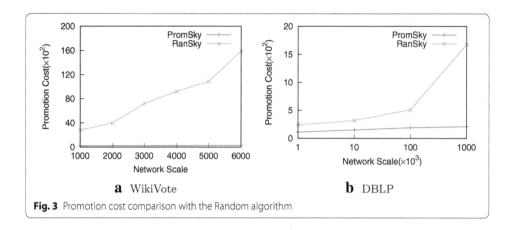

a WikiVote   **b** DBLP

Fig. 3 Promotion cost comparison with the Random algorithm

$$r = \mathrm{PN/CS}, \tag{5}$$

where "r" denotes the successful rate, and "PN" and "CS" are the number of successfully promoted members and the number of all the candidates, respectively.

The skyline authors and potential stars for each year are illustrated in Table 1. From Table 1, we can see each year's skyline authors and potential skyline authors from 1996 to 2016. We think that if the potential skyline author become a skyline author in the next few years, the promotion is successful, otherwise, it fails. We obtain the number of the potential candidates is 20 by merging the duplicated potential stars and removing the potential stars of the year 2016 because it is unable to be verified, and the number of the potential candidates who appear in the next skyline authors is 13. Those names which are in italic represent the successfully promoted candidates. Therefore, we conclude that the successful rate is 65%. However, in the previous research [4], when conducting the experiments on the dataset from 1971 to 2012, we find the successful rate is only 48%. It shows that our algorithm is more accurate than the previous.

Time cost comparisons

We conduct the experiments to compare the time costs of our PromSky algorithm with the SkyBoundary algorithm on two datasets. For the reason of intolerable time complexity, we do not take the RanSky algorithm to be a compared algorithm.

Figure 5 shows the average running time under different network scales. From Fig. 5, we can see that as the network scale grows, the running time also increases and our PromSky algorithm is faster than the SkyBoundary algorithm whatever the network scale is. This is because the candidates in SkyBoundary algorithm are all the non-skyline set but we carry the skyline query over the non-skyline set and take the infra-skyline as the candidates thus remarkably reducing the size of the candidates and controlling the result in a reliable range to a great extent. Besides, by bringing forward the skyline distance, we can reduce the searching space of promotion plans remarkably.

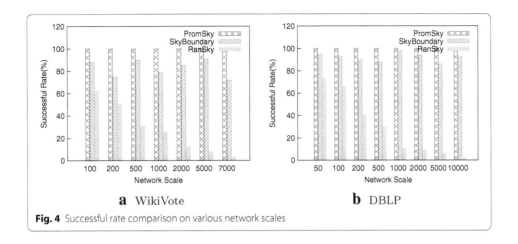

Fig. 4 Successful rate comparison on various network scales

Table 1 Skyline authors and potential stars from 1996 to 2016

Year	Skyline	Potential skyline
1996	Robert L. Glass, David Wilczynski	Robert W. Floyd
1997	Noga Alon, Jean P, Caxton Foster	Peter Kron
1998	Noga Alon, Robert L. Glass, V. Kevin M	Carl Hewitt, Bill Hancock
1999	*Robert W. Floyd*, Noga Alon, Honien Liu	Paul A.D., Alan G. Merten
2000	*Bill Hancock, Peter Kron*	Paul A.D.
2001	*Bill Hancock*, Nan C. Shu	Pankaj K. Agarwal
2002	*Bill Hancock*, Charles W. Bachman, Daniel L. Weller	Pankaj K. Agarwal
2003	Bill Hancock, Daniel L. Weller	Elisa Bertino, Alan G. Merten
2004	*Pankaj K. Agarwal*, Morton M. Astrahan, David R. Warn	Elisa Bertino, Mary Zosel
2005	Gary A. Kildall, Diane Crawford, Hans-Peter Seidel, *Erik D.Demaine*	Carl Hewitt
2006	Noga Alon, Diane Crawford, *Pankaj K. Agarwal*	Ingo H. Karlowsky, Louis Nolin
2007	*Elisa Bertino*, G. RuggiuW, J. Waghorn, M.H. Kay, Erik D. Demaine	T. William Olle
2008	Diane Crawford, *Paul A.D.*	B.M. Fossum
2009	Wen Gao, Xin Li, Jun Wang, P.A. Dearnley, Giampio Bracchi, Paolo Paolini, Ajith Abraham	H. Schenk, Gordon E. Sayre
2010	Xin Li, *B.M. Fossum*, J.K. Iliffe, Wen Gao, *Mary Zosel*, Wei Wang	Paul Mies, Ingo H. Karlowsky
2011	Xin Li, Gordon E. Sayre, T. William Olle	Peter Sandner
2012	H. Vincent Poor, *Peter Sandner*, Ulrich Licht	Yan Zhang
2013	*Ingo H. Karlowsky*, Heidi Anlauff, Günther Zeisel	Guy G. Boulaye
2014	*Yan Zhang*, Yu Zhang, Gordon E. Sayre, Witold Pedrycz	Carl Hewitt
2015	Harold Joseph Highland, Bernard Chazelle	Won Kim
2016	*Won Kim*, Dale E. Jordan, *B.M. Fossum*	Nan C. Shu

Conclusions

In this paper, we propose an improved member promotion algorithm in SNs, which aims at discovering the most potential stars which can be promoted into the skyline with the minimum cost. By adding the attribute of *ReputationRank*, we describe members' importance more precisely. Then we introduce the skyline distance to prune the data points for not

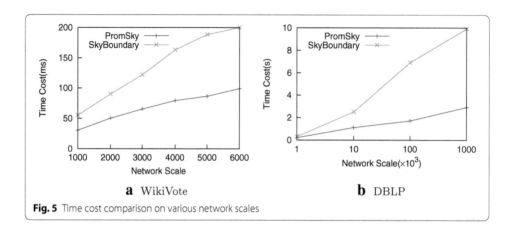

Fig. 5 Time cost comparison on various network scales

being dominated. At the same time, it also helps a lot to reduce the number of promotion plans. Experimental results on the DBLP and WikiVote datasets illustrate the effectiveness and efficiency of our approach.

Authors' contributions

JZ designed the proposed member promotion model and experiments, conceived of the study and performed the experiments analysis. SZ conducted the experiments and drafted the manuscript. Both authors read and approved the final manuscript.

Authors' information

Jiping Zheng received the BS degree from Nanjing University of Information Science & Technology, Nanjing, in 2001, the MS and the Ph.D. degrees from Computer Science Department, Nanjing University of Aeronautics & Astronautics in 2004 and 2007, respectively. From 2007 to 2009, he was a Postdoctoral Fellow at the Department of Computer Science of Tsinghua University, Beijing. From February 2016 to February 2017, he was a Visiting Fellow at the School of Computer Science and Engineering of the University of New South Wales, Sydney, Australia. He is now an associate professor of the College of Computer Science & Technology, Nanjing University of Aeronautics & Astronautics. His research interests include skyline computation, sensor data management and spatial indexes, with an emphasis on data management. He has published more than 30 technical papers in these areas. He is a member of IEEE and ACM, a senior member of China Computer Federation (CCF) and Chinese Institute of Electronics (CIE).

Siman Zhang received the BS degree from Nanjing University of Aeronautics & Astronautics, Nanjing, in 2015. She is a graduate student in College of Computer Science and Technology, Nanjing University of Aeronautics and Astronautics. Her research interests include skyline computation in social networks.

Author details

[1] College of Computer Science and Technology, Nanjing University of Aeronautics and Astronautics, Nanjing, China.
[2] Collaborative Innovation Center of Novel Software Technology and Industrialization, Nanjing, China.

Acknowledgements

This work is partially supported by the National Natural Science Foundation of China under Grant Nos. U1733112, 61702260, the Natural Science Foundation of Jiangsu Province of China under Grant No. BK20140826, the Fundamental Research Funds for the Central Universities under Grant No. NS2015095, Funding of Graduate Innovation Center in NUAA under Grant No. KFJJ20171605. The short version of this manuscript is in CSoNet 2017 [21]. The authors would like to thank for the invitation to submit the extended version to Computational Social Networks.

Competing interests

The authors declare that they have no competing interests.

References

1. Zhang C, Shou L, Chen K, Chen G, Bei Y. Evaluating geo-social influence in location-based social networks. In: 21st ACM international conference on information and knowledge management, CIKM'12, Maui, HI, USA, October 29–November 02, 2012. 2012. p. 1442–51.
2. Kempe D, Kleinberg JM, Tardos É. Maximizing the spread of influence through a social network. Theory Comput. 2015;11:105–47.
3. Z. Peng and C. Wang. Discovering the most potential stars in social networks. In Proceedings of the 3rd International Conference on Emerging Databases, 2011.
4. Peng Z, Wang C. Member promotion in social networks via skyline. World Wide Web. 2014;17(4):457–92.
5. Stephan B, Donald K, Konrad S. The skyline operator. In: ICDE. 2001. p. 421–30.
6. Tan KL, Eng PK, Ooi BC. Efficient progressive skyline computation. In: VLDB. 2001. p. 301–10.

7. Kossmann D, Ramsak F, Rost S. Shooting stars in the sky: an online algorithm for skyline queries. In: VLDB. 2002. p. 275–86.
8. Papadias D, Tao Y, Fu G, Seeger B. Progressive skyline computation in database systems. ACM Trans Database Syst. 2005;30(1):41–82.
9. Pei J, Jiang B, Lin X, Yuan Y. Probabilistic skylines on uncertain data. In: VLDB. 2007. p. 15–26.
10. Chan CY, et.al. Finding k-dominant skylines in high dimensional space. In: SIGMOD. 2006. p. 503–14.
11. Lian X, Chen L. Monochromatic and bichromatic reverse skyline search over uncertain databases. In: SIGMOD. 2008. p. 213–26.
12. Mindolin D, Chomicki J. Discovering relative importance of skyline attributes. Proc VLDB Endowment. 2009;2(1):610–21.
13. Sun S, Huang Z, Zhong H, Dai D, Liu H, Li J. Efficient monitoring of skyline queries over distributed data streams. Knowl Inf Syst. 2010;25:575–606.
14. Jiang B, Pei J. Online interval skyline queries on time series. In: ICDE. 2009. p. 1036–47.
15. Sharifzadeh M, Shahabi C. The spatial skyline queries. In: VLDB. 2006. p. 751–62.
16. Sacharidis D, Papadopoulos S, Papadias D. Topologically sorted skylines for partially ordered domains. In: ICDE. p. 1072–83.
17. Jiang B, Pei J, Lin X, Cheung DW, Han J. Mining preferences from superior and inferior examples. In: SIGKDD. 2008. p. 390–8.
18. Sidiropoulos A, Gogoglou A, Katsaros D, Manolopoulos Y. Gazing at the skyline for star scientists. J Informetr. 2016;10(3):789–813.
19. Katz L. A new status index derived from sociometric analysis. Psychometrika. 1953;18(1):39–43.
20. Huang J, Jiang B, Pei J, Chen J, Tang Y. Skyline distance: a measure of multidimensional competence. Knowl Inf Syst. 2013;34(2):373–96.
21. Zhang S, Zheng J. An efficient potential member promotion algorithm in social networks via skyline. In: The 6th international conference on computational social networks, CSoNet 2017. 2017. p. 678–90.

6

Social learning for resilient data fusion against data falsification attacks

Fernando Rosas[1,2]* ⓘ, Kwang-Cheng Chen[3] and Deniz Gündüz[2]

*Correspondence:
f.rosas@imperial.ac.uk
[1] Centre of Complexity
Science and Department
of Mathematics, Imperial
College London, Kensington,
London SW72AZ, UK
Full list of author information
is available at the end of the
article

Abstract

Background: Internet of Things (IoT) suffers from vulnerable sensor nodes, which are likely to endure data falsification attacks following physical or cyber capture. Moreover, centralized decision-making and data fusion turn decision points into single points of failure, which are likely to be exploited by smart attackers.

Methods: To tackle this serious security threat, we propose a novel scheme for enabling distributed decision-making and data aggregation through the whole network. Sensor nodes in our scheme act following social learning principles, resembling agents within a social network.

Results: We analytically examine under which conditions local actions of individual agents can propagate through the network, clarifying the effect of Byzantine nodes that inject false information. Moreover, we show how our proposed algorithm can guarantee high network performance, even for cases when a significant portion of the nodes have been compromised by an adversary.

Conclusions: Our results suggest that social learning principles are well suited for designing robust IoT sensor networks and enabling resilience against data falsification attacks.

Keywords: Distributed decision-making, Data fusion, Sensor networks, Social networks, Data falsification attacks, Byzantine nodes, Collective behaviour, Multi-agent systems, Social learning, Information cascades

Background

Motivation

Internet of Things (IoT) is expected to play a central role in future digital society. However, to fully adopt this technology, it is crucial to guarantee its security, specially for public utilities whose safety is essential for the well-being of our society [1]. Recent cyber-attacks that created significant damage have been widely reported, e.g. the self-propagating malware *WannaCry* that caused a infamous worldwide network hack in May 2017 [2]. Developing technologies that can guarantee the safety of large information networks, such as IoT, is a challenging but urgent need. As information networks get more closely intertwined within our daily lives, ensuring their security and thus safety is becoming an even more challenging issue.

As the level of security is typically determined by the weakest link, a major dilemma of IoT security lies in the low-complexity sensor networks that are located at the network edge. These sensor networks are usually composed by a large number of autonomous electronic devices, which collect critical information for the control and operation of IoT [3, 4]. By monitoring extensive geographical areas, these networks can enable a wide range of services to society, becoming a key element for the well-being of future smart cities [5, 6]. These networks may also perform sensitive tasks, including the surveillance over military or secure zones, intrusion detection to private property, monitoring of drinkable water tanks and protection from chemical attacks [7, 8].

Although the design of secure wireless sensor networks have been widely studied (e.g. [9–11] and references therein), there remain many open problems of both theoretical and engineering nature [12]. In particular, as the number of sensors is usually very large, precise management of them is challenging or even infeasible. A significant portion of the sensors might be deployed in unprotected areas, where it is impossible to ensure their physical or cyber security (e.g. war zones, or regions easily accessed by adversaries). Furthermore, sensor nodes are generally not tamper-proof due to cost restrictions, and have limited computing and networking capabilities. Therefore, they may not be capable of employing complex cryptographic or security protocols.

The vulnerability of sensor nodes makes them potential victims of cyber/physical attacks driven by intelligent adversaries. Attacks to information networks are usually categorized into *outsider attacks* and *insider attacks*. Outsider attacks include (distributed) denial of service (DoS) attacks, which use the broadcasting nature for wireless communications to disrupt the communications capabilities [10]. In contrast, in insider attacks the adversary "recruits" sensor nodes by malware through cyber/wireless means, or directly by physical substitution [13]. Following the classical *Byzantine generals problem* [14], these "Byzantine nodes" are authenticated, and recognized as valid members of the network. Byzantine nodes can hence generate false data, exhibit arbitrary behaviour, and collude with others to create network malfunctions. In general, insider attacks are considered to be more potentially harmful to information networks than outside attacks.

The effect of Byzantine nodes and data falsification over distributed sensor networks has been intensely studied; the impact over the network performance has been characterized, and various defense mechanisms has been proposed (c.f. [15] for an overview, and also [16–20] for some recent contributions). However, all these works focus on networks with star or tree topology, and rely on centralizing the decision-making in special nodes, called "fusion centers" (FCs), which gather all the sensed data. Therefore, a key element in these approaches is a strong division of labour: ordinary sensor nodes merely sense and forward data, while the processing is done exclusively at the FC corresponding to a *distributed-sensing/centralized-processing* approach. This literature implicitly assume that the FCs are capable of executing secure coding and protocols, and hence, are out of the reach of attackers. However, large information networks might require another kind of mediator devices, known as data aggregators (DAs), which have the capability to access the cloud through high-bandwidth communication links [21]. DAs are attractive targets for insider attacks, as they might also be located in unsafe locations due to the limited range of sensor node radios. Please note that a tampered DA can completely disable the sensing capabilities of all the nodes whose information has been aggregated, generating a single point of failure that is likely to be exploited by smart adversaries [22].

An attractive route to address this issue is to consider *distributed-sensing/distributed-processing* schemes, which avoid centralized decision-making by distributing processing tasks throughout the network [23]. However, the design of practical distributed-sensing/ distributed-processing schemes is a challenging task, as collective computation phenomena usually exhibit highly non-trivial features [24, 25]. In effect, even though the distributed-sensing literature is vast (for classic references c.f. [26–28], and more modern surveys see [3, 4, 29, 30]), the construction of optimal distributed schemes is in general NP-hard [31]. Moreover, although in many scenarios the optimal schemes can be characterized as a set of thresholds for likelihood functions, the determination of these thresholds is usually an intractable problem [26]. For example, homogeneous thresholds can be suboptimal even for networks with similar sensors arranged in star topology [32], being only asymptotically optimal in the network size [33]. Moreover, symmetric strategies are not suitable for more complicated network topologies, requiring heuristic methods.

Distributed decision-making and social learning

In parallel, significant research efforts have been dedicated to analysing *social learning*, which refers to the decision-making processes that take place within social networks [34]. In these scenarios, agents make decisions based on two elements: private information that represents agent's personal knowledge, and social information derived from previous decisions made by the agent's peers [35].

Social learning has been investigated in pioneering works that study sequential decision-making of Bayesian agents over simple social network structures [36, 37]. These models showed how, thanks to social interactions, individuals with weak private signals can harvest information from the decisions of other agents [38]. Interestingly, it was also found that aggregation of rational decisions through *information cascades* could generate suboptimal collective responses, degrading the "wisdom of the crowds" into mere herd behaviour. After these initial findings, researchers have aimed at developing a deeper understanding of information cascades extending the original models by considering more general cost metrics [39–41], and by studying the effects of the network topology on the aggregated behaviour [42–45]. Non-Bayesian learning models have also been explored, where agents use simple rule-of-thumb methods to exchange information [46–52].

Social learning plays a crucial role in many important social phenomena, e.g. in the adoption or rejection of new technology, or in the formation of political opinions [34]. Social learning models are particularly interesting for studying information cascades and herd dynamics, which arises when the social information pushes all the subsequent agents to ignore their own personal knowledge and adopt a homogeneous behaviour [37]. Moreover, there have been a renewed interest in understanding information cascades in the context of e-commerce and digital society [45]. For example, information cascades might have tremendous consequences in online stores where customers can see the opinions of previous customers before deciding to buy a product, or in the emergence of viral media contents based on sequential actions of "like" or "dislike". Therefore, developing a deep understanding of the mechanics behind information cascades, and how they impact social learning, is fundamental for our modern networked society.

The main motivation behind this article is to explore the connections between social learning and secure sensor networks, building a bridge between the research done separately by economists and sociologist on one side and electrical engineers and computer scientists on the other. A key insight for establishing this connection is to realize that

Table 1 Table of correspondances between distributed detection in sensor networks and social learning in social networks

Distributed detection	Social learning
Sensor node	Social agent
Communication range	Social neighbourhood
Environmental variables	State of the world
Noisy measurement	Private information
Local processing	Agent's decision
Bandwidth constraints	Decision sharing

each agent's decision corresponds to a compressed description of his/her private information. Therefore, the fact that agents cannot access the private information of others, but can only observe their decisions, can be understood as a constraint on the communication resources. In this way, social learning can be regarded as an information network that performs distributed inference under communication constraints (see Table 1). Moreover, it would be natural to use social learning principles in the design of distributed-sensing/distributed-processing schemes, with the hope that this might enable additional robustness to decision-making processes in sensor networks.

Contributions

In contrast to almost all the existing research, this work considers powerful topology-aware data falsification attacks, where the adversary knows the network topology and leverages this knowledge to take control of the most critical nodes of the network—either regular nodes, DAs or FCs. This represents a worst-case scenario where the network structure has been disclosed or inferred through network tomography via traffic analysis [53]. The reason why this adversary model has not been popular in the literature might be because traditional distributed-sensing schemes do not offer any resistance against this kind of attack.

This works presents a distributed-sensing/distributed-processing scheme for sensor networks that uses social learning principles in order to deal with a topology-aware adversary. The scheme is a threshold-based data fusion strategy, related to those considered in [26]. However, its relationship with social decision-making allows an intuitive understanding of its mechanisms. For avoiding security threats introduced by FCs, our scheme adopt tandem or serial decision sequencing [27, 54–57]. It is noted that, contrasting with some related literature, our analysis does not focus on optimality aspects of data fusion, but aims to illustrate how distributed decision-making can enable network resilience against powerful topology-aware data falsification attacks. We demonstrate how network resilience hold even when a significant number of nodes have been compromised.

Our work exploits a positive effect of information cascades that have been overlooked before: information cascades make a large number of agents/nodes to hold equally qualified estimators, generating many locations where a network operator can collect aggregated data. Therefore, information cascades are crucial in our solution for avoiding single points of failure. For enabling a better understanding of information cascades, this work extends results presented in [58] providing a mathematical characterization of information cascades under data falsification attacks. In particular, our results clarify the conditions upon which local actions of individual agents can propagate across the network, compromising the collective performance. These results provide a first step towards the clarification of these non-trivial social dynamics, enriching our understanding of decision-making processes in biased social networks.

This paper expands the ideas presented in [59] by developing a formalism that allows considering incomplete or imperfect social information. This formalism is used to overcome the strongest limitation of the scheme presented in [59], namely the fact that each node was required to overhear and store all the previous transmissions in the network. Clearly this cannot take place in a large sensor network, due both to the storage constraints of the nodes, and to the large energy consumption required to transmit and receive across all pairs of nodes [60]. Therefore, this research presents an important step towards practical applications.

The rest of this article is structured as follows: "System model and problem statement" section introduces the system model, describing the network controller and the adversary behaviour. Our social learning data fusion scheme is then described in "Social learning as a data aggregation scheme" section, where some basic statistical properties are explored, and a practical algorithm for implementing the decision rule is derived. "Information cascade" section analyses the mathematical properties of the decision process, providing a geometrical description and a characterization of information cascades. All these ideas are then illustrated in a concrete scenario in "Proof of concept" section. Finally, "Conclusions" section summarizes our main conclusions.

Notation: uppercase letters are used to denote random variables, i.e. X, and lowercase letters their realizations, e.g. x. Boldface letters X and x represent random vectors and their realizations, respectively. Also, $\mathbb{P}_w\{X = x|Y = y\} = \mathbb{P}\{X = x|Y = y, W = w\}$ is used as a shorthand notation. A table summarizing the symbols and notation used through this article can be found in Appendix D.

System model and problem statement

System model

We consider a sensor network of N nodes, each corresponding to an information-processing device that has been deployed in an area of interest. Each node is equipped with sensory equipment to track variables of interest following a scheduled duty cycle. The measurement of the n-th sensor node is denoted by S_n, taking values over a set $\mathcal{S} \subset \mathbb{R}$ that can be discrete or continuous.[1] Based on these signals, the network needs to infer the value of an underlying binary variable W.

We consider networks where all the nodes have equal sensing capabilities, that is, the signals S_n are assumed to be identically distributed. Unfortunately, the general distributed detection problem for arbitrarily correlated signals is known to be NP-hard [31]. Hence,

---

[1] The generalization of our framework and results to vector-valued sensor outputs is straightforward.

for the sake of tractability, it is assumed that the variables $S_1, \ldots, S_N$ are conditionally independent given the event $\{W = w\}$,[2] following a probability distribution denoted by μ_w. It is also assumed that both μ_0 and μ_1 are absolutely continuous with respect to each other [67], i.e. no particular signal determines W unequivocally. This property guarantees that the log-likelihood ratio of these two distributions is always well defined, being given by the logarithm of the corresponding Radon–Nikodym derivative[3] $\Lambda_S(s) = \log \frac{d\mu_1}{d\mu_0}(s)$.

In addition to sensing hardware, each node is equipped with limited computing capability and a radio to wirelessly transit and receive data. Two nodes in the network are assumed to be connected if they can exchange information wirelessly. Note that, sensor nodes usually have a very limited battery budget, which imposes severe restrictions on their communication capabilities [68]. Therefore, it is assumed that each node forwards its data to others only by broadcasting a binary variable X_n. These simple signals do not impose an additional burden on the communication resources, as they could be appended to existent wireless control packages and viceversa, or could be shared by light, ultrasound or other alternative media.

We focus on the case in which the sensing capabilities of each sensor are limited, and hence, any inference about W made based only on the sensed data S_n cannot achieve a high accuracy. Interestingly, due to the nature of wireless broadcasting, nearby transmissions can be overheard and their information can be fused with what is extracted from the local sensor. The information that a node can extract from overhearing transmissions of other nodes is called "social information", contrasting with the "sensorial information" that is obtained from the sensed signal S_n.

Without loss of generality, nodes transmit their signals sequentially according to their indices (i.e. node 1 transmits first, then node 2, etc.).[4] It is assumed that this sequence is randomly chosen, and can be changed by the network operator at any time and be redistributed through the network (c.f. "The sensor network operator and the adversary" section). In general the broadcasted signals $X_1, \ldots, X_{n-1}$ might not be directly observable by the n-th agent because of various restrictions, including range limitations of the node's receiver radio [70], or the limited duty cycles imposed by battery restrictions [68]. Therefore, the social observations obtained by the n-th node are represented by $\boldsymbol{G}_n \in \mathcal{G}_n$, which can be a random scalar, vector, matrix or other mathematical object. Some cases of interest are as follows:

(i) The k previous decisions: $\boldsymbol{G}_n = (X_{n-k}, \ldots, X_{n-1})$.

(ii) The average value of all the previous decisions: $\boldsymbol{G}_n = \frac{1}{n-1} \sum_{k=1}^{n-1} X_k$.

(iii) The decisions of agents connected by an Erdös–Rényi random network with parameter $\xi \in [0, 1]$, i.e. $\boldsymbol{G}_n = (Z_1, \ldots, Z_{n-1}) \in \{0, 1, e\}^{n-1}$, where

$$Z_k = \begin{cases} X_k & \text{with probability } \xi, \\ e & \text{with probability } 1 - \xi. \end{cases} \tag{1}$$

---

[2] The conditional independence of sensor signals is satisfied when the sensor noise is due to local causes (e.g. thermal noise), but do not hold when there exist common noise sources (e.g. in the case of distributed acoustic sensors [61]). For works that consider sensor interdependence see [62–66].

[3] When S_n takes a finite number of values then $\frac{d\mu_1}{d\mu_0}(s) = \frac{\mathbb{P}\{S_n = s | W = 1\}}{\mathbb{P}\{S_n = s | W = 0\}}$, while if S_n is a continuous random variable with conditional p.d.f. $p(S_n | W = w)$ then $\frac{d\mu_1}{d\mu_0}(s) = \frac{p(s | W = 1)}{p(s | W = 0)}$.

[4] Note that the synchronization requirements of this procedure are low, so standard techniques can be used to keep the nodes' local clocks within the required synchronization constraints (see e.g. [69]).

Please note that the Erdös–Rényi model in (iii) has only been used as an illustrative example, and it can be easily generalized to consider the topology of any stochastic network of interest.

In this work, we study the social dynamics based on the properties of the transition probability from state $\boldsymbol{g}' \in \mathcal{G}_{n-1}$ to $\boldsymbol{g} \in \mathcal{G}_n$, as given by the conditional probabilities

$$\beta_w^n(\boldsymbol{g}|x_{n-1}, \boldsymbol{g}') := \mathbb{P}_w\{\boldsymbol{G}_n = \boldsymbol{g}|X_{n-1} = x_{n-1}, \boldsymbol{G}_{n-1} = \boldsymbol{g}'\}, \tag{2}$$

where $x_{n-1} \in \{0, 1\}$. It is also assumed that the social dynamics are causal, meaning that $\boldsymbol{G}_n$ is conditionally independent of S_m given W for all $m \geq n$.

The sensor network operator and the adversary

The network is managed by a network operator, who is an external agent that uses the network as a tool to build an estimate of W. The network operator is opposed by an adversary, whose goal is to disrupt the inference capabilities of the network. For this aim, the adversary controls a group of authenticated Byzantine nodes without being noticed by the network operator, which have been captured by malware through cyber/wireless means, or by physical substitution.

The overall performance of a network of N nodes is defined by the accuracy of the inference of the last node in the decision sequence. As the decision sequence is generated randomly by the network operator, every node is equally likely to be at the end of the decision sequence. It is further assumed that the adversary has no knowledge of the decision sequence, as it can be chosen at run-time and changed regularly. Therefore, as the adversary has no reason to target any particular node in the network, hence, it is reasonable to assume that the adversary captures nodes randomly. Byzantine nodes are, hence, assumed to be uniformly distributed over the network.

For simplicity, we model the strength of the attack with a single parameter p_b, which corresponds to the probability of a node being compromised.[5] Moreover, we assume that the capture probability does not depend on W. Hence, the number of Byzantine nodes, denoted by N^*, is a Binomial random variable with $\mathbb{E}\{N^*\} = p_b N$. Due to the law of large numbers, $N^* \approx p_b N$ for a large network, and hence, p_b is also the ratio of expected Byzantine nodes in the network, which is the traditional metric for attack strength used in the literature.

For enabling data processing and forwarding, the network operator defines a *strategy*, i.e. a data fusion scheme given by a collection of (possibly stochastic) functions $\{\pi_n\}_{n=1}^\infty$, such that $\pi_n : \mathcal{S} \times \mathcal{G}_n \to \{0, 1\}$ for all $n \in \mathbb{N}$. On the other hand, the adversary can freely set the values of the binary signals transmitted by Byzantine nodes. This can be modelled as a random mapping $C: \{0, 1\} \to \{0, 1\}$ that corrupts broadcasted signals. Therefore, the signal broadcasted by the n-th node is given by

$$X_n = \begin{cases} C(\pi_n(S_n, \boldsymbol{G}_n)) & \text{with probability } p_b, \text{ and} \\ \pi_n(S_n, \boldsymbol{G}_n) & \text{otherwise.} \end{cases} \tag{3}$$

Furthermore, as broadcasted signals are binary, the corruption mapping $C(\cdot)$ can be characterized by the conditional probabilities $c_{0|0}$ and $c_{0|1}$, where $c_{i|j} = \mathbb{P}\{C(\pi) = i|\pi = j\}$.

---

[5] This attack model assumes implicitly that the capture of each node is an independent event. Extensions considering cyber-infection propagation properties are possible (c.f. [71]), being left for future studies.

The rest of this work focuses on the case in which the network operator can deduce the corruption function and can estimate the capture risk p_b. Then, the average network miss-detection and false alarm rates for an attack of intensity p_b are defined as

$$\mathbb{P}\{\text{MD}; p_b\} := \mathbb{P}_1\{\pi_N(S_N, \boldsymbol{G}_N) = 0\}, \quad \text{and} \tag{4}$$

$$\mathbb{P}\{\text{FA}; p_b\} := \mathbb{P}_0\{\pi_N(S_N, \boldsymbol{G}_N) = 1\}, \tag{5}$$

respectively (note that p_b implicitly affects the distribution of $\boldsymbol{G}_N$). The case in which these quantities are unknown can be addressed using the current framework with a min-max analysis, which is left for future studies.

Problem statement

Our goal is to develop a resilient strategy, in order to provide a reliable estimation of W even under a significant number of unidentified Byzantine nodes. Note that in most surveillance applications, miss-detections are more important than false alarms, being difficult to estimate the cost of the worst-case scenario. Therefore, the average network performance is evaluated following the Neyman–Pearson criteria, by setting an allowable false alarm rate α and focusing on reducing the miss-detection rate [72]. By denoting by $\mathcal{P}$ the set of all strategies, we have the following optimization problem:

$$\begin{array}{ll} \underset{\{\pi_n\}_{n=1}^{\infty} \in \mathcal{P}}{\text{minimize}} & \mathbb{P}\{\text{MD}; p_b\} \\ \text{subject to} & \mathbb{P}\{\text{FP}; p_b\} \leq \alpha. \end{array} \tag{6}$$

Finding an optimal solution to (6) is a formidable challenge, even for the simple case of networks with start topology and no Byzantine attacks (see [30, 73] and references therein). Therefore, our aim is to develop a sub-optimal strategy that enables resilience, while being suitable for implementation in sensor nodes with limited computational power.

Social learning as a data aggregation scheme

This section describes our proposed data fusion scheme, and explains its function against topology-aware data falsification attacks. In the sequel, "Data fusion rule" section describes and analyses the data fusion rule, then "Decision statistics" section derives basic properties of its statistics, and finally "An algorithm for computing the social log-likelihood" section presents a practical algorithm for its implementation.

Data fusion rule

Let us assume that each sensor node is a rational agent that tries to maximizes the profit of an inference within a social network. Rational agents follow *Bayesian strategies*,[6] which can be elegantly described by the following threshold-based decision rule [72, Chapt. 2]:

$$\frac{\mathbb{P}\{W = 1|S_n, \boldsymbol{G}_n\}}{\mathbb{P}\{W = 0|S_n, \boldsymbol{G}_n\}} \underset{\pi_n=1}{\overset{\pi_n=0}{\gtrless}} \frac{u(0,0) - u(1,0)}{u(1,1) - u(0,1)}. \tag{7}$$

---

[6] Although Bayesian models are elegant and tractable, they assume agents act always rationally [74] and make strong assumptions on the knowledge agents have about posterior probabilities [49]. However, Bayesian models provide an important benchmark, not necessarily due to their accuracy but because they give an important reference point with which other models can be compared [35].

Above, $u(\pi_n, w)$ is a cost assigned to the decision π_n when $W = w$, which can be engineered in order to match the relevance of miss-detections and false alarms [72].

Let us find a simpler expression for the decision rule (7). Due to the causality constraint (c.f. "System model" section), G_n can only be influenced by $S_1, \ldots, S_{n-1}$; and therefore, it is conditionally independent of S_n given W. Using this conditional independence condition, one can find that

$$\frac{\mathbb{P}\{W = 1 | S_n, G_n\}}{\mathbb{P}\{W = 0 | S_n, G_n\}} = e^{\Lambda_S(S_n) + \Lambda_{G_n}(G_n)}, \tag{8}$$

where $\Lambda_S(S_n)$ is the log-likelihood ratio of S_n (c.f. "System model" section) and $\Lambda_{G_n}(G_n)$ is the log-likelihood ratio of G_n. Then, using (8) one can re-write (7) as

$$\Lambda_S(S_n) + \Lambda_{G_n}(G_n) \underset{\pi_n=1}{\overset{\pi_n=0}{\lessgtr}} \tau_0, \tag{9}$$

where $\tau_0 = \log \frac{\mathbb{P}\{W=0\}}{\mathbb{P}\{W=1\}} + \log \frac{u(0,0)-u(1,0)}{u(1,1)-u(0,1)}$. In simple words, (9) states how the n-th node should fuse the private and social knowledge: the evidence is provided by the corresponding log-likelihood terms, which are then simply added and then compared against a fixed threshold.[7]

Further understanding of the above decision rule can be attained by studying it from the point of view of communication theory [58]. We first note that the decision is made not over the raw signal S_n but over the "decision signal" $\Lambda_S(S_n)$. Interestingly, the processing done by the function $\Lambda_S(\cdot)$ might serve for dimensionality reduction, as $\Lambda_S(S_n)$ is always a single number even though S_n may be a matrix or a high-dimensional vector. Due to their construction and the underlying assumptions over S_n (c.f. "System model" section), the variables $\Lambda_S(S_n)$ are identically distributed and conditionally independent given $W = w$. Moreover, by introducing the shorthand notation $\tau_n(G_n) = \tau_0 - \Lambda_{G_n}(G_n)$, one can re-write (9) as

$$\Lambda_S(S_n) \underset{\pi_n=1}{\overset{\pi_n=0}{\lessgtr}} \tau_n(G_n). \tag{10}$$

Therefore, the decision is made by comparing the decision signal with a decision threshold $\tau_n(G_n)$, which can be efficiently computed using the algorithm proposed in "An algorithm for computing the social log-likelihood" section. Note that this represents a comparison between the sensed data, summarized by $\Lambda_S(S_n)$, and the social information carried by $\tau_n(G_n)$.

Decision statistics

Let us find expressions for the probabilities of the actions of the n-th agent, first focusing on the case $n = 1$. Note that

$$\mathbb{P}_w\{\pi_1(S_1) = 0\} = \mathbb{P}_w\{\Lambda_S(S_1) < \tau_0\} = F_w^{\Lambda}(\tau_0), \tag{11}$$

---

[7] As the prior distribution of W is usually unknown, τ_0 is a free parameter of the scheme. Following the discussion in "Problem statement" section, the network operator shall select the lowest value of τ_0 that satisfies the required false alarm rate specified by the Neyman–Pearson criteria.

where $F_w^\Lambda(\cdot)$ is the c.d.f. of Λ_S conditioned on $W = w$. Then, considering the possibility that the first node could be a Byzantine node, one can show that

$$\mathbb{P}_w\{X_1 = 0\} = p_b\mathbb{P}_w\{X_1 = 0| \text{ Byzantine}\} + (1 - p_b)\mathbb{P}_w\{X_1 = 0|\text{not a Byzantine}\}$$
$$= p_b(c_{0|0}F_w^\Lambda(\tau_0) + c_{0|1}[1 - F_w^\Lambda(\tau_0)]) + (1 - p_b)F_w^\Lambda(\tau_0) \tag{12}$$

$$= z_0 + z_1F_w^\Lambda(\tau_0), \tag{13}$$

where we are introducing $z_0 := p_b c_{0|1}$ and $z_1 := 1 - p_b(1 - c_{0|0} + c_{0|1})$ as short-hand notation, which are non-negative constants that summarize the strength of the adversary. In particular, when the adversary is powerless then $z_0 = 0$ and $z_1 = 1$, and hence $\mathbb{P}_w\{\pi_1(S_1) = 0\} = \mathbb{P}_w\{X_1 = 0\}$.

By considering the n-th node, one can find that

$$\mathbb{P}_w\{\pi_n(S_n, G_n) = 0|G_n = g_n\} = \int_{\mathcal{S}} \mathbb{P}_w\{\pi_n(s_n, g_n) = 0|S_n = s\}\mu_w(s)\mathrm{d}s$$
$$= \int_{\mathcal{S}} \mathbb{K}\{\pi_n(g_n, s) = 0\}\mu_w(s)\mathrm{d}s \tag{14}$$

$$= \mathbb{P}_w\{\Lambda_S(s) < \tau_n(g_n)\} \tag{15}$$

$$= F_w^\Lambda(\tau_n(g_n)). \tag{16}$$

The first equality is a consequence of the fact that S_n is conditionally independent of G_n given $W = w$, while the second equality is a consequence that X_n can be expressed as a deterministic function of G_n and S_n, and hence, becomes conditionally independent of W. Above, (16) shows that τ_n is a sufficient statistic for predicting X_n with respect to G_n. Note that $F_w^\Lambda(x)$ can be directly computed from the statistics of the distribution of S_n (c.f. Appendix A). Moreover, using (16) and following a similar derivation as in (12), one can conclude that

$$\mathbb{P}_w\{X_n = 0|G_n = g_n\} = z_0 + z_1F_w^\Lambda(\tau_n(g_n)). \tag{17}$$

Let us now study the statistics of G_n. By using the definition of the transition coefficients $\beta_w^n(g_{n+1}|x_n, g_n)$, one can find that

$$\mathbb{P}_w\{G_{n+1} = g_{n+1}\} = \sum_{g_n \in \mathcal{G}_n}\sum_{x_n \in \{0,1\}} \beta_w^n(g_{n+1}|x_n, g_n)\mathbb{P}_w\{X_n = x_n, G_n = g_n\}. \tag{18}$$

Note that, using the above derivations, the terms $\mathbb{P}_w\{X_n = x_n, G_n = g_n\}$ can be further expressed as

$$\mathbb{P}_w\{X_n = x_n, G_n = g_n\} = \mathbb{P}_w\{X_n = x_n|G_n = g_n\}\mathbb{P}_w\{G_n = g_n\} \tag{19}$$

$$= \lambda(z_0 + z_1F_w^\Lambda(\tau_n(g_n)), x_n)\mathbb{P}_w\{G_n = g_n\}, \tag{20}$$

where $\lambda(p, x) = x(1 - p) + (1 - x)p$. Therefore, a closed form expression can be found for (18) recursively over G_n.

An algorithm for computing the social log-likelihood

The main challenge for implementing (9) as a data processing method in a sensor node is to have an efficient algorithm for computing $\tau_n(\boldsymbol{g}_n)$. Leveraging the above derivations, we develop Algorithm 1 as an iterative procedure for computing τ_n.

Algorithm 1 Computation of the decision threshold

1: **function** COMPUTE_TAU($N, F_0^\Lambda(\cdot), F_1^\Lambda(\cdot), \beta_w^n(\cdot|\cdot,\cdot), \tau_0, z_0, z_1$)
2:     $\tau_1 = \tau_0$
3:     **for** $x_1 \in \{0,1\}$ **do**
4:         $\mathbb{P}_0\{X_1 = x_1, \boldsymbol{G}_1 = 0\} = \lambda(z_0 + z_1 F_0^\Lambda(\tau_1), x_1)$
5:         $\mathbb{P}_1\{X_1 = x_1, \boldsymbol{G}_1 = 0\} = \lambda(z_0 + z_1 F_1^\Lambda(\tau_1), x_1)$
6:     **for** $n = 1, \ldots, N-1$ **do**
7:         **for** $\forall g \in \mathcal{G}_{n+1}$ **do**
8:             $\mathbb{P}_0\{\boldsymbol{G}_{n+1} = \boldsymbol{g}\} = \sum_{\boldsymbol{g}_n \in \mathcal{G}_n} \sum_{x_n \in \{0,1\}} \beta_0^n(\boldsymbol{g}_{n+1}|x_n, \boldsymbol{g}_n)\mathbb{P}_0\{X_n = x_n, \boldsymbol{G}_n = \boldsymbol{g}_n\}$
9:             $\mathbb{P}_1\{\boldsymbol{G}_{n+1} = \boldsymbol{g}\} = \sum_{\boldsymbol{g}_n \in \mathcal{G}_n} \sum_{x_n \in \{0,1\}} \beta_1^n(\boldsymbol{g}_{n+1}|x_n, \boldsymbol{g}_n)\mathbb{P}_1\{X_n = x_n, \boldsymbol{G}_n = \boldsymbol{g}_n\}$
10:            $\Lambda_{\boldsymbol{G}_n}(\boldsymbol{g}) = \log \frac{\mathbb{P}_1\{\boldsymbol{G}_n = \boldsymbol{g}\}}{\mathbb{P}_0\{\boldsymbol{G}_n = \boldsymbol{g}\}}$
11:            $\tau_n(\boldsymbol{g}) = \tau_0 - \Lambda_{\boldsymbol{G}_n}(\boldsymbol{g})$
12:            **for** $x_{n+1} \in \{0,1\}$ **do**
13:                $\mathbb{P}_0\{X_{n+1} = x_{n+1}, \boldsymbol{G}_{n+1} = \boldsymbol{g}\} = \lambda(z_0 + z_1 F_0^\Lambda(\tau_n(\boldsymbol{g}_n)), x_{n+1})\mathbb{P}_0\{\boldsymbol{G}_{n+1} = \boldsymbol{g}\}$
14:                $\mathbb{P}_1\{X_{n+1} = x_{n+1}, \boldsymbol{G}_{n+1} = \boldsymbol{g}\} = \lambda(z_0 + z_1 F_1^\Lambda(\tau_n(\boldsymbol{g}_n)), x_{n+1})\mathbb{P}_1\{\boldsymbol{G}_{n+1} = \boldsymbol{g}\}$
15:     **return** $\tau_N(\cdot)$

The inputs of Algorithm 1 can be classified into two groups. First, the terms $N, F_0^\Lambda(\cdot), F_1^\Lambda(\cdot), \beta_w^n(\cdot|\cdot,\cdot)$ are properties of the network (position of the node within the decision sequence, sensor statistics and social observability, respectively) that the network operator could measure. On the other hand, τ_0, z_0, z_1 are properties of the adversary profile that depend on the prior statistics of W, the rate of compromised nodes p_b and the corruption function defined by $c_{0|0}$ and $c_{0|1}$ (c.f. "The sensor network operator and the adversary" section). In most scenarios, the knowledge of the network controller about these quantities is limited, as attacks are rare and might follow unpredictable patterns. Limited knowledge can still be exploited using e.g. Bayesian estimation techniques [75]. If no knowledge is available for the network controller, then these quantities can be considered free parameters of the strategy that span a range of alternative balances between miss-detections and false positives, i.e. a receiver operating characteristic (ROC) space.

Algorithm 1 initialises from the initial decision threshold τ_0, and explores all the relevant scenarios iteratively in order to build estimations of the likelihood functions that are required to compute τ_N. The computation of the terms $\mathbb{P}_w\{\boldsymbol{G}_n = \boldsymbol{g}\}$ is done following (18), while the ones involving $\mathbb{P}_w\{X_n = x_n, \boldsymbol{G}_n = \boldsymbol{g}\}$ follow (20). Please note that the algorithm's complexity scales gracefully for many cases of interest. For the particular case of nodes with memory of length k (i.e. $\boldsymbol{G}_n = (X_{n-k-1}, \ldots, X_{n-1})$), the complexity of Algorithm 1 is $\mathcal{O}(2^k N)$, and therefore grows linearly with the size of the network, while being limited in the values of k that one can consider. In general, the algorithm complexity scales linearly with N as long as the cardinality of $\mathcal{G}_n$ are bounded, or if a significant portion of the terms $\beta_w^n(\boldsymbol{g}_{n+1}|x_n, \boldsymbol{g}_n)$ are zero.

Information cascade

The term "social learning" refers to the fact that $\pi_n(S_n, \boldsymbol{G}_n)$ becomes a better predictor of W as n grows; and hence, larger networks tend to develop a more accurate inference. However, as the number of shared signals grows, the corresponding "social pressure" can make nodes to ignore their individual measurements to blindly follow the dominant choice, triggering a cascade of homogeneous behaviour. It is our interest to clarify the role of the social pressure in the decision-making of the agents involved in a social network, as information cascades can introduce severe limitations in the asymptotic performance of social learning [44].

Moreover, an adversary can leverage the information cascade phenomenon. In effect, if the number of Byzantine nodes N^* is large enough then a misleading information cascade can be triggered almost surely, making the learning process to fail. However, if N^* is not enough then the network may undo the pool of wrong opinions and end up triggering a correct cascade.

In the sequel, the effect of information cascades is first studied in individual nodes in "Local information cascades" section. Then, the propagation properties of cascades are explored in "Social information dynamics and global cascades" section.

Local information cascades

In general, the decision $\pi_n(S_n, \boldsymbol{G}_n)$ is made based on the evidence provided by both S_n and $\boldsymbol{G}_n$. A *local cascade* takes place in the n-th agent when the information conveyed by S_n is ignored in the decision-making process due to a dominant influence of $\boldsymbol{G}_n$. We use the term "local" to emphasize that this event is related to the data fusion of an individual agent. This idea is formalized in the following definition using the notion of conditional mutual information [76], denoted as $I(\cdot; \cdot|\cdot)$.

Definition 1 The social information $\boldsymbol{g}_n \in \mathcal{G}_n$ generates a *local information cascade* for the n-th agent if $I(\pi_n; S_n|\boldsymbol{G}_n = \boldsymbol{g}_n) = 0$.

The above condition summarizes two possibilities: either π_n is a deterministic function of $\boldsymbol{G}_n$, and hence there is no variability in π_n once $\boldsymbol{G}_n$ has been determined; or there is still variability (i.e. π_n is a stochastic strategy) but it is conditionally independent of S_n. In both cases, the above formulation highlights the fact that the decision π_n contains no information coming from S_n.[8]

Lemma 1 *The variables $\boldsymbol{G}_n \to \tau_n \to \pi_n$ form a Markov Chain (i.e. τ_n is a sufficient statistic of $\boldsymbol{G}_n$ for predicting the decision π_n)*

Proof Using (16) one can find that

$$\mathbb{P}_w\{\pi_n|\tau_n, \boldsymbol{G}_n\} = \lambda(F_w^\Lambda(\tau_n), X_n) = \mathbb{P}_w\{\pi_n|\tau_n\},$$

---

[8] Recall that S_n and $\boldsymbol{G}_n$ are conditionally independent given $W = w$ (c.f. "Data fusion rule" section), and hence there cannot be redundant information about W that is conveyed by S_n and also $\boldsymbol{G}_n$. For a more detailed discussion about redundant information c.f. [77].

and therefore the conditional independency of π_n and $\boldsymbol{G}_n$ given τ_n is clear. $\square$

Let us now introduce the notation $U_s = \operatorname{ess\,sup}_{s \in \mathcal{S}} \Lambda_S(S_n = s)$ and $L_s = \operatorname{ess\,inf}_{s \in \mathcal{S}} \Lambda_S(S_n = s)$ for the essential supremum and infimum of $\Lambda_S(S_n)$, being the signals within $\mathcal{S}$ that most strongly support the hypothesis $\{W = 1\}$ over $\{W = 0\}$ and vice versa.[9] If one of these quantities diverge, this would imply that there are signals $s \in \mathcal{S}$ that provide overwhelming evidence in favour of one of the competing hypotheses. If both are finite then the agents are said to have *bounded beliefs* [44]. As sensory signals of electronic devices are ultimately processed digitally, the number of different signals that an agent can obtain are finite, and hence their supremum is always finite. Therefore, in the sequel we assume that both L_s and U_s are finite. Using these notions, the following proposition provides a characterization for local information cascades.

Proposition 1 *The social information $\boldsymbol{g}_n \in \mathcal{G}_n$ triggers a local information cascade if and only if the agents have bounded beliefs and $\tau_n(\boldsymbol{g}_n) \notin [L_s, U_s]$.*

Proof Let us assume that the agents have bounded beliefs. From the definition of F_w^Λ, which is a cumulative density function, it is clear that if $\tau_n < L_s$ then $F_0^\Lambda(\tau_n) = F_1^\Lambda(\tau_n) = 0$, while if $\tau_n > U_s$ then $F_0^\Lambda(\tau_n) = F_1^\Lambda(\tau_n) = 1$. Therefore, if $\tau_n(\boldsymbol{g}_n) \notin [L_s, U_s]$ then, according to (16), it determines π_n almost surely, making π_n and S_n conditionally independent.

To prove the converse by contrapositive, let us assume that $L_s < \tau_n(\boldsymbol{g}_n) < U_s$. Using again (16) and the definition of U_s and L_s, one can conclude that this implies that $0 < \mathbb{P}_w\{\pi_n = 0 | \boldsymbol{G}_n\} < 1$ for both $w \in \{0, 1\}$. This, in turn, implies that the sets $\mathcal{S}^0(\tau) = \{s \in \mathcal{S} | \Lambda_S(s) < \tau_n(\boldsymbol{G}_n)\}$ and $\mathcal{S}^1(\tau) = \mathcal{S} - \mathcal{S}^0$ both have positive probability under μ_0 and μ_1, which in turn implies the existence of conditional interdependency between π_n and S_n in this case. $\square$

Intuitively, Proposition 1 shows that a local information cascade happens when the social information goes above the most informative signal that could be sensed. Some consequences of this result are explored in the next section.

Social information dynamics and global cascades

It is of great interest to predict when a local information cascade could propagate across the network, disrupting the collective behaviour and hence affecting the network performance. The following definition captures how, during a "global information cascade", the broadcasted signals X_n do not convey information about the corresponding sensor signals anymore.

Definition 2 *The social information $\boldsymbol{g}_n \in \mathcal{G}_n$ triggers a global information cascade if $I(X_m; S_m | \boldsymbol{G}_n = \boldsymbol{g}_n) = 0$ holds for all $m \geq n$.*

---

[9] The essential supremum is the smallest upper bound over $\Lambda_S(S_n)$ that holds almost surely, being the natural measure-theoretic extension of the notion of supremum [78].

A global information cascade is a succession of local information cascades. As Proposition 1 showed that agents are free from local cascades as long as $\tau_n \in [L_s, U_s]$, one can guess that global cascades are related to the dynamics of τ_n. These dynamics are determined by the transitions of G_n, which follows the behaviour dictated by the transition coefficients $\beta_w^n(\cdot|\cdot, \cdot)$. To further study the social information dynamics, we introduce the following definitions.

Definition 3 The collection $\{G_n\}_{n=1}^{\infty}$ is said to have:

1. Strongly consistent transitions if, for any $W = w$, $g \in \mathcal{G}_n$ and $g' \in \mathcal{G}_{n-1}$, $\beta_w^n(g|1, g') > 0$ implies $\tau_n(g) \leq \tau_{n-1}(g')$, while if $\beta_w^n(g|0, g') > 0$ implies $\tau_n(g) \geq \tau_{n-1}(g')$.
2. Weakly consistent transitions if, for all $g \in \mathcal{G}_n$ and $g' \in \mathcal{G}_{n-1}$, $\tau_{n-1}(g') \leq L_s$ and $\mathbb{P}_w\{G_n = g|G_{n-1} = g'\} > 0$ implies $\tau_n(g) \leq L_s$, while $\tau_{n-1}(g') \geq U_s$ and $\mathbb{P}_w\{G_n = g|G_{n-1} = g'\} > 0$ implies $\tau_n(g) \geq U_s$.[10]

Intuitively, strong consistency means that the decision threshold evolves monotonically with respect to the broadcasted signals X_n. Correspondingly, weak consistency implies that τ_n cannot return to the interval $[L_S, U_S]$ once it goes out of it. Moreover, the adjectives "strong" and "weak" reflect the fact that weak consistency only takes place outside the boundaries of the signal likelihood, while the strong consistency affects all the decision space. Moreover, strongly consistent transitions imply weakly consistent transitions when there are no Byzantine nodes, as shown in the next lemma.[11]

Lemma 2 *Strongly consistent transitions satisfy the weak consistency condition if* $p_b = 0$.

Proof See Appendix B.　　　　　　　　　　　　　　　　　　　　　　□

Next, it is shown that if the evolution of G_n becomes deterministic and 1–1 after leaving the interval $[L_s, U_s]$ (henceforth called *weakly invertible transitions*), then it satisfies the weak consistency condition.

Lemma 3 *Weakly invertible transitions imply weakly consistent transitions.*

Proof See Appendix C.　　　　　　　　　　　　　　　　　　　　　　□

Now we present the main result of this section, which is the characterization of information cascades for the case of social information that follows weakly consistent transitions.

---

[10] Note that the condition $\mathbb{P}_w\{G_n = g|G_{n-1} = g'\} > 0$ is equivalent to either $\beta_w^n(g, |0, g')$ or $\beta_w^n(g, |1, g')$ being strictly positive.

[11] It is possible to build examples where weak consistency does not follow from strong consistency when $p_b > 0$.

Theorem 1 *If the social information have weakly consistent transitions, then every local information cascade triggers a global information cascade.*

Proof Let us consider $g_0 \in \mathcal{G}_n$ such that it produces a local cascade in the n-th node. Then, due to Proposition 1, this implies that $\tau_n(g) \notin [L_s, U_s]$ almost surely. This, combined with the weak consistency assumption, implies that $\tau_{n+1}(G_{n+1}) \notin [L_s, U_s]$ almost surely. A second application of Proposition 1 shows that $\mathbb{P}_w\{\pi = 0|G_{n+1}\}$ is equal to 0 o 1. This, in turn, guarantees that $I(\pi_{n+1} : S_{n+1}|G_n = g) = 0$ almost surely, showing that the $(n+1)$-th node experiences a local information cascade because of $G_n = g_0$.

A recursive application of the above argument allows one to prove that $I(\pi_{n+m}; S_{n+m}|G_n = g) = 0$ for all $m \geq 0$, proving the existence of a global cascade. $\quad\square$

This theorem has a number of important consequences. Firstly, it provides an intuitive geometrical description about the nature of global cascades for networks with weak consistency. One can imagine the evolution of $\tau_n(G_n)$ as function of n as a random walk within the interval $[L_s, U_s]$. Because of the weak consistency condition, if the random walk step out of the interval, it will never come back. Moreover, as a consequence of this theorem, the stepping out of $[L_s, U_s]$ is a necessary and sufficient condition to trigger a global information cascade over the network.

Also, note that when $G_n = X^n$ (i.e. each node overhears all previous decision) one can prove that G_n has weakly invertible transitions. Therefore, Theorem 1 is a generalization of Theorem 1 of [58] to the case of a network with Byzantine nodes.

Proof of concept

This section illustrates the main results obtained in "Social learning as a data aggregation scheme" and "Information cascade" sections in a simple scenario. In the following, the scenario is described in "Scenario description" section, and numerical simulations are discussed in "Discussion" section.

Scenario description

Let us consider a sensor network that has surveillance duties over a sensitive geographical area. The sensitive area could correspond to a factory, a drinkable water container or a warzone, whose key variables need to be supervised. The task of the sensor network is, through the observation of these variables, to detect the events $\{W = 1\}$ and $\{W = 0\}$ that correspond to the presence or absence of an attack to the surveilled area, respectively. No knowledge about of the prior distribution of W is assumed.

We consider nodes that have been deployed randomly over the sensitive area, and hence their locations follow a Poisson point process (PPP). The ratio of the area of interest that falls within the range of each sensor is denoted by r. If attacks occur uniformly over the surveilled area, then r is also the probability of an attack taking place under the coverage area of a particular sensor. Note that, due to the limited sensing range, the miss-detection rate of individual nodes is roughly equal to $1 - r$. As r is usually a small number (5% in our simulations), this implies that each node is extremely unreliable without cooperation.

Each node measures its environment using a digital sensor of m levels dynamical range (i.e. $S_n \in \{0, 1, \ldots, m - 1\}$). Under the absence of an attack, the measured signal is assumed to be normally distributed with a particular mean value and variance. For simplicity of the analysis, we assume that when conditioned in $\{W = 0\}$ the signal S_n is distributed following a binomial distribution of parameters (m, q), i.e.

$$\mathbb{P}_0\{S_n = s_n\} = \binom{m}{s_n} q^{s_n} (1 - q)^{m - s_n} := f(s_n; m, q) \tag{21}$$

which, due to the central limit theorem, approximates a Gaussian variable when m is relatively large. Moreover, it is assumed that the sensor dynamical range is adapted to match the mean value on the lower third of the sensor dynamical range, i.e. $\mathbb{E}\{S_n | W = 0\} = m/3$. This naturally imposes the requirement $q = 1/3$.

Following standard statistical approaches, it is further assumed that the sensors observe the environment looking for anomalous events, i.e. when the measurement is larger than the mean value in more than two standard deviations. This may correspond, for example, to when a specific chemical compound trespasses safe concentration values, or when too much movement has been detected over a given time window (see e.g. [79]). Using the fact that $\mathrm{Var}\{S_n\} = mq(1 - q)$, this gives a threshold $T = \mathbb{E}\{S_n\} + 2\sqrt{\mathrm{Var}\{S_n\}} = np + 2\sqrt{nq(1 - q)}$. Therefore, it is assumed that an attack is related to the event of S_n being uniformly distributed in $[T, m]$. Therefore, one finds that

$$\mathbb{P}_1\{S_n = s_n\} = (1 - r)\mathbb{P}_1\{S_n = s_n | \text{attack out of range}\} + r\mathbb{P}_1\{S_n = s_n | \text{attack in range}\}$$
$$= (1 - r)f(s_n; m, q) + r\frac{H(s_n - T)}{m - T}, \tag{22}$$

where $H(x)$ is the discrete Heaviside (step) function given by

$$H(x) = \begin{cases} 1 & \text{if } x \geq 0 \\ 0 & \text{in other case.} \end{cases} \tag{23}$$

In summary, S_n conditioned on $\{W = 1\}$ is modelled as a mixture model between a Binomial and a truncated uniform distribution, where the relative weight between them is determined by r (c.f. Fig. 1, top). Finally, using (21) and (22), the log-likelihood function of the signal S_n can be determined as (see Fig. 1, bottom)

$$\Lambda_{S_n}(s_n) = \log \frac{\mathbb{P}_1\{S_n = s_n\}}{\mathbb{P}_0\{S_n = s_n\}} = \log \left\{ (1 - r) + \frac{rH(s_n - T)}{(m - T)f(s_n; m, q)} \right\}. \tag{24}$$

We are interested in studying how a restricted listening period affects the network performance. Restricted listening periods are usually mandatory for energy-limited IoT devices.[12] For simplicity of the analysis, we focus on scenarios in which a node can overhear the transmissions of all the other nodes, and hence the social information gathered

---

[12] It is well known that the wireless radios of small sensor nodes consume a similar amount of energy while transmitting or receiving data, and hence reducing overhearing periods is key for attaining energy efficiency, and hence long network lifetime [60].

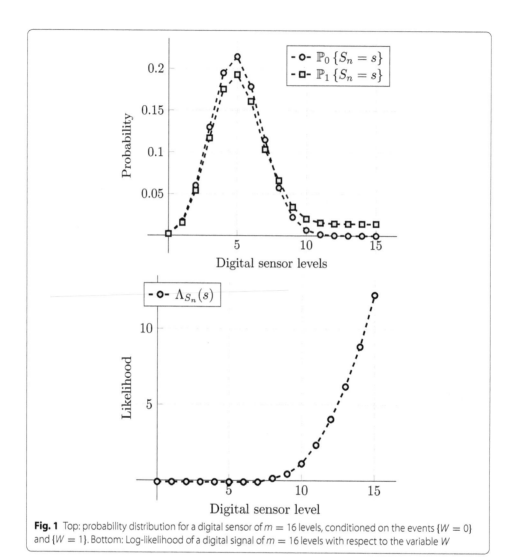

Fig. 1 Top: probability distribution for a digital sensor of $m = 16$ levels, conditioned on the events $\{W = 0\}$ and $\{W = 1\}$. Bottom: Log-likelihood of a digital signal of $m = 16$ levels with respect to the variable W

by the n-th node is $\boldsymbol{G}_n = (X_{n-k-1}, \dots, X_{n-1})$ if $n > k$. Here k is a design parameter, whose impact on the network performance is studied in the next section.

Discussion

We analysed the performance of networks of $N = 300$ sensor nodes, each of which can monitor $r = 5\%$ of the target area. Using the definition given in (4) and (5), combined with (16), miss-detection and false alarm rates are computed as

$$\mathbb{P}\{\text{MD}\} = \sum_{\boldsymbol{g} \in \mathcal{G}_n} F_1^\Lambda(\tau_n(\boldsymbol{g}))\mathbb{P}_1\{\boldsymbol{G}_n = \boldsymbol{g}\} \quad \text{and} \tag{25}$$

$$\mathbb{P}\{\text{FA}\} = \sum_{\boldsymbol{g} \in \mathcal{G}_n} (1 - F_0^\Lambda(\tau_n(\boldsymbol{g})))\mathbb{P}_0\{\boldsymbol{G}_n = \boldsymbol{g}\}, \tag{26}$$

where the terms $\mathbb{P}_w\{\boldsymbol{G}_n = \boldsymbol{g}\}$ are computed using Algorithm 1 (c.f. "An algorithm for computing the social log-likelihood" section). In order to favour the reduction of miss-detections over false alarms $\tau_0 = 0$ is chosen, as it is the lowest value that still allows a

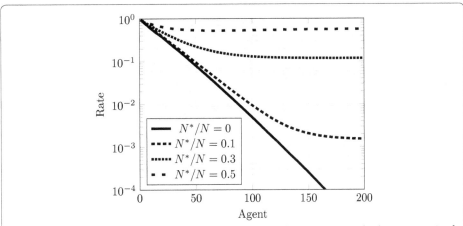

Fig. 2 Performance for the inference of each node for various attack intensities, given by the average ratio of Byzantine nodes $N^*/N = p_b$. Agents overhear the previous $k = 4$ broadcasted signals, and use sensors with dynamical range of $n = 64$

non-trivial inference process.[13] We consider an upper bound of 5% over the tolerable false alarm rate.

Simulations demonstrate that the proposed scheme enables strong network resilience in this scenario, allowing the sensor network to maintain a low miss-detection rate even in the presence of a large number of Byzantine nodes (see Fig. 2). Please recall that if a traditional distributed detection scheme based on centralized decision is used, a topology-aware attacker can cause a miss-detection rate of 100% by just compromising the few nodes that perform data aggregation [i.e. the FC(s)]. Figure 2 shows that nodes that individually would have a miss-detection rate of 95% can improve up to around 10% even when 30% of the nodes are under the control of the attacker. Therefore, by making all the nodes to aggregate data, the network can overcome the influence of Byzantine nodes, generating correct inferences even when a significant fraction of nodes have been compromised.

Please note that, for the case of data falsification attack illustrated by Fig. 2, the miss-detection rate improves until the network size reaches $N = 500$, achieving a performance of $\approx 10^{-12}$ (not shown in the Figure). This result has two important implications. First, this confirms the prediction of Theorem 1 that, if the signal log-likelihood is bounded, then information cascades are eventually dominant, hence stopping the learning process of the network (for a more detailed discussion about this issue please c.f. [58]). Secondly, this result stresses a key difference of our approach with respect to the existent literature about information cascades: *even if information cascades become dominant and perfect social learning cannot be achieved, the achieved performance can still be very high, and hence useful in a practical information-processing setup.*

The network resilience provided by our scheme is influenced by the sensor dynamical range, m, as a higher sensor resolution is likely to provide more discriminative power. Our results show three sharply distinct regimes (see Fig. 3). First, if m is too small ($m \leq 4$) the network performance is very poor, irrespective of the number of Byzantine

---

[13] Simulations showed that if $\tau < 0$ then $X_n = 1$ for all $n \in \mathbb{N}$ independently of the value of W, triggering a premature information cascade.

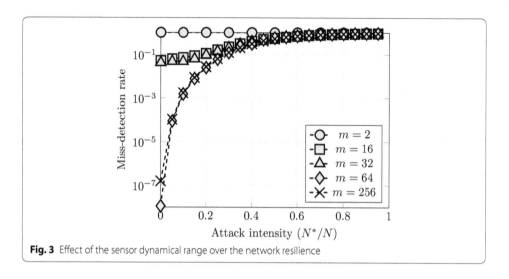

Fig. 3 Effect of the sensor dynamical range over the network resilience

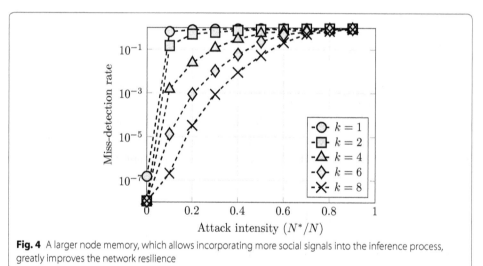

Fig. 4 A larger node memory, which allows incorporating more social signals into the inference process, greatly improves the network resilience

nodes. Secondly, if $8 \leq m \leq 32$ the miss-detection rate without Byzantine nodes is approx. 10% (cf. Fig. 3) and is exponentially degraded by the presence of Byzantine nodes. Finally, if $m \geq 64$ then the performance under no Byzantine nodes is very high, and is degraded super-exponentially by the presence of Byzantine nodes. Interestingly, the point at which the miss-detection rate of this regime goes above 10^{-1} is $N^*/N = 1/3$, having some resemblance with the well-known 1/3 threshold of the Byzantine generals problem [14]. Also, it is intriguing that variations between 8 and 32 levels in the dynamical range provide practically no performance benefits.

Our results also illustrate the effects of the memory size, k, showing that larger values of k provide great benefits for the network resilience (see Fig. 4). In effect, by performing an optimal Bayesian inference over 8 broadcasted signals the network miss-detection rate remains below 10% up to an attack intensity of 50% of Byzantine nodes. Unfortunately, the computation and storage requirements of Algorithm 1 grow exponentially with k, and hence using memories beyond $k = 10$ is not practical for resource-limited sensor networks. Overcoming this limitation is an interesting future line of investigation.

Conclusions

Traditional approaches to data aggregation over information networks are based on a strong division of labour, which discriminates between sensing nodes that merely sense and forward data, and FC that monopolize all the processing and inference capabilities. This generates a single point of failure that is likely to be exploited by smart adversaries, whose interest is the disruption of the network capabilities.

This serious security threat can be overcome by distributing the decision-making process across the network using social learning principles. This approach avoids single points of failure by generating a large number of nodes from where aggregated data can be accessed. In this paper, a social learning data fusion scheme has been proposed, which is suitable to be implemented in sensor networks consisting of devices with limited computational capabilities.

We showed that if the private signals are bounded then each local information cascade triggers a global cascade, extending previous results to the case where an adversary controls a number of Byzantine nodes. This result is highly relevant for sensor networks, as digital sensors are intrinsically bounded, and hence satisfy the assumptions of these results. However, contrasting with the literature, our approach does not focus on the conditions that guarantee perfect asymptotical social learning (i.e. miss-detection and false alarm rates converging to zero), but if their limits are small enough for practical applications. Our results show that this is indeed the case, even when the number of "overheard transmissions is limited.

Moreover, our results suggest that social learning principles can enable significant resilience of an information network against topology-aware data falsification attacks, which can totally disable the detection capabilities of traditional sensor networks. Furthermore, our results illustrate how the network resilience can persist even when the attacker has compromised an important number of nodes.

It is our hope that these results can motivate further explorations on the interface between distributed decision-making, statistical inference and signal processing over technological and social networks and multi-agent systems.

Authors' contributions
All the authors participated in the development of the concepts and the writing of the manuscript. All authors read and approved the final manuscript.

Author details
[1] Centre of Complexity Science and Department of Mathematics, Imperial College London, Kensington, London SW72AZ, UK. [2] Department of Electrical and Electronic Engineering, Imperial College London, Kensington, London SW72AZ, UK. [3] Department of Electrical Engineering, University of South Florida, 4202 E Fowler Ave, Tampa, FL 33620, USA.

Acknowledgements
Fernando Rosas is supported by the European Union's H2020 research and innovation programme, under the Marie Skłodowska-Curie Grant Agreement No. 702981.

Competing interests
The authors declare that they have no competing interests.

Appendix A: Properties of F_w^Λ

For simplicity let us consider the case of real-value signals, i.e. $S_n \in \mathbb{R}$. In this case, the c.d.f. of the signal likelihood is given by

$$F_w^\Lambda(y) = \int_{\mathcal{S}^y} \mathrm{d}\mu_w \tag{27}$$

where $\mathcal{S}^y = \{x \in \mathbb{R} | \Lambda_s(x) \leq y\}$. If Λ_s is an increasing function, then $\mathcal{S}^y = \{x \in \mathbb{R} | x \leq \Lambda_s^{-1}(y)\} = (-\infty, \Lambda_s^{-1}(y)]$ and hence

$$F_w^\Lambda(y) = \int_{-\infty}^{\Lambda_s^{-1}(y)} \mathrm{d}\mu_w = H_w(\Lambda_s^{-1}(y)), \tag{28}$$

where $H_w(s)$ is the cumulative density function (c.d.f.) of S_n for $W = w$. For the general case where Λ_s is an arbitrary (piece-wise continuous) function, then $\mathcal{S}^y$ can be expressed as the union of intervals. Then $\cup_{j=1}^\infty [a_j(y), b_j(y)] = \mathcal{S}^y$ (note that $\Lambda_s(a_j(y)) = \Lambda_s(b_k(y)) = y$) and hence from (27) is clear that

$$F_w^\Lambda(y) = \sum_{j=1}^\infty \int_{a_j(y)}^{b_j(y)} \mathrm{d}\mu_w = \sum_{j=1}^\infty \left[H_w(b_j(y)) - H_w(a_j(y)) \right]. \tag{29}$$

Appendix B: Proof of Lemma 2

Proof Lets assume that the process G_n has strong consistent transitions and consider $g' \in \mathcal{G}_{n-1}$ such that $\tau_{n-1}(g') \leq L_s$. Note that, under these conditions $F_w^\Lambda(\tau_{n-1}(g')) = 0$, and hence

$$\mathbb{P}_w\{X_{n-1} = 1 | G_{n-1} = g'\} = 1 - z_0 - z_1 F_w^\Lambda(\tau_{n-1}(g')) = 1 - p_b c_{0|1} = 0 \tag{30}$$

holds for any $w \in \{0, 1\}$. Moreover, this allows to find that

$$\begin{aligned} \mathbb{P}_w\{G_n = g | G_{n-1} = g'\} &= \sum_{x_n \in \{0,1\}} \beta_w^n(g | x_n, g') \mathbb{P}_w\{X_{n-1} = x_n | G_{n-1} = g'\} \\ &= \beta_w^n(g | 1, g'). \end{aligned} \tag{31}$$

Therefore, due to the strongly consistent transition property, if $\mathbb{P}_w\{G_n = g | G_{n-1} = g'\} = \beta_w^n(g | 1, g') > 0$ then

$$L_s \geq \tau_{n-1}(g') \geq \tau_n(g), \tag{32}$$

proving the weak consistent transition property. The proof for the case of $\tau_{n-1}(g') \geq U_s$ is analogous. $\square$

Appendix C: Proof of Lemma 3

Proof Let us consider $g_0 \in \mathcal{G}_n$ such that $\tau_n(g_0) \notin [L_s, U_s]$. Then, due to the weakly invertible evolution, for each $x \in \{0, 1\}$ there exists $g(x) \in \mathcal{G}_{n+1}$ such that

$$\beta_w^n(\boldsymbol{g}|x,\boldsymbol{g}_0) = \begin{cases} 1 & \text{if } \boldsymbol{g} = \boldsymbol{g}(x), \\ 0 & \text{in other case.} \end{cases} \tag{33}$$

Moreover, note that while the deterministic assumption implies that the event $\{\boldsymbol{G}_n = \boldsymbol{g}_0\}$ could be followed by either $\{\boldsymbol{G}_{n+1} = \boldsymbol{g}(0)\}$ or $\{\boldsymbol{G}_{n+1} = \boldsymbol{g}(1)\}$, the 1–1 assumption requires that $\boldsymbol{g}(0) = \boldsymbol{g}(1)$. With this, note that

$$\Lambda_{\boldsymbol{G}_{n+1}}(\boldsymbol{g}(0)) = \log \frac{\mathbb{P}_1\{\boldsymbol{G}_{n+1} = \boldsymbol{g}(0)\}}{\mathbb{P}_0\{\boldsymbol{G}_{n+1} = \boldsymbol{g}(0)\}}$$

$$= \log \frac{\displaystyle\sum_{\substack{\boldsymbol{g}' \in \mathcal{G}_n \\ x \in \{0,1\}}} \beta_w^n(\boldsymbol{g}(x)|x,\boldsymbol{g}')\mathbb{P}_1\{X_n = x, \boldsymbol{G}_n = \boldsymbol{g}'\}}{\displaystyle\sum_{\substack{\boldsymbol{g}' \in \mathcal{G}_n \\ x \in \{0,1\}}} \beta_w^n(\boldsymbol{g}(x)|x,\boldsymbol{g}')\mathbb{P}_0\{X_n = x, \boldsymbol{G}_n = \boldsymbol{g}'\}} \tag{34}$$

$$= \log \frac{\sum_{x\in\{0,1\}} \mathbb{P}_1\{X_n = x|\boldsymbol{G}_n = \boldsymbol{g}_0\}\mathbb{P}_1\{\boldsymbol{G}_n = \boldsymbol{g}_0\}}{\sum_{x\in\{0,1\}} \mathbb{P}_0\{X_n = x|\boldsymbol{G}_n = \boldsymbol{g}_0\}\mathbb{P}_0\{\boldsymbol{G}_n = \boldsymbol{g}_0\}} \tag{35}$$

$$= \Lambda_{\boldsymbol{G}_{n-1}}(\boldsymbol{g}_0), \tag{36}$$

Above, (34) is a consequence of $\boldsymbol{g}(0) = \boldsymbol{g}(1)$, while (35) is because of the 1-1 condition over the dynamic. Finally, to justify (36) let us first consider

$$\mathbb{P}_w\{X_n = x|\boldsymbol{G}_n = \boldsymbol{g}_0\} = \lambda(z_0 + z_1 F_w^\Lambda(\tau_n(\boldsymbol{g}_0)), x). \tag{37}$$

Because $\tau_n(\boldsymbol{g}_0) \notin [L_s, U_s]$ then $F_w^\Lambda(\tau_n(\boldsymbol{g}_0))$ is either 0 or 1; in any case it does not depend on W. This, in turn, means that $\mathbb{P}_1\{X_n = x|\boldsymbol{G}_n = \boldsymbol{g}_0\} = \mathbb{P}_0\{X_n = x|\boldsymbol{G}_n = \boldsymbol{g}_0\}$, which explains how (36) is obtained.

Please note that (36) shows that, once τ_n leaves $[L_s, U_s]$, it keeps a constant value. This, in turn, shows that weakly deterministic transitions satisfy the weakly consistency condition. $\qquad\square$

Appendix D: List of symbols
Table2 presents a summary of the notation and symbols used in this work.

Table 2 List of symbols and notation

Network properties

N	$\triangleq$ Size of the sensor network
N^*	$\triangleq$ Number of Byzantine nodes
p_b	$\triangleq$ Probability of a given node being compromised

Sensor and social signals

S_n	$\triangleq$ Signal measured by the n-th node
$\mathcal{S}$	$\triangleq$ Set of values that S_n can take
μ_w	$\triangleq$ Distribution of S_n given $W = w$
$\Lambda_S(s)$	$\triangleq$ Log-likelihood of S_n with respect to W
$F_w^\Lambda(s)$	$\triangleq$ c.d.f. of $\Lambda_S(s)$ conditioned on $W = w$
$\boldsymbol{G}_n$	$\triangleq$ Social observations of the n-th node
$\mathcal{G}_n$	$\triangleq$ Set of values that $\boldsymbol{G}_n$ can take
$\Lambda_{\boldsymbol{G}_n}(\boldsymbol{g})$	$\triangleq$ Log-likelihood of $\boldsymbol{G}_n$ with respect to W
$\beta_w^n(\boldsymbol{g}|x_n,\boldsymbol{g}')$	$\triangleq$ Transition probabilities from $\boldsymbol{G}_{n-1}$ to $\boldsymbol{G}_n$ given X_n and W

Data fusion variables

W	$\triangleq$ Target of the networked inference
$u(\boldsymbol{\pi}_n, w)$	$\triangleq$ Node's utility function for deciding $\boldsymbol{\pi}_n$ when $W = w$
τ_n	$\triangleq$ Decision threshold used by the n-th node
$\pi_n(s, \boldsymbol{g})$	$\triangleq$ Data fusion strategy of the n-th node given S_n and $\boldsymbol{G}_n$
X_n	$\triangleq$ Signal broadcasted by the n-th node
$C(\boldsymbol{\pi}_n), c_{0|0}, c_{0|1}$	$\triangleq$ Corruption function, which links $\boldsymbol{\pi}_n$ and X_n
$\mathbb{P}\{MD; p_b\}$	$\triangleq$ Network miss-detection rate
$\mathbb{P}\{FA; p_b\}$	$\triangleq$ Network false alarm rate

Simulation parameters

r	$\triangleq$ Ratio of the area of interest within the sensing range of a single node
m	$\triangleq$ Number of quantization levels of a node's sensor
k	$\triangleq$ Node's memory size

References

1. Kim K-D, Kumar PR. Cyber–physical systems: a perspective at the centennial. Proc IEEE. 2012;100(Special Centennial Issue):1287–308.
2. Response SS. What you need to know about the WannaCry Ransomware. https://www.symantec.com/blogs/threat-intelligence/wannacry-ransomware-attack
3. Veeravalli VV, Varshney PK. Distributed inference in wireless sensor networks. Philos Trans R Soc Lond A. 2012;370(1958):100–17.
4. Barbarossa S, Sardellitti S, Di Lorenzo P. Distributed detection and estimation in wireless. Academic Press library in signal processing: communications and radar signal processing. London: Academic Press; 2013. p. 329.
5. Hancke GP, Hancke GP Jr. The role of advanced sensing in smart cities. Sensors. 2012;13(1):393–425.
6. Difallah DE, Cudre-Mauroux P, McKenna SA. Scalable anomaly detection for smart city infrastructure networks. IEEE Internet Comput. 2013;17(6):39–47.
7. Lambrou TP, Panayiotou CG, Polycarpou MM. Contamination detection in drinking water distribution systems using sensor networks. In: Control Conference (ECC), 2015 European. New York: IEEE; 2015. p. 3298–303.
8. Lambrou TP, Anastasiou CC, Panayiotou CG, Polycarpou MM. A low-cost sensor network for real-time monitoring and contamination detection in drinking water distribution systems. IEEE Sens J. 2014;14(8):2765–72.
9. Perrig A, Stankovic J, Wagner D. Security in wireless sensor networks. Commun ACM. 2004;47(6):53–7.
10. Shi E, Perrig A. Designing secure sensor networks. IEEE Wirel Commun. 2004;11(6):38–43.
11. Pathan A-SK, Lee H-W, Hong CS. Security in wireless sensor networks: issues and challenges. In: The 8th international conference of advanced communication technology, 2006. ICACT 2006, vol. 2. New York: IEEE; 2006. p. 6.
12. Trappe W, Howard R, Moore RS. Low-energy security: limits and opportunities in the internet of things. IEEE Secur Priv. 2015;13(1):14–21. https://doi.org/10.1109/MSP.2015.7.
13. Marano S, Matta V, Tong L. Distributed detection in the presence of Byzantine attacks. IEEE Trans Signal Process. 2009;57(1):16–29.

14. Lamport L, Shostak R, Pease M. The Byzantine generals problem. ACM Trans Program Lang Syst (TOPLAS). 1982;4(3):382–401.

15. Vempaty A, Tong L, Varshney PK. Distributed inference with Byzantine data: state-of-the-art review on data falsification attack. IEEE Signal Process Mag. 2013;30(5):65–75.

16. Nadendla VSS, Han YS, Varshney PK. Distributed inference with M-Ary quantized data in the presence of Byzantine attacks. IEEE Trans Signal Process. 2014;62(10):2681–95. https://doi.org/10.1109/TSP.2014.2314072.

17. Zhang J, Blum RS, Lu X, Conus D. Asymptotically optimum distributed estimation in the presence of attacks. IEEE Trans Signal Process. 2015;63(5):1086–101. https://doi.org/10.1109/TSP.2014.2386281.

18. Kailkhura B, Han YS, Brahma S, Varshney PK. Distributed Bayesian detection in the presence of Byzantine data. IEEE Trans Signal Process. 2015;63(19):5250–63. https://doi.org/10.1109/TSP.2015.2450191.

19. Kailkhura B, Brahma S, Han YS, Varshney PK. Distributed detection in tree topologies with Byzantines. IEEE Trans Signal Process. 2014;62(12):3208–19.

20. Kailkhura B, Brahma S, Dulek B, Han YS, Varshney PK. Distributed detection in tree networks: Byzantines and mitigation techniques. IEEE Trans Inf Forensics Secur. 2015;10(7):1499–512. https://doi.org/10.1109/TIFS.2015.2415757.

21. Chen K-C, Lien S-Y. Machine-to-machine communications: technologies and challenges. Ad Hoc Netw. 2014;18:3–23.

22. Parno B, Perrig A, Gligor V. Distributed detection of node replication attacks in sensor networks. In: 2005 IEEE symposium on security and privacy (S&P'05). New York: IEEE; 2005. p. 49–63.

23. Lin S-C, Chen K-C. Improving spectrum efficiency via in-network computations in cognitive radio sensor networks. IEEE Trans Wirel Commun. 2014;13(3):1222–34.

24. Daniels BC, Ellison CJ, Krakauer DC, Flack JC. Quantifying collectivity. Curr Opin Neurobiol. 2016;37:106–13.

25. Brush ER, Krakauer DC, Flack JC. Conflicts of interest improve collective computation of adaptive social structures. Sci Adv. 2018;4(1):1603311.

26. Tsitsiklis JN. Decentralized detection. Adv Stat Signal Process. 1993;2(2):297–344.

27. Viswanathan R, Varshney PK. Distributed detection with multiple sensors I. Fundamentals. Proc IEEE. 1997;85(1):54–63.

28. Blum RS, Kassam SA, Poor HV. Distributed detection with multiple sensors I. Advanced topics. Proc IEEE. 1997;85(1):64–79.

29. Chen B, Tong L, Varshney PK. Channel aware distributed detection in wireless sensor networks. IEEE Signal Process Mag. 2006;23(4):16–26.

30. Chamberland J-F, Veeravalli VV. Wireless sensors in distributed detection applications. IEEE Signal Process Mag. 2007;24(3):16–25.

31. Tsitsiklis J, Athans M. On the complexity of decentralized decision making and detection problems. IEEE Trans Autom Control. 1985;30(5):440–6.

32. Warren D, Willett P. Optimum quantization for detector fusion: some proofs, examples, and pathology. J Franklin Inst. 1999;336(2):323–59.

33. Chamberland J-F, Veeravalli VV. Asymptotic results for decentralized detection in power constrained wireless sensor networks. IEEE J Sel Areas Commun. 2004;22(6):1007–15.

34. Easley D, Kleinberg J. Networks, crowds, and markets, vol. 1(2.1). Cambridge: Cambridge University Press; 2010. p. 2–1.

35. Acemoglu D, Ozdaglar A. Opinion dynamics and learning in social networks. Dyn Games Appl. 2011;1(1):3–49.

36. Banerjee AV. A simple model of herd behavior. Q J Econ. 1992;107:797–817.

37. Bikhchandani S, Hirshleifer D, Welch I. A theory of fads, fashion, custom, and cultural change as informational cascades. J Political Econ. 1992;100:992–1026.

38. Bikhchandani S, Hirshleifer D, Welch I. Learning from the behavior of others: conformity, fads, and informational cascades. J Econ Perspect. 1998;12(3):151–70.

39. Smith L, Sørensen P. Pathological outcomes of observational learning. Econometrica. 2000;68(2):371–98.

40. Bala V, Goyal S. Conformism and diversity under social learning. Econ Theory. 2001;17(1):101–20.

41. Banerjee A, Fudenberg D. Word-of-mouth learning. Games Econ Behav. 2004;46(1):1–22.

42. Gale D, Kariv S. Bayesian learning in social networks. Games Econ Behav. 2003;45(2):329–46.

43. Gill D, Sgroi D. Sequential decisions with tests. Games Econ Behav. 2008;63(2):663–78.

44. Acemoglu D, Dahleh MA, Lobel I, Ozdaglar A. Bayesian learning in social networks. Rev Econ Stud. 2011;78(4):1201–36.

45. Hsiao J, Chen KC. Steering information cascades in a social system by selective rewiring and incentive seeding. In: to Be included in 2016 IEEE international conference on communications (ICC) 2016.

46. DeMarzo PM, Zwiebel J, Vayanos D. Persuasion bias, social influence, and uni-dimensional opinions. In: Social Influence, and Uni-Dimensional Opinions (November 2001). MIT Sloan Working Paper (4339-01). 2001.

47. Golub B, Jackson MO. Naive learning in social networks and the wisdom of crowds. Am Econ J. 2010;2(1):112–49.

48. Acemoglu D, Ozdaglar A, ParandehGheibi A. Spread of (mis) information in social networks. Games Econ Behav. 2010;70(2):194–227.

49. Jadbabaie A, Molavi P, Sandroni A, Tahbaz-Salehi A. Non-Bayesian social learning. Games Econ Behav. 2012;76(1):210–25.

50. Lalitha A, Sarwate A, Javidi T. Social learning and distributed hypothesis testing. In: 2014 IEEE international symposium on information theory. New York: IEEE; 2014. p. 551–5.

51. Rhim JB, Goyal VK. Distributed hypothesis testing with social learning and symmetric fusion. IEEE Trans Signal Process. 2014;62(23):6298–308.

52. Huang SL, Chen KC. Information cascades in social networks via dynamic system analyses. In: 2015 IEEE international conference on communications (ICC); 2015. p. 1262–7. https://doi.org/10.1109/ICC.2015.7248496.

53. Castro R, Coates M, Liang G, Nowak R, Yu B. Network tomography: recent developments. Stat sci. 2004;19:499–517.

54. Viswanathan R, Thomopoulos SC, Tumuluri R. Optimal serial distributed decision fusion. IEEE Trans Aerospace Electron Syst. 1988;24(4):366–76.

55. Papastavrou JD, Athans M. Distributed detection by a large team of sensors in tandem. IEEE Trans Aerospace Electron Syst. 1992;28(3):639–53.

56. Swaszek PF. On the performance of serial networks in distributed detection. IEEE Trans Aerospace Electron Syst. 1993;29(1):254–60.

57. Bahceci I, Al-Regib G, Altunbasak Y. Serial distributed detection for wireless sensor networks. In: Proceedings. International symposium on information theory, ISIT 2005. New York: IEEE; 2005. p. 830–4.

58. Rosas F, Hsiao J-H, Chen K-C. A technological perspective on information cascades via social learning. IEEE Access. 2017;5:22605–33.

59. Rosas F, Chen K-C. Social learning against data falsification in sensor networks. In: International workshop on complex networks and their applications. New York: Springer; 2017. p. 704–16.

60. Rosas F, Oberli C. Modulation and SNR optimization for achieving energy-efficient communications over short-range fading channels. IEEE Trans Wirel Commun. 2012;11(12):4286–95.

61. Bertrand A. Applications and trends in wireless acoustic sensor networks: a signal processing perspective. In: 2011 18th IEEE symposium on communications and vehicular technology in the Benelux (SCVT); 2011. p. 1–6. https://doi.org/10.1109/SCVT.2011.6101302.

62. Kam M, Zhu Q, Gray WS. Optimal data fusion of correlated local decisions in multiple sensor detection systems. IEEE Trans Aerospace Electron Syst. 1992;28(3):916–20.

63. Chen J-G, Ansari N. Adaptive fusion of correlated local decisions. IEEE Trans Syst Man Cyberne Part C (Appl Rev). 1998;28(2):276–81.

64. Willett P, Swaszek PF, Blum RS. The good, bad and ugly: distributed detection of a known signal in dependent Gaussian noise. IEEE Trans Signal Process. 2000;48(12):3266–79.

65. Chamberland J-F, Veeravalli VV. How dense should a sensor network be for detection with correlated observations? IEEE Trans Inf Theory. 2006;52(11):5099–106.

66. Sundaresan A, Varshney PK, Rao NS. Copula-based fusion of correlated decisions. IEEE Trans Aerospace Electron Syst. 2011;47(1):454–71.

67. Loeve M. Probability theory, vol. 1. New York: Springer; 1978.

68. Karl H, Willig A. Protocols and architectures for wireless sensor networks. Chichester: Wiley; 2007.

69. Sundararaman B, Buy U, Kshemkalyani AD. Clock synchronization for wireless sensor networks: a survey. Ad hoc Netw. 2005;3(3):281–323.

70. Rosas F, Brante G, Souza RD, Oberli C. Optimizing the code rate for achieving energy-efficient wireless communications. In: Wireless communications and networking conference (WCNC), 2014 IEEE. New York: IEEE; 2014. p. 775–80.

71. Karyotis V, Khouzani M. Malware diffusion models for modern complex networks: theory and applications. Cambridge: Morgan Kaufmann; 2016.

72. Poor HV. An introduction to signal detection and estimation. Berlin-Heidelberg: Springer; 2013.

73. Smith P, Hutchison D, Sterbenz JP, Schöller M, Fessi A, Karaliopoulos M, Lac C, Plattner B. Network resilience: a systematic approach. IEEE Commun Mag. 2011;49(7):88–97.

74. Shiller RJ. Conversation, information, and herd behavior. Am Econ Rev. 1995;85(2):181–5.

75. Gelman A, Carlin JB, Stern HS, Dunson DB, Vehtari A, Rubin DB. Bayesian data analysis. Boca Raton: CRC Press; 2014.

76. Cover TM, Thomas JA. Elements of information theory. New Jersey: Wiley; 2012.

77. Rosas F, Ntranos V, Ellison CJ, Pollin S, Verhelst M. Understanding interdependency through complex information sharing. Entropy. 2016;18(2):38.

78. Dieudonne J. Treatise on analysis, vol. II. New York: Associated Press; 1976.

79. McKenna SA, Wilson M, Klise KA. Detecting changes in water quality data. J Am Water Works Assoc. 2008;100(1):74.

7

Cascade source inference in networks: a Markov chain Monte Carlo approach

Xuming Zhai[2], Weili Wu[1,2]* and Wen Xu[2]

*Correspondence:
weiliwu@utdallas.edu
[1] College of Computer Science and
Technology, Taiyuan University of
Technology, Taiyuan 030024, China
[2] Department of Computer Science,
University of Texas at Dallas, 800 W.
Campbell Rd, Richardson, TX 75080,
USA

Abstract

Cascades of information, ideas, rumors, and viruses spread through networks. Sometimes, it is desirable to find the source of a cascade given a snapshot of it. In this paper, source inference problem is tackled under Independent Cascade (IC) model. First, the #P-completeness of source inference problem is proven. Then, a Markov chain Monte Carlo algorithm is proposed to find a solution. It is worth noting that our algorithm is designed to handle large networks. In addition, the algorithm does not rely on prior knowledge of when the cascade started. Finally, experiments on real social network are conducted to evaluate the performance. Under all experimental settings, our algorithm identified the true source with high probability.

Keywords: Social network; Source inference; Markov chain Monte Carlo

Introduction

Modern social and computer networks are common media for cascades of information, ideas, rumors, and viruses. It is often desirable to identify the source of a cascade from a snapshot of the cascade. For example, a good way to stop a rumor is to find out the person that has fabricated it. Similarly, identifying the first computer infected by a virus provides valuable information for catching the author. Therefore, given the network structure and an observed cascade snapshot consisting only the set of infected/active nodes, solving the source inference problem is very useful in many cases. Hereafter, we use infected/active and infect/activate interchangeably.

In the seminal works [1] and [2], source inference problem under susceptible-infected (SI) model is first studied, and a maximum likelihood estimator is proposed with theoretical performance bound when the network is a tree. Based on the same model, many works solve this problem with different extensions. With a priori knowledge of a candidate source set, reference [3] infers the source node using a maximum a posteriori estimator. Wang et al. [4] utilizes multiple independent epidemic observations to single out their common source. Karamchandani and Franceschetti [5] study the case where infected nodes reveal their infection with a probability. When multiple sources are involved, algorithms are proposed in [6] and [7] to find out all of them. The works mentioned above, except [7], are all based on tree networks, while some of them are applicable to general graphs by constructing breadth-first-search trees. More importantly, all of them use SI model, where an infected node will certainly infect a susceptible neighbor after a random period of time. Our work, however, is based on Independent Cascade (IC) model. In the IC model, an active node activates its successor with a certain probability determined by the edge weight.

Although SI model is popular in epidemiological researches because it catches the pattern of epidemics, the IC model is arguably more suitable to depict cascades in social networks, where relationship between peers plays a more important role than time of infection. As an example, suppose Alice bought a new hat, her classmates may or may not imitate the purchase depending on how they agree with her taste. Those who do not appreciate her taste are unlikely to change their minds even Alice wears her hat every day. These people are now immune from the influence of Alice's new hat, though they may still be persuaded by someone they appreciate more.

Although the IC model is popular in social network researches, finding source in the IC model is rarely studied. Using a model similar to the IC with identical edge weight, reference[8] studies the problem of inferring both links and sources given multiple observed cascades. Under the IC model, reference [9] solves the problem of finding sources that are expected to generate cascades most similar to the observation. Surprisingly, this problem is fundamentally different from source inference problem, which finds the source that most likely has started the observed cascade. For example, when a cascade that infects all nodes is observed in the simple linear network in Fig. 1, node c is the optimal result for the problem defined in [9] because it is expected to generate a cascade with least difference from the observed one. However, it is obvious that c cannot be responsible for a cascade that spreads through all three nodes.

In this paper, we work on the problem of detecting the source node that is responsible for a given cascade. We first formulate the source inference problem in the IC model and prove its #P-completeness. Then, a Markov chain Monte Carlo (MCMC) algorithm is proposed to solve the inference problem. It is worth noting that our algorithm scales with observed cascade size rather than network size, which is very important due to the huge size of social networks nowadays. Another advantage of our algorithm is that it is designed to deal with snapshot of cascades taken either before or after termination. More importantly, our algorithm does not require prior knowledge of the starting time of the cascade, which is usually unknown in practical scenarios. To evaluate the performance of our algorithm, experiments are done in a real network. Experimental results demonstrate the effectiveness of our algorithm.

Problem formulation

Propagation model

In this work, we model a social network as a weighted directed graph $G(V, E)$ with weights $w_{i,j} \in (0, 1]$ associated with each edge $(i, j) \in E$ representing the probability

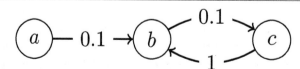

Fig. 1 Example of a simple case of source inference problem: if all three nodes are found active, then node a must be the source

of i successfully influencing j. The propagation procedure of a cascade in the network is depicted by the well-known IC model [10]. The cascade starts with all nodes inactive except a source node s, which we assume is activated at time τ_0. At every time step $\tau > \tau_0$, every node i that was activated at $\tau - 1$ has a single chance to influence each of its inactive successors through the directed edge with success probability specified by the weight of the edge. If the influence is successful, then the successor is activated at time τ and will be able to influence its inactive successors at the next time step. The process terminates when no new node is activated.

An important fact about the IC model is that each active node has only one chance of influencing each of its neighbors. To put it another way, there is only one chance for each edge to participate in the propagation with success rate specified by the weight. Since edge weights are fixed and independent of the cascade, we can flip the biased coins even before the cascade starts to determine whether each edge will help the propagation. This gives an alternative process consisting of two steps that also simulates the IC model. First, a subgraph G' of the original network G is taken by 1) keeping all vertices and 2) filtering edges according to their weights, i.e.,

$$\forall v \in G, \quad v \in G',$$
$$\forall (i, j) \in G, \quad \Pr((i, j) \in G') = w_{i,j}. \tag{1}$$

Then, every node i reachable from source s in G' is active, with its activation time set to $\tau + d_{G'}(s, i)$, where $d_{G'}(s, i)$ is the distance, i.e., number of edges in the directed shortest path, from s to i in G'.

It is easy to verify that the alternative process is equivalent to the previous one. Moreover, the alternative view builds the equivalence between sampling subgraphs of network and simulating cascades on it. Due to this convenience, we extensively use the alternative view in the following sections.

Source inference problem

Suppose in a given network G, an unnoticed cascade starts from an unknown source node s^* at time τ_0. Later at time $\tau_0 + \tau$, the cascade is discovered and the set of active nodes A_τ is identified without knowing their corresponding activation time. Note that A_τ can be viewed as a snapshot of the cascade at time τ. Now, we want to find the node $\hat{s}$ that most likely had started the cascade. Thus,

$$\hat{s} = \arg\max_s \Pr(A_\tau | G, s, \tau), \tag{2}$$

where $\Pr(A_\tau | G, s, \tau)$ denotes the probability of a cascade on G starting from s having snapshot A_τ at time τ. According to the alternative view of the IC model defined in the 'Propagation model' section and suppose G' is sampled according to (1), we have

$$\Pr(A_\tau | G, s, \tau) = \Pr(A_\tau = \{i \mid d_{G'}(s, i) \leq \tau\}). \tag{3}$$

The following theorem shows the intractability of source inference problem, i.e., solving (2) given G, τ, and A_τ.

Theorem 1. *Source inference problem is #P-complete.*

This theorem is proven by constructing a polynomial-time Turing reduction from s-t connectedness problem [11] to source inference problem. Please refer to Appendix 1 for the detailed proof.

Source inference algorithm

Basic algorithm

We use $\mathcal{R}(G', s, \tau)$ to denote the set of nodes in G' reachable from s within distance τ, i.e.,

$$\mathcal{R}(G', s, \tau) = \{i \mid d_{G'}(s, i) \leq \tau\}.$$

Then, the probability shown in (3) can also be written as

$$\Pr(A_\tau | G, s, \tau) = \sum_{G' \subseteq G} \Pr_\mathcal{G}(G') I(A_\tau = \mathcal{R}(G', s, \tau)) \tag{4}$$

$$= \mathbb{E}_{G' \sim \mathcal{G}}[I(A_\tau = \mathcal{R}(G', s, \tau))], \tag{5}$$

where $\mathcal{G}$ represents the distribution of subgraphs of G defined by (1), $\Pr_\mathcal{G}(G')$ denotes the probability mass function (PMF) of G' in distribution $\mathcal{G}$, i.e.,

$$\Pr_\mathcal{G}(G') = \prod_{(i,j) \in G} w_{i,j}^{I((i,j) \in G')} (1 - w_{i,j})^{I((i,j) \notin G')} \tag{6}$$

and I is an indicator function defined as

$$I(c) = \begin{cases} 1 & \text{if condition } c \text{ is true,} \\ 0 & \text{otherwise.} \end{cases}$$

Because of the #P-completeness of source inference problem, calculating exact value of (4) is #P-hard.

A trivial method to approximate the value is to estimate the expectation in (2) by randomly sampling graphs in $\mathcal{G}$. But this method is still impractical. To show this, we define $\mathcal{S} = \{G' \mid G' \subseteq G\}$ as the set of all subgraphs of G, which is also the support of $\mathcal{G}$. Then, a subset of $\mathcal{S}$ is defined as

$$\mathcal{S}' = \{G' \mid G' \subseteq G, \exists s, s \rightsquigarrow A_\tau \subseteq G'\},$$

where $s \rightsquigarrow A_\tau \subseteq G'$ denotes "every node in A_τ is reachable from s in G'". Now, notice that $A_\tau = \mathcal{R}(G', s, \tau) \implies G' \in \mathcal{S}'$ and that the ratio $|\mathcal{S}|/|\mathcal{S}'|$ can be exponential to $|G|$, which means almost all subgraphs of G will make the indicator function in equals 0. As an example, consider a linear graph $G_L(V_L, E_L)$ where $V_L = \{v_1, v_2, \ldots, v_n\}$ and $E_L = \{(v_k, v_{k+1}) \mid 1 \leq k < n\}$. Suppose $A_\tau = V_L$ and $\tau = n$, then $|\mathcal{S}| = 2^{n-1}$ whereas $s \rightsquigarrow A_\tau \subseteq G'$ only if $G'_L = G_L$ and $s = v_1$.

To overcome this problem, we want to sample G' from set $\mathcal{S}'$ rather than $\mathcal{S}$. On set $\mathcal{S}'$, we define a new sampling distribution, denoted as $\mathcal{G}'$, whose PMF is

$$\Pr_{\mathcal{G}'}(G') = \begin{cases} \Pr_{\mathcal{G}'}(G')/Z & \text{if } G' \in \mathcal{S}', \\ 0 & \text{otherwise,} \end{cases}$$

$$Z = \sum_{G' \in \mathcal{S}'} \Pr_{\mathcal{G}'}(G'). \tag{7}$$

Notice that set $\mathcal{S}'$ is independent of any candidate source node, so is the normalization factor Z. Therefore, with (7), we have

$$\mathbb{E}_{G' \sim \mathcal{G}}[I(A_\tau = \mathcal{R}(G', s, \tau))] \propto \mathbb{E}_{G' \sim \mathcal{G}'}[I(A_\tau = \mathcal{R}(G', s, \tau))].$$

Consequently, we can solve source inference problem (2) by solving

$$\hat{s} = \arg\max_s \mathbb{E}_{G' \sim \mathcal{G}'}[I(A_\tau = \mathcal{R}(G', s, \tau))]. \tag{8}$$

Now the problem is how to sample from $\mathcal{S}'$ with probability defined in (7). However, one can easily show that calculating factor Z is #P-hard, which makes calculating (7) impractical. Therefore, it is unlikely to be possible to directly sample from set $\mathcal{S}'$. Fortunately, the probability ratio between any two subgraphs is easy to compute; thus, we can use Metropolis algorithm to sample distribution $\mathcal{G}'$ in a Markov chain Monte Carlo.

Algorithm 1: Local move

    Input: G'_k, G, w, A_τ

    Output: G'_{k+1}

1 choose $(i, j) \in G$ uniformly randomly;

2 **if** $(i, j) \in G'_k$ **then**   `// remove edge`

3     $G'_{k+1} = G'_k \setminus \{(i, j)\}$;

4     $p = (1 - w_{i,j})/w_{i,j}$;

5 **else**   `// add edge`

6     $G'_{k+1} = G'_k \cup \{(i, j)\}$;

7     $p = w_{i,j}/(1 - w_{i,j})$;

8 **if** $\exists i, i \rightsquigarrow A_\tau \subseteq G'_{k+1}$ **then**

9     $p = \min\{p, 1\}$;

10 **else**

11     $p = 0$;

12 with probability $1 - p$, set $G'_{k+1} = G'_k$;   `// reject`

13 **return** G'_{k+1};

Algorithm 1 describes a local move from a subgraph in $\mathcal{S}'$ to another. Each local move will add/remove an edge to/from the previous subgraph G'_k. The new subgraph G'_{k+1} is either accepted or rejected depending on the probability ratio $\Pr_{\mathcal{G}'}(G'_{k+1})/\Pr_{\mathcal{G}'}(G'_k)$ defined in $\mathcal{G}'$. Starting from any subgraph in $\mathcal{S}'$, running Algorithm 1 iteratively will produce a Markov chain whose states represent subgraphs in $\mathcal{S}'$ and whose stationary distribution is exactly the same as (7).

With the help of local move in Algorithm 1, Algorithm 2 infers the most likely source node responsible for the cascade snapshot A_τ taken at time τ. Input parameter K is used to indicate the number of samples to take by this algorithm. With line 3, the algorithm starts with whole graph G as the initial sample, which is obviously in $\mathcal{S}'$. During every iteration of the while-loop, a subgraph in $\mathcal{S}'$ is sampled, and all possible source vertices are found and recorded. After the while-loop ends, $count[i]/K$ is the estimation of $\mathbb{E}_{G' \sim \mathcal{G}'}[I(A_\tau = \mathcal{R}(G', i, \tau))]$. Hence, the returned value of Algorithm 2 is an approximate solution of (8).

A more practical approach

Algorithm 2 has some drawbacks in practical scenarios. First, the whole network may be orders of magnitude larger than the cascade snapshot in question. However, Algorithm 2

Algorithm 2: Basic source inference algorithm

Input: instance: G, w, A_τ, τ; parameter: K

Output: s

1 create new array *count* with size $|V|$ and default value 0;

2 $k = 0$;

3 $G'_k = G$;   `// initial sample in` $\mathcal{S}'$

4 **while** $k < K$ **do**

5      $\mathcal{C} = \{i \mid \mathcal{R}(G'_k, i, \tau) = A_\tau\}$;

6   **for** $i \in \mathcal{C}$ **do**

7   **if** $A_\tau == \mathcal{R}(G'_k, i, \tau)$ **then**

8              $count[i] = count[i] + 1$;

9   run Algorithm 1 with G'_k G, w, A_τ to get G'_{k+1};

10     $k = k + 1$;

11 $s = \arg\max_i count[i]$;

12 **return** s;

---

scales with the size of full network rather than the snapshot, which is unfavorable here. Second, when the source node of a cascade is unknown, the starting time of the cascade is usually also absent. In these cases, inferring source node without knowing τ is desired. In this section, we will handle these two problems.

Based on the cascade snapshot A_τ, we can classify edges in E into three disjoint subsets

$$E_1 = \{(i, j) \mid (i, j) \in E, i, j \in A_\tau\}, \tag{9}$$

$$E_2 = \{(i, j) \mid (i, j) \in E, i \in A_\tau, j \notin A_\tau\},$$

$$E_3 = \{(i, j) \mid (i, j) \in E, i \notin A_\tau\}.$$

And E_2 can be further split into subsets according to the source node of edges:

$$E_{2,u} = \{(i, j) \mid (i, j) \in E_2, i = u\}.$$

Then we define three subgraphs of $G(V, E)$ accordingly: $G_1(A_\tau, E_1)$, $G_2(V, E_2)$, and $G_3(V, E_3)$. Note that G_1 only contains nodes in A_τ because edges in G_1 are all between nodes in A_τ. Furthermore, we partition each sampled subgraph G' into G'_1, G'_2 and G'_3, where $G'_k = G' \cap G_k$. With these definitions, we have the following lemma.

Lemma 1. *If we define subgraph $G_1(A_\tau, E_1)$ consisting of only edges between nodes in A_τ, the condition*

$$A_\tau = \mathcal{R}(G', s, \tau) \tag{10}$$

is equivalent to the combination of

$$A_\tau = \mathcal{R}(G'_1, s, \tau) \tag{11}$$

and

$$\forall i \in A_\tau, \quad d_{G'_1}(s, i) = \tau \ \lor \ E_{2,i} \cap E' = \varnothing, \tag{12}$$

where $G'_1 = G' \cap G_1$.

Proof. Eq. 10 can be split to 1) any node in A_τ must be within distance τ from s, i.e.,

$$A_\tau \subseteq \mathcal{R}(G', s, \tau), \tag{13}$$

and 2) any node outside A_τ must have distance from s larger than τ, i.e.,

$$\mathcal{R}(G', s, \tau) \setminus A_\tau = \varnothing. \tag{14}$$

Hence, the shortest path from s to any node $i \in A_\tau$ is within G_1, which implies $\forall i \in A_\tau$, $d_{G'}(s, i) = d_{G'_1}(s, i)$ and thus (11). Further, (12) means any node i with $d_{G'}(s, i) < \tau$ must not be able to activate its neighbors outside A_τ, which is necessary to ensure (14).

On the other hand, (11) guarantees (13) and (12) ensures $\forall i \notin A_\tau, d_{G'}(s, i) > \tau$ which leads to (14). $\qquad\square$

From Lemma 1, it is straightforward to get the following corollaries.

Corollary 1. *The indicator function in (4) is equivalent to*

$$I(A_\tau = \mathcal{R}(G', s, \tau)) = I(A_\tau = \mathcal{R}(G'_1, s, \tau))$$
$$\cdot \prod_{(i,j)\in G'_2} I(d_{G'_1}(s, i) = \tau).$$

Corollary 2. $I(A_\tau = \mathcal{R}(G', s, \tau))$ *is independent of* G'_3.

In addition, because $G' = G'_1 \cup G'_2 \cup G'_3$ and edge sets in G'_k are disjoint, (6) can be rewritten as the product of three terms

$$\Pr_{\mathcal{G}}(G') = \prod_{(i,j)\in G} w_{i,j}^{I((i,j)\in G')} (1 - w_{i,j})^{I((i,j)\notin G')}$$
$$= \prod_{k=1}^{3} \Pr_{\mathcal{G}k}(G'_k), \tag{15}$$

where

$$\Pr_{\mathcal{G}k}(G'_k) = \prod_{(i,j)\in G_k} w_{i,j}^{I((i,j)\in G'_k)} (1 - w_{i,j})^{I((i,j)\notin G'_k)}. \tag{16}$$

Now we have Theorem 2 that speedup the algorithm.

Theorem 2. *Define distribution* $\mathcal{G}'_1$ *of graphs in* $\mathcal{S}'_1 = \{G'_1 \mid G'_1 \subseteq G_1, \exists s, s \rightsquigarrow A_\tau \subseteq G'_1\}$ *with PMF proportional to* $\Pr_{\mathcal{G}_1}(G'_1)$. *Then, we have*

$$\Pr(A_\tau \mid G, s, \tau) \propto \mathbb{E}_{G'_1 \sim \mathcal{G}'_1}[f(G'_1, s, \tau)], \tag{17}$$

where

$$f(G'_1, s, \tau) = I(A_\tau = \mathcal{R}(G'_1, s, \tau)) \prod_{\substack{(i,j)\in G_2 \\ d_{G'_1}(s,i)<\tau}} (1 - w_{i,j}). \tag{18}$$

The proof of Theorem 2 is shown in Appendix 2.

Theorem 2 shows that sampling subgraphs of G_1, rather than the whole network G, is sufficient to infer the cascade source, which greatly accelerates the algorithm when the whole network is much larger than the cascade snapshot A_τ.

Next, we deal with unknown cascade starting time, i.e., unknown τ. First, due to the fact that node set in G_1 is A_τ,

$$A_\tau = \mathcal{R}(G_1', s, \tau) \iff A_\tau \subseteq \mathcal{R}(G_1', s, \tau)$$
$$\iff s \rightsquigarrow A_\tau \subseteq G_1' \wedge \tau \geq \epsilon_{G_1'}(s),$$

where $\epsilon_{G_1'}(s)$ is the eccentricity of node s in G_1', defined as

$$\epsilon_{G_1'}(s) = \max_{i \in G_1'} d_{G_1'}(s, i). \tag{19}$$

As a result, for any given G_1' and s such that $s \rightsquigarrow A_\tau \subseteq G_1'$, there are three possible values for function $f(G', s, \tau)$ in (18):

$$f(G', s, \tau) = \begin{cases} 0, & \tau < \epsilon_{G_1'}(s), \\ \displaystyle\prod_{\substack{(i,j) \in G_2 \\ d_{G_1'}(s,i) < \epsilon_{G_1'}(s)}} (1 - w_{i,j}), & \tau = \epsilon_{G_1'}(s), \\ \displaystyle\prod_{(i,j) \in G_2} (1 - w_{i,j}), & \tau > \epsilon_{G_1'}(s). \end{cases} \tag{20}$$

Here, the values for all three cases are independent of τ. Then, we have Theorem 3 that deals with unknown cascade starting time.

Theorem 3. *Suppose samples $G_{1,k}'$, $k = 1, 2, \ldots, K$ are taken with distribution $\mathcal{G}_1'$, then we can approximate (17) by*

$$\mathbb{E}_{G_1' \sim \mathcal{G}_1'}[f(G_1', s, \tau)] \approx \frac{1}{K}\left(A(s, \tau) + W \cdot \sum_{\tau' < \tau} C(s, \tau')\right),$$

where

$$A(s, \tau) = \sum_{k: \tau = \epsilon_{G_{1,k}'}(s)} \prod_{\substack{(i,j) \in G_2 \\ d_{G_{1,k}'}(s,i) < \epsilon_{G_{1,k}'}(s)}} (1 - w_{i,j}),$$

$$W = \prod_{(i,j) \in G_2} (1 - w_{i,j}), \tag{21}$$

$$C(s, \tau') = \sum_{k: \tau' = \epsilon_{G_{1,k}'}(s)} 1.$$

Proof. Because samples $G_{1,k}'$ are taken with distribution $\mathcal{G}_1'$, we have

$$\mathbb{E}_{G_1' \sim \mathcal{G}_1'}[f(G_1', s, \tau)] \approx \frac{1}{K} \sum_{k=1}^{K} f(G_{1,k}', s, \tau). \tag{22}$$

Substituting (20) into the summation of (22) proves the theorem.   □

With both Theorems 2 and 3, Algorithm 2 can be improved to Algorithm 3 which overcomes problems of large network and unknown τ.

In Algorithm 3, we only consider τ' ranging from 1 to $|A_\tau|$ because 1) $\epsilon_{G_{1,k}'}(s)$ ranges from 1 to $|A_\tau| - 1$ given $|A_\tau| > 1$ and $s \rightsquigarrow A_\tau \subseteq G_{1,k}'$; 2) if $\tau >= |A_\tau|$, the cascade must have terminated, thus $\forall \tau > |A_\tau|$, $\Pr(A_\tau|G, s, \tau) = \Pr(A_\tau|G, s, |A_\tau|)$. The input time range $[\tau_l, \tau_u]$ represents limited knowledge of τ. If the exact starting time of the cascade

---

Algorithm 3: Advanced source inference algorithm

Input: instance: G, w, A_τ; time range $[\tau_l, \tau_u]$; parameter: K

Output: s

1 create new tables *accu*, *count* and *result* with size $|A_\tau| \times |A_\tau|$ and default value 0;

2 create graph $G_1(A_\tau, E_1)$ according to (9);

3 $k = 0$;

4 $G'_{1,k} = G'_1$;

5 calculate W by (21);

6 **for** $i \in A_\tau$ **do**

7 $\quad \lfloor \ W_i = \prod_{j \in V \backslash A_\tau : (i,j) \in G} (1 - w_{i,j})$;

8 **while** $k < K$ **do**

9 $\quad \mathcal{C} = \{i \mid i \rightsquigarrow A_\tau \subseteq G'_{1,k}\}$;

10 $\quad$ **for** $i \in \mathcal{C}$ **do**

11 $\quad\quad \tau' = \epsilon_{G'_{1,k}}(i)$ by (19);

12 $\quad\quad w' = W$;

13 $\quad\quad$ **for** $j \in A_\tau, d_{G'_{1,k}}(i,j) == \tau'$ **do**

14 $\quad\quad\quad \lfloor \ w' = w'/W_j$;

15 $\quad\quad accu[i][\tau'] = accu[i][\tau'] + w'$;

16 $\quad\quad count[i][\tau'] = count[i][\tau'] + 1$;

17 $\quad$ run Algorithm 1 with $G'_{1,k}$ G_1, w, A_τ to get $G'_{1,k+1}$;

18 $\quad k = k + 1$;

19 **for** $i \in A_\tau$ **do**

20 $\quad c = 0$;

21 $\quad$ **for** $\tau' = 1, \ldots, |A_\tau|$ **do**

22 $\quad\quad result[i][\tau'] = accu[i][\tau'] + W \times c$;

23 $\quad\quad c = c + count[i][\tau']$;

24 $s = \arg\max_i \sum_{\tau'=\tau_l}^{\tau_u} result[i][\tau']$;

25 **return** s;

---

is known, we can use $\tau_l = \tau_u = \tau$. On the contrary, if nothing at all is known about τ, $\tau_l = \min_i \epsilon_{G'_1}(i)$ and $\tau_u = |A_\tau|$ may be used instead.

It should be noted that for any sample G'_1, line 9 in Algorithm 3 can be done in $O(|G'_1|)$ time. First, condensation $C(G'_1)$ is calculated, which needs linear time. Then, since $C(G'_1)$ is a directed acyclic graph, there is at least one strong component in $C(G'_1)$ that has no predecessor. If there is exactly one such component, it is the set $\mathcal{C}$; if there is more than one, $\mathcal{C} = \varnothing$. This method also applies to line 8 in Algorithm 1 and line 5 in Algorithm 2.

Experimental results

In this section, we conduct experiments of our cascade source inference algorithm (Algorithm 3, with $K = 10^6$) on real network dataset. The network used is from WikiVote dataset ([12, 13]), which consists of all Wikipedia voting data from the inception of Wikipedia till January 2008. The dataset has 7115 nodes and 103,689 directed unweighted edges. Each node represents a Wikipedia user participating in elections, while each directed node (i, j) means user i voted for user j. We use this unweighted dataset because we cannot find a social network dataset with influence probability available despite our best effort. Since the dataset is unweighted, we use reciprocal of in-degree of the destination node as the weight of an edge. With uniformly randomly chosen source nodes, cascades are then generated on the network according to the IC model. To make the experiment challenging, we discard cascades with less than 20 candidate sources. Here, candidate source set is not active nodes set A_τ, but set of nodes from which all active nodes are reachable in G_1, i.e., $\{i \mid i \leadsto A_\tau \subseteq G_1\}$. We use 200 cascades in our experiments. Figure 2a, b shows histograms of the number of active nodes and candidate sources among these cascades.

To compare our proposed algorithm with existing algorithm, we also implement the algorithm proposed by [9]. In that paper, they proposed three algorithms ("DP", "Sort", and "OutDegree") to find a set of k sources. In our case where single source generates the cascade, their DP algorithm and Sort' algorithm are equivalent. In the experiment below, we use this algorithm and call it "Effector" algorithm.

First, we take snapshot at $\tau = |A_\tau|$, i.e., after cascades terminate and do the experiment with exact knowledge of τ. Figure 3a shows the distribution of error distances, which is defined as the distance between inferred source node and true source node assuming edges are undirected. To compare with, the error distance of random guess among A_τ is also shown in Fig. 1c. It is clear that all source nodes inferred by our algorithm are within two hops around the source node, and 24 % of the inferred nodes are true sources. In comparison, the Effector algorithm has fewer results with 0 or 1 error distance. To further evaluate the algorithm, we make the algorithms output a list of candidate source nodes sorted in descending order of likelihood, rather than merely the most likely source node. This output is sometimes more useful because it answers queries like "what's the 5 most

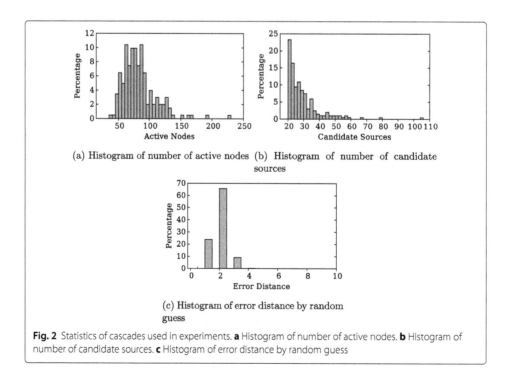

(a) Histogram of number of active nodes (b) Histogram of number of candidate sources

(c) Histogram of error distance by random guess

Fig. 2 Statistics of cascades used in experiments. **a** Histogram of number of active nodes. **b** Histogram of number of candidate sources. **c** Histogram of error distance by random guess

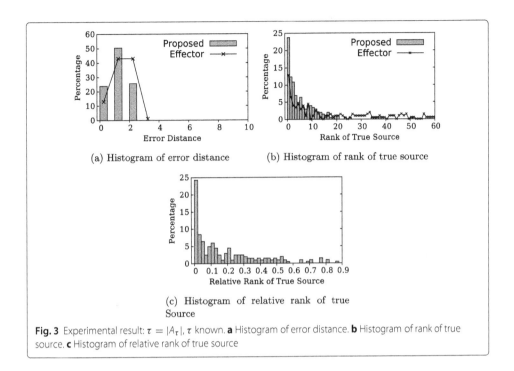

(a) Histogram of error distance   (b) Histogram of rank of true source

(c) Histogram of relative rank of true Source

Fig. 3 Experimental result: $\tau = |A_\tau|$, τ known. **a** Histogram of error distance. **b** Histogram of rank of true source. **c** Histogram of relative rank of true source

likely source of the cascade". Figure 3b shows the distribution of rank of the true source node in the ordered list. In more than half of total experiments, the true source is among top 4 candidates output by our algorithm. The Effector algorithm, however, has a much heavier tail with far less results with lower ranks. In fact, there are 15 % of the results with a rank higher than 60 which is not shown in the figure. Figure 3c shows distribution of relative ranks, i.e., rank divided by candidate set size. Only our algorithm is shown in this figure because the Effector algorithm does not calculate candidate set and their output list include many nodes not in the candidate set due to the reason explained by Fig. 1 in the 'Introduction' section. In more than 50 % of the experiments, our output that has relative rank of the true source is less than or equal to 0.1.

Then, we do experiments with snapshots taken at $\tau = 8$, when most of the cascades are yet to terminate. The results are shown in Fig. 4. Similarly, our proposed algorithm performs better than the Effector algorithm. In 55 % of the experiments, our algorithm has true source node among top 4 candidates, and in half of experiments, we have true source node with relative rank no larger than 0.1.

To evaluate the performance of our source inference algorithm when exact cascade starting time is absent, we conduct another experiment on the snapshot taken at $\tau = 8$ with input time range $[0, 16]$. As shown in Fig. 5, our algorithm effectively infers the source nodes even without exact knowledge of cascade starting time. In the experiment, 57 % of the true source nodes are among top 4 candidates, and in half of the cases, the true source ranked top 10 % in the output list.

Conclusion

We considered cascade source inference problem in the IC model. First the #P-completeness of this problem was proven. Then, a Markov chain Monte Carlo algorithm was proposed to approximate the solution. Our algorithm was designed with two major

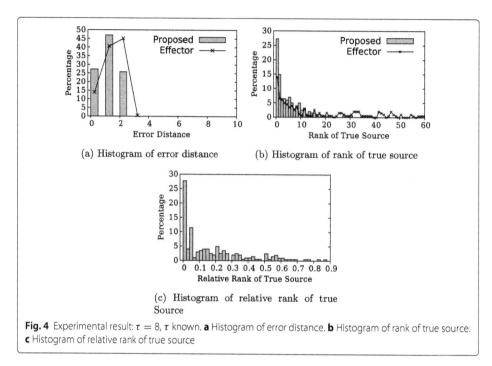

(a) Histogram of error distance   (b) Histogram of rank of true source

(c) Histogram of relative rank of true Source

Fig. 4 Experimental result: $\tau = 8$, τ known. **a** Histogram of error distance. **b** Histogram of rank of true source. **c** Histogram of relative rank of true source

advantages: 1) it scales with the observed cascade snapshot rather than the whole network and thus is applicable to enormous modern social networks and 2) it does not require any knowledge about the starting time of the cascade, which is a common and practical scenario in cascade source inference problem. To demonstrate the performance of our algorithm, experiments on real social network were conducted. As shown above, our algorithm performs well no matter when the cascade snapshot is taken or whether the cascade starting time is known. In all these experiments, around 25 % of the true sources are correctly identified, about half of them are among the top 4 or top 10 % of the candidates.

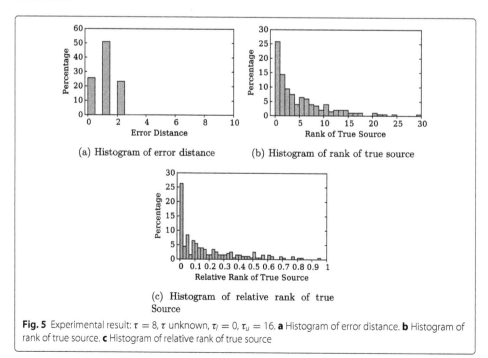

(a) Histogram of error distance   (b) Histogram of rank of true source

(c) Histogram of relative rank of true Source

Fig. 5 Experimental result: $\tau = 8$, τ unknown, $\tau_l = 0$, $\tau_u = 16$. **a** Histogram of error distance. **b** Histogram of rank of true source. **c** Histogram of relative rank of true source

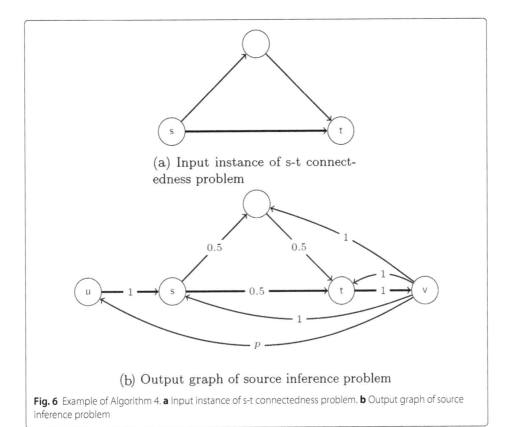

(a) Input instance of s-t connectedness problem

(b) Output graph of source inference problem

Fig. 6 Example of Algorithm 4. **a** Input instance of s-t connectedness problem. **b** Output graph of source inference problem

Appendix 1

Proof of Theorem 1

We will prove Theorem 1 by constructing a polynomial-time Turing reduction from s-t connectedness problem to source inference problem. S-t connectedness problem is given a directed graph $\hat{G}(\hat{V}, \hat{E})$ and two nodes $s, t \in \hat{V}$, output the number of subgraphs of $\hat{G}$ in which there is a path from s to t, i.e. , Connectedness$(\hat{G}, s, t) = |\{\hat{E}' \subseteq \hat{E} \mid s \leadsto t \subseteq \hat{E}'\}$. This problem is known to be #P-complete [11].

A key part of the proof is Algorithm 4 which converts an instance of s-t connectedness problem to an instance of source inference problem with properties listed in Lemma 2. An simple example of this algorithm is shown in Fig. 6.

Algorithm 4: Conversion from an instance of s-t connectedness problem to an instance of source inference problem

Input: Parameter $p \in (0, 1]$; instance $\hat{G}(\hat{V}, \hat{E})$, $s, t \in \hat{V}$.

Output: $G(V, E)$, w, A_τ, τ.

1 $V = \hat{V} \cup \{u, v\}, u, v \notin \hat{V}$;

2 $E = \hat{E} \cup \{(v, u), (u, s), (t, v)\} \cup \{(v, j) \mid \forall j \in \hat{V}\}$;

3 $w_{v,u} = p, w_{u,s} = 1, w_{t,v} = 1$;

4 $w_{v,j} = 1, \forall j \in \hat{V}$;

5 $w_{i,j} = 0.5, \forall (i, j) \in \hat{E}$;

6 $A_\tau = V$;

7 $\tau = |V|$;

8 **return** $G(V, E)$, w, A_τ, τ;

Lemma 2. *Given input parameter p and instance $\hat{G}(\hat{V}, \hat{E})$, $s, t \in \hat{V}$, the output instance $G(V, E)$, w, A_τ, τ of Algorithm 4 has the following properties:*

1. $\Pr(A_t|G, v, \tau) = \Pr(A_t|G, t, \tau) = p;$
2. $\Pr(A_t|G, i, \tau < p, \forall i \in \hat{V}, i \neq t;$
3. $\Pr(A_t|G, u, \tau) = \text{Connectedness}(\hat{G}, s, t) \cdot 0.5^{|\hat{E}|}.$

Proof. In this proof, we use $i \rightsquigarrow j \subseteq G$ to denote the existence of a path from i to j in graph G. In addition, $i \rightsquigarrow V \subseteq G$ means $\forall j \in V, j \neq i, i \rightsquigarrow j \subseteq G$.

According to the algorithm, output snapshot A_τ contains all vertices, and $\tau = |V|$ guarantees that $d_{G'}(i, j) < \tau$ if $i \rightsquigarrow j \subseteq G'$. Therefore, due to (3), the output instance has

$$\Pr(A_\tau|G, i, \tau = \Pr(i \rightsquigarrow V \subseteq G'),$$

which means considering reachability rather than distance is sufficient in the remaining part of the proof.

Now, due to line 4 in Algorithm 4, every node in $\hat{V}$ is reachable from v in every subgraph G' sampled via (1). And because $w_{t,v} = 1$ (by line 3), for any subgraph G',

$$t \rightsquigarrow \hat{V} \subseteq G',$$

$$v \rightsquigarrow \hat{V} \subseteq G',$$

$$\forall i \in V, \quad i \rightsquigarrow t \subseteq G' \Longleftrightarrow i \rightsquigarrow v \subseteq G' \Longleftrightarrow i \rightsquigarrow \hat{V} \subseteq G'. \tag{23}$$

Thus property 1 is straightforward:

$$\Pr(A_t|G, t, \tau) = \Pr(A_t|G, v, \tau)$$
$$= \Pr(v \rightsquigarrow V \subseteq G')$$
$$= \Pr(v \rightsquigarrow u \subseteq G')$$
$$= p.$$

On the other hand, since the new node u has only one incoming edge (v, u), we have $\forall i \in \hat{V}, i \neq t, i \rightsquigarrow u \subseteq G'$ implies $i \rightsquigarrow t \subseteq G'$. Therefore, we have the proof for property 2: for any $i \in \hat{V}, i \neq t$,

$$\Pr(A_t|G, i, \tau) = \Pr(i \rightsquigarrow V \subseteq G')$$
$$= \Pr(i \rightsquigarrow t \subseteq G') \cdot p$$
$$< p,$$

where the last inequality is because every incoming edge of t has weight 0.5 according to line 5 in Algorithm 4.

To prove property 3, we first note that s is the only successor of u and $w_{u,s} = 1$, with (23), we have

$$u \rightsquigarrow V \subseteq G' \Longleftrightarrow s \rightsquigarrow t \subseteq G'.$$

And therefore,

$$\Pr(A_t|G, u, \tau) = \Pr(u \rightsquigarrow V \subseteq G') = \Pr(s \rightsquigarrow t \subseteq G'). \tag{24}$$

Because $\hat{G} \subset G$, sampling subgraphs G' of G can be viewed as sampling subsets of $\hat{E}$ followed by sampling subsets of $E \setminus \hat{E}$. Since any path from s to t consists only edges in $\hat{E}$, $\Pr(s \rightsquigarrow t \subseteq G')$ is fully determined by sampling $\hat{E}$, or equivalently, sampling subgraphs of $\hat{G}$. As a result,

$$\Pr(s \rightsquigarrow t \subseteq G') = \text{Connectedness}(\hat{G}, s, t) \cdot 0.5^{|\hat{E}|}, \tag{25}$$

because every subset of $\hat{E}$ has probability $0.5^{|\hat{E}|}$ to be selected via (1) according to line 5 in Algorithm 4. Now property 3 follows from (24) and (25). ☐

Proof. First, to show source inference problem is in #P, we note that calculating $\Pr(A_t|G, i, \tau)$ is in #P since it is the sum of probabilities of all subgraphs of G with $i \rightsquigarrow V \subseteq G$. So source inference problem, i.e., finding node i that maximize $\Pr(A_t|G, i, \tau)$, is also in #P.

Since graph $\hat{G}$ has $2^{|\hat{E}|}$ subgraphs, Connectedness$\hat{G}, s, t$ must be an integer in range $[0, 2^{|\hat{E}|}]$. Therefore, $\Pr(A_t|G, u, \tau)$ of the output instance of Algorithm 4 must be in set $\{k \cdot 0.5^{|\hat{E}|} \mid k \in \mathbb{N}, k \leq 2^{|\hat{E}|}\}$. A binary search algorithm, i.e., Algorithm 5, can solve s-t connectedness problem by solving source inference problem.

Algorithm 5: Solution of s-t connectedness problem with oracle for source inference problem

---

Input: $\hat{G}(\hat{V}, \hat{E}), s, t \in \hat{V}$.
Output: $k = \text{Connectedness}\hat{G}, s, t$
1 **if** t *is not reachable from* s **then**
2   **return** 0;
3 $m = 2^{|\hat{E}|}, n = 1$;
4 **while** $m \neq n$ **do**
5     $p = (m + n)/2 \cdot 0.5^{|\hat{E}|}$;
6   run Algorithm 4 with $p, \hat{G}, s, t$ to get G, w, A_τ, τ;
7   solve source inference problem G, w, A_τ, τ to get x;
8   **if** $x == u$ **then**
9        $n = (m + n + 1)/2$;
10   **else**
11        $m = (m + n - 1)/2$;
12 **return** m;

In Algorithm 5, there will be $|\hat{E}|$ iterations of while-loop. Hence, only polynomial number of queries to the oracle will be made. All other operations can be done in polynomial time. Therefore, this algorithm shows a polynomial-time Turing reduction from s-t connectedness problem to source inference problem. Since s-t connectedness problem is #P-complete and source inference problem is in #P, Theorem 1 is proven. ☐

Appendix 2

Proof of Theorem 2

The proof is shown from Eqs. (26) to (33). Here, Eq. (27) follows from (15); (28) is due to the equivalence between sampling $G' \subseteq G$ and sampling $G'_k \subseteq G_k, k = 1, 2, 3$, separately;

(29) results from Corollary 2 and the fact that $\Pr_{\mathcal{G}_k}(G'_k)$ depends only on G'_k respectively; (30) is simply due to $\sum_{G'_3 \subseteq G_3} \Pr_{\mathcal{G}_3}(G'_3) = 1$; (31) is by Corollary 1.

To further transform the (32), we split G_2 to $G_{2,\tau}(V, E_{2,\tau})$ and $G_{2,\hat{\tau}}(V, E_{2,\hat{\tau}})$, where

$$
E_{2,\tau} = \bigcup_{\substack{i \in A_\tau \\ d_{G'_1}(s,i) = \tau}} E_{2,i},
$$

$$
E_{2,\hat{\tau}} = \bigcup_{\substack{i \in A_\tau \\ d_{G'_1}(s,i) < \tau}} E_{2,i}.
$$

Then, with given subgraph $G'_1 \subseteq G_1$, sampling subgraph $G'_2 \subseteq G_2$ is essentially sampling $G'_{2,\tau} \subseteq G_{2,\tau}$ and $G'_{2,\hat{\tau}} \subseteq G_{2,\hat{\tau}}$, which leads to (34). Since the first summation in (34) is the sum probability of all possible subgraphs of $G_{2,\tau}$, which is 1, we have (35). Because only one specific subgraph $G'_{2,\hat{\tau}} \subseteq G_{2,\hat{\tau}}$, namely, $G'_{2,\hat{\tau}} = G_{2,\hat{\tau}}$, satisfies $\forall (i,j) \in G_{2,\hat{\tau}}$, $I((i,j) \notin G'_{2,\hat{\tau}}) > 0$, we have (36). Then, substituting (36) into (31) gives (32). According to the definition of distribution $\mathcal{G}'_1$, we have (33) and prove Theorem 2.

$$
\Pr(A_\tau | G, s, \tau) = \sum_{G' \subseteq G} \Pr_{\mathcal{G}}(G') I(A_\tau = \mathcal{R}(G', s, \tau)) \tag{26}
$$

$$
= \sum_{G' \subseteq G} \prod_{k=1}^{3} \Pr_{\mathcal{G}_k}(G'_k) I(A_\tau = \mathcal{R}(G', s, \tau)) \tag{27}
$$

$$
= \sum_{G'_1 \subseteq G_1} \sum_{G'_2 \subseteq G_2} \sum_{G'_3 \subseteq G_3} \prod_{k=1}^{3} \Pr_{\mathcal{G}_k}(G'_k) I(A_\tau = \mathcal{R}(G', s, \tau)) \tag{28}
$$

$$
= \sum_{G'_1 \subseteq G_1} \left[\Pr_{\mathcal{G}_1}(G'_1) \cdot \sum_{G'_2 \subseteq G_2} \left[\Pr_{\mathcal{G}_2}(G'_2) I(A_\tau = \mathcal{R}(G', s, \tau)) \cdot \sum_{G'_3 \subseteq G_3} \left[\Pr_{\mathcal{G}_3}(G'_3) \right] \right] \right] \tag{29}
$$

$$
= \sum_{G'_1 \subseteq G_1} \left[\Pr_{\mathcal{G}_1}(G'_1) \cdot \sum_{G'_2 \subseteq G_2} \left[\Pr_{\mathcal{G}_2}(G'_2) I(A_\tau = \mathcal{R}(G', s, \tau)) \right] \right] \tag{30}
$$

$$
= \sum_{G'_1 \subseteq G_1} \left[\Pr_{\mathcal{G}_1}(G'_1) I(A_\tau = \mathcal{R}(G'_1, s, \tau)) \cdot \sum_{G'_2 \subseteq G_2} \left[\Pr_{\mathcal{G}_2}(G'_2) \prod_{(i,j) \in G'_2} I(d_{G'_1}(s,i) = \tau) \right] \right] \tag{31}
$$

$$
= \sum_{G'_1 \subseteq G_1} \left[\Pr_{\mathcal{G}_1}(G'_1) I(A_\tau = \mathcal{R}(G'_1, s, \tau)) \cdot \prod_{\substack{(i,j) \in G_2 \\ d_{G'_1}(s,i) < \tau}} (1 - w_{i,j}) \right] \tag{32}
$$

$$
\propto \mathbb{E}_{G'_1 \sim \mathcal{G}'_1} \left[I(A_\tau = \mathcal{R}(G'_1, s, \tau)) \cdot \prod_{\substack{(i,j) \in G_2 \\ d_{G'_1}(s,i) < \tau}} (1 - w_{i,j}) \right], \tag{33}
$$

where (32) is due to

$$\sum_{G_2' \subseteq G_2} \left[\Pr_{\mathcal{G}_2}(G_2') \prod_{(i,j) \in G_2'} I(d_{G_1'}(s,i) = \tau) \right]$$

$$= \sum_{G_2' \subseteq G_2} \left[\prod_{(i,j) \in G_2} w_{i,j}^{I((i,j) \in G_2')}(1 - w_{i,j})^{I((i,j) \notin G_2')} \cdot \prod_{\substack{(i,j) \in G_2 \\ d_{G_1'}(s,i) < \tau}} I((i,j) \notin G_2') \right] \qquad \text{(by (16))}$$

$$= \sum_{G_2' \subseteq G_2} \left[\prod_{\substack{(i,j) \in G_2 \\ d_{G_1'}(s,i) = \tau}} w_{i,j}^{I((i,j) \in G_2')}(1 - w_{i,j})^{I((i,j) \notin G_2')} \cdot \prod_{\substack{(i,j) \in G_2 \\ d_{G_1'}(s,i) < \tau}} (1 - w_{i,j})I((i,j) \notin G_2') \right]$$

$$= \sum_{G_{2,\tau}' \subseteq G_{2,\tau}} \left[\prod_{(i,j) \in G_{2,\tau}} w_{i,j}^{I((i,j) \in G_{2,\tau}')}(1 - w_{i,j})^{I((i,j) \notin G_{2,\tau}')} \right] \cdot \sum_{G_{2,\hat{\tau}}' \subseteq G_{2,\hat{\tau}}} \left[\prod_{(i,j) \in G_{2,\hat{\tau}}} (1 - w_{i,j})I((i,j) \notin G_{2,\hat{\tau}}') \right] \qquad (34)$$

$$= \sum_{G_{2,\hat{\tau}}' \subseteq G_{2,\hat{\tau}}} \left[\prod_{(i,j) \in G_{2,\hat{\tau}}} (1 - w_{i,j})I((i,j) \notin G_{2,\hat{\tau}}') \right] \qquad (35)$$

$$= \prod_{(i,j) \in G_{2,\hat{\tau}}} (1 - w_{i,j}). \qquad (36)$$

Authors' contributions

XZ proved the theorems and did the algorithm design and experiment. WW and WX contributed to the problem formulation and organized this research. All authors read and approved the final manuscript.

Competing interests

The authors declare that they have no competing interests.

Acknowledgements

This work was supported in part by the China National Science Foundation (CNSF) under Grant No. F020809.

References

1. Shah, D, Zaman, T: Rumors in a network: who's the culprit? IEEE Trans. Inf. Theory. **57**(8), 5163–5181 (2011)
2. Shah, D, Zaman, T: Rumor centrality: a universal source detector. In: Proceedings of the 12th ACM SIGMETRICS/PERFORMANCE Joint International Conference on Measurement and Modeling of Computer Systems, pp. 199–210. ACM, New York, (2012)
3. Dong, W, Zhang, W, Tan, CW: Rooting out the rumor culprit from suspects. In: 2013 IEEE International Symposium on Information Theory, pp. 2671–2675. IEEE, New York, (2013)
4. Wang, Z, Dong, W, Zhang, W, Tan, CW: Rumor source detection with multiple observations: fundamental limits and algorithms. In: Proceedings of the 2014 ACM International Conference on Measurement and Modeling of Computer Systems - SIGMETRICS '14, pp. 1–13. ACM, New York, (2014)
5. Karamchandani, N, Franceschetti, M: Rumor source detection under probabilistic sampling. In: 2013 IEEE International Symposium on Information Theory, pp. 2184–2188. IEEE, New York, (2013)
6. Luo, W, Tay, WP, Leng, M: Identifying infection sources and regions in large networks. IEEE Trans. Signal Process. **61**(11), 2850–2865 (2013)
7. Prakash, BA, Vreeken, J, Faloutsos, C: Spotting culprits in epidemics: how many and which ones? In: 2012 IEEE 12th International Conference on Data Mining, pp. 11–20. IEEE, New York, (2012)
8. Mannila, H, Terzi, E: Finding links and initiators: a graph-reconstruction problem. In: Proceedings of the 2009 SIAM International Conference on Data Mining - SDM'09, pp. 1209–1219. SIAM, Philadelphia, (2009)
9. Lappas, T, Terzi, E, Gunopulos, D, Mannila, H: Finding effectors in social networks. In: Proceedings of the 16th ACM SIGKDD International Conference on Knowledge Discovery and Data Mining - KDD '10, pp. 1059–1068. ACM, New York, (2010)
10. Kempe, D, Kleinberg, J, Tardos, E: Maximizing the spread of influence through a social network. In: Proceedings of the Ninth ACM SIGKDD International Conference on Knowledge Discovery and Data Mining - KDD '03, pp. 137–146. ACM, New York, (2003)
11. Valiant, LG: The complexity of enumeration and reliability problems. SIAM J. Comput. **8**(3), 410–421 (1979)
12. Leskovec, J, Huttenlocher, D, Kleinberg, J: Predicting positive and negative links in online social networks. In: Proceedings of the 19th International Conference on World Wide Web - WWW '10, p. 641. ACM, New York, (2010)
13. Leskovec, J, Huttenlocher, D, Kleinberg, J: Signed networks in social media. In: Proceedings of the 28th International Conference on Human Factors in Computing Systems - CHI '10, p. 1361, New York, NY, USA, (2010)

8

Analysis and control of information diffusion dictated by user interest in generalized networks

Eleni Stai[*] [ID], Vasileios Karyotis and Symeon Papavassiliou

*Correspondence:
estai@netmode.ntua.gr
School of Electrical
and Computer Engineering,
National Technical
University of Athens (NTUA),
15780 Zografou, Athens,
Greece

Abstract

The diffusion of useful information in generalized networks, such as those consisting of wireless physical substrates and social network overlays is very important for theoretical and practical applications. Contrary to previous works, we focus on the impact of user interest and its features (e.g., interest periodicity) on the dynamics and control of diffusion of useful information within such complex wireless-social systems. By considering the impact of temporal and topical variations of users interests, e.g., seasonal periodicity of interest in summer vacation advertisements which spread more effectively during Spring–Summer months, we develop an epidemic-based mathematical framework for modeling and analyzing such information dissemination processes and use three indicative operational scenarios to demonstrate the solutions and results that can be obtained by the corresponding differential equation-based formalism. We then develop an optimal control framework subject to the above information diffusion modeling that allows controlling the trade-off between information propagation efficiency and the associated cost, by considering and leveraging on the impact that user interests have on the diffusion processes. By analysis and extensive simulations, significant outcomes are obtained on the impact of each network layer and the associated interest parameters on the dynamics of useful information diffusion. Furthermore, several behavioral properties of the optimal control of the useful information diffusion with respect to the number of infected/informed nodes and the evolving user interest are shown through analysis and verified via simulations. Specifically, a key finding is that low interest-related diffusion can be aided by utilizing proper optimal controls. Our work in this paper paves the way towards this user-centered information diffusion framework.

Keywords: User interests, Information diffusion, Generalized networks, SIS epidemic model, Time-varying interests, Optimal control, Pontryagin's Maximum Principle, Hamilton–Jacobi–Bellman equation

Introduction

Analyzing and controlling information diffusion in complex networks is of high research and practical interest nowadays. "Information" may appear in diverse forms, useful or malicious, each with different diffusion dynamics and demanding different types of control. Malicious information, e.g., a dangerous computer virus, might have catastrophic outcomes calling for suppressive control, while marketing advertisements can be exploited for maximizing online revenues and may be enhanced by an amplifying type of control.

To better facilitate the increased needs for effective information exchange, continuing technological advances in wireless and wired communications and the development of online social networks have given rise to "generalized" network systems. The latter consist of a physical layer, i.e., a wireless medium, and a social overlay, where social encounters develop, forming combined cyber-physical, e.g., social-wireless networks, referred to as generalized networks [1]. According to [2], generalized networks, even when consisting of a physical (e.g., wireless multihop) and only one social network can significantly improve information spread. In this paper, we focus on social-wireless types of generalized networks, while other types may be straightforwardly considered.

Motivated by the above observations on networks and information proliferation, in this paper, we focus on the diffusion dynamics and control of useful information in generalized networks. Various relevant works on the topic exist in the literature ("Related work and contributions"). However, albeit, they bear a specific drawback by not accounting for the evolution of user interest on the information diffused. Typically, humans interact with each other and exchange content on the basis of features such as "topics of information". In particular, during an encounter, humans may not care for information that is out of their interest range at that particular time, thus not participating in the diffusion of the corresponding topic. Therefore, communicating information is highly affected by user interests and their temporal evolution, since not every contact does necessarily imply information transfer for all the topics under diffusion. It rather depends both on human preferences and their interconnections (physical and social topology).

Several real-world examples indicate the dependence of information diffusion dynamics on the temporal and topical variation of user interests [3–5]. For instance, advertisements on summer vacations are expected to have a more successful spread outcome during the Spring and Summer months, while being hobbled during Fall and Winter months, highlighting an emergent seasonal periodicity with respect to user interests. Secondly, news on a soccer match might not be well spread within the members of a dance group, while they are expected to be quickly spread within the members of a soccer club. The first of the above cannot be expressed by the current models of information diffusion which do not segregate the diffusion success rate with respect to seasonal dependence, while the second case implies a non-homogeneous information rate across populations with different characteristics. As a result, for a realistic inclusion of users' interests in the information diffusion model, the interests should be considered time varying, e.g., reflecting the evolving seasonal behavior of human beings [6]. The second example further implies the need of explicitly taking into account the subject of users' interests, when designing information diffusion models.

Thus, in this paper we introduce and develop for the first time an information diffusion modeling framework that takes into account both user interests' differentiation and their possible temporal variability (e.g., periodicity). Furthermore, we provide an optimal control framework on top of the information diffusion model that allows for trading-off diffusion efficiency with the associated cost, leveraging on the impact that user interest has on information dissemination dynamics. To the best of our knowledge, there is limited literature in the field of optimal control over diffusion dynamics described by epidemic modeling with time-evolving parameters [6, 7]. Incorporating control, will benefit information spreading, particularly when there is limited interest on the useful information being diffused, in which case, it can be mapped to, e.g., advertising campaigns or other incentives provided to users in an optimized way with respect to cost. An example of explicit control is the provision of incentives to users, e.g., in the form of competition, rewards, reputation, etc., to participate in information propagation when their interest itself in the propagated topic is limited, decreasing in this way the probability that information propagation on a specific subject deceases fast enough. Significant outcomes are provided on the impact of each topological layer (social or wireless) and the associated interest parameters on the dynamics and control of information diffusion over complex social-wireless topologies, via analysis, numerical evaluations and simulations of relevant scenarios. Furthermore, the properties/behavior of the optimal controls on information diffusion are extensively studied.

The rest of the paper is organized as follows. "Related work and contributions" describes related literature and positions our work within the existing relevant literature, while "System model, notation and assumptions" presents the employed system model. "Information diffusion modeling and analysis without control" analyzes the proposed information diffusion model and the examined application scenarios. In the sequel, "Optimal control framework for information diffusion" introduces the information diffusion optimal control framework, while "Simulation and numerical results without applying control" and "Simulation results, numerical results and discussion in controlled information diffusion" present and thoroughly discuss the performed simulation results and numerical evaluations without and with control, respectively. Finally, "Conclusions" concludes the paper.

Related work and contributions

Due to the importance of information nowadays, studying the properties of its diffusion along with the possibility of control has attracted considerable interest. In this paper, we focus on two important facets of information diffusion, namely the dynamics of information spreading and its optimal control.

Regarding the dynamics of information diffusion, the earliest and most frequently encountered approaches were inspired by epidemiological models [8, 9]. Some of the most recent ones are [1, 10–13], while more can be found in the references therein. More specifically, both stochastic and deterministic epidemic models exist for information propagation [7, 14], where the nodes having received the information are denoted as "infected". Stochastic epidemic models treat information propagation as a discrete time process (Discrete Time Markov Chain) [7, 14] being more suitable for small-scale systems whereas deterministic epidemic models assume continuous processes relying on the law of large numbers and applying differential equations or inclusions [15, 16], thus being more suitable for large-scale systems. In this paper, we will apply a deterministic epidemic model. Most of deterministic models consider the evolution of the cumulative system state/number of infected individuals (macroscopic modeling), denoted as "population dynamics", assuming homogeneous infection rates for all population members. On the other hand, the deterministic "network" models study the state of each individual separately and also segregate infection rates between different pairs of individuals [7].

However, system state transitions (i.e., population dynamics) depend on the state transition models developed for each individual, e.g., susceptible–infected–susceptible (SIS), etc. [7, 8]. Contrary to deterministic network models, a typical assumption when considering population dynamics is that of homogeneous mixing, where contact patterns between individuals are considered highly homogeneous [17]. Both types of models, stochastic and deterministic, account for the endogenous (transition that takes place owe to internal individual operation, e.g., recovery transition) and exogenous (transitions dictated by external factors, e.g., infection transition) transition rates expressing the topological and operational, endogenous or exogenous, factors that affect the evolution of the system [7].

Information dissemination epidemic models have been developed for different network topologies, e.g., wireless networks [18], social networks [8] and multiple social networks [3], and generalized networks [1]. More specifically, epidemic models, e.g., SIS, susceptible–infected–removed (SIR) and susceptible–infected (SI) [6, 8] have been adopted and adapted over diverse network topologies to describe the spreading of useful or malicious information. In this work, we mainly focus on the diffusion of useful information over generalized networks based on the SIS epidemic model. Our model lies between the frameworks of population dynamics and network models, since we study system state transitions while considering neighborhood relations in a node-degree sense.

Furthermore, to the best of our knowledge, the impact of user interests and their temporal variability analyzed in this work have been considered in the literature in a limited degree, e.g., [3, 4, 19]. In [3], the authors aim at finding the minimum number of seed users who can spread the information to all users interested in the specific topic over multiple online social networks (where some users belong in more than one online social networks simultaneously). The work in [19] studies the role of information diffusion to the evolution of the network topology considering the link formation process with respect to sources/retransmitters of the information, based on users' preferences. User interests in the information topics being propagated are also inferred and considered in [4] to detect active links in the diffusion of a given message over the network. Generally, most of the previous works, except from taking into account contact-related and topological factors affecting information diffusion dynamics [1, 13], they occasionally regard static users' interests [3, 4], but not the user interest temporal variability. In a closer spirit to our approach, [6] studies the spatio-temporal dynamics of information diffusion via partial differential equations, while incorporating time decreasing users' interest on the propagated messages. A similar study is performed for the case of malware dissemination over the Internet in [15]. Specifically, in [15], the infection rate decreases with time while this time dependence is shown via experimentation to model better the Code Red worm propagation. The reason for such decreasing infection rate is that worm spread over the Internet can be slowed down by countermeasures employed by users and congestion points arising over Internet. As in [15], in our approach, the introduction of the time evolving users' interests in the information propagation decisions along with the consideration of a network substrate abolishes the homogeneity assumption. However, contrary to [15] and [6], in this work we are not restricted to decreasing with time users' interests, but we apply diverse function forms of the latter (e.g., periodic).

Apart from analyzing the spreading, controlling the information diffusion over various types of networks via explicit, e.g., [7, 10, 20–22] or implicit control, e.g., [16], is highly important. A thorough overview of the current framework of controlling epidemics can be found in [7], including heuristic feedback methods and optimal control policies for both population dynamics and deterministic network models along with spectral control policies for the latter. The authors usually adopt optimal control frameworks for obtaining features allowing the control of the corresponding diffusion properties, which are modeled via differential equations (deterministic models). The work in [20], studies the possible attack strategies of malware over wireless networks and the extent of damage they can sustain. The control parameters consist of the transmission range and media scanning rate of the worm targeting at accelerating its spread. Malware information dissemination is also studied in [10], where the control signal distribution time is determined, aiming to minimize the number of infected nodes and the cost of control. Similar approaches for malware quarantining and filtering (e.g., configurable firewall) are developed and analyzed in [21–23]. These problem approaches, although different in various scopes compared to the target of this paper, they resemble and serve as driving forces to our proposed model and analysis.

Considering implicit control, in [16], malware information propagation is studied and analyzed over a homogeneous mixing network, where control takes the form of updates to nodes from an external source to which nodes reply via a best response (game theoretic) scheme. Also, in [16], there is an implicit introduction (i.e., via the time-varying state of the system) of time-varying behavior on the parameters of the information diffusion epidemic model. However, this takes place in a more restricted sense and with a different scope (i.e., malware propagation) compared to our work.

Our work dealing with non-malicious information, identifies a major driving force for the successfulness of diffusion, namely user interest and its temporal properties, opening up new directions for the optimal control of useful information diffusion taking into account these aspects as well. Moreover, although our approach adopts a similar problem formulation and analytical approach as in [20], contrary to [7, 10, 20–22], the state constraint, i.e., the epidemic-based differential equation of the evolution of the number of infected nodes, has time-varying parameters due to the temporal dependence of users' interests considered in this paper.

System model, notation and assumptions

We focus on information diffusion and its optimal control in generalized networks, where the substrate is a wireless multihop network, i.e., user devices. Two different spreading pathways develop in such networks, namely information diffusion via either Multimedia Messaging Service (MMS) in the social layer or via WiFi/bluetooth (P) in the physical substrate [1] (Fig. 1). The former acts as a "long-range" information spread, since nodes communicating directly at the social layer may be actually separated by many hops in the physical layer. MMS transfers act as diffusion shortcuts. On the contrary, P-type information transfers act as local information ripples over short-range areas around information processors.

We consider a wireless multihop network of N nodes uniformly and independently distributed on a square region of side L. Each node has a transmission radius R. For

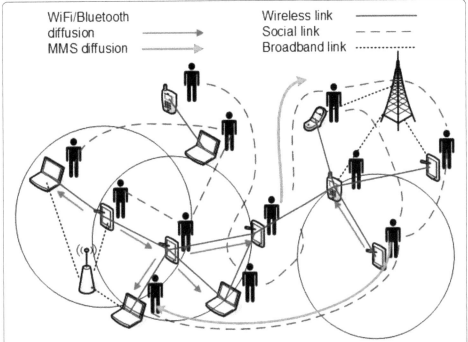

Fig. 1 The considered information diffusion mechanisms over generalized networks. WiFi/Bluetooth diffusion (*purple arrows*) includes all neighbors within the transmission range of the user (physical layer), while MMS diffusion (*green arrows*) may take place with only specific neighbors of a user in social layer depending on their interest values in the propagated information

simplicity, mobility is ignored, since compared to an MMS type of information spreading, the corresponding long-range information spreading achieved by mobility, which is essentially of P type, will lead to a similar, but smaller effect, as also argued in [1].

We assume M classes of information denoted by $m = 1...M$, as in [24]. Each class consists of messages on a specific topic, e.g., summer vacations advertisements. Information diffusion is studied separately for each class; however, interactions among separate classes are taken into consideration in the information diffusion model's probabilistic setting. Each node i is characterized by its interest in class m at time t, denoted as $R_i^m(t)$, where $\sum_{\forall m} R_i^m(t) \leq 1$, $\forall i$ (e.g., normalization over all classes). The information diffusion process proposed in this paper is based on the Susceptible–Infected–Susceptible (SIS) epidemic model [9]. We consider the following mapping. A node i is considered Infected (i.e., informed) for a specific class m of information if it possesses at least one message belonging in this class, otherwise i is considered Susceptible (i.e., not informed) for class m. This means that an informed/not-informed node is mapped to an infected/susceptible state correspondingly, in epidemiology terms. More precisely, the transition from the susceptible state to the infected state for a particular class takes place when a node receives information about this class, while an infected node transits back to the susceptible state when it deletes all messages for this class.

In the rest of the paper, we will employ the notation provided in Table 1. If the network is directed, the out-degree is considered. $f_1(x), f_2(x), f_3(x)$ are general functions that will be used in the information diffusion model. Finally, the system model will be further enhanced in "Optimal control framework for information diffusion", where the optimal

Table 1 Notation and explanation of symbols.

Symbol	Interpretation
$I^m(t)$	Number of Infected nodes for class m
$S^m(t)$	Number of Susceptible nodes concerning class m
$\mathcal{I}^m(t)$	Set of Infected nodes concerning class m
$\mathcal{N}_S(i)$	Set of node i's friends in the social layer
$\mathcal{N}_P(i)$	Set of connections of i in the wireless network (physical layer)
$0 \leq p_1, p_2, q \leq 1$	Probabilities defined in the proposed information diffusion model
N_S^{avg}	The average degree of all nodes in the social layer
$f_1(x)$	$f_1(x) : [0,1] \to [0,1]$ monotonically increasing on x
$f_2(x)$	$f_2(x) : [0,1] \to [0,1]$ monotonically decreasing on x
$f_3(x)$	$f_3(x) : [0,1] \to [0,1]$ monotonically increasing on x

control framework over the information dissemination modeling framework in generalized networks is introduced.

Information diffusion modeling and analysis without control

In this section, we describe the proposed information diffusion process that considers users' social features/interests. Its analysis via epidemic modeling leads to the incorporation of the impact of nodes' interests on the information diffusion dynamics. With respect to information diffusion, a node i is expected to perform/experience one of the following actions at each time t.

1. For the classes for which i is infected/informed:

    (a) i diffuses information about class m with probability $f_1(R_i^m(t))$ (also denoted as $f_1(t)$ for simplicity),

    (b) i deletes all messages about class m with probability $qf_2(R_i^m(t))$, where the parameter q is introduced to control the deletion process and $f_2(R_i^m(t))$ will be also denoted as $f_2(t)$ for simplicity.

    We consider that the duration of each time slot permits only the completion of one action, thus only one class m will be selected and either (a) or (b) will happen. This means that

    $$\sum_{m:\ i \in \mathcal{I}^m(t)} (f_1(R_i^m(t)) + qf_2(R_i^m(t))) \leq 1.$$

2. Node i performs another action—which is not of interest for the information diffusion—with probability equal to $1 - \sum_{m:\ i \in \mathcal{I}^m(t)} (f_1(R_i^m(t)) + qf_2(R_i^m(t)))$.

If choosing one class m for action (a) (with probability $f_1(R_i^m(t))$), node i performs one of the following:

- with probability p_1, node i employs an MMS type of transmission, including as receivers each $j \in \mathcal{N}_S(i)$ selected with probability $f_3(R_j^m(t))$ (also denoted as $f_3(t)$ for simplicity), where $f_3(R_j^m(t))$ for all $j \in \mathcal{N}_S(i)$ does not form a probability distribution,
- with probability p_2, node i broadcasts to all its $\mathcal{N}_P(i)$ neighbors (P-type action).

Note that $p_1 + p_2 \leq 1$.

The above diffusion process requires that there is always an infected node for every class to maintain the spreading. However, all infected nodes for a particular class may delete their information for this class, thus disrupting its diffusion. Exogenous impact such as the optimal control which will be introduced in "Optimal control framework for information diffusion", may be leveraged to alleviate in a certain degree such phenomena of extinction of a whole information class. In the case of P-type contacts, we do not consider the interests of users receiving a P-induced message, as the latter is broadcasted indiscriminately to all of them.

In the following, we model the dynamics of the evolution of the number of infected nodes for each class m, $I^m(t)$, via differential equations that approximate the system evolution. Specifically, the approximate dynamics of $I^m(t)$ are captured by the following ordinary differential equation (ODE),

$$
\begin{aligned}
\frac{\mathrm{d}I^m(t)}{\mathrm{d}t} &= p_1 f_1^{\mathrm{avg}}(t) f_3^{\mathrm{avg}}(t) \frac{S^m(t)}{N} I^m(t) N_s^{\mathrm{avg}} \\
&\quad + p_2 N \frac{\pi R^2}{L^2} \frac{S^m(t)}{N} I^m(t) f_1^{\mathrm{avg}}(t) \\
&\quad - q I^m(t) f_2^{\mathrm{avg}}(t),
\end{aligned}
\tag{1}
$$

where $f_3^{\mathrm{avg}}(t)$ is the average or the expected value of all f_3 functions over the network at time t for the corresponding class m. Functions $f_1^{\mathrm{avg}}(t)$, $f_2^{\mathrm{avg}}(t)$ are similarly defined. The initial conditions are $I^m(0) = I_0^m, \forall m$, i.e., I_0^m nodes are initially infected for each information class m via the social layer.

The ODE (1) has a unique solution when $f_1^{\mathrm{avg}}(t)$, $f_2^{\mathrm{avg}}(t)$, $f_3^{\mathrm{avg}}(t)$ are continuous functions with respect to time (Cauchy–Lipschitz Theorem [25]). The right-hand side is obviously Lipschitz continuous with respect to I^m. This fact has an impact on the design of possible forms for the interests' functions $R_i^m(t)$, $\forall m, i$, which should be continuous in time. It also has impact on the design of possible formats for the functions $f_1^{\mathrm{avg}}(t)$, $f_2^{\mathrm{avg}}(t)$, $f_3^{\mathrm{avg}}(t)$.

A suitable selection for the functions f_1, f_2, f_3 in the working example scenarios that follow is:

$$
\begin{aligned}
f_1(R_i^m(t)) &= \frac{R_i^m(t)}{2M}, \\
f_2(R_i^m(t)) &= \frac{1 - R_i^m(t)}{2M}, \\
f_3(R_j^m(t)) &= R_j^m(t).
\end{aligned}
\tag{2}
$$

This configuration is not restrictive in the sense that others may be designed for other scenarios/applications. It is important to note that Eq. (1) is approximate since averages or expected values of the functions f_1, f_2, f_3 are used. However, such an approximate form can be used to demonstrate the important characteristics of information diffusion dynamics in specific interesting cases that will be examined via appropriately designed scenarios in the sequel.

Scenario 1: periodic users' interests

In this scenario, two classes of information are considered. The time continuous interests' functions take sinusoidal forms to express users' time periodicity of their interest with respect to the propagated information. Specifically, $R_i^1(t) = 1 - A_i \sin^2(a(t + b_i)) + B_i$, $\forall i$, for class $m = 1$, where $a > 0$ determines the period of users' interests and A_i, b_i, B_i are appropriately defined constants. Then, $R_i^2(t) = A_i \sin^2(a(t + b_i)) - B_i$, $\forall i$, so that $R_i^1(t) + R_i^2(t) = 1$, $\forall t, i$. Note that, we consider the same frequency for all sinusoidal interests assuming the propagation of information that intrigues the attention of all users over specific time periods such as vacations, summer sports, Halloween, etc.

Based on the configuration for the functions f_1, f_2, f_3 defined above (Eq. 2), their average values for class 1 become

$$f_1^{\text{avg}}(t) = \frac{1 - A \sin^2(a(t + b)) + B}{2M},$$

$$f_2^{\text{avg}}(t) = \frac{A \sin^2(a(t + b)) - B}{2M},$$

$$f_3^{\text{avg}}(t) = 1 - A \sin^2(a(t + b)) + B,$$

where $b_i = b$, $\forall i$, and the constants A, B are computed by averaging the interests over all users at time t. The average values of functions f_1, f_2, f_3 for class 2 are defined similarly.

We can also assume that $f_1^{\text{avg}}(t)$, $f_2^{\text{avg}}(t)$, $f_3^{\text{avg}}(t)$ represent the expected values of the corresponding functions of users' interests at time t. Thus, users' interests will vary randomly according to a distribution with mean value $1 - A \sin^2(a(t + b)) + B$ for class 1, letting the complementary interest (i.e., with mean value $A \sin^2(a(t + b)) - B$) to be assigned to class 2.

In this case, the ODE (1) for class 1, becomes

$$\frac{dI^1(t)}{dt} = \frac{p_1 N_s^{\text{avg}}}{N}(N - I^1(t))I^1(t)\frac{(1 - A \sin^2(a(t + b)) + B)^2}{2M}$$

$$+ p_2 \frac{\pi R^2}{L^2}(N - I^1(t))I^1(t)\frac{(1 - A \sin^2(a(t + b)) + B)}{2M}$$

$$- qI^1(t)\frac{(A \sin^2(a(t + b)) - B)}{2M}, \tag{3}$$

and similarly, the ODE (1) for class 2, can be written as

$$\frac{dI^2(t)}{dt} = \frac{p_1 N_s^{\text{avg}}}{N}(N - I^2(t))I^2(t)\frac{(A \sin^2(a(t + b)) - B)^2}{2M}$$

$$+ p_2 \frac{\pi R^2}{L^2}(N - I^2(t))I^2(t)\frac{(A \sin^2(a(t + b)) - B)}{2M}$$

$$- qI^2(t)\frac{(1 - A \sin^2(a(t + b)) + B)}{2M}. \tag{4}$$

The solution of both Eqs. (3), (4) takes a complex form which does not provide any intuition regarding the dynamics of change of the number of infected nodes for each class, $I^1(t)$, $I^2(t)$. For this reason, we apply a finite difference approach to approximate them as follows. Let $M_1(t)$ be the right-hand side of Eq. (3) and $M_2(t)$ be the right-hand side of Eq. (4). Then, the finite difference scheme with sufficiently small time step $\Delta t > 0$ and $t \geq 0$ yields:

$$I^1(t + \Delta t) = I^1(t) + M_1(t) \cdot \Delta t, \tag{5}$$

$$I^2(t + \Delta t) = I^2(t) + M_2(t) \cdot \Delta t. \tag{6}$$

It can be observed that when $1 - A\sin^2(a(t + b)) + B \cong 0$, $M_1(t) \cong -\frac{qI^1(t)}{2M}$, thus $I^1(t + \Delta t) < I^1(t)$ for that time periods, while complementarily $S^1(t + \Delta t) > S^1(t)$. The converse holds for the time periods where $1 - A\sin^2(a(t + b)) + B \cong 1$. Therefore, the periodicity of user interests is reflected in the information diffusion dynamics, where it is possible that the number of infected nodes does not converge to a specific value but rather fluctuates according to a time period determined by user interest periodicity.

Scenario 2: comparison of information diffusion dynamics among groups with different characteristics

In this scenario, we apply constant interests to study how information of a specific subject spreads in groups characterized by different features such as in the second example described in the introductory section ("Background"). This special case is similar to the SIS models developed in literature [8, 9] in the sense that the parameters applied in the ODEs describing the dynamics of information diffusion are constant, contrary to the time varying parameters $(f_1^{\text{avg}}(t), f_2^{\text{avg}}(t), f_3^{\text{avg}}(t))$ considered in this paper. Therefore, the already existing schemes [26] constitute special cases of our proposed diffusion model.

In this framework, we consider two groups and one information class (e.g., class 1). For both groups $R_i^1(t) = a$, $\forall i, 0 < a < 1$, where for the first group a is close to 1 while in the second group a gets closer to 0. In this particular case of constant interests, the solution of Eq. (1) attains a less complex form than in Scenario 1. However, we will use again the finite difference approximation of Eqs. (5), (6), where the definitions of $M_1(t)$, $M_2(t)$ are based on constant interests adapted for the two groups correspondingly, to get more intuition about the derived convergence in the number of infected nodes. Specifically, as it will be verified via simulation and numerical results in "Simulation and numerical results without applying control", a higher constant interest by users implies convergence of the number of infected nodes to a higher value.

Scenario 3: increasing vs. decreasing users' interest

In this scenario, there exist two classes of information, while the population has increasing interest for the one class and decreasing for the other. The appropriate interest functions for this case are formulated, $\forall i$, as follows:

$$R_i^1(t) = B\frac{At}{At + C}, \quad R_i^2(t) = B\frac{C}{At + C}, \tag{7}$$

where A, B, C are constants.

Again, we will use the finite difference approximation of Eqs. (5), (6), where the definitions of $M_1(t)$, $M_2(t)$ for each class correspondingly are based on Eq. (7).

Optimal control framework for information diffusion

In this section, we introduce an optimal control framework for the previously presented information diffusion model for a specific class m. The objective in this optimal control problem is to maximize the number of infected (informed) nodes for a topic/class m by applying an exogenous aid/force, i.e., the control, while taking into account associated control costs, e.g., advertising cost. The motivation behind this is twofold. First it might be necessary to apply a control action to boost users' interest to increase information spreading. Secondly, more resources might be required (by increasing a control signal) when users are more interested in a topic to conserve resources by not wasting them when users are not interested in the propagated information. Thus, this approach will allow affecting the information diffusion over the susceptible (non-informed) users, via properly controlling user interests.

Assuming the control signal is given by a function $u(.) = \{u(t)|t \in [0, T]\}$, we aim at maximizing the objective function:

$$J(u(.)) = \int_0^T \left(k_1 I^m(t) + k_2 u(t)\right) dt + k_I I^m(T), \tag{8}$$

where $k_1, k_I \geq 0$, $k_2 \leq 0$ are parameters expressing the trade-off between control cost and diffusion efficiency. Parameters k_1, k_2 refer to the operation during a specific time interval within $[0, T]$ and k_I refers to the final state of the system. We aim at finding an optimal control $u^*(.)$ such that:

$$J(u^*(.)) = \max_{u(.)} J(u(.)). \tag{9}$$

The control problem will be solved subject to the approximate dynamics of the evolution of the number of informed nodes, which is similar to Eq. (1):

$$\begin{aligned}
\frac{dI^m(t)}{dt} &= \frac{N_s^{avg} p_1}{N} f_1^{avg}(t) f_3^{avg}(t)(N - I^m(t)) I^m(t) g_1(u(t)) \\
&\quad + p_2 \frac{\pi R^2}{L^2} f_1^{avg}(t) I^m(t)(N - I^m(t)) g_1(u(t)) \\
&\quad - q I^m(t) f_2^{avg}(t) g_2(u(t)),
\end{aligned} \tag{10}$$

with $I^m(0) = I_0^m$ ($S^m(0) = N - I_0^m$). Also the following state conditions should hold:

$$N = I^m(t) + S^m(t), \ 0 \leq I^m(t) \leq N, \ t \in [0, T], \tag{11}$$

for every t. Note that Eq. (10) differs from Eq. (1) due to the introduction of the control $u(t)$ in the summands of its right-hand side, where the probabilities $f_1^{avg}(t)$, $f_2^{avg}(t)$ have been replaced with $f_1^{avg}(t) g_1(u(t))$, $f_2^{avg}(t) g_2(u(t))$. The control $u(.)$ depends on the controller's budget for topic m, while the control region is defined as $\Omega = \{u(.) : [0, T] \rightarrow \Re | u_{min} \leq u(t) \leq u_{max}, \forall t\}$ and also each $u(.)$ is a piece-wise continuous function such that its left and right limits exist. Functions g_1, g_2 are non-negative, differentiable and either convex or concave with respect to u. While g_1 is increasing with u, g_2 is decreasing, and $g_1, g_2 : [u_{\min}, u_{\max}] \to [0, 1]$. The control might take the form of incentives for increasing user interest, or it may exploit the increased user interest to reinforce information spreading, while such behavior will be explored in the following.

The next proposition allows us to ignore the state constraints expressed in Eq. (11) in the rest of the analysis.

Proposition 1 *For any $u(.) \in \Omega$, the state function $I^m(.) : [0, T] \to \mathfrak{R}$ that satisfies $I^m(0) = I_0^m$, also satisfies Eq. (11).*

Proof Let t_0 be the first time instant in $[0, T]$ where $I^m(t_0) = 0$ or $I^m(t_0) = N$.

- If $I^m(t_0) = 0$ then $S^m(t_0) = N$ and $\frac{dI^m(t)}{dt}|_{t=t_0^+} = 0$, meaning that $I^m(t) = 0$, for every $t > t_0, t \leq T$.
- If $I^m(t_0) = N$ then $S^m(t_0) = 0$. Thus, $\frac{dI^m(t)}{dt}|_{t=t_0^+} = -qN f_2^{\text{avg}}(t_0) g_2(u(t_0)) < 0$, since $f_2^{\text{avg}}(t_0), g_2(u(t_0)) > 0$, meaning that $I^m(t_0^+) \leq N$. Similarly for all other $t' \in (t_0, T]$ where $I^m(t') = N$. $\qquad\square$

The following proposition proves that the number of infected nodes for class m, $I^m(t)$ is strictly positive for every $t \in [0, T]$.

Proposition 2 *We have that $I^m(t) \geq I_0^m e^{-q f_{2\max}^{\text{avg}} g_2(u_{\min})t} \geq 0, \forall t \in [0, T]$.*

Proof It holds that $\frac{dI^m(t)}{dt} \geq -qI^m(t)f_2^{\text{avg}}(t)g_2(u(t))$, which means that $\frac{I^m(t)'}{I^m(t)} \geq -qf_{2\max}^{\text{avg}}g_2(u_{\min})$, where $f_{2\max}^{\text{avg}} = \max_{\forall t} f_2^{\text{avg}}(t)$ and since g_2 is decreasing with u. Thus, $\ln I^m(t) \geq -qf_{2\max}^{\text{avg}}g_2(u_{\min})t + \ln I^m(0)$, yielding $I^m(t) \geq I_0^m e^{-q f_{2\max}^{\text{avg}} g_2(u_{\min})t}$, for every $t \in [0, T]$. $\qquad\square$

Definition 1 The pair $(I^m(.), u(.))$ is an admissible pair if the following hold: (i) $u(.) \in \Omega$, (ii) the state $(I^m(.))$ constraint of Eq. (10) holds. Then $u(.)$ is called an admissible control [20].

Definition 2 An admissible control $u(.)$ is an optimal control, if $J(u(.)) \geq J(\underline{u}(.))$ for all admissible controls $\underline{u}(.)$ [20].

Based on these two definitions, we will apply Pontryagin's Maximum Principle [20, 27–29] to determine the optimal control's functional form and study its properties. Let us denote as $\lambda(t)$ the adjoint/costate variable of the Pontryagin's Maximum Principle [27] at time $t \in [0, T]$. First, we define the Hamiltonian function, $\mathcal{H}$, at time t as:

$$
\begin{aligned}
\mathcal{H}(I^m(t), u(t), \lambda(t)) = {} & k_1 I^m(t) + k_2 u(t) \\
& + \lambda(t) \Bigg[\frac{N_s^{\text{avg}} p_1}{N} f_1^{\text{avg}}(t) f_3^{\text{avg}}(t)(N - I^m(t)) I^m(t) g_1(u(t)) \\
& + p_2 \frac{\pi R^2}{L^2} f_1^{\text{avg}}(t) I^m(t)(N - I^m(t)) g_1(u(t)) \\
& - q I^m(t) f_2^{\text{avg}}(t) g_2(u(t)) \Bigg].
\end{aligned}
\tag{12}
$$

Assuming that $u^*(.)$ is the optimal control value and $I^{m^*}(.)$ is the corresponding state trajectory, i.e., the one solving Eq. (10) for $u^*(.)$, according to Pontryagin's Maximum Principle [27], there exists a function $\lambda^*(.) : [0, T] \to \mathfrak{R}$ such that

$$\frac{\mathrm{d}\lambda^*(t)}{\mathrm{d}t} = -\frac{\partial \mathcal{H}}{\partial I^m} = -k_1 - \lambda^*(t)\left[\frac{N_s^{\text{avg}}p_1}{N}f_1^{\text{avg}}(t)f_3^{\text{avg}}(t)(N - 2I^{m^*}(t))g_1(u^*(t))\right.$$

$$+ p_2\frac{\pi R^2}{L^2}f_1^{\text{avg}}(t)(N - 2I^{m^*}(t))g_1(u^*(t))$$

$$\left. - qf_2^{\text{avg}}(t)g_2(u^*(t))\right], \tag{13}$$

$$\lambda^*(T) = k_I (\text{transversality condition}), \tag{14}$$

where $\lambda^*(.)$ is the optimal costate (adjoint) function and also the optimal control, $u^*(.)$, is computed as:

$$u^*(t) = u(t) \in \arg\max_{\underline{u}\in\Omega} \mathcal{H}(I^{m^*}(t), \underline{u}, \lambda^*(t)), \ 0 \le t \le T. \tag{15}$$

For simplicity, from now on we omit the symbol $*$ from the optimal values. We can prove the following proposition which will be useful in studying the properties of the optimal control function.

Proposition 3 *We have that $\lambda(t) > 0$ for $t \in [0, T)$.*

Proof We follow a similar proof to the one of Lemma 2 in [20]. First we show that $\lambda(t)$ is strictly positive over an interval of non-zero length towards the end of $[0, T)$. It holds that $\lambda(T) = k_I \ge 0$. If $k_I > 0$, this statement holds due to continuity. If $k_I = 0$, then from (13) and for $t = T$ we have: $\frac{d\lambda(t)}{dt}|_{t=T} = -k_1 < 0$, i.e., descending from positive values before reaching the value $k_I = 0$, and this statement also holds.

As $t' < T$, consider the latest time in $[0, T)$ that $\lambda(t') = 0$, i.e., $\lambda(t) > 0$ for $t' < t < T$. Then, $\frac{d\lambda(t)}{dt}|_{t=t'+} = -k_1 < 0$ which is impossible since for $t > t'$, λ is positive and thus it should increase from the zero value. The latter statement concludes the proof of Proposition 3. □

Let us now omit the time dependence over the employed notation for brevity reasons. We can define the functional:

$$\phi(u) = k_2 u + \lambda\left[\frac{N_s^{\text{avg}}p_1}{N}f_1^{\text{avg}}f_3^{\text{avg}}(N - I^m)I^m g_1(u)\right.$$

$$+ p_2\frac{\pi R^2}{L^2}f_1^{\text{avg}}I^m(N - I^m)g_1(u)$$

$$\left. - qI^m f_2^{\text{avg}}g_2(u)\right], \tag{16}$$

and search for an optimal u, i.e., such that $\phi(u) \geq \phi(\underline{u})$ for all admissible $\underline{u} \in \Omega$. The functional $\phi(u)$ is derived by the Hamiltonian (Eq. 12) for a particular time, considering only the terms that depend on u.

Given the possible forms of the functions g_1, g_2 with respect to the control u (convex or concave), the following cases can be identified:

1. g_1 convex and g_2 concave. Then ϕ is convex with respect to u. Due to convex maximization, the optimal control will be necessarily at the extrema of the range of the control, determined by comparison as:

$$u^* = \begin{cases} u_{\min} & \text{if } \phi(u_{\min}) > \phi(u_{\max}), \\ u_{\max} & \text{if } \phi(u_{\min}) < \phi(u_{\max}). \end{cases} \tag{17}$$

2. g_1 concave and g_2 convex. Then ϕ is concave with respect to u. In this case, a concave maximization takes place, where the maxima of $\phi(u)$ occur at the points where the partial derivative with respect to u is zero, or at the extrema of the range of the control, determined by comparison. The equation $\frac{\partial \phi}{\partial u} = 0$ becomes:

$$-\frac{k_2}{\lambda} = \frac{\partial g_1(u)}{\partial u} \left[\frac{N_s^{\text{avg}} p_1}{N} f_1^{\text{avg}} f_3^{\text{avg}} (N - I^m) I^m \right.$$
$$\left. + p_2 \frac{\pi R^2}{L^2} f_1^{\text{avg}} I^m (N - I^m) \right]$$
$$- \frac{\partial g_2(u)}{\partial u} q I^m f_2^{\text{avg}}, \tag{18}$$

where $\lambda > 0$ from Proposition 3. If u' is the solution of the above, then the optimal control becomes:

$$u^* = \max\left\{ u_{\min}, \min\{u', u_{\max}\} \right\}. \tag{19}$$

In this case based on the explicit forms of functions g_1, g_2, we can study possible relations/properties of the optimal control with respect to users' interests, as it will be performed in the following sections.

3. g_1 concave and g_2 concave. We have

$$\frac{\partial^2 \phi(u)}{\partial u^2} = \lambda \left[\frac{N_s^{\text{avg}} p_1}{N} f_1^{\text{avg}} f_3^{\text{avg}} (N - I^m) I^m \frac{\partial^2 g_1(u)}{\partial u^2} \right.$$
$$+ p_2 \frac{\pi R^2}{L^2} f_1^{\text{avg}} I^m (N - I^m) \frac{\partial^2 g_1(u)}{\partial u^2}$$
$$\left. - q I^m f_2^{\text{avg}} \frac{\partial^2 g_2(u)}{\partial u^2} \right], \tag{20}$$

where $A_1 = \frac{N_s^{\text{avg}} p_1}{N} f_1^{\text{avg}} f_3^{\text{avg}} (N - I^m) I^m \frac{\partial^2 g_1(u)}{\partial u^2} + p_2 \frac{\pi R^2}{L^2} f_1^{\text{avg}} I^m (N - I^m) \frac{\partial^2 g_1(u)}{\partial u^2} \leq 0$

and $B_1 = q I^m f_2^{\text{avg}} \frac{\partial^2 g_2(u)}{\partial u^2} \leq 0$. Thus, $\frac{\partial^2 \phi(u)}{\partial u^2} \leq 0$ if $|A_1| \geq |B_1|$, that leads to a concave maximization as in case 2 above, or $\frac{\partial^2 \phi(u)}{\partial u^2} \geq 0$ if $|A_1| \leq |B_1|$, that leads to a convex maximization as in case 1 above.

4. g_1 convex and g_2 convex. Then $\frac{\partial^2 g_1(u)}{\partial u^2} \geq 0$, $\frac{\partial^2 g_2(u)}{\partial u^2} \geq 0$. Thus, $\frac{\partial^2 \phi(u)}{\partial u^2} \geq 0$ if $|A_1| \geq |B_1|$, that leads to a convex maximization as in case 1 above, or $\frac{\partial^2 \phi(u)}{\partial u^2} \leq 0$ if $|A_1| \leq |B_1|$, that leads to a concave maximization as in case 2 above.

We should note that the controller applies one kind of control with aim to increase $I^m(t)$ trading-off cost, but this impacts in a different way each part of the information propagation equation (i.e., Eq. 10) via the functions $g_1(u), g_2(u)$.

At this point, we study the case 2 more extensively, by choosing a (non-restrictive) specific form for the control functions $g_1(u)$, $g_2(u)$, as follows:

$$
\begin{aligned}
g_1(u) &= 1 + \frac{\ln(1 + u)}{\ln(1 + u_{\max})}, \\
g_2(u) &= \frac{\ln(1 + u_{\max}) - \ln(1 + u))}{\ln(1 + u_{\max})}.
\end{aligned} \tag{21}
$$

This choice serves the purpose of boosting the number of infected (informed) nodes for the examined class by increasing probabilities of communicating/transferring knowledge via $g_1(u) > 1$ in the first and second summands of the right-hand side of Eq. (10), and by decreasing probabilities of knowledge "deletion" via $g_2(u) < 1$ in the last summand of the right-hand side of Eq. (10). Then, after computing $\frac{\partial g_1(u)}{\partial u}$, $\frac{\partial g_2(u)}{\partial u}$, replacing them in Eq. (18) and solving the latter, the optimal control takes the following formula:

$$
u^* = \left\{ -1 - \frac{\lambda \Gamma}{k_2} \right\}_{u_{\min}}^{u_{\max}}, \tag{22}
$$

where $\{ \}_{u_{\min}}^{u_{\max}}$ expresses projection to $[u_{\min}, u_{\max}]$ and

$$
\Gamma = \frac{1}{\ln(1 + u_{\max})} \left[\frac{N_s^{\mathrm{avg}} p_1}{N} f_1^{\mathrm{avg}} f_3^{\mathrm{avg}} (N - I^m) I^m + p_2 \frac{\pi R^2}{L^2} f_1^{\mathrm{avg}} I^m (N - I^m) \right.
$$
$$
\left. + q I^m f_2^{\mathrm{avg}} \right]. \tag{23}
$$

At this point, we study some properties of Γ (Eq. 23) that will assist in the interpretation of the observable behavior of the optimal control in "Simulation results, numerical results and discussion in controlled information diffusion". First, we study the dependence of Γ on the values of interest for the examined class m, i.e., R_{avg}^m. By considering Eq. (2) providing the types of $f_1^{\mathrm{avg}}, f_2^{\mathrm{avg}}, f_3^{\mathrm{avg}}$, Γ is increasing with R_{avg}^m, i.e., $\frac{\partial \Gamma}{\partial R_{\mathrm{avg}}^m} > 0$ if

$$
I^m < N - \frac{q}{\frac{N_s^{\mathrm{avg}} p_1 2 R_{\mathrm{avg}}^m}{N} + \frac{p_2 \pi R^2}{L^2}} = I_{TH}. \tag{24}
$$

Therefore, Γ will become an increasing function of interest for class m only if the number of infected nodes for class m becomes less that the threshold I_{TH}. This behavior is also expected for the optimal control itself, u^* (Eq. 22), since by Proposition 3 it holds $-\frac{\lambda}{k_2} > 0$ (if ignoring the dependence of λ on R_{avg}^m). This fact, which will be verified via numerical evaluations in "Simulation results, numerical results and discussion in controlled information diffusion", indicates the targeted trade-off between information spread and cost, while leveraging users' interests for class m. If the number of infected nodes for class m is high enough, higher that I_{TH}, the optimal control saves resources when the corresponding user interest for class m increases. When the number of infected nodes falls below I_{TH}, the control increases with user interest, aiming to leverage from higher values of interest to drastically boost the number of infected nodes for class m. This behavior emerges also in the case of power control in a wireless channel, where high power values are optimal under good channel conditions, to exploit the maximum possible data transfer rates [30]. Since I_{TH} (Eq. 24) is time varying, as R_{avg}^m evolves with time ("Information diffusion modeling and analysis without control"), the monotony of Γ may also change with time. Generally, higher values of R_{avg}^m lead to a higher range of values of the number of infected nodes for which Γ is increasing with interest for class m.

Obviously, Γ is a concave function of I^m, attaining its maximum at
$I_{max}^m = \frac{FR_{avg}^m + G(\frac{1}{R_{avg}^m} - 1) + K}{DR_{avg}^m + E}$, where $F = \frac{N_S^{avg} p_1}{2M}$, $E = \frac{p_2 \pi R^2}{L^2 M}$, $D = \frac{N_S^{avg} p_1}{MN}$, $G = \frac{q}{2M}$, $K = \frac{p_2 \pi R^2 N}{L^2 2M}$. Note that I_{max}^m is decreasing with interest when $(FE + GD - DK)(R_{avg}^m)^2 - 2GDR_{avg}^m - GE < 0$, where D, E, F, G, K, are determined by the parameters of the system. In this case, for higher values of interest it is intuitively expected that the optimal control (Eq. 22) will achieve its maximum on a lower value of I^m, if ignoring any dependence of λ on the examined parameters, i.e., I^m, R_{avg}^m.

Computing the optimal control value

Although Eqs. (17, 19) provide the form of the optimal control, computing the optimal control value is more complex, demanding the knowledge of the value of the adjoint variable, λ, for each t. In this section, we construct the Hamilton–Jacobi–Bellman (HJB) equation [27–29] and solve it via a numerical approach to obtain optimal control values within the control time interval ([0, T]).

Definition 3   We define the Value function $V(I^m, t)$, where $I^m(t) = I^m \in \mathfrak{R}$, $0 \leq t \leq T$, as follows:

$$V(I^m, t) = \sup_{u(.) \in \Omega} J(u(.)), \quad V(I^m, T) = k_I I^m \text{ (final condition)}.$$

Actually, the Value function is obtained by varying the starting time of control within the control interval [0, T] and the initial value of infected nodes for class m. The HJB equation is formulated as the following partial differential equation:

$$\frac{dV(I^m, t)}{dt} + \max_{u \in \Omega} \mathcal{H}\left(I^m, u, \frac{\partial V(I^m, t)}{\partial I^m}\right) = 0,$$

$$V(I^m, T) = k_I I^m,$$

$$(25)$$

where $\mathcal{H}$ is the Hamiltonian function defined in Eq. (12). Also, at each time $t \in [0, T]$, we have $\frac{\partial V(I^{m*}(t), t)}{\partial I^m} = \lambda^*(t)$, where the symbol $*$ again is used for denoting the optimal values obtained for $u^*(t)$. At this point, we will solve numerically the HJB equation [31] (Eq. 25) to compute the Value function for each $t \in [0, T)$. Then, the optimal control values will be obtained via Eqs. (17, 19) if replacing λ with $\frac{\partial V}{\partial I^m}$ both computed at the examined time t. Applying a finite difference scheme and denoting as $u(t)$ the optimal control value, Eq. (25) takes the following form:

$$\frac{V(I^m, t) - V(I^m, t - \Delta t)}{\Delta t} + k_1 I^m + k_2 u(t)$$

$$+ \frac{V(I^m + \Delta I^m, t) - V(I^m - \Delta I^m, t)}{2\Delta I^m} \left[\frac{N_s^{avg} p_1}{N} f_1^{avg}(t) f_3^{avg}(t)(N - I^m) I^m g_1(u(t)) \right.$$

$$\left. + p_2 \frac{\pi R^2}{L^2} f_1^{avg}(t) I^m (N - I^m) g_1(u(t)) - q I^m f_2^{avg}(t) g_2(u(t)) \right] = 0, \tag{26}$$

$$V(I^m, T) = k_I I^m,$$

where ΔI^m, Δt are the steps of state and time and Eq. (26) is solved backwards since we know the Value function at the end, T, of the control time interval. Specifically, we compute the Value function for all $I^m \in \{1, 2, ..., N\}$ at time $0 \leq t - \Delta t < T$ from the corresponding ones at time t. When computing the optimal control values via Eqs. (19), (17) we replace λ with $\frac{\partial V}{\partial I^m}\big|_t = \frac{V(I^m + \Delta I^m, t) - V(I^m - \Delta I^m, t)}{2\Delta I^m}$. Furthermore, in the numerical solution of the HJB, we apply as a boundary condition for the partial derivative of the Value function with respect to state the following $\frac{\partial V}{\partial I^m}\big|_{t=T} = \frac{\partial V}{\partial I^m}\big|_{t=T-\Delta t}$.

Simulation and numerical results without applying control

In this section, we present simulation and numerical results for each users' interest scenario of "Information diffusion modeling and analysis without control". Specifically, the simulation results refer to the realization of the diffusion model described in "Information diffusion modeling and analysis without control" in MATLAB, while numerical results refer to the approximate solution (via finite difference scheme) of the ODEs in each scenario with the same parameters as in the corresponding simulation.

The simulation setting is as follows. We consider a generalized network, the wireless substrate of which consists of a wireless multihop network with $N = 500$ nodes deployed over a square region with side $L = 350m$ and with homogeneous transmission radius among nodes equal to $R = 25m$. All simulation results are obtained as averages over several wireless topologies (#2) and multiple repetitions (#3) for the diffusion at each topology. Furthermore, we examine two overlaying social network topologies over the same set of nodes as the wireless substrate, namely one scale-free and one small-world [32]. For the scale-free network topology, the social degree for each node is drawn from the power-law distribution with exponent 3, as observed for many social networks [33] (specifically the probability density function is $f(x) = \left(\frac{2}{x}\right)^3$, $x \geq 2$), and the corresponding social layer's neighbors of each node are chosen randomly. The small-world topology is constructed following the Watts & Strogatz paradigm [34]. For both topologies, $N_S^{avg} \cong 4$. However, the degree distribution in the small-world topology is much more homogeneous than the corresponding one of the scale-free social topology. Also, the scale-free topology presents low average path length, which is a small-world feature [32]. Note that the value Δt should be appropriately small, so that the solution of the ODE derived via the finite difference scheme (Eqs. 5, 6), approximates closely the precise solution of the ODE. We chose $\Delta t = 0.4$. Finally, 10 nodes out of 500 are initially infected (e.g., via MMS) for each class in all simulation and numerical results that follow.

Scenario 1: information diffusion dynamics in the case of periodic users' interests

In this scenario, we consider that the users' interests vary uniformly and randomly with mean value $1 - \frac{1}{4} \sin^2(\frac{\pi}{180}(t + 100)) - \frac{1}{7}$ for the first class and $\frac{1}{4} \sin^2(\frac{\pi}{180}(t + 100)) + \frac{1}{7}$ for the second class with the constraint that the interests of one node for the two classes are complementary (i.e., in the corresponding scenario of "Information diffusion modeling and analysis without control", $A = \frac{1}{4}$, $B = -\frac{1}{7}$, $a = \frac{\pi}{180}$, $b = 100$). Therefore, the period of the interests' functions is one year, a fact that can be reflected in realistic situations as the ones explained in "Background". The values of p_1, p_2, q will be specified in each simulation case.

Fig. 2a compares the dynamics of the information diffusion for class 1 as derived by numerically solving Eq. (3) with the results obtained via simulations according to the proposed diffusion model in "Information diffusion modeling and analysis without control". The same is illustrated in Fig. 2b for class 2 (where the numerical results are obtained via numerically solving Eq. 4). The involved parameters take the values $p_1 = p_2 = 0.5$, i.e., P and MMS types of transfer take place with the same probability in case of diffusion and $q = 0.2$. The results are the same independently of the social topology, i.e., small-world or scale-free.

The periodic behavior of users' interests is also reflected in the dynamics of information diffusion, as expected from the discussion in "Information diffusion modeling and analysis without control", and the number of infected nodes does not converge to a specific value as predicted by the conventional models in the literature [1, 13]. We observe that for class 1, the numerical results approximate well the ones obtained from simulations. In the case of class 2, i.e., in the case of lower interest for the information under propagation, it can be stated that the numerical results mostly overestimate the number of infected nodes. This observation can be explained by the fact that in the simulations, the number of infected nodes may become zero when all nodes delete their messages for a particular class, whereas according to Proposition 2, the theoretical number of infected nodes is always greater than zero. Thus, in the simulation it becomes likely that the information propagation for a class terminates (a fact that becomes more probable when interest values are lower), whereas in theory there is always enough quantity of infected nodes to spread information if the users' interest for the latter increases.

The results in Fig. 3a, b concern only the case of P type, while the results in Fig. 4a, b refer to the case of applying MMS type alone. By comparing these figures, it is observed

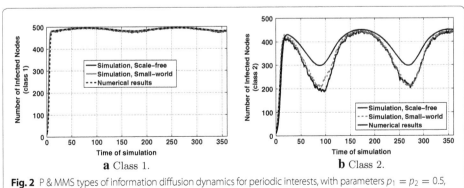

a Class 1.   **b** Class 2.

Fig. 2 P & MMS types of information diffusion dynamics for periodic interests, with parameters $p_1 = p_2 = 0.5$, $q = 0.2$

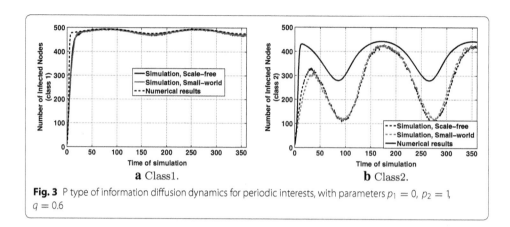

Fig. 3 P type of information diffusion dynamics for periodic interests, with parameters $p_1 = 0$, $p_2 = 1$, $q = 0.6$

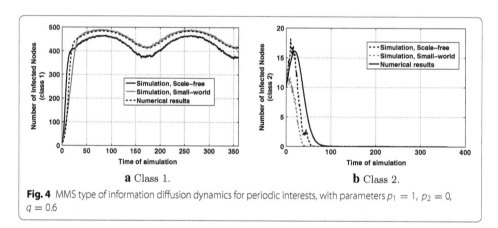

Fig. 4 MMS type of information diffusion dynamics for periodic interests, with parameters $p_1 = 1$, $p_2 = 0$, $q = 0.6$

that P type plays a significant role in maintaining the diffusion alive with respect to class 2 in which users' interest for the diffused information attains lower values. Generally, P type further boosts information spreading for both classes. In Fig. 4a, for class 1, the diffusion dynamics over the small-world topology approximate much closer the numerical results than over the scale-free topology, whereas in the other cases, both topologies present similar behavior.

To conclude for this scenario, the theoretical model overestimates the volume of the information spreading, especially for class 2, which is characterized by lower values of interest. Also, the behavior in both cases of social topologies, i.e., small-world and scale-free, does not differentiate significantly.

Scenario 2: information diffusion dynamics in the presence of groups with different characteristics

In this evaluation scenario, based on the description of "Information diffusion modeling and analysis without control", we consider one information class and two groups with different interests in this information class. Group 1 has an interest value of 0.8 and Group 2 has an interest value of 0.2. Fig. 5a, b indicate that the interest plays significant role in the number of infected nodes to which the dynamics of information diffusion converge. In Group 1 the participants of which are highly interested in this information class, finally all nodes become infected. The parameters' values are specified in the legends of the figures.

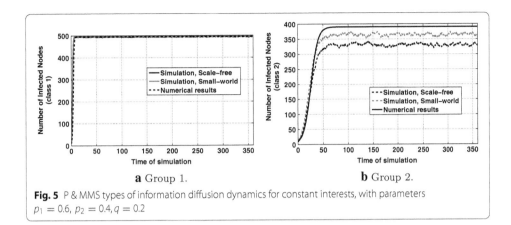

Fig. 5 P & MMS types of information diffusion dynamics for constant interests, with parameters $p_1 = 0.6$, $p_2 = 0.4$, $q = 0.2$

It is also observed that for high interest the approximation of the theoretical model to the simulation results is satisfactory, while for lower interest, the theoretical model overestimates the simulation results. However, in the latter case (Fig. 5b), the diffusion dynamics over the small-world topology obtained via simulations lie much closer to the numerical results. In Fig. 5a, where interest values are higher, both social topologies present similar behavior concerning the information diffusion dynamics.

Scenario 3: information diffusion dynamics in the case of increasing vs. decreasing users' interests

The results regarding this evaluation scenario are shown in Fig. 6a, b, where $A = 5$, $C = 10$, $B = 0.5$ in Eq. (7). Fig. 6a, demonstrates the dynamics of information diffusion for the first class, where it is observed that the number of infected nodes initially presents a steep increase and then it increases with much lower rate. Regarding the information diffusion dynamics for class 2, from Fig. 6b it is observed that there is an initial increase which later deflates, due to the decreasing with time user interests, eventually yielding zero number of infected nodes for the simulation results and close to zero number of infected nodes for the numerical results (Proposition 2). Such dynamics cannot be captured by previous state-of-the art information diffusion models using constant diffusion parameters.

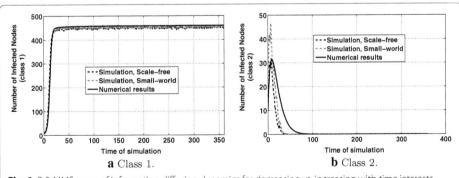

Fig. 6 P & MMS types of information diffusion dynamics for decreasing vs. increasing with time interests, with parameters $p_1 = 0.5$, $p_2 = 0.5$, $q = 0.4$

Simulation results, numerical results and discussion in controlled information diffusion

In this section, we further study and evaluate the introduction of control—as described in "Optimal control framework for information diffusion"—in the three scenarios of "Simulation and numerical results without applying control". The values of the parameters that are used in "Simulation and numerical results without applying control" remain the same, except otherwise mentioned. Additionally, we consider $u_{\min} = 0$, $u_{\max} = 30$, $\Delta I^m = 1$, $\forall\, m$, $\Delta t = 10^{-4}$, $k_1 = 1$, $k_2 = -3$, $k_I = 1$, $T = 2$, and finally, the topology on the social layer is considered as scale free. Note that $\Delta t << \Delta I^m$ so that the HJB solution converges [31]. The control is applied to only one class (or equivalently one group for constant interests) and specifically, we chose the class $m = 2$ (or equivalently Group 2 for constant interests), to evaluate how information diffusion behaves under low values of interest when introducing control, and compare this behavior with the case when no control is applied (similarly to "Simulation and numerical results without applying control"). In the following subsections, in each scenario, we compare the numerical (derived via Eq. 10 using Eq. 21) and simulation results with and without control regarding the number of infected nodes for the second class/group, while we also study several properties and the behavior of the optimal control itself. We adapt the diffusion model of "Information diffusion modeling and analysis without control" to introduce control by replacing the probabilities $f_1^{\mathrm{avg}}(t)$, $f_2^{\mathrm{avg}}(t)$ with $f_1^{\mathrm{avg}}(t)g_1(u(t))$, $f_2^{\mathrm{avg}}(t)g_2(u(t))$, as implied by comparing Eq. (10) with Eq. (1). Every simulation runs for 200 time steps, i.e., the control time $T = 2$ is divided into smaller time intervals each having a duration of 0.01.

Scenario 1: controlled information diffusion dynamics in the case of periodic users' interests

Similar to "Scenario 1: information diffusion dynamics in the case of periodic users' interests", we consider that the users' interests vary uniformly and randomly with mean value $1 - \frac{1}{4}\sin^2(\frac{\pi}{0.5}(t + 0.2)) - \frac{1}{7}$ for the first class and $\frac{1}{4}\sin^2(\frac{\pi}{0.5}(t + 0.2)) + \frac{1}{7}$ for the second class with the constraint that the interests of one node for the two classes are complementary.

Fig. 7 presents the dynamics of the information diffusion for class 2 when applying periodic interests as defined above. Specifically, Fig. 7a depicts the dynamics of information diffusion for the second class derived from simulations with and without control. We observe that similar to the results of "Scenario 1: information diffusion dynamics in the case of periodic users' interests" the periodicity of users' interests is also reflected to the dynamics of information diffusion, while the introduction of control significantly improves the expected number of infected nodes (there is an increase of one hundred nodes) and reduces the amplitude of the sinusoidal curve, i.e., the variance of the number of infected nodes. Fig. 7b depicts the same comparison when the dynamics of information diffusion are derived via Eq. (10). Note that Eq. (10) is solved numerically in a similar way to Eq. (6), demanding more running time to converge due to the small value of Δt, which is the reason why the running time in Fig. 7b is more than two periods. Comparing Fig. 7a, b, we observe that the introduction of control leads to a much closer approximation of the simulation results from the numerical ones, compared to the

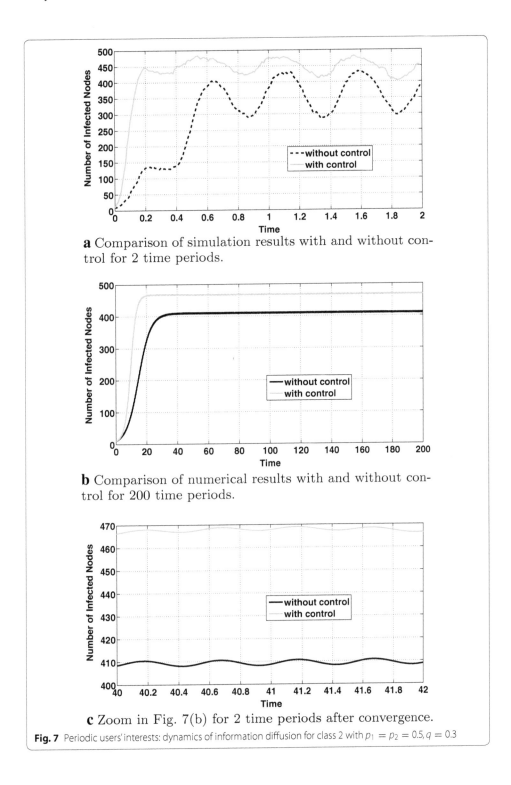

a Comparison of simulation results with and without control for 2 time periods.

b Comparison of numerical results with and without control for 200 time periods.

c Zoom in Fig. 7(b) for 2 time periods after convergence.

Fig. 7 Periodic users' interests: dynamics of information diffusion for class 2 with $p_1 = p_2 = 0.5, q = 0.3$

absence of control that is also discussed in "Scenario 1: information diffusion dynamics in the case of periodic users' interests". Finally, Fig. 7c zooms in two specific periods of Fig. 7b, after the convergence of the numerical solution of Eq. (10), to indicate in a clearer way the periodicity in the information diffusion dynamics.

Figure 8 studies the behavior of the optimal control with respect to the number of infected nodes and the users' evolving interest for the class $m = 2$. From Fig. 8b, we observe that the optimal control is a concave function of the number of infected nodes

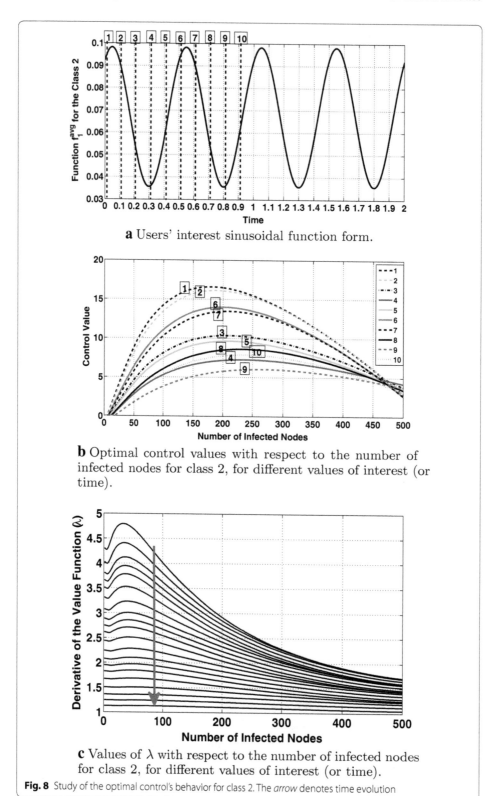

a Users' interest sinusoidal function form.

b Optimal control values with respect to the number of infected nodes for class 2, for different values of interest (or time).

c Values of λ with respect to the number of infected nodes for class 2, for different values of interest (or time).

Fig. 8 Study of the optimal control's behavior for class 2. The *arrow* denotes time evolution (for all times), achieving its maximum value at a different number of infected nodes, $I_{\max}^m$, at each time or value of interest. This behavior is intuitively expected from the analysis of "Optimal control framework for information diffusion" with respect to Γ (Eq. (23)), although it ignores the dependence of the adjoint variable λ on the number of infected nodes. Furthermore, comparing Fig. 8a, b, we observe that $I_{\max}^m$ decreases with interest which can be intuitively explained by the fact that for our considered parameters the corresponding condition stated at the end of "Optimal control framework for information diffusion" is satisfied. More specifically, higher values of interest, e.g., points 1, 2, 6, 7 of the users' interest sinusoidal function in Fig. 8a lead to lower values of $I_{\max}^m$ as it is observed in the corresponding optimal control curves 1, 2, 6, 7 in Fig. 8b. Moreover, comparing Fig. 8a, b and more specifically the interest values 1, 2, ..., 10 in Fig. 8a with their corresponding control curves in Fig. 8b, it can be observed that the values of the optimal control follow a sinusoidal-like evolution being aligned with the sinusoidal evolution of users' interest. The decreasing with time trend in the optimal control values, which cannot be explained by the Γ function (Eq. 23, "Optimal control framework for information diffusion"), can be justified by the decreasing values of the adjoint variable λ with time as shown in Fig. 8c where time is indicated by the arrow.

Finally, Fig. 9 shows the monotonicity of the optimal control with respect to interest for different values of the number of infected nodes for class $m = 2$. The applied parameters in these simulations lead to a threshold value I_{TH} ("Optimal control framework for information diffusion") at most (considering the maximum value of users' interest) equal to 473 nodes. Thus, it is expected that when $I^{m=2} > 473$ nodes the optimal control will be decreasing with interest and the opposite will hold for $I^{m=2} < 473$ nodes. This expectation is verified in Fig. 9, where the monotonicity change is performed around $I^{m=2} = 470$ nodes, while below 470 the optimal control value increases with interest (Fig. 9a–e) and above this value (Fig. 9g, h) it decreases with interest balancing in this way the cost with the information propagation efficiency as also discussed in "Optimal control framework for information diffusion". Note that in Fig. 9, the ticks on the horizontal axis are not simple interest values, but they are the values of interest over a two-period time interval as shown in Fig. 8a. Therefore, time has also impact on the adjoint variable λ affecting the optimal control values leading, e.g., here to decreasing optimal control values with time as it can be observed in all subfigures of Fig. 9. Time evolution is denoted by the arrows in each subfigure of Fig. 9.

Scenario 2: controlled information diffusion dynamics in the presence of groups with different characteristics

In this section, we consider constant users' interests adopting the same parameter values as in "Scenario 2: information diffusion dynamics in the presence of groups with different characteristics". Fig. 10 presents the dynamics of the information diffusion for Group 2 and indicates several properties of the optimal control. Specifically, Fig. 10a depicts the dynamics of information diffusion for Group 2 derived from simulations and computed numerically both cases with and without control (Eqs. 1, 10). As in the case of periodic users' interests, the introduction of control increases the number of infected nodes. Note that the numerical results of Eq. (10) refer to a time interval of length 2 after convergence (see also the discussion in "Scenario 1: information diffusion dynamics in

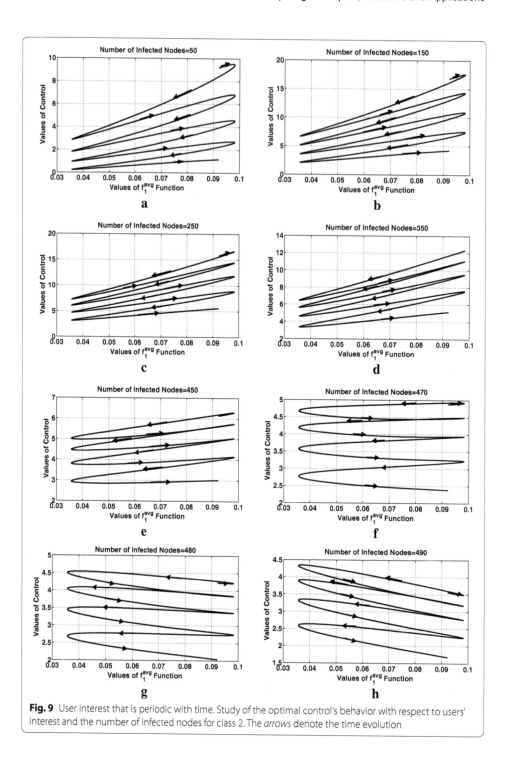

Fig. 9 User interest that is periodic with time. Study of the optimal control's behavior with respect to users' interest and the number of infected nodes for class 2. The *arrows* denote the time evolution

the case of periodic users' interests"). As it is shown in Fig. 10a, introducing control leads to a tighter approximation of the simulation results from the numerical ones, compared to the absence of control.

Figure 10c studies the behavior of the optimal control with respect to the number of infected nodes and time for the class $m = 2$. As in Fig. 8b, we observe that the optimal control is a concave function of the number of infected nodes (for all times) while I_{max}^m

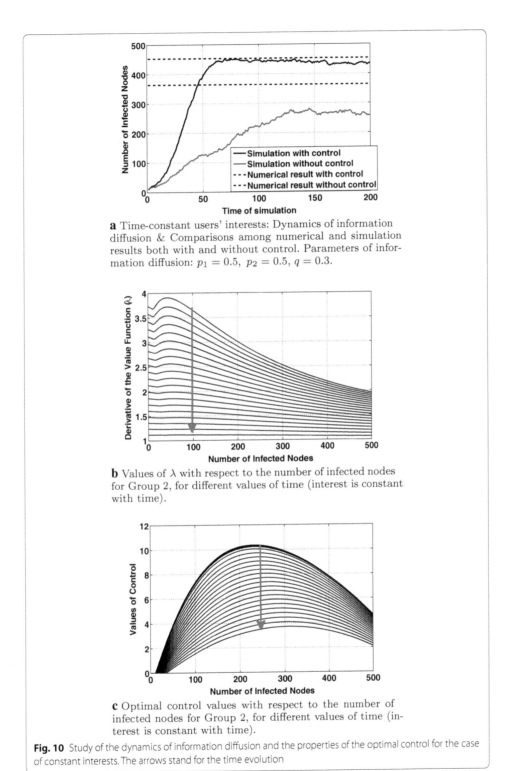

a Time-constant users' interests: Dynamics of information diffusion & Comparisons among numerical and simulation results both with and without control. Parameters of information diffusion: $p_1 = 0.5$, $p_2 = 0.5$, $q = 0.3$.

b Values of λ with respect to the number of infected nodes for Group 2, for different values of time (interest is constant with time).

c Optimal control values with respect to the number of infected nodes for Group 2, for different values of time (interest is constant with time).

Fig. 10 Study of the dynamics of information diffusion and the properties of the optimal control for the case of constant interests. The arrows stand for the time evolution

remains approximately stable (due to the consideration of constant interests). The optimal control values decrease with time (indicated by the arrow) due to the decreasing values of the adjoint variable λ with time as shown in Fig. 10b.

Scenario 3: controlled information diffusion dynamics in the case of decreasing with time users' interests

In this section, we consider users' interests that decrease with time using the same parameters/interest functions with "Scenario 3: information diffusion dynamics in the case of increasing vs. decreasing users' interest". Figure 11 presents the dynamics of the information diffusion for class 2 and indicates several properties of the optimal control. Specifically, Fig. 11a depicts the dynamics of information diffusion for the second class ($m = 2$) derived from simulations and computed numerically both cases with and without control (Eqs. 1, 10). We observe that the decrease of users' interests is reflected to the dynamics of information diffusion, although the later exhibits a much smaller decreasing rate. As in the cases of periodic and constant users' interests, the introduction of control increases the number of infected nodes. Note that the numerical results of Eq. (10) refer to a time interval of length 2 after convergence (see also the discussion in "Scenario 1: controlled information diffusion dynamics in the case of periodic users' interests"). As it is shown in Fig. 11a, introducing control leads to a tighter approximation of the simulation results from the numerical ones compared to the absence of control.

Figure 11c studies the behavior of the optimal control with respect to the number of infected nodes and the users' evolving interest for the class $m = 2$. As in Fig. 8b, we observe that the optimal control is a concave function of the number of infected nodes (for all times), achieving its maximum value at a different number of infected nodes, $I_{\max}^m$, for different times (or values of interest) while $I_{\max}^m$ values decrease with interest, as explained in "Scenario 1: controlled information diffusion dynamics in the case of periodic users' interests". The optimal control values decrease with time (indicated by the arrow) due to the decreasing values of users' interests and the decrease of the adjoint variable λ with time as shown in Fig. 11b. Finally, Fig. 12 shows the monotonicity of the optimal control with respect to user interest for different values of the number of infected nodes for class $m = 2$. The deployed parameters lead to a threshold value of at most $I_{TH} = 475$ ("Optimal control framework for information diffusion") (considering the maximum value of users' interest). Below $I_{TH} = 475$ the optimal control value increases with interest (Fig. 12a–e) and above this value (Fig. 12f, g) it decreases with interest. The dependence of the adjoint variable λ on time affects the optimal control values, impacting the monotonicity of the optimal control with respect to user interest and the number of infected nodes, as shown in Fig. 12f, g where the optimal control becomes increasing instead of decreasing (which is expected) with user interest after a specific time. Time evolution is denoted by the arrows in each subfigure of Fig. 12.

Conclusions

In this paper, we introduced a novel framework for modeling and controlling useful information diffusion in generalized networks that takes into account user interests and their features, i.e., interest periodicity or interest dependence on the topic of the propagated information. The epidemic equations were numerically solved and compared with simulation results for three indicative operational scenarios, yielding significant results on the impact of each associated factor (e.g., topology layer, interest values and time variedness) on diffusion dynamics. Furthermore, optimal controls were obtained and studied over each information class, while simulation and numerical results are provided for

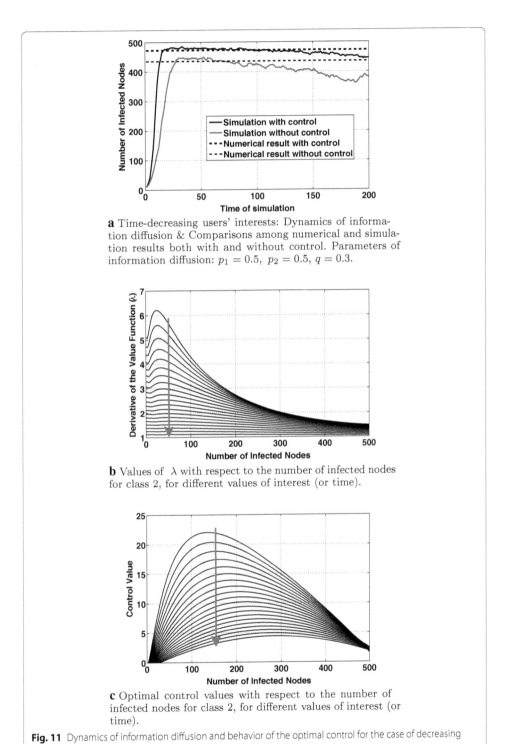

a Time-decreasing users' interests: Dynamics of information diffusion & Comparisons among numerical and simulation results both with and without control. Parameters of information diffusion: $p_1 = 0.5$, $p_2 = 0.5$, $q = 0.3$.

b Values of λ with respect to the number of infected nodes for class 2, for different values of interest (or time).

c Optimal control values with respect to the number of infected nodes for class 2, for different values of interest (or time).

Fig. 11 Dynamics of information diffusion and behavior of the optimal control for the case of decreasing with time user interests. The *arrows* stand for the time evolution

the cases where user interest is low and diffusion needs boosting to improve the efficiency of useful information spreading. Interesting behavioral properties of the optimal controls with respect to their dependence on the evolving users' interests and the number of infected nodes are shown via analysis (on an intuitive basis) and numerical

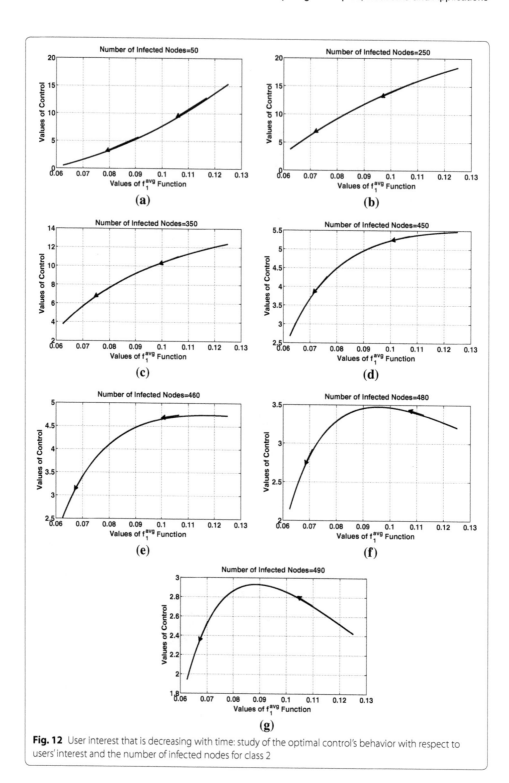

Fig. 12 User interest that is decreasing with time: study of the optimal control's behavior with respect to users' interest and the number of infected nodes for class 2

evaluations. Our future work will focus on studying the cases where interest classes may have correlations, and the impact that these correlations may have on the corresponding controls.

Analysis and control of information diffusion dictated by user interest...

169

Authors' contributions

ES contributed to the development and analysis of the proposed framework for modeling and studying information diffusion. She also developed the evaluation part and participated in the manuscript writing. VK contributed in the development and analysis of the framework, participated in the design of the study, in the sequence alignment and contributed in the manuscript writing. SP participated in the design of the study and its coordination. All authors read and approved the final manuscript.

Acknowledgements

This research is co-financed by the European Union (European Social Fund) and Hellenic national funds through the Operational Program 'Education and Lifelong Learning' (NSRF 2007-2013).

Competing interests

The authors declare that they have no competing interests.

References

1. Cheng, S.-M., Ao, W.C., Chen, P.-Y., Chen, K.-C.: On modeling malware propagation in generalized social networks. Commun. Lett. IEEE **15**(1), 25–27 (2011)
2. Yagan, O., Qian, D., Zhang, J., Cochran, D.: Conjoining speeds up information diffusion in overlaying social-physical networks. Sel. Areas Commun. IEEE J. **31**(6), 1038–1048 (2013)
3. Shen, Y., Dinh, T.N., Zhang, H., Thai, M.T.: Interest-matching information propagation in multiple online social networks. In: Proceedings of the 21st ACM International Conference on Information and Knowledge Management. CIKM '12 (2012)
4. Varshney, D., Kumar, S., Gupta, V.: Modeling information diffusion in social networks using latent topic information. In: Huang, D.-S., Bevilacqua, V., Premaratne, P. (eds.) Intelligent Computing Theory. Lecture Notes in Computer Science, vol. 8588, pp. 137–148 (2014)
5. Weng, L., Flammini A., Menczer F.: Unifying Themes in Complex Systems Volume VIII: Proc. 8th International Conference on Complex Systems (ICCS), (2011)
6. Wang, F., Wang, H., Xu, K., Wu, J., Jia, X.: Characterizing information diffusion in online social networks with linear diffusive model. In:Distributed Computing Systems (ICDCS), 2013 IEEE 33rd International Conference On, pp. 307–316 (2013)
7. Nowzari, C., Preciado, V.M., Pappas, G.J.: Analysis and control of epidemics: A survey of spreading processes on complex networks. arXiv:1505.00768v2 [math.OC], 53 (2015)
8. Hethcote, H.W.: Recent advances in information diffusion and influence maximization of complex social networks. Society for Industrial and Applied Mathematics (SIAM). Review **42**(4), 599–653 (2000)
9. Daley, D.J., Gani, J.: Epidemic Modeling: An Introduction. Cambridge University Press, Cambridge (2001)
10. Chen, P.-Y., Cheng, S.-M., Chen, K.-C.: Optimal control of epidemic information dissemination over networks. Cybern. IEEE Trans. **44**(12), 2316–2328 (2014)
11. Yang, J., Leskovec, J.: Modeling information diffusion in implicit networks. Proceedings of the 2010 IEEE International Conference on Data Mining. ICDM '10, pp. 599–608. IEEE Computer Society, Washington, DC (2010)
12. Guille, A., Hacid, H., Favre, C., Zighed, D.A.: Information diffusion in online social networks: a survey. SIGMOD Rec. **42**(2), 17–28 (2013)
13. Chou, Y.-F., Huang, H.-H., Cheng, R.-G.: Modeling information dissemination in generalized social networks. Commun. Lett. IEEE **17**(7), 1356–1359 (2013)
14. Allen, L.J.S.: An introduction to stochastic epidemic models. Mathematical Epidemiology Lecture Notes in Mathematics, vol. 1945, pp. 81–130. Springer Berlin Heidelberg (2008)
15. Zou, C.C., Gong, W., Towsley, D.: Code red worm propagation modeling and analysis. Proceedings of the 9th ACM Conference on Computer and Communications Security. CCS '02, pp. 138–147. ACM, New York (2002)
16. Theodorakopoulos, G., Le Boudec, J.-Y., Baras, J.S.: Selfish response to epidemic propagation. Autom. Control IEEE Trans. **58**(2), 363–376 (2013)
17. Bansal, S., Grenfell, B.T., Meyers, L.A.: When individual behaviour matters: homogeneous and network models in epidemiology. J. R. Soc. Interface **4**(16), 879–891 (2007)
18. Scellato, S., Mascolo, C., Musolesi, M., Latora, V.: Epcast: Controlled dissemination in human-based wireless networks using epidemic spreading models. Bio-Inspired Computing and Communication (Lecture Notes in Computer Science) **5151**, 295–306 (2008)
19. Weng, L., Ratkiewicz, J., Perra, N., Gonçalves, B., Castillo, C., Bonchi, F., Schifanella, R., Menczer, F., Flammini, A.: The role of information diffusion in the evolution of social networks. In: Proceedings of the 19th ACM SIGKDD International Conference on Knowledge Discovery and Data Mining. KDD '13 (2013)
20. Khouzani, M.H.R., Sarkar, S., Altman, E.: Maximum damage malware attack in mobile wireless networks. Netw. IEEE ACM Trans. **20**(5), 1347–1360 (2012)
21. Khouzani, M.H.R., Altman, E., Sarkar, S.: Optimal quarantining of wireless malware through reception gain control. Autom. Control IEEE Trans. **57**(1), 49–61 (2012)
22. Bloem, M., Alpcan, T., Basar, T.: An optimal control approach to malware filtering. In:Decision and Control, 2007 46th IEEE Conference On, pp. 6059–6064 (2007)

23. Forster, G.A., Gilliga, C.A.: Optimizing the control of disease infestations at the landscape level. Proc. Natl. Acad. Sci. USA **104**(12), 4984–4989 (2007)
24. Valerio, L., Conti, M., Pagani, E., Passarella, A.: Autonomic cognitive-based data dissemination in opportunistic networks. In:World of Wireless, Mobile and Multimedia Networks (WoWMoM), 2013 IEEE 14th International Symposium and Workshops on A, pp. 1–9 (2013)
25. Arnold, V.I.: Ordinary Differential Equations. The MIT Press, Cambridge MA, USA (1978)
26. Zhang, H., Mishra, S., Thai, M.T.: Recent advances in information diffusion and influence maximization of complex social networks. Opportunistic Mobile Social Networks, pp. 37–69. CRC Press (2014)
27. Evans, L.C.: An Introduction to Mathematical Optimal Control Theory, Version 2. University of California, Berkeley, **(unpublished)**
28. Yong, J., Zhou, X.Y.: Stochastic Controls. Hamiltonian Systems and HJB Equations. Springer, New York, USA (1999)
29. Fleming, W.H., Sooner, H.M.: Controlled Markov Processes and Viscosity Solutions, 2nd edn. Springer-Verlag, New York (2006)
30. Stai, E., Loulakis, M., Papavassiliou, S.: Congestion & power control of wireless multihop networks over stochastic ltf channels. In:IEEE Wireless Communications and Networking Conference (WCNC) (2015)
31. Causon, D.M., Mingham, C.G.: Introductory Finite Difference Methods for PDEs. Ventus Publishing ApS, Frederiksberg, Capital Region of Denmark (2010)
32. Karyotis, V., Stai, E., Papavassiliou, S.: Evolutionary Dynamics of Complex Communications Networks. CRC Press - Taylor & Francis Group, Boca Raton (2013)
33. Albert, R., Barabási, A.-L.: Statistical mechanics of complex networks. Rev. Mod. Phys. **74**, 47–97 (2002)
34. Watts, D.J., Strogatz, S.H.: Collective dynamics of 'small-world' networks. Nature **393**, 440–442 (1998)

9

Factorization threshold models for scale-free networks generation

Akmal Artikov[1,3]*, Aleksandr Dorodnykh[1], Yana Kashinskaya[1,2] and Egor Samosvat[3]

*Correspondence:
artikov.akmalzhon@phystech.edu
[1] Moscow Institute of Physics and Technology (SU), Moscow, Russia
Full list of author information is available at the end of the article

Abstract

Background: Several models for producing scale-free networks have been suggested; most of them are based on the preferential attachment approach. In this article, we suggest a new approach for generating scale-free networks with an alternative source of the power-law degree distribution.

Methods: The model derives from matrix factorization methods and geographical threshold models that were recently proven to show good results in generating scale-free networks. We associate each node with a vector having latent features distributed over a unit sphere and with a weight variable sampled from a Pareto distribution. We join two nodes by an edge if they are spatially close and/or have large weights.

Results and conclusion: The network produced by this approach is scale free and has a power-law degree distribution with an exponent of 2. In addition, we propose an extension of the model that allows us to generate directed networks with tunable power-law exponents.

Keywords: Scale-free networks, Matrix factorization, Threshold models

Background

Most social, biological, topological and technological networks display distinct nontrivial topological features demonstrating that connections between the nodes are neither regular nor random at the same time [1]. Such systems are called *complex networks*. On of the well-known and well-studied classes of complex networks is *scale-free networks* whose degree distribution $P(k)$ follows a power law $P(k) \sim k^{-\alpha}$, where α is a parameter whose value is typically in the range $2 < \alpha < 3$. Many real networks have been reported to be scale-free [2].

Generating scale-free networks is an important problem because they usually have useful properties, such as high clustering [3], robustness to random attacks [4] and easy achievable synchronization [5]. Several models for producing scale-free networks have been suggested; most of them are based on the preferential attachment approach [1]. This approach forces existing nodes of higher degrees to gain edges added to the network more rapidly in a "rich-get-richer" manner. This paper offers a model with another explanation of scale-free property.

Our approach is inspired by *matrix factorization*, a machine learning method being successfully used for link prediction [6]. The main idea is to approximate a network adjacency matrix by a product of matrices V and V^T, where V is the matrix of nodes' latent features vectors. To create a generative model of scale-free networks, we sample latent features V from some probabilistic distribution and try to generate a network adjacency matrix. Two nodes are connected by an edge if the dot product of their latent features exceeds some threshold. This threshold condition is influenced by the *geographical threshold models* that are applied to scale-free network generation [7]. Because of the methods used (adjacency matrix factorization and threshold condition), we call our model the *factorization threshold model*.

A network produced in such a way is scale-free and follows power-law degree distribution with an exponent of 2, which differs from the results for basic preferential attachment models [8–10] where the exponent equals 3. We also suggest an extension of our model that allows us to generate directed networks with a tunable power-law exponent.

This paper is organized as follows. "Related work" section provides information about related works that inspired us. The formal description of our model in the case of an undirected fixed size network is presented in "Model description" section, which is followed by a discussion of how to generate growing networks. In "Generating sparse networks" section, the problem of making resulting networks sparse is considered. "Degree distribution" section shows that our model indeed produces scale-free networks. Extensions of our model, which allows to generate directed networks with a tunable power-law exponents and some other interesting properties, will be discussed in "Model modifications" section. "Conclusion" section concludes the paper.

Related work

In this section, we consider related works that encouraged us to create a new model for complex networks generation.

Matrix factorization

Matrix factorization is a group of algorithms where a given matrix R is factorized into two smaller matrices Q and P such that: $R \approx Q^T P$ [11].

There is a popular approach in *recommendation systems* which is based on matrix factorization [12]. Assume that users express their preferences by rating some items, this can be viewed as an approximate representation of their interests. Combining known ratings, we get partially filled matrix R, the idea is to approximate unknown ratings using matrix factorization $R \approx Q^T P$. A geometrical interpretation is the following. The rows of matrices Q and P can be seen as latent features vectors $\vec{q}_i$ and $\vec{p}_u$ of items and users, respectively. The dot product $(\vec{q}_i, \vec{p}_u)$ captures an interaction between an user u and an item i, and it should approximate the rating of the item i by the user u: $R_{ui} \approx (\vec{q}_i, \vec{p}_u)$. Mapping of each user and item to latent features is considered as an optimization problem of minimizing distance between R and $Q^T P$ that is usually solved using stochastic gradient descent (SGD) or alternating least squares (ALS) methods.

Furthermore, matrix factorization was suggested to be used for link prediction in networks [6]. Link prediction refers to the problem of finding missing or hidden links which probably exist in a network [13]. In [6] it is solved via matrix factorization: a network adjacency matrix A is approximated by a product of the matrices V and V^T, where V is the matrix of nodes' latent features.

Geographical threshold models

Geographical threshold models were recently proven to have good results in scale-free networks generation [7]. We are going to briefly summarize one variation of these models [14].

Suppose the number of nodes to be fixed. Each node carries a randomly and independently distributed weight variable $w_i \in \mathbb{R}$. Also, the nodes are uniformly and independently distributed with specified density in a $\mathbb{R}^d$. A pair of nodes with weights w, w' and Euclidean distance r are connected if and only if:

$$(w + w') \cdot h(r) \geq \theta, \tag{1}$$

where θ is the model threshold parameter and $h(r)$ is the distance function that is assumed to decrease in r. For example, we can take $h(r) = r^{-\beta}$, where $\beta > 0$.

First, exponential distribution of weights with the inverse scale parameter λ has been studied. This distribution of weights leads to scale-free networks with a power-law exponent of 2: $P(k) \propto k^{-2}$. It is interesting that the exponent of a power law does not depend on the λ, d and β in this case. Second, Pareto weight distribution with scale parameter w_0 and shape parameter a has been considered. In this case, a tunable power-law degree distribution has been achieved: $P(k) \propto k^{-1-\frac{a\beta}{d}}$.

There are other variations of this approach: uniform distribution of coordinates in the d-dimensional unit cube [15], lattice-based models [16, 17] and even networks embedded in fractal space [18].

Model description

We studied theoretically matrix factorization by turning it from a trainable supervised model into a generative probabilistic model. When matrix factorization is used in machine learning, the adjacency matrix A is given and the goal is to train the model by tuning the matrix of latent features V in such way that $A \approx V^T V$. In our model, we make the reverse: latent features V are sampled from some probabilistic distribution and we generate a network adjacency matrix A based on $V^T V$.

Formally our model is described in the following way:

$$\begin{cases} A_{ij} = \mathrm{I}\left[(\vec{v}_i, \vec{v}_j) \geq \theta\right] \\ \vec{v}_i = w_i \vec{x}_i \in \mathbb{R}^d \\ w_i \sim \mathrm{Pareto}(a, w_0), \ \vec{x}_i \sim \mathrm{Uniform}(S^{d-1}) \\ i = 1 \ldots n, \ j = 1 \ldots n \end{cases}$$

- Network has n nodes and each node is associated with a d-dimensional latent features vector $\vec{v}_i$.
- Each latent features vector $\vec{v}_i$ is a product of weight w_i and direction $\vec{x}_i$.
- Directions $\vec{x}_i$ are i.i.d. random vectors uniformly distributed over the surface of $(d-1)$-sphere.
- Weights are i.i.d. random variables distributed according to Pareto distribution with the following density function $f(w)$:

$$f(w) = \frac{a}{w_0} \left(\frac{w_0}{w}\right)^{a+1} \ (w \geq w_0). \tag{2}$$

- Edges between nodes i and j appear if a dot product of their latent features vectors $(\vec{v}_i, \vec{v}_j)$ exceeds a threshold parameter θ.

Therefore, we take into consideration both node's importance w_i and its location x_i on the surface of a $(d-1)$-sphere (that can be interpreted as the earth in the case of $\vec{x}_i \in S^2 \subset \mathbb{R}^3$). Thus, inspired by the matrix factorization approach we achieved the following model behavior: the edges in our model are assumed to be formed when a pair of nodes is spatially close and/or has large weights. Actually, compared with the geographical threshold models, we use dot product to measure proximity of nodes instead of Euclidean distance.

We have defined our model for fixed size networks, but in principle, our model can be generalized for the case of growing networks. The problem is that a fixed threshold θ when the size of a network tends to infinity with high probability leads to a complete graph. But real networks are usually sparse.

Therefore, to introduce *growing factorization threshold models* we use a threshold function $\theta := \theta(n)$ which depends on the number of nodes n in the network. Then for every value of network size n we have the same parameters except of threshold θ. This means that at every step, when a new node will be added to the graph, some of the existing edges will be removed. In the next section, we will try to find threshold functions which lead to sparse networks.

To preserve readability of the proofs, we consider only the case $d = 3$ because proofs for higher dimensions can be derived in a similar way. However, we will give not only mean-field approximations but also strict probabilistic proofs, which to the best of our knowledge have not been done for geographical threshold models yet and can be likely applied in the other works too.

Generating sparse networks

The aim of this section is to model sparse growing networks. To do this, we need to find a proper threshold function.

First, we have studied the growth of the real networks. For example, Fig. 1 shows the growth of a citation graph. The data was obtained from the SNAP[1] database. It can be seen that the function $y(x) = 4.95x \log x - 40x$ is a good estimation of the growth rate of this network. That is why we decided to focus on the linearithmic or sub-linearithmic growth rate of the model (here and subsequently, by the growth of the model we mean the growth of the number of edges).

Analysis of the expected number of edges

Let $M(n)$ denote the number of edges in the network of size n. To find its expectation, we need the two following lemmas.

Lemma 1   *The probability for a node with weight w to be connected to a random node is*

$$
P_e(w) = \begin{cases} \frac{1}{2}\left(1 - \frac{a\theta}{w(a+1)w_0}\right), & w > \frac{\theta}{w_0}, \\ \frac{1}{2}\frac{w_0^a}{\theta^a(a+1)}w^a, & w \le \frac{\theta}{w_0}. \end{cases} \tag{3}
$$

---

[1] https://snap.stanford.edu/data/.

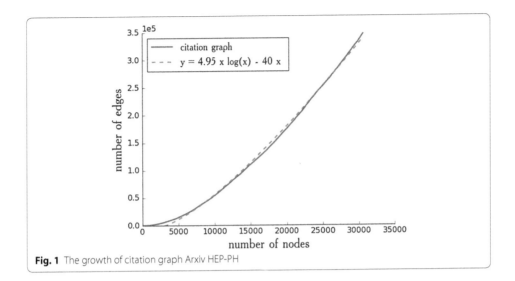

Fig. 1 The growth of citation graph Arxiv HEP-PH

Lemma 2 *The edge probability in the network is*

$$P_e = \begin{cases} \frac{1}{2} - \frac{1}{2}\frac{a^2}{(a+1)^2}\frac{\theta}{w_0^2}, & \theta < w_0^2, \\ \frac{w_0^{2a}}{2\theta^a}\left(\frac{a(\ln\theta - 2\ln w_0)}{a+1} - \frac{a^2}{(a+1)^2} + 1\right), & \theta \geq w_0^2. \end{cases} \tag{4}$$

To improve readability, we moved the proofs of Lemmas 1 and 2 to Appendix.

The next theorem shows that our model can have any growth which is less than quadratic.

Theorem 1 *Denote as $R(n)$ such function that $R(n) = o(n^2)$ and $R(n) > 0$. Then there exists such threshold function $\theta(n)$ that the growth of the model is $R(n)$:*

$$\exists N \quad EM(n) = R(n) \quad (n \geq N).$$

Proof It easy to check that P_e is a continuous function of θ. The intermediate value theorem states that $P_e(\theta)$ takes any value between $P_e(\theta = 0) = 1/2$ and $P_e(\theta = \infty) = 0$ at some point within the interval.

Since $R(n) = o(n^2)$ and positive, there exists N such that for all $n \geq N$, $0 < R(n) < \frac{1}{2} \times \frac{n(n-1)}{2}$.

It means that the equation $EM(n) = R(n)$ is feasible for all $n \geq N$. $\square$

Taking into account Theorem 1, we obtain parameters for the linearithmic and linear growths of the expected number of edges.

Theorem 2 *Suppose the following threshold function: $\theta(n) = Dn^{\frac{1}{a}}$ where D is a constant. Then the growth of the model is linearithmic:*

$$EM(n) = An\ln n(1 + o(1)) \quad \left(n \geq \frac{w_0^{2a}}{D^a}\right),$$

where A is a constant depending on the Pareto distribution parameters.

Proof We can rewrite inequality $n \geq \frac{w_0^{2a}}{D^a}$ as $Dn^{\frac{1}{a}} \geq w_0^2$ and apply Lemma 2 in the case $\theta(n) = Dn^{\frac{1}{a}} \geq w_0^2$

$$EM = \frac{n(n-1)}{2} \frac{w_0^{2a}}{2\theta^a} \left(\frac{a(\ln\theta - 2\ln w_0)}{a+1} - \frac{a^2}{(a+1)^2} + 1 \right). \tag{5}$$

If we replace θ by $Dn^{\frac{1}{a}}$, we obtain

$$
\begin{aligned}
EM(n) &= \frac{n(n-1)w_0^{2a}}{4(Dn^{\frac{1}{a}})^a} \left(\frac{a(\ln(Dn^{\frac{1}{a}}) - 2\ln w_0)}{a+1} - \frac{a^2}{(a+1)^2} + 1 \right) \\
&= \frac{(n-1)w_0^{2a}}{4D^a} \left(\frac{\ln n}{a+1} - \frac{a^2}{(a+1)^2} + 1 + \frac{a(\ln D - 2\ln w_0)}{a+1} \right) \\
&= An \ln n(1 + o(1)).
\end{aligned}
$$

Theorem 3 *Suppose that the growth of the model is sub-linearithmic:* $\frac{EM(n)}{n\ln n} = o(1)$, *then* $\frac{n^{\frac{1}{a}}}{\theta(n)} = o(1)$.

Proof Let us consider another model with a threshold function $\theta'(n) = Dn^{\frac{1}{a}}$ and the expected number of edges $EM'(n)$. According to Theorem 2 and the condition $\frac{EM(n)}{n\ln n} = o(1)$ there exists a natural number N_D such that

$$\forall n \geq N_D \quad EM'(n) = An \ln n(1 + o(1)) \geq EM(n).$$

This also means that for all $n \geq N_D$ we have $\theta(n) \geq \theta'(n)$. Therefore

$$\forall n \geq N_D \quad \frac{n^{\frac{1}{a}}}{\theta(n)} \leq \frac{n^{\frac{1}{a}}}{\theta'(n)} = \frac{1}{D}.$$

By the arbitrariness of the choice of D, we have $\frac{n^{\frac{1}{a}}}{\theta(n)} = o(1)$. $\square$

Concentration theorem

In this section, we will find the variance of the number of the edges and prove the concentration theorem

Proofs of the following lemmas can be found in the Appendix.

Lemma 3 *Suppose that* x, y *and* z *are random nodes. Let* $P_<$ *be the probability for the node* x *to be connected to both nodes* y *and* z. *Then the variance of the number of edges* M *is*

$$\text{Var}(M) = \frac{n(n-1)}{2}P_e(1 - P_e) + n\frac{(n-1)(n-2)}{2}(P_< - P_e^2),$$

Lemma 4 *Suppose that* x, y *and* z *are random nodes. Let* $P_<$ *be the probability for the node* x *to be connected to both nodes* y *and* z. *Then*

$$P_< = \begin{cases} \frac{1}{4}\frac{w_0^{2a}}{\theta^{2a}(a+1)^2}[\theta^a - w_0^{2a}] + \frac{1}{4}\frac{w_0^{2a}}{\theta^a}\left[1 - 2\frac{a^2}{(a+1)^2} + \frac{a^3}{(a+1)^2(a+2)}\right], & \theta \geq w_0^2, \\ \frac{1}{4} - \frac{1}{2}\frac{a^2\theta}{(a+1)^2}\frac{1}{w_0^2} + \frac{1}{4}\frac{a^3\theta^2}{(a+1)^2(a+2)}\frac{1}{w_0^4}, & \theta < w_0^2. \end{cases}$$

Combining these results, we get the following theorem that will be needed to prove the concentration theorem

Theorem 4 *If $\theta \geq w_0^2$, the variance is*

$$\mathrm{Var}(M) = EM + n\frac{(n-1)(n-2)}{2}\left[A\frac{1}{\theta^a} + B\frac{1}{\theta^{2a}}\right] - \frac{2(n-2)}{n(n-1)}(EM)^2,$$

where A and B are constants which depend on the Pareto distribution parameters.

Proof According to Lemmas 3 and 4 in case of $\theta \geq w_0^2$, the variance is

$$\mathrm{Var}(M) = \frac{n(n-1)}{2}P_e(1-P_e) + n\frac{(n-1)(n-2)}{2}(P_< - P_e^2). \tag{6}$$

$$P_< = \frac{1}{4}\frac{w_0^{2a}}{\theta^{2a}(a+1)^2}[\theta^a - w_0^{2a}] + \frac{1}{4}\frac{w_0^{2a}}{\theta^a}\left[1 - 2\frac{a^2}{(a+1)^2} + \frac{a^3}{(a+1)^2(a+2)}\right] \tag{7}$$

According to Lemma 2, the expected number of edges is

$$EM = \frac{n(n-1)}{2}P_e. \tag{8}$$

Combining (8) and (6), we obtain

$$\mathrm{Var}(M) = EM(1-P_e) + n\frac{(n-1)(n-2)}{2}P_< - EM(n-2)P_e$$

$$= EM + n\frac{(n-1)(n-2)}{2}P_< - \frac{2(n-2)}{n(n-1)}(EM)^2.$$

Therefore,

$$P_< = \frac{1}{4}\frac{w_0^{2a}}{\theta^{2a}(a+1)^2}[\theta^a - w_0^{2a}] + \frac{1}{4}\frac{w_0^{2a}}{\theta^a}\left[1 - 2\frac{a^2}{(a+1)^2} + \frac{a^3}{(a+1)^2(a+2)}\right]$$

$$= \frac{1}{\theta^a}C_1 - \frac{1}{\theta^{2a}}C_2 + \frac{1}{\theta^a}C_3 = A\frac{1}{\theta^a} + B\frac{1}{\theta^{2a}},$$

where C_1, C_2, C_3, A and B are constants depending on the Pareto distribution parameters.
Finally, we obtain

$$\mathrm{Var}(M) = EM + n\frac{(n-1)(n-2)}{2}\left[A\frac{1}{\theta^a} + B\frac{1}{\theta^{2a}}\right] - \frac{2(n-2)}{n(n-1)}(EM)^2.$$

$\square$

Theorem 5 *Concentration theorem If $\theta(n)$ and $EM(n)$ tends to infinity as $n \to \infty$ and $\frac{n^3}{(EM(n))^2\theta(n)^a} = o(1)$, then*

$$\forall \varepsilon > 0 \quad P(|M - EM| \geq \varepsilon \cdot EM) \xrightarrow{n\to\infty} 0,$$

where M is the number of edges in the graph.

Proof According to Chebyshev's inequality, we have

$$P(|M - EM| \geq \varepsilon \cdot EM) \leq \frac{\mathrm{Var}(M)M}{\varepsilon^2 \cdot (EM)^2}. \tag{9}$$

Let us estimate the right part of the inequality. Using Theorem 4, we get

$$\frac{\text{Var}(M)}{\varepsilon^2 \cdot (EM)^2} = \frac{1}{\varepsilon^2 EM} + \frac{O(n^3)}{(EM)^2}\left[A\frac{1}{\theta^a} + B\frac{1}{\theta^{2a}}\right] + O\left(\frac{1}{n}\right)$$

$$= \frac{1}{\varepsilon^2 EM} + \frac{O(n^3)}{(EM)^2}\frac{1}{\theta^a}\left[1 + \frac{B}{A\theta^{2a}}\right] + O\left(\frac{1}{n}\right)$$

Using the conditions of the theorem, we obtain

$$\frac{\text{Var}(M)}{\varepsilon^2 \cdot (EM)^2} \to 0 \text{ as } n \to \infty.$$

$\square$

Combining Theorems 2, 3 and 5, we obtain the following corollary.

Corollary 1   *Suppose that one of the following conditions holds:*
- *The threshold function $\theta(n)$ equals $Dn^{\frac{1}{a}}$*
- $\frac{n}{EM(n)} = O(1)$ *and* $\frac{EM(n)}{n\ln n} = o(1)$

Then

$$\forall \varepsilon > 0 \quad P(|M - EM| \geq \varepsilon \cdot EM) \xrightarrow[n\to\infty]{} 0,$$

where M is the number of edges in the graph.

In this way, we have proved that the number of edges in the graph does not deviate much from its expected value. It means that having the linearithmic or the sub-linearithmic growth of the expected number of edges we also have the same growth for the actual number of edges.

Degree distribution

In this section, we show that our model follows power-law degree distribution with an exponent of 2 and give two proofs. The first is a mean-field approximation. It is usually applied for a fast checking of hypotheses. The second one is a strict probabilistic proof. To the best of our knowledge it has not been considered in the context of the geographic threshold models yet.

To confirm our proofs, we carried out a computer simulation and plotted complementary cumulative distribution of node degree which is shown on Fig. 2. We also used a discrete power-law fitting method, which is described in [2] and implemented in the network analysis package igraph.[2] We obtained $\alpha = 2.16$, $x_{\min} = 4$ and a quite large p-value of 0.9984 for the Kolmogorov–Smirnov goodness of fit test.

Theorem 6   *Let $P(k)$ be the probability of a random node to have a degree k. If $\frac{n^{\frac{1}{a}}}{\theta(n)} = o(1)$, then there exist such constants C_0 and N_0 such that $\forall\, k(n) : \forall\, n > N_0\ k(n) < C_0 n$ we have*

$$P(k) = (1 + o(1))k^{-2}.$$

---

[2] http://igraph.org/.

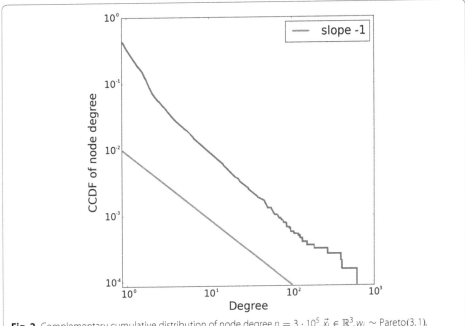

Fig. 2 Complementary cumulative distribution of node degree $n = 3 \cdot 10^5$, $\vec{x}_i \in \mathbb{R}^3$, $w_i \sim$ Pareto(3, 1), $\theta = 66.9$

Mean-field approximation

This approximation gives power law only for nodes with weights $w \leq \frac{\theta}{w_0}$. But the expected number of nodes with weights not satisfying this inequality Em is extremely small

$$Em = nP\left(w > \frac{\theta}{w_0}\right) = n\left(\frac{w_0^2}{\theta}\right)^a = o(1).$$ (10)

As it was shown in Lemma 1, the probability of the node $\vec{v}_i = w_i \vec{x}_i$ with weight $w_i = w \leq \frac{\theta}{w_0}$ to have an edge to another random node is

$$P_e(w) = \frac{w_0^a}{2\theta^a(a+1)}w^a.$$

Let $k_i(w)$ be the degree of the node v_i. Then

$$k_i(w) = \sum_{i \neq j} I[v_i \text{ is connected to } v_j],$$

where I stands for the indicator function.

As all nodes are independent, we get

$$Ek_i(w) = (n-1)P_e(w).$$

In the mean-field approximation, we assume that $k_i(w)$ is really close to its expectation and we can substitute it by $(n-1)P_e(w)$ in the following expression for the degree distribution $P(k) = f(w)\frac{dw}{dk}$, where $f(w)$ is a density of weights. Thus,

$$P(k) = \frac{2aw_0^a\theta^a(a+1)}{(n-1)w^{2a}} \propto k^{-2}$$

$\square$

Note that we have not used conditions on $k(n)$ and $\theta(n)$ yet, they are needed to estimate residual terms in the following rigorous proof.

Proof Degree k_i of the node v_i is a binomial random variable. Using the probability $P_e(w)$ of the node v_i with weight $w_i = w$ to have an edge to another random node, we can get the probability that k_i equals k:

$$P(k_i = k | w_i = w) = \binom{n-1}{k}(P_e(w))^k(1 - P_e(w))^{n-k-1}.$$

To get the total probability, we need to integrate this expression with respect to w

$$P(k_i = k) = \binom{n-1}{k}\int_{w_0}^{\infty}(P_e(w))^k(1 - P_e(w))^{n-k-1}\frac{aw_0^a}{w^{a+1}}dw.$$

Because of $P_e(w)$ is a composite function, the integral breaks up into two parts.

$$I_1 = \int_{w_0}^{\theta/w_0}(P_e(w))^k(1 - P_e(w))^{n-k-1}\frac{aw_0^a}{w^{a+1}}dw,$$

$$I_2 = \int_{\theta/w_0}^{\infty}(P_e(w))^k(1 - P_e(w))^{n-k-1}\frac{aw_0^a}{w^{a+1}}dw.$$

Thus,

$$P(k_i = k) = \binom{n-1}{k}(I_1 + I_2).$$

For estimating I_1 we can use the formula $P_e(w) = \frac{1}{2}\frac{w_0^a}{\theta^a(a+1)}w^a$ from Lemma 1. After making the substitution to integrate with respect to $P_e(w)$ and using the incomplete beta-function, we get

$$I_1 = \frac{w_0^{2a}}{2\theta^a a(a+1)} \cdot \left(B\left(\frac{1}{2(a+1)}; k-1, n-k\right) - B\left(\frac{w_0^{2a}}{2\theta^a(a+1)}; k-1, n-k\right)\right).$$

For I_2 we can derive an upper bound. Note that for $w \geq \theta/w_0$ we have

$$P_e(w) = \frac{1}{2}\left(1 - \frac{a\theta}{w(a+1)w_0}\right) < \frac{1}{2}$$

$$1 - P_e(w) \leq 1 - P_e(\theta/w_0) = \frac{1}{2}\left(1 + \frac{a}{a+1}\right) = \varepsilon_0 < 1.$$

Therefore, we obtain the following upper estimate

$$I_2 = O\left(\frac{(\varepsilon_0)^{n-k-1}}{2^k}\int_{\theta/w_0}^{\infty}\frac{aw_0^a}{w^{a+1}}dw\right) = O\left(\frac{(\varepsilon_0)^{n-k-1}}{\theta^a 2^k}\right).$$

We now combine estimates for I_1, I_2 and the following estimates for the incomplete beta-function:

$$B(x; a, b) = O\left(\frac{x^a}{a}\right),$$

$$B(x; a, b) = B(a, b) + O\left(\frac{(1-x)^b}{b}\right),$$

$$\frac{1}{B(d-1, n-d)} = \frac{\Gamma(n-1)}{\Gamma(d-1)\Gamma(n-d)} = O\left(\frac{n^{d-1}}{\Gamma(d-1)}\right).$$

This gives us

$$P(k_i = k) = \binom{n-1}{k}\frac{w_0^{2a}}{2\theta^a a(a+1)}\left[B(k-1, n-k) + O\left(\frac{\left(1 - \frac{1}{2(a+1)}\right)^{n-k}}{n-k}\right)\right.$$

$$\left. - O\left(\frac{\left(\frac{w_0^{2a}}{2\theta^a(a+1)}\right)^{k-1}}{k-1}\right) + O\left(\frac{(\varepsilon_0)^{n-k-1}}{\theta^a 2^k}\right)\right]$$

$$= \binom{n-1}{k}\frac{w_0^{2a}}{2\theta^a a(a+1)}B(k-1, n-k)$$

$$\left[1 + O\left(\frac{(\varepsilon_1)^{n-k}n^{k-1}}{(n-k)\Gamma(k-1)}\right) + O\left(\frac{\left(\frac{w_0^{2a}}{2\theta^a(a+1)}\right)^{k-1}n^{k-1}}{(k-1)\Gamma(k-1)}\right)\right.$$

$$\left. + O\left(\frac{(\varepsilon_0)^{n-k-1}}{\theta^a 2^k}\frac{n^{k-1}}{\Gamma(k-1)}\right)\right].$$

Let us introduce the following notations:

$$A = O\left(\frac{(\varepsilon_1)^{n-k}n^{k-1}}{(n-k)\Gamma(k-1)}\right), \text{ where } \varepsilon_1 = 1 - \frac{1}{2(a+1)},$$

$$B = O\left(\frac{\left(\frac{w_0^{2a}}{2\theta^a(a+1)}\right)^{k-1}n^{k-1}}{(k-1)\Gamma(k-1)}\right),$$

$$C = O\left(\frac{(\varepsilon_0)^{n-k-1}}{\theta^a 2^k}\frac{n^{k-1}}{\Gamma(k-1)}\right), \text{ where } \varepsilon_0 = \frac{1}{2}\left(1 + \frac{a}{a+1}\right).$$

Using $\frac{n}{\theta^a(n)} = o(1)$, for $k(n) < C_0 n$ we get

$$B = O\left(\frac{\left(\frac{w_0^{2a}}{2(a+1)}\right)^{k-1}(\frac{n}{\theta^a})^{k-1}}{\Gamma(k)}\right) = o(1).$$

If $k(n)$ is a bounded function, then since $\varepsilon_0 < 1$ and $\varepsilon_1 < 1$ we have

$$A = O\left((\varepsilon_1)^{\frac{n-k}{k-1}} n^{k-1}\right) = o(1),$$
$$C = O\left((\varepsilon_0)^{n-k} n^{k-1}\right) = o(1).$$

If $k(n) \to \infty$ as $n \to \infty$, using Stirling's approximation $\Gamma(k-1) \sim \sqrt{2\pi(k-2)}\left(\frac{e}{k-2}\right)^{k-2}$ we get

$$A = O\left(\frac{k-2}{(n-k)\sqrt{k-2}}\left((\varepsilon_1)^{\frac{n-k}{k-1}}\frac{n}{k-2}\right)^{k-1}\right),$$
$$C = O\left(\frac{\sqrt{k-2}}{\theta a}\left((\varepsilon_0)^{\frac{n-k-1}{k-1}}\frac{n}{k-2}\right)^{k-1}\right).$$

Since $\varepsilon^x x \to 0$ for $\varepsilon < 1$ as $x \to \infty$ there exist constants C_0 and N_0 such that for $n > N_0$ and $k(n) < C_0 n$ we have $(\varepsilon_1)^{\frac{n-k}{k-1}}\frac{n}{k-2} < 1$ and $(\varepsilon_0)^{\frac{n-k-1}{k-1}}\frac{n}{k-2} < 1$. This implies that $A = o(1)$ and $C = o(1)$.

Thus, we obtain

$$P(k_i = k) = (1 + o(1))\binom{n-1}{k}B(k-1, n-k) = (1 + o(1))k^{-2}. \tag{11}$$

□

Note that regardless of the shape parameter of the Pareto distribution of weights we always generate networks with a degree distribution following a power law with an exponent equals 2. In the next section, we modify our model to change the exponent of the degree destribution and some other properties of the resulting networks.

Model modifications

In this section, we will show how to modify our model to get new properties and how these modifications will affect the degree distribution.

Directed network

Many real networks are directed. To model them and obtain an exponent of the power law that differs from 2, we changed the condition for the existence of an edge. There will be a directed edge (v_i, v_j), if and only if

$$(w_i^\alpha \vec{x}_i, w_j^\beta \vec{x}_j) \geq \theta, \quad \alpha, \beta > 0.$$

As it follows from the next theorem this modification allows us to tune an exponent of the power law.

Theorem 7 *Let $P_{out}(k)$ be the probability of an random node to have out-degree k, $P_{in}(k)$ in-degree k. If $n^{\max\{\alpha,\beta\}/a}/\theta(n) = o(1)$, then there exist constants C_0 and N_0 such that $\forall k(n) : \forall n > N_0 \; k(n) < C_0 n$ we have*

$$P_{out}(k) = (1 + o(1))k^{-1-\alpha/\beta}, P_{in}(k) = (1 + o(1))k^{-1-\beta/\alpha}.$$

Proof Here is a proof for the out-degree distribution. The case of the in-degree distribution is similar.

First, let us compute $P_e(w)$—the probability of the node $\vec{v}_i = w_i\vec{x}_i$ with weight $w_i = w$ to have an edge to another random node.

$$P_e(w) = \int\limits_{w_0}^{\infty} f(w') \int\limits_{\substack{x' \in S(0,1) \\ (w^\alpha x, (w')^\beta x') \geq \theta}} \frac{1}{4\pi}dx'dw'. \tag{12}$$

Similar to Lemma 1 we get

$$P_e(w) = \int\limits_{\max\{w_0,\theta^{1/\beta}/w^{\alpha/\beta}\}}^{\infty} \frac{aw_0^a}{(w')^{a+1}} \frac{1}{2}\left(1 - \frac{\theta}{w^\alpha(w')^\beta}\right)dw'. \tag{13}$$

Thus, we obtain

$$P_e(w) = \begin{cases} \frac{1}{2}\left(1 - \frac{a\theta}{w^\alpha(a+\beta)w_0^\beta}\right), & w > \left(\frac{\theta}{w_0^\alpha}\right)^{1/\beta}, \\ \frac{w^{a\alpha/\beta}w_0^a}{2\theta^{a/\beta}}\left(\frac{1}{a} - \frac{1}{\beta+a}\right), & w \leq \left(\frac{\theta}{w_0^\alpha}\right)^{1/\beta}. \end{cases} \tag{14}$$

Like in Theorem 6, we have

$$P(k_i = k) = \binom{n-1}{k} \int\limits_{w_0}^{\infty} (P_e(w))^k (1 - P_e(w))^{n-k-1} \frac{aw_0^a}{w^{a+1}}dw.$$

The rest of the proof is similar to the corresponding steps of Theorem 6, so we omit details here. □

With $\alpha = \beta$ this model turns into an undirected case with the power-law exponent equals 2 that agrees with Theorem 6.

Functions of dot product

In our model because of the condition $w_i w_j(\vec{x}_i, \vec{x}_j) \geq \theta \geq 0$ node $\vec{v}_i$ can only be connected to the node $\vec{v}_j$ if an angle between $\vec{x}_i$ and $\vec{x}_j$ is less than $\pi/2$. This is a constraint on the possible neighbors of a node that restricts the scope of our model.

We can solve this issue by changing the condition for the existence of an edge:

$$w_i^\alpha w_j^\beta h((\vec{x}_i, \vec{x}_j)) \geq \theta, \tag{15}$$

where $h : [-1, 1] \to \mathbb{R}$. On Fig. 3 is an example of how it works in $\mathbb{R}^2$.

Theorem 8 Let $P_{out}(k)$ be the probability of an random node to have out-degree k, $P_{in}(k)$—in-degree k. If $n^{\max\{\alpha,\beta\}/a}/\theta(n) = o(1)$ and $h : [-1, 1] \to \mathbb{R}$-continuous, strictly

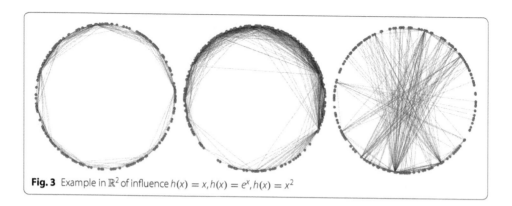

Fig. 3 Example in $\mathbb{R}^2$ of influence $h(x) = x, h(x) = e^x, h(x) = x^2$

increasing function, positive at least in one point from $(-1, 1)$, then there exist constants C_0 and N_0 such that $\forall k(n) : \forall n > N_0 \; k(n) < C_0 n$ we have

$$P_{out}(k) = k^{-1-\alpha/\beta}(1 + o(1)), P_{in}(k) = k^{-1-\beta/\alpha}(1 + o(1)).$$

Short scheme of proof

Here is the scheme of proof for the out-degree distribution. The case of the in-degree is similar.

Restrictions on the function h allow us to modify the proof of the directed case. The main difference is a value of the probability $P_e(w)$ of a node $\vec{v}_i = w_i \vec{x}_i$ with the weight $w_i = w$ to have an edge to another random node.

$$P_e(w) = \int_{w_0}^{\infty} \frac{aw_0^a}{(w')^{a+1}} \int_{\substack{x' \in S^2 \\ w^\alpha (w')^\beta h((x,x')) \geq \theta}} \frac{1}{4\pi} \mathrm{d}x' \mathrm{d}w'. \tag{16}$$

We will denote by I the inner integral:

$$\int_{\substack{x' \in S^2 \\ w^\alpha (w')^\beta h((x,x')) \geq \theta}} \frac{1}{4\pi} \mathrm{d}x' \mathrm{d}w'. \tag{17}$$

We can rewrite inequality (15) as $h((x,x')) \geq \frac{\theta}{w^\alpha (w')^\beta}$ and notice that $\frac{\theta}{w^\alpha (w')^\beta} \in (0, +\infty)$. Let us consider $h([-1, 1]) = [r, q]$, on this interval function h is invertable. We examine the mutual position of $[r, q]$ and $(0, +\infty)$. The definition of h implies that $[r, q] \cap (0, +\infty) \neq \emptyset$. This gives us the next two cases.

A. The first case is $[r, q] \subset (0, +\infty)$. If $\frac{\theta}{w^\alpha (w')^\beta} \in [r, q]$, then we may invert h and the inner integral I is equal to $2\pi \left(1 - h^{-1}\left(\frac{\theta}{w^\alpha (w')^\beta}\right)\right)$. If $\frac{\theta}{w^\alpha (w')^\beta} > q$, then the inequality (15) is not satisfied and $I = 0$. If $0 < \frac{\theta}{w^\alpha (w')^\beta} < r$, then the inequality (15) is satisfied for any pair of x and x', $I = 4\pi$, the surface area of S^2.

To deal with $P_e(w)$, we need to compare w_0 with boundaries for each range of $\frac{\theta}{w^\alpha (w')^\beta}$

1. If $w_0 < \frac{\theta^{1/\beta}}{w^{\alpha/\beta} q^{1/\beta}}$, then

$$P_e(w) = \int\limits_{w_0}^{\frac{\theta^{1/\beta}}{w^{\alpha/\beta} q^{1/\beta}}} 0 dw' + \int\limits_{\frac{\theta^{1/\beta}}{w^{\alpha/\beta} q^{1/\beta}}}^{\frac{\theta^{1/\beta}}{w^{\alpha/\beta} r^{1/\beta}}} \frac{aw_0^a}{(w')^{a+1}} \frac{1}{2}\left[1 - h^{-1}\left(\frac{\theta}{w^\alpha (w')^\beta}\right)\right] dw'$$

$$+ \int\limits_{\frac{\theta^{1/\beta}}{w^{\alpha/\beta} r^{1/\beta}}}^{\infty} 4\pi \frac{aw_0^a}{(w')^{a+1}} dw'.$$

2. If $\frac{\theta^{1/\beta}}{w^{\alpha/\beta} q^{1/\beta}} \leq w_0 < \frac{\theta^{1/\beta}}{w^{\alpha/\beta} r^{1/\beta}}$, then

$$P_e(w) = \int\limits_{w_0}^{\frac{\theta^{1/\beta}}{w^{\alpha/\beta} r^{1/\beta}}} \frac{aw_0^a}{(w')^{a+1}} \frac{1}{2}\left[1 - h^{-1}\left(\frac{\theta}{w^\alpha (w')^\beta}\right)\right] dw' + \int\limits_{\frac{\theta^{1/\beta}}{w^{\alpha/\beta} r^{1/\beta}}}^{\infty} 4\pi \frac{aw_0^a}{(w')^{a+1}} dw'.$$

3. Last case is $w_0 \geq \frac{\theta^{1/\beta}}{w^{\alpha/\beta} r^{1/\beta}}$. But $\theta(n)$ grows with n, and for big enough n this inequality will not be satisfied.

B. The second case is $[r, q] \not\subset (0, +\infty)$, which implies $r \leq 0$. If $\frac{\theta}{w^\alpha (w')^\beta} \in (0, q]$, then $I = 2\pi\left(1 - h^{-1}\left(\frac{\theta}{w^\alpha (w')^\beta}\right)\right)$. If $\frac{\theta}{w^\alpha (w')^\beta} > q$, then $I = 0$. This gives

$$P_e(w) = \int\limits_{\max(w_0, \frac{\theta^{1/\beta}}{w^{\alpha/\beta} q^{1/\beta}})}^{\infty} \frac{aw_0^a}{(w')^{a+1}} \frac{1}{2}\left[1 - h^{-1}\left(\frac{\theta}{w^\alpha (w')^\beta}\right)\right] dw'$$

It remains only to show that $P_{out}(k) = k^{-2}(1 + o(1))$. But now it is easy to see that the influence of every kind of the principal parts of the integral for $P_e(w)$ has been already examined in previous theorems for degree distributions. For example,

$$\int\limits_{\frac{\theta^{1/\beta}}{w^{\alpha/\beta} q^{1/\beta}}}^{\frac{\theta^{1/\beta}}{w^{\alpha/\beta} r^{1/\beta}}} \frac{aw_0^a}{(w')^{a+1}} \frac{1}{2}\left[1 - h^{-1}\left(\frac{\theta}{w^\alpha (w')^\beta}\right)\right] dw' = \frac{w_0^a w^{2a\alpha/\beta}}{\beta\theta^{a/\beta}} \int\limits_{r}^{q} (1 - h^{-1}(t)) t^{a/\beta - 1} dt,$$

what is proportional to the one we got in Theorem 7. Therefore, we are not giving here additional details. $\qquad\square$

For example, described class of functions contains functions like e^x and $x^{2m+1} + c$, $m \in \mathbb{N}$, for a proper constant c.

Of course, not only this small class of functions $h(x)$ has no influence on the degree distribution. For example, it is easy to show that $h(x) = x^{2m}, m \in \mathbb{N}$ also has this property. In this way, a proof will be different only in the computation of $P_e(w)$.

Conclusion

In our work, we suggest a new model for scale-free networks generation, which is based on the matrix factorization and has a geographical interpretation. We formalize it for fixed size and growing networks. We proof and validate empirically that degree distribution of resulting networks obeys power law with an exponent of 2.

We also consider several extensions of the model. First, we research the case of the directed network and obtain power-law degree distribution with a tunable exponent. Then, we apply different functions to the dot product of latent features vectors, which give us modifications with interesting properties.

Further research could focus on the deep study of latent features vectors distribution. It seems that not only a uniform distribution over the surface of the sphere should be considered because, for example, cities are not uniformly distributed over the surface of Earth. Besides, we want to try other distributions of weights.

Authors' contributions

This work is the result of a close joint effort in which all authors contributed almost equally to defining and shaping the problem definition, proofs, algorithms, and manuscript. The research would not have been conducted without the participation of any of the authors. All authors read and approved the final manuscript.

Author details

[1] Moscow Institute of Physics and Technology (SU), Moscow, Russia. [2] Skolkovo Institute of Science and Technology, Moscow, Russia. [3] Yandex, Moscow, Russia.

Competing interests

The authors declare that they have no competing interests.

Appendix

Proof of Lemma 1

For a node x with the weight w, the probability to be connected to a random node is represented by

$$P_e(w) = \int_{w_0}^{\infty} f(w') \int_{\substack{x' \in S^2 \\ ww'(x,x') \geq \theta}} \frac{1}{4\pi} dx' dw'. \tag{18}$$

We can rewrite inequality $ww'(x,x') \geq \theta$ as $(x,x') \geq \frac{\theta}{ww'}$. If $\frac{\theta}{ww'} \in [0,1]$, this inequality defines the spherical cap of the area $2\pi(1 - \frac{\theta}{ww'})$. Therefore, we have

$$P_e(w) = \int_{\max\{w_0, \theta/w\}}^{\infty} f(w') 2\pi \left(1 - \frac{\theta}{ww'}\right) \frac{1}{4\pi} dw'. \tag{19}$$

If we substitute $f(w')$ from (2), we obtain

$$P_e(w) = \int_{\max\{w_0, \theta/w\}}^{\infty} \frac{a}{w_0} \left(\frac{w_0}{w'}\right)^{a+1} \frac{1}{2} \left(1 - \frac{\theta}{ww'}\right) dw'. \tag{20}$$

If $w \leq \theta/w_0$, then

$$P_e(w) = \int\limits_{\theta/w}^{\infty} \frac{a}{2w_0} \left(\frac{w_0}{w'}\right)^{a+1} \left(1 - \frac{\theta}{ww'}\right) dw' = \int\limits_{\theta/w}^{\infty} \frac{a}{2w_0} \left(\frac{w_0}{w'}\right)^{a+1} dw' - \int\limits_{\theta/w}^{\infty} \frac{a}{2w_0} \left(\frac{w_0}{w'}\right)^{a+1} \frac{\theta}{ww'} dw'$$

$$= \frac{aw_0^a}{2} \frac{1}{a(\theta/w)^a} - \frac{aw_0^a\theta}{2w} \frac{1}{(a+1)(\theta/w)^{a+1}} = \frac{1}{2} \frac{w_0^a}{\theta^a(a+1)} w^a.$$

If $w > \theta/w_0$, then

$$P_e(w) = \int\limits_{w_0}^{\infty} \frac{a}{w_0} \left(\frac{w_0}{w'}\right)^{a+1} 2\pi \left(1 - \frac{\theta}{ww'}\right) \frac{1}{4\pi} dw' = \frac{aw_0^a}{2} \int\limits_{w_0}^{\infty} \frac{1}{w'^{a+1}} dw' - \frac{aw_0^a\theta}{2w} \int\limits_{w_0}^{\infty} \frac{1}{w'^{a+2}} dw'$$

$$= \frac{aw_0^a}{2} \frac{1}{aw_0^a} - \frac{aw_0^a\theta}{2w} \frac{1}{(a+1)w_0^{a+1}} = \frac{1}{2} \left(1 - \frac{a\theta}{w(a+1)w_0}\right).$$

Proof of Lemma 2

The edge probability is represented by

$$P_e = \int\limits_{w_0}^{\infty} \int\limits_{S^2} \int\limits_{w_0}^{\infty} \int\limits_{\substack{x' \in S^2 \\ ww'(x,x') \geq \theta}} f(w)f(w') \frac{1}{16\pi^2} dx' dw' dx dw. \tag{21}$$

Using (18), we obtain

$$P_e = \int\limits_{w_0}^{\infty} \int\limits_{S(0,1)} \frac{1}{4\pi} f(w)P_e(w) dx dw = \int\limits_{w_0}^{\infty} f(w)P_e(w) dw. \tag{22}$$

If $\theta < w_0^2$, then for all $w \in [w_0, \infty)$ $P_e(w)$ equals to $\frac{1}{2}\left(1 - \frac{a\theta}{w(a+1)w_0}\right)$. Using it, we get

$$P_e = \int\limits_{w_0}^{\infty} \frac{1}{2}\left(1 - \frac{a\theta}{w(a+1)w_0}\right) a \frac{w_0^a}{w^{a+1}} dw$$

$$= \frac{1}{2} - \int\limits_{w_0}^{\infty} \frac{1}{2}\left(\frac{a\theta}{w(a+1)w_0}\right) a \frac{w_0^a}{w^{a+1}} dw$$

$$= \frac{1}{2} - \frac{1}{2}a^2\theta \frac{w_0^{a-1}}{a+1} \int\limits_{w_0}^{\infty} \frac{1}{w^{a+2}} dw$$

$$= \frac{1}{2} - \frac{1}{2}a^2\theta \frac{w_0^{a-1}}{a+1} \frac{1}{a+1} \frac{1}{w_0^{a+1}}$$

$$= \frac{1}{2} - \frac{1}{2} \frac{a^2}{(a+1)^2} \frac{\theta}{w_0^2}.$$

If $\theta \geq w_0^2$, then

$$
P_e = \int\limits_{w_0}^{\theta/w_0} \frac{1}{2} \frac{w_0^a}{\theta^a(a+1)} w^a a \frac{w_0^a}{w^{a+1}} dw + \int\limits_{\theta/w_0}^{\infty} \frac{1}{2}\left(1 - \frac{a\theta}{w(a+1)w_0}\right) a \frac{w_0^a}{w^{a+1}} dw
$$

$$
= \frac{1}{2}\frac{w_0^a}{\theta^a(a+1)} a w_0^a \int\limits_{w_0}^{\theta/w_0} \frac{1}{w} dw + \frac{1}{2} a w_0^a \int\limits_{\theta/w_0}^{\infty} \frac{1}{w^{a+1}} - \frac{a^2 w_0^{a-1}\theta}{2(a+1)} \int\limits_{\theta/w_0}^{\infty} \frac{1}{w^{a+2}} dw
$$

$$
= \frac{1}{2}\frac{w_0^{2a} a}{\theta^a(a+1)}(\ln \theta - 2\ln w_0) + \frac{w_0^{2a}}{2\theta^a} - \frac{a^2}{2(a+1)^2}\frac{w_0^{2a}}{\theta^a}.
$$

Proof of Lemma 3

Let us enumerate pairs of nodes. Each pair of nodes i has an edge indicator I_{e_i}.

By definition, we have

$$
\mathrm{Var}(M) = \mathbb{E}(M^2) - \mathbb{E}(M)^2 = \mathbb{E}(I_{e_1} + \cdots + I_{e_{n(n-1)/2}})^2 - (\mathbb{E}I_{e_1} + \cdots + \mathbb{E}I_{e_{n(n-1)/2}})^2
$$

$$
= \sum_i \mathbb{E}I_{e_i}^2 + 2\sum_{i\neq j}\mathbb{E}I_{e_i}I_{e_j} - \sum_i (\mathbb{E}I_{e_i})^2 - 2\sum_{i\neq j}\mathbb{E}I_{e_i}\mathbb{E}I_{e_j}.
$$

$I_{e_1}, \cdots, I_{e_{n(n-1)/2}}$ is the sequence of identically distributed random variables, so their expected value is the same and equals to P_e.

Since $\mathbb{E}I_{e_i}^2 = \mathbb{E}I_{e_i} = P_e$, it follows that

$$
\mathbb{E}I_{e_i}I_{e_j} - \frac{n(n-1)}{2}(P_e)^2 - 2\sum_{i\neq j}\mathbb{E}I_{e_i}\mathbb{E}I_{e_j} = \frac{n(n-1)}{2}P_e(1-P_e) + 2\sum_{i\neq j}\mathbb{E}I_{e_i}I_{e_j} - 2\sum_{i\neq j}\mathbb{E}I_{e_i}\mathbb{E}I_{e_j}.
$$

If edges e_i and e_j do not have mutual nodes, then I_{e_i} and I_{e_j} are independent variables. Therefore, $\mathbb{E}(I_{e_i}I_{e_j}) = \mathbb{E}(I_{e_i})\mathbb{E}(I_{e_j}) = P_e^2$. We get

$$
\mathrm{Var}(M) = \frac{n(n-1)}{2}P_e(1-P_e) + \sum_{v=1}^{n}\sum_{\substack{w=1 \\ w\neq v}}^{n}\sum_{\substack{z=w+1 \\ z\neq v}}^{n}(\mathbb{E}I_{e(v,w)}I_{e(v,z)} - \mathbb{E}I_{e(v,w)}\mathbb{E}I_{e(v,z)})
$$

$$
= \frac{n(n-1)}{2}P_e(1-P_e) + \sum_{v=1}^{n}\sum_{\substack{w=1 \\ w\neq v}}^{n}\sum_{\substack{z=w+1 \\ z\neq v}}^{n}(\mathbb{E}I_{e(v,w)}I_{e(v,z)} - P_e^2)
$$

$\mathbb{E}I_{e(v,w)}I_{e(v,z)}$ is exactly equal to $P_<$.

Proof of Lemma 4

It can be easily seen that

$$
P_< = \int\limits_{w_0}^{\infty} P_e(w)^2 f(w) dw.
$$

If $\theta < w_0^2$ we have

$$P_< = \int\limits_{w_0}^{\infty} \frac{1}{4}\left(1 - \frac{a\theta}{w(a+1)w_0}\right)^2 a\frac{w_0^a}{w^{a+1}}\,dw$$

$$= \frac{1}{4}aw_0^a\int\limits_{w_0}^{\infty}\frac{1}{w^{a+1}}\,dw - \frac{1}{2}\frac{a^2\theta w_0^{a-1}}{a+1}\int\limits_{w_0}^{\infty}\frac{1}{w^{a+2}}\,dw + \frac{1}{4}\frac{a^3\theta^2 w_0^{a-2}}{(a+1)^2}\int\limits_{w_0}^{\infty}\frac{1}{w^{a+3}}\,dw$$

$$= \frac{1}{4} - \frac{1}{2}\frac{a^2\theta}{(a+1)^2}\frac{1}{w_0^2} + \frac{1}{4}\frac{a^3\theta^2}{(a+1)^2(a+2)}\frac{1}{w_0^4}.$$

If $\theta \geq w_0^2$, then

$$P_< = \int\limits_{w_0}^{\theta/w_0}\frac{1}{4}\frac{w_0^{2a}}{\theta^{2a}(a+1)^2}w^{2a}a\frac{w_0^a}{w^{a+1}}\,dw + \int\limits_{\theta/w_0}^{\infty}\frac{1}{4}\left(1 - \frac{a\theta}{w(a+1)w_0}\right)^2 a\frac{w_0^a}{w^{a+1}}\,dw.$$

Computing the first integral, we get

$$\int\limits_{w_0}^{\theta/w_0}\frac{1}{4}\frac{w_0^{2a}}{\theta^{2a}(a+1)^2}w^{2a}a\frac{w_0^a}{w^{a+1}}\,dw = \frac{1}{4}\frac{w_0^{2a}}{\theta^{2a}(a+1)^2}aw_0^a\int\limits_{w_0}^{\theta/w_0}w^{a-1}\,dw$$

$$= \frac{1}{4}\frac{w_0^{2a}}{\theta^{2a}(a+1)^2}[\theta^a - w_0^{2a}].$$

And for the second one, we have

$$\int\limits_{\theta/w_0}^{\infty}\frac{1}{4}\left(1 - \frac{a\theta}{w(a+1)w_0}\right)^2 a\frac{w_0^a}{w^{a+1}}\,dw = \int\limits_{\theta/w_0}^{\infty}\frac{1}{4}a\frac{w_0^a}{w^{a+1}}\,dw - \int\limits_{\theta/w_0}^{\infty}\frac{1}{2}\frac{a\theta}{w(a+1)w_0}a\frac{w_0^a}{w^{a+1}}\,dw$$

$$+ \int\limits_{\theta/w_0}^{\infty}\frac{1}{4}\frac{a^2\theta^2}{w^2(a+1)^2w_0^2}a\frac{w_0^a}{w^{a+1}}\,dw$$

$$= \frac{1}{4}aw_0^a\int\limits_{\theta/w_0}^{\infty}\frac{1}{w^{a+1}}\,dw - \frac{1}{2}\frac{a^2\theta w_0^{a-1}}{a+1}\int\limits_{\theta/w_0}^{\infty}\frac{1}{w^{a+2}}\,dw$$

$$+ \frac{1}{4}\frac{a^3\theta^2 w_0^{a-2}}{(a+1)^2}\int\limits_{\theta/w_0}^{\infty}\frac{1}{w^{a+3}}\,dw$$

$$= \frac{1}{4}w_0^a\frac{w_0^a}{\theta^a} - \frac{1}{2}\frac{a^2\theta w_0^{a-1}}{(a+1)^2}\frac{w_0^{a+1}}{\theta^{a+1}} + \frac{1}{4}\frac{a^3\theta^2 w_0^{a-2}}{(a+1)^2(a+2)}\frac{w_0^{a+2}}{\theta^{a+2}}$$

$$= \frac{1}{4}\frac{w_0^{2a}}{\theta^a} - \frac{1}{2}\frac{a^2}{(a+1)^2}\frac{w_0^{2a}}{\theta^a} + \frac{1}{4}\frac{a^3}{(a+1)^2(a+2)}\frac{w_0^{2a}}{\theta^a}.$$

This gives us $P_<$ in the case of $\theta \geq w_0^2$:

$$P(<) = \frac{1}{4}\frac{w_0^{2a}}{\theta^{2a}(a+1)^2}[\theta^a - w_0^{2a}] + \frac{1}{4}\frac{w_0^{2a}}{\theta^a}\left[1 - 2\frac{a^2}{(a+1)^2} + \frac{a^3}{(a+1)^2(a+2)}\right].$$

References

1. Albert R, Barabási A-L. Statistical mechanics of complex networks. Rev Mod Phys. 2002;74(1):47.
2. Clauset A, Shalizi CR, Newman ME. Power-law distributions in empirical data. SIAM Rev. 2009;51(4):661–703.
3. Colomer-de-Simon P, Boguná M. Clustering of random scale-free networks. Phys Rev E Stat Nonlin Soft Matter Phys. 2012;86:026120 (preprint arXiv:1205.2877).
4. Callaway DS, Newman ME, Strogatz SH, Watts DJ. Network robustness and fragility: percolation on random graphs. Phys Rev Lett. 2000;85(25):5468.
5. Moreno Y, Pacheco AF. Synchronization of kuramoto oscillators in scale-free networks. EPL (Europhys Lett). 2004;68(4):603.
6. Menon AK, Elkan C. Link prediction via matrix factorization. In: Gunopulos D, Hofmann T, Malerba D, Vazirgiannis M, editors. Machine learning and knowledge discovery in databases: European conference, ECML PKDD 2011, Athens, September 5–9, 2011, Proceedings, Part II. Berlin: Springer; 2011. p. 437–52.
7. Hayashi Y. A review of recent studies of geographical scale-free networks. arXiv preprint physics/0512011; 2005.
8. Barabási A-L, Albert R. Emergence of scaling in random networks. Science. 1999;286(5439):509–12.
9. Bollobás B, Riordan O, Spencer J, Tusnády G, et al. The degree sequence of a scale-free random graph process. Random Struct Algorithms. 2001;18(3):279–90.
10. Holme P, Kim BJ. Growing scale-free networks with tunable clustering. Phys Rev E. 2002;65(2):026107.
11. Lee DD, Seung HS. Algorithms for non-negative matrix factorization. In: Advances in neural information processing systems; 2001. p. 556–562.
12. Koren Y, Bell R, Volinsky C. Matrix factorization techniques for recommender systems. Computer. 2009;8:30–7.
13. Liben-Nowell D, Kleinberg J. The link-prediction problem for social networks. J Am Soc Inf Sci Technol. 2007;58(7):1019–31.
14. Masuda N, Miwa H, Konno N. Geographical threshold graphs with small-world and scale-free properties. Phys Rev E. 2005;71(3):036108.
15. Morita S. Crossovers in scale-free networks on geographical space. Phys Rev E. 2006;73(3):035104.
16. Rozenfeld AF, Cohen R, Ben-Avraham D, Havlin S. Scale-free networks on lattices. Phys Rev Lett. 2002;89(21):218701.
17. Warren CP, Sander LM, Sokolov IM. Geography in a scale-free network model. Phys Rev E. 2002;66(5):056105.
18. Yakubo K, Korošak D. Scale-free networks embedded in fractal space. Phys Rev E. 2011;83(6):066111.

10

Efficient network generation under general preferential attachment

James Atwood[1][*], Bruno Ribeiro[2] and Don Towsley[1]

*Correspondence:
jatwood@cs.umass.edu
[1] School of Computer Science,
University of Massachusetts
Amherst, 01003, Amherst, MA, USA
Full list of author information is
available at the end of the article

Abstract

Preferential attachment (PA) models of network structure are widely used due to their explanatory power and conceptual simplicity. PA models are able to account for the scale-free degree distributions observed in many real-world large networks by sequentially introducing nodes that attach preferentially to existing nodes with high degree. The ability to efficiently generate instances from PA models is a key asset in understanding both the models themselves and the real networks that they represent. Surprisingly, little attention has been paid to the problem of efficient instance generation. In this paper, we show that the complexity of generating network instances from a PA model depends on the preference function of the model, provides efficient data structures that work under any preference function, and presents empirical results from an implementation based on these data structures. We demonstrate that, by indexing growing networks with a simple augmented heap, we can implement a network generator which scales many orders of magnitude beyond existing capabilities (10^6 to 10^8 nodes). We show the utility of an efficient and general PA network generator by investigating the consequences of varying the preference functions of an existing model. We also provide 'quicknet,' a freely available open-source implementation of the methods described in this work.

Keywords: Preferential; Attachment; Network; Science

Introduction

There is a clear need for scalable network generators, as the ability to efficiently generate instances from models of network structure is central to understanding both the models and the real networks that they represent. Ideally, researchers of communication and social networks should be able to generate networks on the same scale as the real networks they study, and many interesting networks, such as the World Wide Web and Facebook, have millions to billions of nodes. Furthermore, network generation is the primary tool both for empirically validating the theoretical behavior of models of network structure and for investigating behaviors that are not captured by theoretical results. The generation of very large networks is of particular importance for these tasks because theoretically derived behavior is often asymptotic.

However, the generation of large networks is difficult because of its high complexity. In the case of preferential attachment (PA), arguably the most widely used generative model of networks, a nonlocal distribution over node degrees must be both sampled from and updated at each time-step. If we naively index this distribution, we will need to update every node at every time-step, which implies that generating a network will have complexity of at least $O\left(|V|^2\right)$.

PA models are of particular interest because they account for the scale-free distribution of degree observed in many large networks [1]. For instance, scale-free degree distributions have been observed in the World Wide Web [2-4], the Internet [5-7], telephone call graphs [8,9], bibliographic networks [10], and social networks [11].

Preferential attachment models generate networks by sequentially introducing nodes that prefer to attach to nodes with high degree. While many extensions to this model class exist, all members share the same basic form: At each time-step, a node is sampled from the network with probability proportional to its degree, a new node is introduced to the network, and an edge is added from the new node to the sampled node. This behavior has important implications for implementation. First, PA is inherently sequential, because the next action taken depends on the state of the network, and the state of the network changes at each time-step. This implies that the algorithm is not easily parallelized. Second, network nodes must be indexed such that they can be efficiently sampled by degree, and, because we are introducing a new node at each time-step, the index must also support efficient insertion. Third, the relevant distribution over nodes is nonlocal, in that the introduction of a new node and edge affects the probability of every node in the network through the normalization factor.

Much of the work in modeling network structure has focused on the asymptotic regime. A model is defined, and a limiting degree distribution (as $|V|$ approaches infinity) is obtained analytically. Less effort has focused on generating finite networks. In the following sections, we provide a robust framework for generating networks via PA. This framework easily scales to millions of nodes on commodity hardware. We also provide 'quicknet,' a freely available open-source C implementation of the framework [12].

The remainder of the paper is structured as follows. In the 'Complexity' section, we analyze the complexity of generating networks from PA models. The 'Implementation' section describes candidate methods for efficiently implementing preferential attachment generators and presents results from a simulator which implements them. The 'Applications' section describes several applications of a PA network generator which scales to many millions of nodes. We describe related work in the 'Related work' section and present conclusions and future work in the 'Conclusion' and 'Future work' sections, respectively.

Complexity

In this section, we then provide a formal definition of a PA model, then describe two existing PA models as examples. This is followed by an analysis of the complexity of generating networks from PA models.

Definitions

In this section, we provide a framework for representing general preferential attachment models. Note that the idea of a general PA model is not new to this work and that the formulation presented here is only used to facilitate algorithmic analysis. For a detailed treatment of general preferential attachment, please see 'The Organization of Random Growing Networks' by Krapivsky and Redner [13].

Let $G_t = (V_t, E_t)$ be the network that results from t iterations of a PA simulation. V_t is the set vertices (or nodes) within the network, and E_t is the set of edges between elements of V_t. Let $T(G_t)$ be the worst case time complexity of generating G_t; that is, the worst case time complexity of a preferential attachment simulation of t iterations.

Recall that the number of iterations required to generate a network with $|V|$ nodes via PA is $\Theta(|V|)$. Accordingly, we will omit t and frame our discussion of complexity $T(G)$ in terms of $|V|$.

Let $A = \{a_1, a_2, \ldots, a_{|A|}\}$ be a set of attributes that can be defined on a network node. Let $X_v = \{x_{va_1}, x_{va_2}, \ldots, x_{va_{|A|}}\} \in \mathbb{R}^{|A|}$ be a setting of A for node $v \in V$, and let $\lambda_{va_i} \in \mathbb{R}$ be the fitness of node v for attribute a_i. Let:

$$f = \left\{ f_{a_i}(x_{va_i}, \lambda_{va_i}) : \mathbb{R} \times \mathbb{R} \to \mathbb{R}^+ \mid a_i \in A \right\}$$

be a set of functions, where $f_{a_i} \in f$ maps $x_{va_i} \in \mathbb{R}$ and $\lambda_{va_i} \in \mathbb{R}$ to a preference mass $\mu_{va_i} \in \mathbb{R}^+$. The 'preference mass' μ_{va_i} is a nonnegative real value that is proportional to the probability of selecting v by a_i under the PA model. We will refer to the elements of f as the 'preference functions' of the PA model. Note that, in this work, we restrict our attention to the set of degree-related attributes D (i.e., in-degree, out-degree, and total degree) with settings $x_{vd} \in \mathbb{N} \forall d \in D$. This implies that the elements of f are defined over the natural numbers:

$$f = \left\{ f_d(x_{vd}, \lambda_{vd}) : \mathbb{N} \times \mathbb{R} \to \mathbb{R}^+ \mid d \in D \right\}$$

The restriction is purely elective; any attribute with real-valued settings could be specified.

A PA model has one or more preference functions. Price's model, for example, has a single linear preference function. Krapivsky's model has two: one for in-degree and another for out-degree. A 'linear preferential attachment model' only admits linear preference functions of the form $g(x, \lambda) = c_1 x + \lambda$, a 'quadratic preferential attachment model' only admits quadratic preference functions of the form $g(x, \lambda) = c_2 x^2 + c_1 x + \lambda$ and so on.

Description of considered models
Price's model
Figure 1 describes Price's algorithm. Briefly, at each time-step, a node is sampled from the network with probability proportional to its in-degree, a new node is introduced to the network, and a directed edge is added from the new node to the sampled node. Notice that a node is added at each time-step, so that the generation of a network with $|V|$ nodes takes $|V|$ steps.

Krapivsky's model
Figure 1 also describes the algorithm of Krapivsky et al. At each step, the algorithm of Price's model is followed with probability p, and a 'preferential edge step' is taken with probability $1 - p$. During a preferential edge step, two nodes, n_o and n_i, are sampled from the network by out- and in-degree, respectively, and an edge is added from n_o to n_i. Note that a node is no longer added at every step; rather, a node is added at a given step with probability p. This implies that the number of iterations required to generate a network with $|V|$ nodes is a random variable with expected value $|V|/p$. $|V|/p$ is $\Theta(|V|)$

```
Price(n,λ):
    G ← G₀
    for i ← 1 to n − |G₀| do
        existing_node ← sample_in_degree(G, λ)
        new_node = add_node(G)
        add_edge(G, new_node, existing_node)
    end for
    return G


Krapivsky(n, p, λ, μ):
    G ← G₀
    while |V| < n do
        u ← uniform draw
        if u < p then
            existing_node ← sample_in_degree(G, λ)
            new_node = add_node(G)
            add_edge(G, new_node, existing_node)
        else
            existing_node_tail ← sample_in_degree(G, λ)
            existing_node_head ← sample_out_degree(G, μ)
            add_edge(G, existing_node_tail, existing_node_head)
        end if
    end while
    return G
```

Figure 1 Generating a network with _n_ nodes under Price and Krapivsky's models. G_0 is some small seed network. λ and μ are scalers which give the fitness of nodes for incoming and outgoing edges, respectively.

$\forall p$, so asymptotically, this is no different than Price's model. More generally, the number of iterations required to generate a network with $|V|$ nodes via a PA model is $\Theta(|V|)$.

Generation complexity

We obtain a trivial lower bound on $T(G)$ by noting that, in order to generate G, we must at the very least output $|V|$ nodes, so $T(G) = \Omega(|V|)$.

A discussion of the upper bound follows. Recall that the salient problem in generating networks from a PA model is indexing the network's nodes in such a way that sampling, insertion, and incrementation can be accomplished efficiently. Tonelli et al. [14] provide a clever method for accomplishing all three tasks in constant time, provided that the preference function is linear and the fitness is both uniform across all nodes and constant. Given constant insertion and sampling times, the generation of a network with $|V|$ nodes takes $O(|V|)$ time. Considering that the lower bound is $\Omega(|V|)$, we have the asymptotically tight bound of $T(G) = \Theta(|V|)$.

However, this method does not extend to nonlinear preferential attachment (see 'Related work' section for details). We can improve performance by shifting to data structures which provide $O(\log|V|)$ insertion, sampling, and incrementation, giving an overall complexity of $T(G) = O(|V|\log|V|)$.

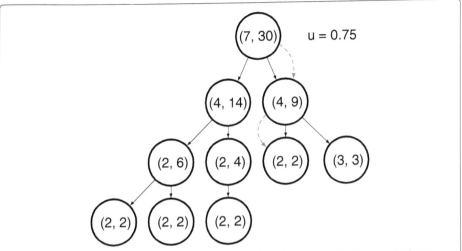

Figure 2 An example of an augmented tree structure. Each node is annotated with (μ_n, μ_s), where μ_n the node mass and μ_s is the subtree mass. The preference function associated with this tree is $f(d) = d + 2.0$. The sample path through the tree structure is illustrated for $u = 0.75$.

We accomplish this with a set of augmented tree structures. Each tree supports a preference function of the model by indexing the preference mass assigned to each node in the network by that preference function. Each item in the tree indexes a node in the network. The tree items are annotated with the preference mass of the network node under the preference function and the subtree mass, which is the total preference mass of the subtree that has the item as root; see Figure 2. Note that we refer to 'items' in the tree rather than the more typical 'nodes'; this is to avoid confusion between elements of the tree and elements of the network. We can sample from such a structure by recursively comparing the properly normalized subtree mass of a given item and its children to a uniform random draw; see Figures 2 and 3.

Note that, at each iteration of a standard PA simulation, we must sample a node, update that node's mass, and insert a new node. In what follows, we show that each of these steps can be accomplished in asymptotically logarithmic time.

Implementation

The tree structure that we described in the previous section can be implemented in a number of different ways that each have a generation time of $O(|V|\log|V|)$. They differ in their computational time for finite $|V|$. In this section, we empirically evaluate a set of realizations of the annotated tree structure. Specifically, we investigate a simple binary max-heap where priority is defined by node mass and a set of binary treaps with various sort and priority keys.

Note that, in the discussion of the heap-based and treap-based implementations of the tree structure, we will often refer to a 'sort invariant' and a 'heap invariant'. The sort invariant states that, for any three nodes $Y \leftarrow X \rightarrow Z$ where Y and Z are the left and right children of parent X, respectively, and a 'sort key' k that is associated with each item, $Y.k \leq X.k \leq Z.k$. The heap invariant states that for any three nodes $Y \leftarrow X \rightarrow Z$ (defined in the same fashion) and some 'priority key' p associated with each item, $X.p \geq Y.p$ and $X.p \geq Z.p$.

```
Sample(tree):
    sampled_node ← NULL
    u ← uniform sample
    if tree.root != NULL then
        sampled_node ← SampleItem(tree, tree.root, 0., u)
    end if
    return sampled_node


SampleItem(item, η, u):
    if item.left != NULL then
        if u < (η + item.left.subtree_mass) / tree.total_mass then
            return SampleItem(tree, item.left, η, u)
        end if
        η ← η + item.left.subtree_mass
    end if
    η ← η + item.node_mass
    if u < observed_mass / tree.total_mass then
        return item.node
    end if
    if item.right != NULL then
        return SampleItem(tree, item.right, η, u)
    end if
```

Figure 3 General algorithm to sample from the augmented tree structure. η is the mass observed thus far, and u is a sample from the standard uniform distribution.

We first describe the binary maximum heap. We annotate each item in the heap with a node mass, which is defined by the preference function, and a subtree mass, which is initialized to the node mass. When inserting a new item i, i's node mass is added to all traversed items, so that the subtree mass remains accurate upon insertion. Sampling is accomplished via the algorithm of Figure 3. Node mass may only increase, so we implement an augmented version of increase-key which maintains subtree mass under exchanges; see Figure 4 for a diagram of the exchange operation. The increase-key operation supports the Increment operation, which is described below. We set priorities to be equivalent to node masses so that the most probable nodes can be accessed more quickly.

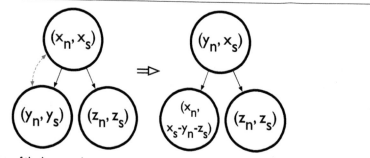

Figure 4 A diagram of the heap exchange process in the augmented heap. Each node is annotated with (μ_n, μ_s), where μ_n the node mass and μ_s is the subtree mass. Note that exchanges maintain the subtree mass invariant.

The PA process is supported by the binary maximum heap via the operations Sample, Increment, and Insert. As previously mentioned, sampling is performed via the algorithm of Figure 3. Increment increases an item's mass and then performs heap exchanges to account for any violation of the heap invariant; it is described in Figure 5. Insert adds an item to the index, appropriately updating the subtree masses of any parent items; see Figure 6.

Note that, if we were to annotate each item with a node's *probability* mass rather than *preference* mass, insertion would be a linear time operation. When a new node is introduced, the probability of every existing node decreases because the normalization factor increases. Thus, upon insertion, every item's probability mass would need to be updated. There are $|V|$ items, so insertion becomes a $\Theta(|V|)$ operation in this situation. Conversely, the preference mass of each node is unaffected by the introduction of a new node. Insertion in this scenario is a $O(\log|V|)$ operation; see Figures 6 and 7.

We use Price's model as an illustrative example. Recall that, in Price's model, a new node is introduced at each time-step and an edge from the new node to an existing node is added preferentially. We first identify an existing node via Sample. We then create a new node and add an edge from the new node to the existing node. Increment is called on the existing node to reflect the change in preference mass due to the new incoming edge. Finally, the new node is added to the index via Insert. Sample, Increment, and Insert are $O(\log|V|)$ operations, which implies that a single iteration is $O(\log|V|)$ and that a simulation with $|V|$ iterations is $O(|V|\log|V|)$. Generating a network with $|V|$ nodes takes $\Theta(|V|)$ iterations, so $T(G) = O(|V|\log|V|)$.

The augmented heap is implemented via a dynamic array that provides amortized constant insertion time at the cost of some wasted space. We sought to avoid this wastage by instead using some sort of binary tree, where insertion can be defined according to some ordinal value rather than an index into an underlying array. Binary treaps are an extension of binary trees that maintain a heap invariant over a random priority assigned to each item, guaranteeing that the tree is balanced in expectation [15].

The treap-based tree structure supports two operations: Insert and Sample-Destructive. Sample-Destructive is built on the Sample procedure that is given in Figure 3.

```
Increment(heap,item,new_mass):
        additional_mass ← new_mass - item.mass
        item.mass ← new_mass
        item.subtree_mass += additional_mass
        while item != heap.root && parent(item).mass ¡ item.mass do
            parent(item).subtree_mass += additional_mass
            heap_exchange(heap, item, parent(item))
            item ← parent(item);
        end while
        while item != heap.root do
            parent(item).subtree_mass += additional_mass
            item ← parent(item);
        end while
```

Figure 5 The Increment operation of the heap-based tree structure. The constant-time operation heap_exchange is demonstrated in Figure 4. The two while loops collectively over an item's $O(\log|V|)$ ancestors, so Increment is a $O(\log|V|)$ operation.

```
Insert(heap, item):
    heap.add(item)
    node_mass ← item.node_mass
    while item has a parent do
        item ← parent(item)
        item.subtree_mass += node_mass
    end while
```

Figure 6 The Insert operation of the heap-based tree structure. Note that each item has $O(\log|V|)$ ancestors, so Insert is a $O(\log|V|)$ operation.

It alters the procedure so that the sampling operation is destructive; that is, the sampled item is removed from the treap. The Insert operation inserts an item so that the sort invariant is maintained, much like one would insert an item into a binary tree. After the item is inserted, the heap invariant may have been violated, so tree rotations are performed until the heap invariant has been restored.

Figure 8 shows the empirical runtime of each of these structures as a function of generated network size. All networks were generated from Krapivsky's model. The binary heap consistently took significantly less time than the treap-based methods to generate networks of several different sizes.

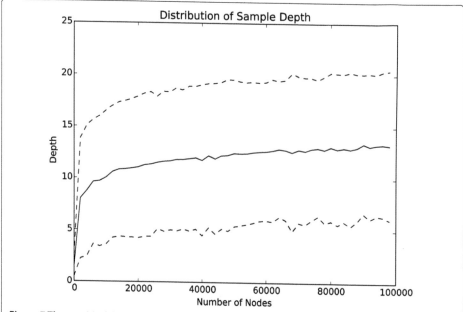

Figure 7 The empirical distribution of the depth of a sampled node within the heap as a function of network size. The solid line indicates the expected depth, and the dashed lines provide the 95% confidence interval. Note that the expected depth grows logarithmically with size of the network, which is consistent with the theoretical bounds presented in the 'Implementation' section.

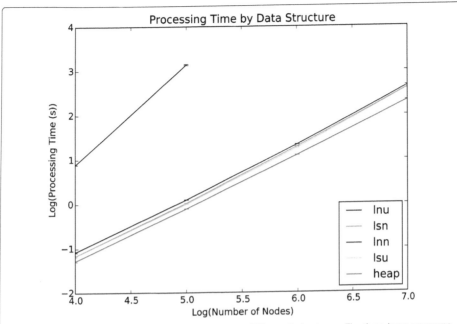

Figure 8 The empirical runtime of the simulator using different index types. The three-letter acronyms in the legend indicate the preference function type ('l' for linear), the sort key ('s' for subtree mass or 'n' for node mass), and the definition of priority ('n' for node mass or 'u' for uniform) for different variants of the treap structure. Twenty networks were generated for each configuration and size. Error bars, barely visible, indicate the 95% confidence interval.

Applications

We validate our generation model by generating sets of networks from the Krapivsky model and comparing the marginal degree distributions inferred from the generated networks with the asymptotic value predicted by the model. We then use the generator to explore some interesting questions. Specifically, we analyze the effect of changing the fitnesses of the Krapivsky model from a constant value to a random variable with various distributions. We also analyze the robustness of Krapivsky's model to superlinear preference functions.

Validating the network generator

We validate our framework by comparing the inferred exponents of the marginal distributions of generated networks with the known (theoretical, asymptotic) values for the exponents. We generated 10 networks with 10^7 nodes each. Figure 9 shows a plot of the base-10 logarithm of both degree an complementary cumulative distribution. The exponents of the marginal degree distributions were inferred via linear regression. We find, as expected, that they both exhibit power-law behavior (evident in the linearity) and that the inferred exponents of the distributions are in relatively good agreement with asymptotic theoretical values. Note that, while networks with 10^7 nodes are very large, they are still finite; we believe that this accounts for the small discrepancy between the inferred exponents and the theoretic values.

Exploring extensions to Krapivsky's model
Pareto fitness

We use our network generator to investigate the effects of altering the Krapivsky model. Specifically, we generated networks from a variant where the fitnesses assigned to each

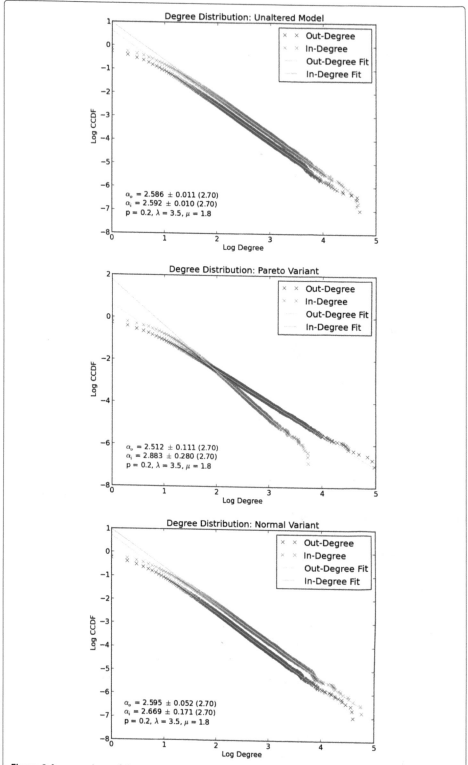

Figure 9 A comparison of the generated and theoretical marginal distributions of in- and out-degree under Krapivsky's model. The model was parameterized with $\lambda = 3.5$ and $\mu = 1.8$, and 10 networks with 10^7 nodes were generated. We plot the degree distribution of a single example network. Three variants are investigated: The unaltered model (top), a model with Pareto-distributed fitnesses (center), and a model with normally distributed fitnesses (bottom). $\alpha_o = \mu_o \pm 2\sigma_{SE}(\alpha_o^*)$ specifies the inferred exponent of the marginal out-degree distribution, where μ_o is the observed mean of the exponent, σ_{SE} is the standard error, and α_o^* is the predicted exponent for the unaltered model. The same form holds for α_i.

node were sampled from a Pareto distribution, rather than assigning the same constant value to each node. Results can be seen in Figure 9. The distribution of in-degree fitness is $\frac{\lambda d_m^\lambda}{d^{\lambda+1}}$ and has expected value $\frac{\lambda d_m}{\lambda-1}$. The parameter d_m is set to $(\lambda-1)$ so that the expected value of the distribution simplifies to λ. The same form was used for the out-degree fitness. Note that this variant still exhibits scale-free behavior, that the inferred exponents are in better agreement with the predicted values than the exponents inferred from the simulation of the unaltered model, and that the variance of the inferred exponents is higher.

Normal fitness

We also simulated a variant of the Krapivsky model where fitnesses were sampled from a truncated normal distribution. Results can be seen in Figure 9. In-degree fitnesses were sampled from $N(\lambda, (\lambda/4)^2)$ and out-degree fitnesses from $N(\lambda, (\lambda/4)^2)$. The variances were chosen such that the probability of sampling a negative fitness is very small (less than 10^{-4}); the distributions were truncated so that any negative samples were replaced with zero. Note that scale-free behavior is still observed and that the inferred exponents of the marginal distributions of in- and out-degree are in very close agreement with the simulation of the original model.

Robustness to superlinear preference functions

Superlinear preference functions increase the strength of the 'rich-get-richer' effect. This can lead to situations where one node quickly overtakes all others and is thus a component of most of the edges in the network. In the extreme case, a star will form; all edges will be connected to the outlier node. We investigate the robustness of Krapivsky's model to superlinear preference functions by plotting the ratio $\frac{d_{max}}{|E|}$, were d_{max} is the maximum degree, as a function of the preference function exponent α; see Figure 10. $\frac{d_{max}}{|E|}$ will approach one as the network approaches a star formation.

There is an interesting side effect to the transition from scale-free to star-structured networks. As the network becomes more star-like, the probability of selecting the most probable node tends to increase. The most probable node always sits at the top of the heap, so it can be accessed in constant time. So, the closer a network's structure is to a star formation, the larger the probability that an iteration of a PA algorithm will be constant time. For a star structured network in the limit, every iteration will be constant time and the generation of a network with $|V|$ nodes will be $\Theta(|V|)$. This behavior is apparent for finite $|V|$; we have observed that the runtime of the generator tends to decrease as α increases.

Related work

Summary

This work is concerned with the problem of efficiently generating networks from PA models. Some examples of PA models include the models of Price (directed networks with scale-free in-degrees) [16], Barabási and Albert (undirected networks with scale-free degrees) [17], Krapivsky et al. (directed networks with nonindependent in and out-degrees which exhibit marginally scale-free behavior) [18], and Capocci et al. (like Krapivsky's model, but with reciprocation) [19].

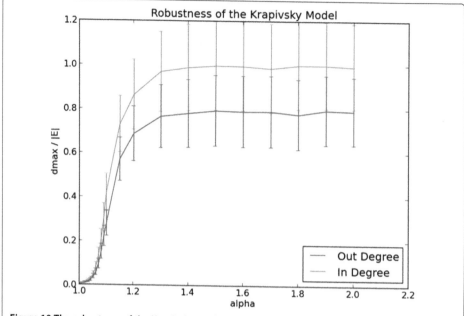

Figure 10 The robustness of the Krapivsky model to superlinear preference functions. α indicates the exponent of a preference function of the form $f(d) = d^\alpha + c$. d_{max} is the maximum degree of the generated network; $\frac{d_{max}}{|E|}$ gives the proportion of edges that involve the maximum degree node. $\frac{d_{max}}{|E|} = 1$ indicates a star formation. Note that there is a phase transition from scale-free to star-structured networks between $\alpha = 1.0$ and $\alpha = 1.2$. One-hundred networks with 10^6 nodes each was generated for each value of α. Error bars indicate the 95% confidence interval.

There has been some prior work in efficiently generating networks from PA models. Ren and Li [20] describe the simulation of a particular linear PA model, RX, but do not address the general problem of simulating networks from models with general preference functions. Hruz et al. [21] and D'Angelo and Ferreti [22] provide methods for parallelizing the simulation of linear PA but do not treat the nonlinear case. Machta and Machta [23] analyze the general case for the PRAM shared-memory parallel architecture. To the best of our knowledge, our work is the first to address the problem of efficient generation from PA models under possibly nonlinear preference functions using a sequential model of computation.

Tonelli et al. [14] provide a method for computing an iteration of the linear Yule-Simon cumulative advantage process in constant time. This method can naturally be extended to network generation through linear PA. However, the extension to nonlinear PA is very inefficient in both time and space, as shown in the next section.

Extension to nonlinear PA

Let u be an array of integers and F a real number. Consider a preferential attachment model with a linear preference function $f(d) = ad + b$, where a is the coefficient of the preferential attachment model, d is a node's in-degree, and b is a fitness value which is the same for all nodes. Assume that, like Price's model, each new node is introduced with an outgoing edge which attaches preferentially to an existing node. When a node n is inserted into the network, n's fitness is added to F, and a label identifying the node that n attaches to is appended to u. It is easy to see that the probability of selecting node i after the nth insertion is proportional to $a|d_i^n| + F$. The real number, F, can be thought of as indexing the probability mass due only to the fitness of each node in the network, whereas the array of integers, u, indexes the mass due to the degrees of nodes. Tonelli et al. provide a constant-time algorithm for sampling from this structure in their paper.

The array, u, stores a collection of integers which map to node labels. Each time a node is attached to, that node's label is appended to u. The real number, F, stores the sum of all of the individual fitnesses b. We sample from this structure as follows. Let K be the length of u, a be the linear coefficient of the process, and r be a random variable uniformly distributed on the interval $[0, K + nb]$. If $r > K$, then the quantity round $\left(\frac{r-K}{b}\right) + 1$ provides the label of the node. Otherwise, the quantity round $\left(\frac{r}{a}\right) + 1$ specifies an index into u which in turn specifies a node label. Both calculations take constant time, so sampling does as well.

Notice that this generation algorithm relies on two assumptions: the preferential attachment scheme must be linear, and the fitnesses must be the same for all nodes. To understand the first assumption, consider a model with a quadratic preference function $f(d) = ad^2 + b$. In order to index a node's transition from degree d to degree $d + 1$, we must append $(d + 1)^2 - d^2 = 2d + 1$ entries to u. Indexing a node of degree d is thus an $O(d)$ operation, and the array u requires $\sum_{v \in V} d_v^2$ entries. More generally, under a preference function of degree α, indexing a node's transition from d to $d + 1$ requires $O\left(d^{\alpha-1}\right)$ operations, and the array u will have $\sum_{v \in V} d_v^\alpha$ entries.

The second assumption is necessary for the real number F to map directly to a node index. The generation algorithm also assumes that the fitnesses of each node are the same. Imagine if, instead of adding each node's fitness to a real number F, we had an array z with one entry for each node, and that each entry in z contained an identifying label. We could sample a label from z in constant time simply by uniformly choosing an index into z and returning the label in z at that index. Now consider the situation where fitnesses are real-valued and not the same. We can no longer sample from z simply by sampling an index of the array, because different indices now imply different fitnesses, and thus different probability masses. We could account for this by annotating each item in z with the node's fitness value, but then, sampling would entail a search and be an $O(\log|V|)$ operation.

So, when extended to nonlinear preferential attachment, the algorithm of Tonelli et al. becomes very inefficient. Note also that the extension only holds when the preference function is a polynomial.

Conclusion

We provide an efficient framework for simulating preferential attachment under general preference functions which scales to millions of nodes. We validate this framework empirically and show applications in the generation and comparison of large networks.

Future work

We have shown that, for nonlinear preferential attachment, the complexity of generating a network with $|V|$ nodes is both $\Omega(|V|)$ and $O(|V|\log|V|)$. Future work could provide asymptotically tighter bounds. Furthermore, generation methods that focus on creating disk-resident or distributed networks could potentially scale to much larger sizes than the in-memory approach proposed in this paper.

Competing interests

The authors declare that they have no competing interests.

Authors' contributions

JA wrote the implementation and the initial manuscript under the supervision of BR and DT. JA, BR, and DT all contributed to the final manuscript. All authors read and approved the final manuscript.

Acknowledgements

This work was supported by the MURI ARO grant 66220-9902 and NSF grant CNS-1065133.

Author details

[1]School of Computer Science, University of Massachusetts Amherst, 01003, Amherst, MA, USA. [2]School of Computer Science, Carnegie Mellon University, 15213, Pittsburgh, PA, USA.

References

1. Newman, MEJ: The structure and function of complex networks. SIAM Rev. **45**(2), 167–256 (2003)
2. Barabási, A-L, Albert, R, Jeong, H: Internet: diameter of the World-Wide Web. Nature. **401**(6749), 130–131 (1999)
3. Barabási, A-L, Albert, R, Jeong, H: Scale-free characteristics of random networks: the topology of the world-wide web. Physica A: Stat. Mech. Appl. **281**(1–4), 69–77 (2000)
4. Broder, A, Kumar, R, Maghoul, F, Raghavan, P, Rajagopalan, S, Stata, R, Tomkins, A, Wiener, J: Graph structure in the web. Comput networks. **33**(1), 309–320 (2000)
5. Chen, Q, Chang, H, Govindan, R, Jamin, S: The origin of power laws in Internet topologies revisited. In: INFOCOM 2002. Twenty-First Annual Joint Conference of the IEEE Computer and Communications Societies. Proceedings. IEEE, pp. 608–617. IEEE, (2002)
6. Faloutsos, M, Faloutsos, P, Faloutsos, C: On power-law relationships of the internet topology. ACM SIGCOMM Comput Commun Rev. **29**(4), 251–262 (1999)
7. Vázquez, A, Pastor-Satorras, R, Vespignani, A: Large-scale topological and dynamical properties of the Internet. Phys. Rev. E. **65**(6), 066130 (2002)
8. Aiello, W, Chung, F, Lü, L: A random graph model for massive graphs. In: the Thirty-second Annual ACM Symposium, pp. 171–180. ACM, New York, (2000)
9. Aiello, W, Chung, F, Lu, L: Random evolution in massive graphs. Found Comput Sci (2001)
10. de Solla Price, DJ: Networks of scientific papers. Science. **169**, 510–515 (1965)
11. Ribeiro, B, Gauvin, W, Liu, B, Towsley, D: On MySpace account spans and double Pareto-like distribution of friends. In: INFOCOM. NFOCOM IEEE Conference on Computer Communications Workshops, New York, USA, (2010)
12. Quicknet Implementation. https://github.com/hackscience/quicknet
13. Krapivsky, P, Redner, S: Organization of growing random networks. Phys. Rev. E. **63**(6), 066123 (2001)
14. Tonelli, R, Concas, G, Locci, M: Three efficient algorithms for implementing the preferential attachment mechanism in Yule-Simon stochastic process. WSEAS Trans. Inf. Sci. App. **7**(2), 176–185 (2010)
15. Aragon, CR, Seidel, RG: Randomized search trees. In: Foundations of Computer Science, 1989, 30th Annual Symposium on, pp. 540–545. IEEE, (1989)
16. Price, D. d. S: A general theory of bibliometric and other cumulative advantage processes. J. Am. Soc. Inform. Sci. **27**(5), 292–306 (1976)
17. Barabási, AL, Albert, R: Emergence of scaling in random networks. Science, 509–512 (1999)
18. Krapivsky, P, Rodgers, G, Redner, S: Degree distributions of growing networks. Phys. Rev. Lett. **86**(23), 5401–5404 (2001)
19. Capocci, A, Servedio, V, Colaiori, F, Buriol, L. S, al, e: Preferential attachment in the growth of social networks: the Internet encyclopedia Wikipedia. Phys. Rev. E. **74**(3), 036116 (2006)
20. Ren, W, Li, J: A fast algorithm for simulating scale-free networks. ICCTA, 264–268 (2009)
21. Hruz, T, Geisseler, S, Schöngens, M: Parallelism in simulation and modeling of scale-free complex networks. Parallel Comput. **36**(8), 469–485 (2010)
22. D'Angelo, G, Ferretti, S: Simulation of scale-free networks. In: Proceedings of the 2nd International Conference on Simulation Tools and Techniques, p. 20. ICST (Institute for Computer Sciences, Social-Informatics and Telecommunications Engineering), (2009)
23. Machta, B, Machta, J: Parallel dynamics and computational complexity of network growth models. Phys. Rev. E. **71**(2), 026704 (2005)

11

Efficient influence spread estimation for influence maximization under the linear threshold model

Zaixin Lu[*], Lidan Fan, Weili Wu, Bhavani Thuraisingham and Kai Yang

*Correspondence:
zaixinlu@utdallas.edu
Department of Computer Science,
University of Texas at Dallas, 800 W.
Campbell Road, Richardson, TX
75080, USA

Abstract

Background: This paper investigates the influence maximization (IM) problem in social networks under the linear threshold (LT) model. Kempe et al. (ACM SIGKDD Conference on Knowledge Discovery and Data Mining, pp. 137–146, 2003) showed that the standard greedy algorithm, which selects the node with the maximum marginal gain repeatedly, brings a $\frac{e-1}{e}$-factor approximation solution to this problem. However, Chen et al. (International Conference on Data Mining, pp. 88–97, 2010) proved that the problem of computing the expected influence spread (EIS) of a node is #P-hard. Therefore, to compute the marginal gain exactly is computational intractable.

Methods: We step-up on investigating efficient algorithm to compute EIS. We show that the EIS of a node can be computed by finding cycles through it, and we further develop an exact algorithm to compute EIS within a small number of hops and an approximation algorithm to estimate EIS without the hop constraint. Based on the proposed EIS algorithms, we finally develop an efficient greedy based algorithm for IM.

Results: We compare our algorithm with some well-known IM algorithms on four real-world social networks. The experimental results show that our algorithm is more accurate than others in finding the most influential nodes, and it is also better than or competitive with them in terms of running time.

Conclusions: IM is a big topic in social network analysis. In this paper, we investigate efficient influence spread estimation for IM under the LT model. We develop two influence spread estimation algorithms and a new greedy based algorithm for IM under the LT model. The performance of the proposed algorithms are analyzed theoretically and evaluated through simulations.

Keywords: Social network analysis; Expected influence spread estimation; Influence maximization; Linear threshold model

Background

Social network is a multidisciplinary research area for both academia and industry, including social network modeling, social network analysis, and data mining. An interesting problem in social network analysis is influence maximization (IM), which can be applied in marketing to deploy business strategies. Typically, IM is the problem that given a graph G as a social network, an influence spread model and an integer k select the top

k nodes as seeds to maximize the expected influence spread (EIS) through G. One corresponding issue in marketing is product promotion. In order to advertise a new product efficiently within a limited budget, a company may choose a few people as seeds who will be given free samples. It is likely that those people will recommend others, such as their friends, relatives or co-workers, to try this product. Eventually, a great number of people may adopt the product due to such 'word-of-mouth' effect [1-6]. Intuitively, the initial seed selection is a key factor that will impact on the success of the product promotion. Therefore, it is important to design applicative influence spread model and efficient search algorithm to find the most influential people in social networks.

IM was first investigated as an combinatorial optimization problem by Kempe et al. in [5]. They considered two influence spread models, namely, Independent Cascade (IC; [2,3]) and Linear Threshold (LT; [7,8]), and proved a series of theoretical results. After that, the two models have been extensively studied (please see, e.g., [9-15] for recent works). In this paper, we focus upon the LT model. Let S be a set of initially active nodes; the influence, under the LT model, propagates in a threshold manner. That is, a node v is activated if and only if the sum of influence it receives from its active neighbors exceeds a threshold $\lambda(v)$ chosen uniformly at random.

As we understand, a crucial part of IM is how to compute the EIS given a node, since only we know the EIS of each node, and then we could find a seed set to maximize the combinatorial EIS. The exact EIS computation was left as an open problem in [5] and has attracted a great deal of attentions in recent years (see, e.g., [9-11,13,15,16]). In [11], Chen et al. proved that computing the exact EIS under the LT model is #P-hard. Therefore, a polynomial time exact solution does not exist unless $P = \text{NP}$. But based on the observations in [11,15], the influence diminishes rapidly during the diffusion in many real-world social networks under the LT model. In other words, the influence spread of a seed is limited within a small number of hops. It has been shown that the influence spread under the LT model can be computed by searching simple paths starting from the seeds [11,15]. Therefore, we can define a hop constraint T such that given a seed v, we only take paths within T hops to estimate the EIS of v. The main contributions of this paper are as follows:

1. We develop an exact algorithm for computing the EIS within four hops. Instead of finding simple paths, we compute the EIS of a node by finding cycles through it. In this study, a cycle of length l is defined as a path visiting a node twice and visiting other $l - 2$ nodes exactly once. The detailed algorithm is given in the 'Methods' section.

2. For the case that $T > 4$, we develop an approximation algorithm to estimate EIS based on random walk. The experimental results in the 'Results and discussion' section show that more precise and quick results can be obtained by using a combination of our exact and approximation algorithms rather than using methods based on simple path.

3. When applying the standard greedy algorithm to IM, it will repeatedly run EIS estimation (EISE) until the top k influential nodes are selected. To further reduce the running time, we construct two lists to save the influence diffused by each node and the active probability of each node, respectively. Moreover, we develop two algorithms to update the two lists when adding a new seed so that the next one with the maximum marginal gain can be directly obtained without running the EISE.

The update algorithms are represented in the 'Influence maximization' section. It is able to say that the two lists contain all the information for doing the seed selection, and they can be easily and quickly updated by our update algorithms.

4.   We compare our algorithm with some well-known IM algorithms on four real-world social networks. The experimental results show that our algorithm is more accurate than others in finding the most influential nodes, and it is also better than or competitive with them in terms of running time.

The rest of this paper is organized as follows: The 'Related work' section introduces the related works. 'Problem description' section gives the problem descriptions of both EISE and IM. 'Methods' and 'Influence maximization' sections study the two problems, respectively. In detail, 'A deterministic algorithm' section efficiently solves the EISE assuming that the influence spread is negligible after four hops. 'A randomized algorithm' section presents an approximation algorithm for general EISE. The 'Influence maximization' section presents a fast method to solve IM by using the algorithms proposed in the 'Methods' section. Finally, 'Results and discussion' section gives the simulation results, and the 'Conclusion' section concludes this paper.

Related work

In the literature, the IM problem has been extensively studied under the IC and LT models. Kempe et al. in [5] first showed that it is NP-hard to determine the optimum for IM under the two models, and by showing that the EIS function is monotone and submodular, they proved that the standard greedy algorithm brings a $\frac{e-1}{e}$-factor approximation solution. In mathematics, a set function $f : 2^\Omega = \mathbb{R}^+$ is monotone and submodular if $\forall S_2 \subseteq S_1$, we have $f(S_1) \geq f(S_2)$ and $f(S_1 \cup \{u\}) - f(S_1) \geq f(S_2 \cup \{u\}) - f(S_2)$, where u is an arbitrary item. In such cases, a $\frac{e-1}{e}$-factor approximation solution can be obtained by picking the item with the maximum marginal gain repeatedly [17]. In [5], how to compute the exact marginal gain (i.e., compute the EIS increment when adding a node) under the two models was left as an open problem, and they estimated it by running the Monte Carlo (MC) simulation, which is not computational efficient (e.g., it takes days to select 50 seeds in a moderate size graph of 30K nodes [11]). Motivated by improving the running time performance, many algorithms have been proposed. Leskovec et al. developed a Cost-Effective Lazy Forward (CELF) algorithm, which is up to 700 times faster than the greedy algorithm with Monte Carlo simulation [16]. But as the results shown in [9], CELF still cannot be applied to find seeds in large social networks, and it takes several hours to select 50 seeds in a graph with tens of thousands of nodes. To further reduce the running time, Goyal et al. [13] developed an extension of CELF, called CELF++, which was showed 0.35 to 0.55 faster than CELF. In [9], Chen et al. proposed two new greedy algorithms, namely NewGreedy and MixedGreedy. NewGreedy reduces the running time by deleting edges having no contribution to influence spread (similar idea was also proposed in [18]), and MixedGreedy which is a combination of NewGreedy and CELF (it uses NewGreedy as the first step and applies CELF for the remaining rounds). Based on the experiments, they showed that MixedGreedy is much faster than both NewGreedy and CELF.

Based on the IC model, Chen et al. also proposed a new influence spread model, called Maximum Influence Arborescence (MIA), to further reduce the running time of EISE.

The efficiency of MIA was demonstrated in [10]. Besides selecting nodes greedily, Wang et al. [19] proposed a community-based algorithm for mining the top k influential nodes under the IC model, and Jiang et al. in [14] proposed a heuristic algorithm based on Simulated Annealing.

In terms of LT model, after Kempe et al. proposed the greedy algorithm [5], the most recent works for IM under this model are [10,12,15]. In [10], Chen et al. proved that the EIS under LT model can be computed in linear time in a directed acyclic graph, and they proposed an algorithm called Local Directed Acyclic Graph (LDAG). Given a general graph, it first converts the original graph into small acyclic graphs, and it only considers the EIS of a node within its local graph when computing the marginal gain. In [12], Narayanam and Narahari developed an algorithm for the LT model that selects the nodes based on the Shapley Value. In [15], Goyal et al. proposed an algorithm called SIMPATH, which estimates the EIS by searching for the simple paths starting from seeds. Since it is computationally expensive to find all the simple paths, they adopted a parameter η to prune them. They also applied the vertex cover optimization to cut down the number of iterations. Based on their experimental results, SIMPATH showed its merits from the aspects of running time and seed quality.

Problem description

Many introductions about the LT model and IM problem can be found in detail in papers cited above. Here, for the sake of completeness, we give a brief description for the LT model and formal definitions for IM and EISE.

Definition 1. Let $G(V, E)$ be a directed graph; we define

- $N_{\text{in}}(v)$ (respectively $N_{\text{out}}(v)$) to be the set of incoming (respectively outgoing) neighbors of v ($\forall v \in V$).
- $\lambda(v)$ to be the threshold of v, which is a real number in the range of $[0, 1]$ chosen uniformly at random.
- $x(v)$ to be a 0 to 1 variable which indicates whether v is active or not.

According to Definition 1, given a weighted directed graph $G(V, E, w)$, where $w(e) \in [0, 1]$ ($\forall e \in E$) is a weight function, the sum of influence v receives can be formulated as $\sum_{u \in N_{\text{in}}(v)} x(u)w(u, v)$. Without loss of generality, we assume $\sum_{u \in N_{\text{in}}(v)} w(u, v) \leq 1$ ($\forall v \in V$). In the LT model, time is discrete. Given a seed set S, at time 0, we have $\forall v \in S$, $x(v) = 1$, and $\forall u \in (V \backslash S)$, $x(u) = 0$. At any particular time t, a node $v \in V$ becomes active if $\sum_{u \in N_{\text{in}}(v)} x(u)w(u, v) \geq \lambda(v)$. Finally, the influence spread process stops at a time slot when there is no newly activated node.

Definition 2. *EISE*: Given a weighted directed graph $G(V, E, w)$ and a set $S \subseteq V$ of nodes, EISE is the problem of estimating the expected number of active nodes at the end of the influence spread. EISE_T is the problem that given an integer T, estimates the expected number of nodes that are active at time T.

For the rest of this paper, given a seed set S, we denote by $\sigma(S)$ the expected number of nodes that are eventually active and denote by $\sigma_T(S)$ the expected number of nodes that are activated within T time slots. We can say that $\sigma(S)$ is an expected number among the probability distributions of active nodes given S and $\sigma_T(S)$ is a time limited version of $\sigma(S)$.

Definition 3. *IM:* Given a weighted directed graph $G(V, E, w)$ and a parameter k, the IM problem is to find a seed set S of cardinality k to maximize $\sigma(S)$.

As the experimental results shown in [15], under the LT model, the EIS is negligible after a small number of hops (usually three or four hops) in many real-world social networks. Therefore, to solve the IM problem, it is sufficient to compute $\sigma_T(S)$ instead of $\sigma(S)$ for some small value of T.

Methods
We first present a deterministic algorithm for computing the exact value of $\sigma_T(v)$ for the case that $T \leq 4$ in the 'A deterministic algorithm' section and then present a randomized algorithm for estimating $\sigma_T(v)$ for $T \geq 5$ in the 'A randomized algorithm' section.

Definition 4. In this study, we define

- a path is a sequence of nodes, each of which is connected to the next one in the sequence; and a path with no repeated nodes is called a simple path.
- a cycle is a path such that the first node appears twice and the other nodes appear exactly once; and a simple cycle is a cycle such that the first and last nodes are the same.

A deterministic algorithm
According to the observation in [15], the EIS of a node v after three or four hops is negligible in most cases. Therefore, we are interested in how to compute $\sigma_T(v)$ for $T \leq 4$. In [11], it has been shown that the EIS of a seed set S under the LT model can be formulated as

$$\sigma(S) = \sum_{\pi \in \mathcal{P}(S)} \prod_{e \in \pi} w(e) + |S| \quad [15],$$

where $\mathcal{P}(S)$ denotes the set of simple paths starting from nodes in S, π denotes an element in $\mathcal{P}(S)$, and e denotes an edge in π. Thus, $\forall v \in V$, we have

$$\sigma(v) = \sum_{\pi \in \mathcal{P}(v)} \prod_{e \in \pi} w(e) + 1,$$

where $\mathcal{P}(v)$ denotes the set of simple paths starting from node v.

As an example shown in Figure 1, considering v_0 is an active node, then the probability that v_4 can be activated by v_0 is $w(0, 1)w(1, 4) + w(0, 2)w(2, 4) + w(0, 3)w(3, 4)$, which is

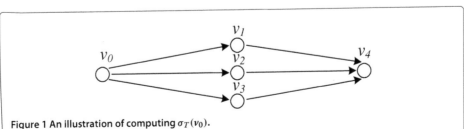

Figure 1 An illustration of computing $\sigma_T(v_0)$.

the sum of weight products of all the simple paths from v_0 to v_4. Although the example is easy to understand, in a general graph G, it requires exponential time to enumerate all the simple paths. Thus, to compute the exact value of $\sigma(v)$ is computational intractable, and a hop constraint T is used in this paper to balance the accuracy of EISE and the program efficiency in terms of running time.

In order to find a node v with the maximum $\sigma_T(v)$, we have to compute $\sigma_T(v)$ for all the nodes $v \in V$. Let $\sigma_0(v) = 1$ $(\forall v \in V)$; we first consider the simple case that $T = 1$. In such cases, we have $\sigma_1(v) = \sigma_0(v) + \sum_{u \in N_{\text{out}}(v)} w(v, u)$, because there is only direct influence spread without propagation. When $T > 1$, we can compute $\sigma_T(v)$ by recursively finding all the simple paths of length no more than T, starting from v, which requires $O(\Delta^T)$ time by using the depth-first search (DFS) algorithm, and Δ denotes the node maximum degree. Thus, let G be a weighted directed graph; computing $\sigma_T(v)$ for all the nodes in G requires $O(n\Delta^T)$ time if we use the above simple path method [15], where n denotes the number of nodes in G. To further improve the running time performance, we develop a dynamic programming (DP) approach to compute $\sigma_T(v)$ for $T \leq 4$. It is based on searching cycles instead of simple paths.

As an example shown in Figure 2, there are three types of cycles of length 4, and only the third one is a simple cycle. Let $C_l(v)$ denote the set of cycles of length l, starting from v, and let

$$\varrho_T(v) = \sum_{l=2\cdots T} \sum_{\pi \in C_l(v)} \prod_{e \in \pi} w(e),$$

we have

$$\sigma_T(v) = \sigma_0(v) + \sum_{u \in N_{\text{out}}(v)} w(v, u) \cdot (\sigma_{T-1}^{V \setminus v}(u))$$

$$= \sigma_0(v) + \sum_{u \in N_{\text{out}}(v)} w(v, u) \cdot (\sigma_{T-1}(u))$$

$$- \varrho_T(v),$$

where $\sigma_{T-1}^{V \setminus v}(u)$ denotes the EIS of node u in the induced graph of $V \setminus v$ within $T - 1$ hops, and $\varrho_T(v)$ denotes the invalid influence spread involving cycles.

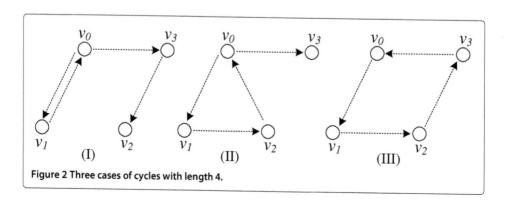

Figure 2 Three cases of cycles with length 4.

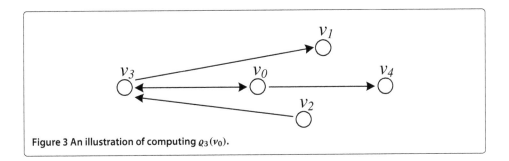

Figure 3 An illustration of computing $\varrho_3(v_0)$.

Figure 3 shows an example, in which v_3 and v_4 are v_0's outgoing neighbors. It is easy to see $\sigma_2(v_3) = 1 + w(3, 0) + w(3, 1) + w(3, 0)w(0, 4)$ and $\sigma_2(v_4) = 1$. Thus,

$$\sigma_0(v_0) + \sum_{u \in N_{\text{out}}(v_0)} w(v_0, u) \cdot (\sigma_2(u))$$

$$= w(0, 3) + w(0, 4) + w(0, 3)w(3, 0) + w(0, 3)w(3, 1)$$

$$+ w(0, 3)w(3, 0)w(0, 4) + 1,$$

in which the terms $w(0, 3)w(3, 0)$ and $w(0, 3)w(3, 0)w(0, 4)$ have to be removed since they involve cycles. The rest of this section is devoted to investigating how to compute $\varrho_T(v)$ for $T \leq 4$.

Lemma 1. *Given a weighted directed graph $G(V, E, w)$ and an arbitrary node $v \in V$, $\varrho_T(v)$ can be computed in $O\left(\Delta^2\right)$ time when $T \leq 4$.*

A brief description for the idea of our method is presented before the formal algorithm and its proof. Firstly, $\varrho_T(v)$ involves all the cycles of length no more than T, starting from v. In order to compute $\varrho_4(v)$ efficiently, we divide $\varrho_4(v)$ into three parts: $\sum_{\pi \in \mathcal{C}_l(v)} \prod_{e \in \pi} w(e)$ $(l = 2, 3, 4)$ to carry on the analysis. If each part can be computed in $O(\Delta^2)$ time, $\varrho_4(v)$, which is the sum of them, can be obtained in $O(\Delta^2)$ time. Secondly, considering $\mathcal{C}_l(v)$ $(2 \leq l \leq 4)$, we can further classify the cycles in $\mathcal{C}_l(v)$ into $l - 1$ types. Note that a cycle of length l, starting from v, consists of a sequence of $l + 1$ nodes, two of which are v and others are distinct. Therefore, we can label a cycle according to the position in the sequence where the second v appears. $\forall v \in V$, let $\mathcal{C}_T^l(v)$ denote the set of cycles of length T, whose lth node is v, we have

$$\varrho_T(v) = \sum_{l=2,\cdots,T} \sum_{\pi \in \mathcal{C}_l(v)} \prod_{e \in \pi} w(e)$$

$$= \sum_{l=2,\cdots,T} \sum_{l'=3,\cdots,l+1} \sum_{\pi \in \mathcal{C}_l^{l'}(v)} \prod_{e \in \pi} w(e).$$

In order to compute $\varrho_T(v)$, our method will compute each $\sum_{\pi \in \mathcal{C}_l^{l'}(v)} \prod_{e \in \pi} w(e)$ separately.

Proof. We will prove Lemma 1 by showing that $\sum_{\pi \in \mathcal{C}_l(v)} \prod_{e \in \pi} w(e)$ can be computed in $O(\Delta^2)$ time when $l = 4$, and for the case that $l < 4$, $\sum_{\pi \in \mathcal{C}_l(v)} \prod_{e \in \pi} w(e)$ can be computed in $O(\Delta^2)$ time or less via a similar method. As we have mentioned above, there are only three types of cycles of length 4, as shown in Figure 2.

Consider case (I). Such a cycle consists of a simple cycle of length 2 and a simple path of length 2. Let $\mathcal{P}_2(v)$ denote the set of simple paths of length 2, starting from v, and $\mathcal{C}_2^3(v)$ denote the set of simple cycles of length 2 through v. $\mathcal{P}_2(v)$ can be obtained in $O(\Delta^2)$ time by DFS, and $\mathcal{C}_2^3(v)$ can be obtained by finding the set of nodes that are both incoming and outgoing neighbors of v, i.e.,

$$\mathcal{C}_2^3(v) = \left\{ (v, u, v) : u \in N_{\text{out}}(v) \cap N_{\text{in}}(v) \right\}.$$

The intersection of two lists can be obtained in linear time if the two lists are sorted. Let $I(v) = N_{\text{out}}(v) \cap N_{\text{in}}(v)$ and $\kappa = \sum_{u \in I(v)} w(v, u)w(u, v)$; we have

$$\sum_{\pi \in \mathcal{C}_4^3(v)} \prod_{e \in \pi} w(e)$$

$$= \sum_{\pi \in \mathcal{P}_2(v)} \sum_{u \in I(v) \setminus \pi} w(v, u)w(u, v) \prod_{e \in \pi} w(e)$$

$$= \sum_{\pi \in \mathcal{P}_2(v)} \left(\kappa - \sum_{u \in \pi \cap I(v)} w(v, u)w(u, v) \right) \prod_{e \in \pi} w(e)$$

$$= \sum_{\pi \in \mathcal{P}_2(v)} \left(\kappa - \sum_{u \in \pi \setminus v} w(v, u)w(u, v) \right) \prod_{e \in \pi} w(e),$$

in which $I(v) \setminus \pi$ denotes the set of nodes in $I(v)$ but not in π, $e \in \pi$ denotes an edge in π, and $u \in \pi$ denotes a node in π. Note that if $u \notin I(v)$, we have $(v, u) \notin E$ or $(u, v) \notin E$. In such cases, $w(v, u)w(u, v) = 0$. Therefore, $\sum_{u \in \pi \cap I(v)} w(v, u)w(u, v) = \sum_{u \in \pi \setminus v} w(v, u)w(u, v)$. Since $\mathcal{P}_2(v)$ consists of at most Δ^2 elements, each of which includes only two edges, $\sum_{\pi \in \mathcal{P}_2(v)} (\kappa - \sum_{u \in \pi \setminus v} w(v, u)w(u, v)) \prod_{e \in \pi} w(e)$ can be computed in $O(\Delta^2)$ time.

Consider case (II). $\sum_{\pi \in \mathcal{C}_4^4(v)} \prod_{e \in \pi} w(e)$ can be computed by a similar method. A cycle in $\mathcal{C}_4^4(v)$ consists of a simple cycle of length 3, in which the first and last nodes are v. Therefore, instead of directly constructing a set of simple cycles of length 3, we can construct a set $\mathcal{P}_2(v)$ of simple paths of length 2. Let $l(\pi)$ denote the last node of a path $\pi \in \mathcal{P}_2(v)$ and let $\tau = \sum_{u \in N_{\text{out}}(v)} w(v, u)$; we have

$$\sum_{\pi \in \mathcal{C}_4^4(v)} \prod_{e \in \pi} w(e)$$

$$= \sum_{\pi \in \mathcal{P}_2(v)} w(l(\pi), v) \left(\sum_{u \in N_{\text{out}}(v) \setminus \pi} w(v, u) \right) \prod_{e \in \pi} w(e)$$

$$= \sum_{\pi \in \mathcal{P}_2(v)} w(l(\pi), v) \left(\tau - \sum_{u \in \pi \setminus v} w(v, u) \right) \prod_{e \in \pi} w(e),$$

in which $w(l(\pi), v) = 0$ if $l(\pi) \notin N_{\text{in}}(v)$. Therefore, $\sum_{\pi \in \mathcal{C}_4^4(v)} \prod_{e \in \pi} w(e)$ can also be computed in $O(\Delta^2)$ time.

Consider case (III). The analysis is somewhat more complicated. Instead of computing $\sum_{\pi \in \mathcal{C}_4^5(v)} \prod_{e \in \pi} w(e)$ directly, we first show that $\sum_{\pi \in (\mathcal{C}_4^5(v) \cup \mathcal{C}'(v))} \prod_{e \in \pi} w(e)$ can be computed in $O(\Delta^2)$ time, where $\mathcal{C}'(v)$ denotes the set of cycles as shown in Figure 4. That is, cycles consist of three nodes in which the first two nodes are visited twice. Let $\rho_2(v, v')$ denote the probability that v' is reachable from v with exact two hops, i.e.,

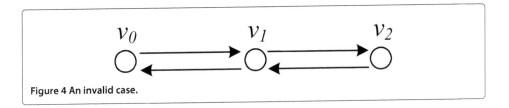

Figure 4 An invalid case.

$\rho_2(v, v') = \sum_{u \in N_{out}(v) \cap N_{in}(v')} w(v, u) w(u, v')$. Let $N_{out}^2(v)$ be the set of nodes that are reachable from v with exact two hops. To compute $\rho_2(v, v')$ for all the nodes $v' \in N_{out}^2(v)$, we can build up an outgoing tree rooted at v, in which the nodes are repeatable among different paths. This can be done in $O(\Delta^2)$ time by DFS. In addition, let $N_{in}^2(v)$ be the set of nodes that can reach v with exact two hops, we can build up an incoming tree rooted at v to compute $\rho_2(v', v)$ for all the nodes $v' \in N_{in}^2(v)$ in the same way. Then, we have

$$\sum_{\pi \in (\mathcal{C}_4^5(v) \cup \mathcal{C}'(v))} \prod_{e \in \pi} w(e)$$

$$= \sum_{v' \in N_{out}^2(v) \cap N_{in}^2(v)} \rho_2(v, v') \rho_2(v', v),$$

which can be computed in $O(\Delta^2)$ time. It is easy to see

$$\sum_{\pi \in \mathcal{C}_4^5(v)} \prod_{e \in \pi} w(e)$$

$$= \sum_{\pi \in (\mathcal{C}_4^5(v) \cup \mathcal{C}'(v))} \prod_{e \in \pi} w(e) - \sum_{\pi \in \mathcal{C}'(v)} \prod_{e \in \pi} w(e).$$

Therefore, to show $\sum_{\pi \in \mathcal{C}_4^5(v)} \prod_{e \in \pi} w(e)$ can be computed in $O(\Delta^2)$ time, it is sufficient to show that $\sum_{\pi \in \mathcal{C}'(v)} \prod_{e \in \pi} w(e)$ can be computed in $O(\Delta^2)$ time. We have

$$\sum_{\pi \in \mathcal{C}'(v)} \prod_{e \in \pi} w(e)$$

$$= \sum_{v' \in I(v)} \sum_{u \in I(v')} w(v, v') w(v', u) w(u, v') w(v', v),$$

where $I(v) = N_{out}(v) \cap N_{in}(v)$ and $I(v') = N_{out}(v') \cap N_{in}(v')$. Therefore, $\sum_{\pi \in \mathcal{C}'(v)} \prod_{e \in \pi} w(e)$ can be computed in $O(\Delta^2)$ time.

In sum, we prove $\sum_{\pi \in \mathcal{C}_4(v)} \prod_{e \in \pi} w(e)$ $(\forall v \in V)$ can be computed in $O(\Delta^2)$ time. It can be shown that $\sum_{\pi \in \mathcal{C}_l(v)} \prod_{e \in \pi} w(e)$ $(l < 4)$ can be computed in $O(\Delta^2)$ time or less by a similar method. Therefore, it requires only $O(\Delta^2)$ time to compute $\varrho_4(v)$ $(\forall v \in V)$. $\square$

Theorem 1. *Given a weighted directed graph $G(V, E, w)$, Algorithm 1 can compute $\sigma_4(v)$ for all the nodes $v \in V$ in $O(n\Delta^2)$ time, where n denotes the number of nodes in V, and Δ denotes the maximum node degree.*

Algorithm 1 EISE$_4$

0: input: a weighted directed graph $G = (V, E, w)$.

1: let $\sigma_1(v) = \sum_{u \in N_{out}(v)} w_{v,u} \ (\forall v \in V)$;

2: **for** $l = 2 \cdots 4$ **do**

3: $\quad \sigma_l(v) = \sigma_1(v) - \varrho_l(v) + \sum_{u \in N_{out}(v)} w_{v,u} \cdot \sigma_{l-1}(u)$;

4: **end for**

5: output: a list of $\sigma_4(v)$ for all the nodes $v \in V$.

Proof. Without considering the possible numerical computation error, the solution of Algorithm 1 is exact, and the time complexity analysis easily follows the algorithm. The computation of $\sigma_l(v)$ only depends on $\sigma_{l-1}(u)$ ($u \in N_{out}(v)$) and $\varrho_l(v)$. Therefore, $\sigma_4(v)$ for all the nodes $v \in V$ can be computed by a DP approach. The number of subproblems is $O(n)$ and each subproblem can be solved in $O(\Delta^2)$ time. Therefore, Algorithm 1 requires $O(n\Delta^2)$ time. $\square$

Compared with the method based on a simple path, which requires $O(\Delta^4)$ time to compute $\sigma_4(v)$ for a node v, the core advantage of Algorithm 1 is its running time performance. Based on our experiments in the 'Results and discussion' section, when $T \leq 4$, Algorithm 1 can compute the $\sigma_T(v)$ for all the nodes in a moderate size graph in about 1 s.

A randomized algorithm

Theorem 1 shows that Algorithm 1 can efficiently compute $\sigma(v)$, if the EIS from node v is negligible after four hops. For the case that the EIS within a large number T hops is not negligible, it has been shown that computing $\sigma_T(v)$ is #P-hard [11]. To estimate $\sigma_T(v)$ approximately, we can use MC simulation, i.e., simulate the influence spread process a sufficient number of times, re-choosing the thresholds uniformly at random, and use the arithmetic mean of the results instead of the EIS. Let $X_1, X_2, \cdots, X_r$ be the numbers of active nodes at time T for r runs, and let $E[\overline{X}]$ be the EIS within time T. By Hoeffding's inequality [20], we have

$$\Pr\left(|\overline{X} - E[\overline{X}]| \geq \epsilon\right) \leq \exp\left(-\frac{2\epsilon^2 r^2}{\sum_{i=1}^{r}(b_i - a_i)^2}\right),$$

where a_i and b_i are the lower and upper bounds for X_i, respectively. Apparently, $a_i \geq 0$ and $b_i \leq n$, where n is the number of nodes in the graph. Thus, $\forall 0 < \delta < 1$, when $r \geq \frac{n \ln \frac{1}{\delta}}{2\epsilon^2}$, the probability that $|\overline{X} - E[\overline{X}]| \geq \epsilon$ is at most δ. Therefore, the EIS estimated by using MC simulation with a sufficient number of runs is nearly exact. However, as the experiments shown in [5,11,15], applying the MC simulation to estimate the EIS is computational expensive, and the standard greedy algorithm with MC simulation (run 10,000 times to get the average) requires days to select 50 seeds in some real-world social networks with tens of thousands of nodes.

To improve the computation efficiency, we developed a randomized algorithm, computing $\sigma_T(v)$ for $T \geq 5$. We first give the main idea of our method. Recall that the EIS of a node v can be computed by searching simple paths starting from v; thus, $\sigma_T(v) = \sum_{\pi \in \mathcal{P}_T(v)} \prod_{e \in \pi} w(e)$. Let $\text{avg}(\mathcal{P}_T(v))$ be the arithmetic mean of $\prod_{e \in \pi} w(e)$ for all the elements $\pi \in \mathcal{P}_T(v)$, and let $|\cdot|$ be the number of elements in '·'; we have $\sigma_T(v) = \text{avg}(\mathcal{P}_T(v))|\mathcal{P}_T(v)|$. However, obtaining $\text{avg}(\mathcal{P}_T(v))$ and $|\mathcal{P}_T(v)|$ requires the knowledge of $\mathcal{P}_T(v)$ and is therefore as difficult as the original problem. We propose an alternative approach. Instead of computing $\sigma_T(v)$ directly, we relax $\mathcal{P}_T(v)$ to $\acute{\mathcal{P}}_T(v)$ that contains all the paths starting from v, instead of simple paths. Let $x(\pi \in \mathcal{P}_T(v))$ be a 0 to 1 variable denote whether π is a simple path or not; we have

$$\sigma_T(v) = \sum_{\pi \in \acute{\mathcal{P}}_T(v)} x(\pi \in \mathcal{P}_T(v)) \prod_{e \in \pi} w(e).$$

The next question is how to estimate $\text{avg}(\acute{\mathcal{P}}_T(v))$ and $|\acute{\mathcal{P}}_T(v)|$ to obtain $\sigma_T(v)$.

Lemma 2. *Given a directed graph $G(V, E)$ and an integer T, there is a polynomial time algorithm to compute $|\acute{\mathcal{P}}_T(v)|$ for all the nodes $v \in V$.*

Proof. We can compute $|\acute{\mathcal{P}}_T(v)|$ by iteration or recursion. $\forall 1 \leq l \leq T$, we have

$$\begin{cases} |\acute{\mathcal{P}}_l(v)| = |\mathcal{P}_l(v)| = |N_{\text{out}}(v)|, & l = 1 \\ |\acute{\mathcal{P}}_l(v)| = \sum_{u \in N_{\text{out}}(v)} |\acute{\mathcal{P}}_{l-1}(v)|, & \text{otherwise.} \end{cases}$$

$|\acute{\mathcal{P}}_1(v)|$ equals to the number of outgoing neighbors of v, and $|\acute{\mathcal{P}}_l(v)|$ ($l > 1$) can be obtained by a DP approach. Since there are $O(nT)$ subproblems and each subproblem can be solved in $O(\Delta)$ time, $|\acute{\mathcal{P}}_T(v)|$ can be obtained in $O(nT\Delta)$ time. $\square$

Theorem 2. *Let ϵ and δ be two positive constants in the range of $(0, 1)$. There is a random walk algorithm such that given a weighted directed graph $G(V, E, w)$ and a node $v \in V$, it gives a $(1 \pm \epsilon)$-factor approximation solution to $\text{avg}(\acute{\mathcal{P}}_T(v))$ in $O\left(\frac{1}{\epsilon^2} \ln \frac{1}{\delta} + nT\Delta\right)$ time with probability greater than $1 - \delta$.*

Proof. We can use uniform random sampling, which selects elements with equal probability from $\acute{\mathcal{P}}_T(v)$. By Lemma 2, we can obtain $|\acute{\mathcal{P}}_T(v)|$ for all the nodes $v \in V$ in $O(nT\Delta)$ time. Let the probability $\Pr(y_{i+1} = u'|y_i = u) = \frac{|\acute{\mathcal{P}}_{T-i}(u')|}{|\acute{\mathcal{P}}_{T-i+1}(u)|}$ and $\Pr(y_1 = v) = 1$; then, a path of length T can be generated by taking T successive random steps. $\forall$ a path $\pi = (v_1, v_2, \cdots, v_T)$ in $\acute{\mathcal{P}}_T(v)$, we have

$$\Pr(\pi) = \prod_{i=1,\cdots,T-1} \Pr(y_{i+1} = v_{i+1}|y_i = v_i)$$

$$= \prod_{i=1,\cdots,T} \frac{|\acute{\mathcal{P}}_{T-i}(v_{i+1})|}{|\acute{\mathcal{P}}_{T-i+1}(v_i)|} = \frac{1}{|\acute{\mathcal{P}}_T(v)|}.$$

Therefore, we can generate paths $\pi_1, \pi_2, \cdots, \pi_r$ uniformly at random. By Hoeffding's inequality, we have

$$\Pr\left(\frac{|\sum_{i=1,\cdots,r} \prod_{e \in \pi_i} w(e)r}{-} \text{avg}\left(\acute{\mathcal{P}}_T(v)\right)| \geq \epsilon\right)$$

$$\leq \exp\left(-\frac{2\epsilon^2 r^2}{\sum_{i=1}^{r} \left(\max_{\pi \in \acute{\mathcal{P}}_T(v)} \prod_{e \in \pi} w(e)\right)^2}\right),$$

where $\max_{\pi \in \acute{\mathcal{P}}_T(v)} \prod_{e \pi} w(e)$ is the maximum weight product of a path of length T starting from v. Since $w(e) \leq 1$ $(\forall e \in E)$, we have $\max_{\pi \in \acute{\mathcal{P}}_T(v)} \prod_{e \pi} w(e) \leq 1$. Thus, Theorem 2 is proved. $\qquad\qquad\qquad\qquad\qquad\qquad\qquad\qquad\qquad\qquad\qquad\qquad\qquad\qquad\qquad\square$

Based on Theorem 2, we now describe our randomized algorithm for computing $\sigma_T(v)$ for all the nodes $v \in V$. It runs in $O(nT\Delta + nr)$ time, where r is a constant and does not depend on the input graph.

In Algorithm 2, it first computes $|\acute{\mathcal{P}}_T(v)|$ (step 1) and then estimates $\sigma_T(v)$ by uniform random sampling. As far as the running time, the most time-consuming part is steps 2 to 8, in which r is independent of the input graph. It is clear that when r is small, the accuracy of EISE is low, but the estimation time is short, and vice verse. Compared with MC simulation, Algorithm 2 is much faster. In order to estimate the EIS of a node, it only generates a constant number of paths, while if MC simulation is applied instead of Algorithm 2, each time we have to re-choose the thresholds for all the nodes, and the time complexity is $O((|V| + |E|)r)$, when most of the edges are accessed each time. In the experiment, we observed that the error is less than 3% when $T = 5$, using an appropriate number of samples ($r = 1,000$).

Algorithm 2 EISE$_T$

0: input: a weighted directed graph $G = (V, E, w)$ and two integers T and r.

1: construct $|\acute{\mathcal{P}}_l(v)|$ $(1 \leq l \leq T)$ for all the nodes $v \in V$;

2: **for** $v \in V$ **do**

3:     let $\sigma_T(v) = 0$;

4:     **for** $i = 1, \cdots, r$ **do**

5:         let π_r be the path of length T, generated by the random walk technique;

6:         $\sigma_T = \sigma_T + x(\pi_r \in \mathcal{P}_T(v)) \prod_{e \in \pi_r} w(e)$;

7:     **end for**

8: **end for**

9: $\sigma_T(v) = \sigma_T(v) \frac{|\acute{\mathcal{P}}_l(v)|}{r}$;

10: output: a list of $\sigma_T(v)$ for all the nodes $v \in V$.

Influence maximization

Considering the computational efficiency, we define a hop constraint for EISE, and we present two algorithms in 'Methods' section to compute $\sigma_T(v)$ in v's local area (T hops). The proposed algorithms are worth applying to solve the IM problem greedily. Given a weighted directed graph $G(V, E, w)$, the standard greedy algorithm will run EISE $O(n)$ times to select a seed, where n denotes the number of nodes. To further reduce the running time, we construct an influence list IL to store the EIS of nodes in the induced graph of $G \backslash S$, where S is the current seed set. Let $v_1, v_2, \cdots, v_n$ be the nodes in the input graph. Given a parameter T, initially we have IL $= \{l_1 = \sigma_T(v_1), \cdots, l_n = \sigma_T(v_n)\}$, since $S = \emptyset$. After adding a node v_i into S, all the nodes, whose local area include v_i, have to be updated. Instead of running EISE, we update them by building an incoming tree rooted at v_i (Algorithm 3).

Algorithm 3 Update$_{IL}$

0: input: $G = (V, E, w)$, v, S, and IL.

1: construct an incoming tree of depth T rooted at v in the induced graph of $G \backslash S$ (without loss of generality, assume that the simple paths are $\pi_1, \pi_2, \cdots, \pi_m$);

2: **for** $i = 1 \cdots m$ **do**

3:     let $i_0, i_1, \cdots, i_T$ be the nodes visited by π_i sequentially and $l_{i_0}, l_{i_1}, \cdots, l_{i_T}$ be the corresponding elements in IL (in which $i_0 = v$);

4:     **for** $j = 1 \cdots T$ **do**

5:        $l_{i_j} = l_{i_j} - \prod_{l=1}^{j} w(i_l, i_{l-1})(1 + \sigma_{T-j}^{V \backslash S \backslash \{i_1, \cdots, i_j\}}(v))$;

6:     **end for**

7: **end for**

8: output: IL.

In Algorithm 3, the incoming tree is node repeated, including all the simple path of length T ending at v. $\prod_{l=1}^{j} w(i_l, i_{l-1})$ denotes the EIS from i_j to i_0 via path $(i_j, i_{j-1}, \cdots, i_0)$, where $i_0 = v$, and $\sigma_{T-j}^{V \backslash S \backslash \{i_1, \cdots, i_j\}}(v)$ denotes the EIS of v in the induce graph of $V \backslash S \backslash \{i_1, \cdots, i_j\}$. Thus, $\prod_{l=1}^{j} w(i_l, i_{l-1})(1 + \sigma_{T-j}^{V \backslash S \backslash \{i_1, \cdots, i_j\}}(v))$ denotes the entire influence diffused from i_j through path $(i_j, i_{j-1}, \cdots, i_1, \pi)$, where π is a path of length no more than $T - j$ starting from v and does not contain any node in $\{i_1, i_2, \cdots, i_j\}$. It is clear that after steps 2 to 7, $\forall u \in (V \backslash S)$, the influence diffused from u through v is removed from the corresponding element in IL. Consider now the running time. Algorithm 3 generates at most $O(\Delta^j)$ nodes in depth j $(1 \leq j \leq T)$. For each node i_j in depth j, $\sigma_{T-j}^{V \backslash S \backslash \{i_1, \cdots, i_j\}}(v)$ can be computed by building an outgoing tree of depth $T - j$ rooted at v, which can be done by DFS in $O(\Delta^{T-j})$ time. Therefore, Algorithm 3 runs in $O(\Delta^T)$ time, considering T as a constant. Compared with running EISE for all the nodes, it is much faster when T and Δ are relatively small.

In addition to IL, we construct another list, namely, probability list PL, to store the nodes' active probabilities at time T. When $S = \emptyset$, obviously PL $= \{p_1 = 0, \cdots, p_n = 0\}$. Similarly, after adding a node v_i into S, the active probabilities of nodes in v_i's local area need to be updated. The algorithm of updating PL is given in Algorithm 4.

Algorithm 4 UpdatePL

0: input: $G = (V, E, w)$, v, S, and PL.

1: construct an outgoing tree of depth T rooted at v in the induced graph of $G \backslash S$ (without loss of generality, assume the simple paths are $\pi_1, \pi_2, \cdots, \pi_m$);

2: **for** $i = 1 \cdots m$ **do**

3:     let $i_0, i_1, \cdots, i_T$ be the nodes visited by π_i sequentially and $p_{i_0}, p_{i_1}, \cdots, p_{i_T}$ be the corresponding elements in PL;

4:     **for** $j = 1 \cdots T$ **do**

5:        $p_{i_j} = p_{i_j} + (1 - p_v) \prod_{l=0}^{j-1} w(i_l, i_{l+1})$;

6:     **end for**

7: **end for**

8: output: PL.

Algorithm 4 searches the simple paths of length T starting from v and updates the active probability of a node i_j according to step 5, in which $\prod_{l=0}^{j-1} w(i_l, i_{l+1})$ is the influence spread from v to i_j through path $(i_0, \cdots, i_j)$, and $1 - p_v$ is the increment of v' active probability when it is added into S. In the outgoing tree, there are $O(\Delta^T)$ nodes; thus, PL can be updated in $O(\Delta^T)$ time.

Assume v_i is a newly added node; then, the marginal gain is $l_i(1 - p_i)$. Since both Algorithms 3 and 4 run in $O(\Delta^T)$ time, we can find the node with the maximum marginal gain in $O(\Delta^T + n)$ time. Next, we present an algorithm, which consists of two steps, for influence maximization based on a time parameter T (IMT). Given a weighted directed graph $G(V, E, w)$, the first step is to compute the EIS of each node $v \in V$. Such computation is based on the assumption that the EIS is negligible after T hops. The second step contains two parts, the first part is to choose a node with the maximum marginal gain and the second part is to update the two lists: IL and PL. Let v be the last added node; the updating is limited to the local area of v (T hops from v).

The running time of Algorithm 5 highly depends on T and the maximum degree Δ. In [15], when estimating the EIS of a node by searching simple paths, a parameter η is used to prune a path once its influence spread is less than η. To further reduce the running time, when building the incoming and outgoing trees (step 6), we prune the paths in the same way. It is worthy to mention that in [15], the EISE of a node v misses all the outgoing simple paths of v whose product of weights is less than η. When building the incoming (respectively outgoing) tree rooted at v, our algorithm also neglects a number of paths; however, the losses are now evenly distributed to all the nodes in v's local area. Thus, the impact is less significant.

Algorithm 5 IMT

0: input: a weighted directed graph $G = (V, E, w)$ and two integers T and k.

1: let $S = \emptyset$;

2: let IL be the list resulted by Algorithm 1 and Algorithm 2 and let PL $= 0$;

3: **while** $|S| < k$ **do**

4:     let v_i be the node in $V \backslash S$ that has the maximum $l_i \cdot (1 - p_i)$;

5:     add v into S;

6:     update IL and PL by Algorithm 3 and Algorithm 4;

7: **end while**

8: output: S.

Results and discussion

We perform three experiments to evaluate the proposed algorithms. The performance metrics are average influence spread (AIS) and program running time (PRT). Since our algorithm is based on a parameter T, we will first analyze how it impacts the time performance and the quality of seed selection. In the second experiment, we will compare IMT (Algorithm 5) with some well-known IM algorithms in terms of AIS. In the last experiment, we will investigate the accuracy of our EISE (Algorithms 1 and 2) and the accuracy of SIMPATH [15]. The data sets used in this paper are introduced in detail in the 'Simulation environments' section, and the algorithms are described in the 'Algorithms' section.

Simulation environments

The experiments are conducted on four real-world networks: 'Hep', 'Phy', 'Amazon', and 'Flixster', which have been widely used for evaluating IM algorithms under different models [5,9-11,15]. The dataset statistics are summarized in Table 1. Briefly, 'Hep' and 'Phy' are academic author networks extracted from http://www.arXiv.org, where nodes denote authors and edges denote collaborations. 'Amazon' is a product network, where nodes denote products and edge (u, v) denote product v which is often purchased with product u. 'Flixster' is a social network allowing users to rate movies, in which nodes denote users and edges denote friendships.

In all types of social networks, let $\deg_{in}(v) = |N_{in}(V)|$ be the in-degree of node v; we use a classic method proposed in [5] to add the weights to edges, i.e., $w(u, v) = c(u, v)/\deg_{in}(v)$, where $c(u, v)$ is the number of edges from u to v.

Algorithms

For the comparison purposes, we evaluate some well-known algorithms designed for IM under the LT model and some model independent heuristics for IM as follows:

- MC: The greedy algorithm with MC simulation and CELF optimization. Each time, we simulate 10K runs to get the EIS of a seed set.
- LDAG: The LDAG algorithm proposed in [11]. As recommended by the authors, the pruning threshold $\eta = \frac{1}{320}$.
- SP: The SIMPATH algorithm proposed in [15]. As recommended by the authors, the pruning threshold $\eta = \frac{1}{1,000}$.
- MAXDEG: A heuristic algorithm [5] based on the notion of 'degree centrality', considers higher-degree nodes are more influential.
- PR: The PAGE-RANK algorithm proposed for ranking the importance of pages in web graphs. We can compute the PR value for each node by the power method with a damping value between 0 and 1. In the experiments, it is set to 0.15, and the algorithm stops when two consecutive iterations differ for at most 10^{-4}.
- RANDOM: The RANDOM algorithm chooses the nodes uniformly at random. It was proposed in [5] as a baseline method for comparison purposes.

We run 10K MC simulations to approximate the AIS of seed set S resulted by the above algorithms. All the experiments are run on a PC with a 2.6-Ghz processer and 6-GB memory.

Experimental results

To understand how effectively the hop constraint T can help us to balance the algorithm efficiency and quality of seed selection, we run IMT on the four data sets, with T varying

Table 1 Statistics of datasets

Dataset	Hep	Phy	Amazon	Flixster
Number of nodes	12K	37K	257K	720K
Number of edges	60K	348K	1.2 million	10 million
Maximum out-degree	64	178	5	1,010
Maximum in-degree	62	178	420	319

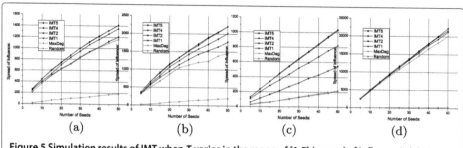

Figure 5 Simulation results of IMT when _T_ varies in the range of [1,5] (spread of influence). (a) Hep, **(b)** Phy, **(c)** Amazon, and **(d)** Flixster.

in the range of $[1, 5]$. The simulation results are shown in Figure 5 and Table 2, in which MaxDeg and Random are considered as baselines. When $T \leq 4$, the EIS is estimated by Algorithm 1; and when $T = 5$, it is estimated by Algorithm 2 with parameter $r = 1,000$. Figure 5 shows the AIS of seed sets resulted by IMT, MaxDeg, and Random. First, the AIS of IMT in all the datasets is non-decreasing as T increases. This agrees with our intuition in that increasing the number of hops brings more accurate EISE. Second, the increments of AIS are tiny when increasing T from 4 to 5, which implies that the seed quality of $IMT_{T=4}$ is as good as that of IMT5. From Figure 5, we also can get that the performance of $IMT_{T=2}$ is much better than that of $IMT_{T=1}$ for the first three data sets, and it is slightly worse than $IMT_{T=4}$. In the 'Flixster' data set, all the algorithms perform similarly, except Random, which is always the worst one in all the experiments.

Consider now the running time performance. Table 2 shows the PRT of IMT, in which the file reading and writing time are not counted. When $T \leq 4$, on the first three data sets, IMT is extremely fast, since the maximum out-degree in those data sets is not large. For instance, $IMT_{T=4}$ only requires less than 1 s to finish in 'Hep'. In 'Flixster', IMT is fast when $T \leq 2$, and it is relatively slow when $T \geq 4$. When $T = 5$, the PRT of IMT increases in certain degree for all the data sets. It is reasonable since in such a case, Algorithm 1 does not work, and Algorithm 2 is applied.

According to the first experiment, one notes that, in general, $IMT_{T=4}$ is an efficient algorithm for seed selection. When the running time is of first priority or the data set is extremely large, $IMT_{T=2}$ is a good replacement.

In the second experiment, we compare $IMT_{T=2}$ and $IMT_{T=4}$ with the algorithms introduced in the 'Algorithms' section. The results are exhibited in Figure 6. Since MC is not scalable, its results are omitted for the last three data sets. As shown in Figure 6a, $IMT_{T=4}$ and MC perform similarly in 'Hep'. SP is about 2% lower than $IMT_{T=4}$ and MC in spread achieved when the number of seeds is 35, and its performance matches $IMT_{T=4}$ and MC when the number of seeds is greater or equal to 40. In the other three data sets, $IMT_{T=4}$

Table 2 Running time performance (seconds)

Dataset	Hep	Phy	Amazon	Flixster
$IMT_{T=1}$	0.14	0.28	0.37	1.32
$IMT_{T=2}$	0.26	0.41	0.53	2.57
$IMT_{T=3}$	0.46	0.92	1.01	30.54
$IMT_{T=4}$	0.73	2.44	2.41	126.95
$IMT_{T=5}$	5.71	11.18	81.83	363.42

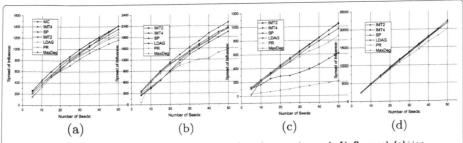

Figure 6 Simulation results of multiple methods on four datasets (spread of influence). (a) Hep, **(b)** Phy, **(c)** Amazon, and **(d)** Flixster.

is able to produce seed sets of the highest quality, and $IMT_{T=2}$ is also compatible with other algorithms in terms of AIS. In general, $IMT_{T=4}$ is the best one. In 'Phy', $IMT_{T=4}$ outperforms SP by about 0% to 10%, and in 'Amazon' and 'Flixster', they perform similarly. $IMT_{T=2}$ outperforms PR and LDAG in 'Hep' and 'Amazon', and they perform similarly in 'Phy'. In 'Flixster', all the methods perform well. More than 20K nodes can be activated by the seed set resulted by any algorithm in 'Flixster'. It is probably because there are a lot of high-degree nodes in 'Flixster' (as shown in Table 1, the maximum degree node in 'Flixster' has 1,010 outgoing neighbors).

Although MC is able to produce high-quality seed sets, it is not scabble. In terms of PRT, $IMT_{T=2}$ is orders of magnitude faster than MC, and $IMT_{T=4}$ is also much faster than MC. According to the experiments, MC takes 8,532.6 s to finish in 'Hep'. As shown in Table 2, the running time of $IMT_{T=2}$ and $IMT_{T=4}$ is only 0.26 and 0.73 s, respectively. Therefore, IMT is much more scalable than MC. In sum, IMT is better than other algorithms in terms of AIS except MC, and it is more suitable than MC for finding seed set in large social networks.

Finally, we would also like to evaluate the accuracy of our EISE algorithms. To do this, we compute the EIS for the most influential node in each data set by our EISE algorithms and by the SP algorithm, respectively. The results are compared with the exact solutions. Figure 7 shows the comparisons, in which 'Ext' denotes the exact EIS_T which is computed by enumerating all the simple paths of length no more than T. Our results exactly match the exact solutions when $T \leq 4$, which validates our conclusion in the 'A deterministic algorithm' section ($EISE_4$ is exact). For the case that $T = 5$, when $r = 1,000$, the errors of EISE are about 1%, 2%, 0.1%, and 1% in the four data sets, where r denotes the number of uniform random samples. When $r = 10,000$, the error is much lower. Compared with the

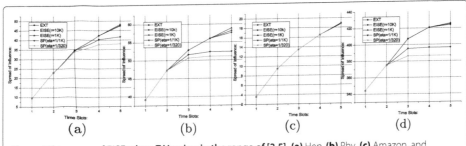

Figure 7 Accuracy of EISE when T Varying in the range of [2,5]. (a) Hep, **(b)** Phy, **(c)** Amazon, and **(d)** Flixster.

SP method with a pruning threshold η, EISE is much more accurate in computing the EIS in data sets: 'Hep', 'Phy', and 'Flixster'. In 'Amazon', the results of both EISE and SP match the exact solution. Note that in the second experiment, $IMT_{T=4}$ outperforms SP in 'Hep' and 'phy', and they perform similarly in 'Amazon'. Thus, we can say that an accurate EISE algorithm is indeed important for solving the IM problem.

Conclusion

IM is a big topic in social network analysis. In this paper, we investigate efficient influence spread estimation for IM under the LT model. We analyze the problem both theoretically and practically. By adding a hop constraint T, we show that the influence estimation problem can be solved efficiently when T is small, and it can be approximated well by uniform random sampling. Based on the two points, we develop a new algorithm called IMT for the LT model. The efficiency of IMT is demonstrated through simulations on four real-world social networks.

In future research, we plan to extend our work to other influence propagation models such as the IC model. Furthermore, we will study constraints under which the optimal solution for IM can be obtained.

Competing interests
The authors declare that they have no competing interests.

Authors' contributions
ZL, LF, and KY formulated the problem and did the algorithm design and implementation. WW and BT contributed to the theoretical part of algorithm design and organized this research. All authors read and approved the final manuscript.

Acknowledgements
This research work was supported in part by the US National Science Foundation (NSF) under grants CNS 1016320 and CCF 0829993.

References

1. Domingos, P, Richardson, M: Mining the network value of customers. In: 2001 ACM SIGKDD Conference on Knowledge Discovery and Data Mining, pp. 57–66 San Francisco, CA, USA, (August 26-29, 2001)
2. Goldenberg, J, Libai, B, Muller, E: Using complex systems analysis to advance marketing theory development. Acad. Market. Sci. Rev. **9**(3), 1-18 (2001)
3. Goldenberg, J, Libai, B, Muller, E: Talk of the network: a complex systems look at the underlying process of word-of-mouth. Marketing Lett. **12**(3), 211–223 (2001)
4. Richardson, M, Domingos, P: Mining knowledge-sharing sites for viral marketing. In: the 2002 International Conference on Knowledge Discovery and Data Mining, pp. 61–70 Edmonton, AB, Canada, (July 23-25, 2002)
5. Kempe, D, Kleinberg, J, Tardos, É: Maximizing the spread of influence through a social network. In: The 2003 ACM SIGKDD Conference on Knowledge Discovery and Data Mining, pp. 137–146 Washington, DC, USA, (August 24-27, 2003)
6. Ma, H, Yang, H, Lyu, MR, King, I: Mining social networks using heat diffusion processes for marketing candidates selection. In: The 2008 ACM Conference on Information and Knowledge Management, pp. 233–242 Napa Valley, CA, USA, (October 26-30, 2008)
7. Granovetter, M: Threshold models of collective behavior. Am. J. Sociol. **83**(6), 1420–1443 (1978)
8. Schelling, T: Micromotives and Macrobehavior. W.W. Norton, New York, USA, (1978)
9. Chen, W, Wang, Y, Yang, S: Efficient influence maximization in social networks. In: The 2009 ACM SIGKDD Conference on Knowledge Discovery and Data Mining, pp. 199–208 Paris, France, (June 28 - July 01, 2009)
10. Chen, W, Wang, C, Wang, Y: Scalable influence maximization for prevalent viral marketing in large-scale social networks. In: The 2010 ACM SIGKDD Conference on Knowledge Discovery and Data Mining, pp. 1029–1038 Washington DC, DC, USA, (July 25-28, 2010)
11. Chen, W, Yuan, Y, Zhang, L: Scalable influence maximization in social networks under the linear threshold model. In: The 2010 International Conference on Data Mining, pp. 88–97 Sydney, Australia, (December 14-17, 2010)
12. Narayanam, R, Narahari, Y: A Shapley value based approach to discover influential nodes in social networks. IEEE Trans. Automation Sci. Eng. **8**(1), 130–147 (2011)
13. Goyal, A, Lu, W, Lakshmanan, LVS: CELF++: optimizing the greedy algorithm for influence maximization in social networks. In: The 2011 International World Wide Web Conference, pp. 47–48 Hyderabad, India, (March 28 - April 01, 2011)

14. Jiang, Q, Song, G, Cong, G, Wang, Y, Si, W, Xie, K: Simulated annealing based in influence maximization in social networks. In: The 2011 AAAI Conference on Artificial Intelligence. San Francisco, CA, USA, (August 7-11, 2011)

15. Goyal, A, Lu, W, Lakshmanan, LVS: SIMPATH: an efficient algorithm for influence maximization under the linear threshold model. In: The 2011 IEEE International Conference on Data Mining, pp. 211–220 Vancouver, Canada, (December 11-14, 2011)

16. Leskovec, J, Krause, A, Guestrin, C, Faloutsos, C, VanBriesen, J, Glance, NS: Cost-effective outbreak detection in networks. In: The 2007 ACM SIGKDD Conference on Knowledge Discovery and Data Mining, pp. 420–429 San Jose, CA, USA, (August 12-15, 2007)

17. Nemhauser, G, Wolsey, L, Fisher, M: An analysis of the approximations for maximizing submodular set functions. Math. Program. **14**(1978), 265–294 (1978)

18. Kimura, M, Saito, K, Nakano, R: Extracting influential nodes for information diffusion on social network. In: The 2007 AAAI Conference on Artificial Intelligence, pp. 1371–1376 Vancouver, British Columbia, (July 22-26, 2007)

19. Wang, Y, Cong, G, Song, G, Xie, K: Community-based greedy algorithm for mining top-*k* influential nodes in mobile social networks. In: The 2010 ACM SIGKDD Conference on Knowledge Discovery and Data Mining, pp. 1039–1048. Washington DC, DC, USA, (July 25-28, 2010)

20. Hoeffding, W: Probability inequalities for sums of bounded random variables. J. Am. Stat. Assoc. **58**(301), 13–30 (1963)

12

Sentiment leaning of influential communities in social networks

Borut Sluban[1]*, Jasmina Smailović[1], Stefano Battiston[2] and Igor Mozetič[1]

*Correspondence:
borut.sluban@ijs.si
[1] Department of Knowledge Technologies, Jožef Stefan Institute, Ljubljana, Slovenia
Full list of author information is available at the end of the article

Abstract

Social media and social networks contribute to shape the debate on societal and policy issues, but the dynamics of this process is not well understood. As a case study, we monitor Twitter activity on a wide range of environmental issues. First, we identify influential users and communities by means of a network analysis of the retweets. Second, we carry out a content-based classification of the communities according to the main interests and profile of their most influential users. Third, we perform sentiment analysis of the tweets to identify the leaning of each community towards a set of common topics, including some controversial issues. This novel combination of network, content-based, and sentiment analysis allows for a better characterization of groups and their leanings in complex social networks.

Keywords: Social networks; Communities; Sentiment analysis; Influence

Introduction

Environmental and sustainability issues are among the major societal concerns today. The formulation of environmental policies is often a result of the interaction between antagonistic interest groups, including policy makers (governments and international organizations), advocacy groups representing the interest of specific industry sectors, and civic activists. The motivation for this research is to contribute to a better understanding of the dynamics of advocacy and activism around policy issues. We expect that the results will help policymakers in monitoring the response of various interest groups to the proposed regulations and policy targets.

The explosive growth of social media and user-generated contents on the Web provides a potentially relevant and rich source of data. This work is based on data from Twitter [1], a social networking and micro blogging service with over 270 million monthly active users, generating over 500 million tweets per day.

We collect a broad range of tweets related to the environmental issues and address the following research questions:

- Can one identify influential communities and environmental topics of interest?
- Are there differences in their leanings towards various environmental topics?

Our results indicate that there are observable differences in sentiment leanings towards various environmental issues between the major communities.

There are several aspects of Twitter data analysis that are relevant for this research. On the one hand, Twitter is a social network, and several types of networks can be constructed from the data, e.g., followers, mention, or retweet networks. Network analysis algorithms then yield interesting network properties, such as communities, modularity, various, and centralities. On the other hand, Twitter data can also be analyzed for its contents, by applying text mining and sentiment analysis algorithms. A novelty of our research is that we combine both types of analysis. We detect influential communities, identify discussion topics, and assign sentiment of the communities towards selected topics.

There are three different ways how users on Twitter interact: 1) a user follows posts of other users, 2) a user can respond to other user's tweets by mentioning them, and 3) a user can forward interesting tweets by retweeting them. Based on these three interaction types, Cha et al. [2] define three measures of influence of the user on Twitter: *indegree influence* (the number of followers, indicating the size of his audience), *mention influence* (the number of mentions of the user, indicating his ability to engage others in conversation), and *retweet influence* (the number of retweets, indicating the ability of the user to write content of interest to be forwarded to others). They find that mention and retweet influence are correlated, but that indegree alone reveals little about the user's actual influence. This is also known as *the million follower fallacy* [3]. Instead of the number of followers, they show that it is more influential to have an active audience who mentions or retweets the user. Suh et al. [4] analyze factors which have a positive impact on the number of retweets: URLs, hashtags, the number of followers and followees, the age of the account, but not the number of past tweets. Bakshy et al. [5] quantify the influence on Twitter by tracking the diffusion of URLs through retweet cascades. They find that the longest retweet cascades tend to be generated by the most influential users in the past.

Closely related to our research is the work by Conover et al. [6], albeit applied to the problem of political polarization. They construct both retweet and mention networks from political tweets and apply community detection. It turns out that the retweet network exhibits clear community segregation (to the left- and right-leaning users), while the mention network is dominated by a single community. In [7], they compare the predictive accuracy of the community-based model to two content-based (full text tweets and hashtags-only) models. The community-based model constructed from the retweet network clearly outperforms the content-based models (with the accuracy of 95 vs. 91 %).

The above research indicates that the retweet influence seems to be the most promising measure of influence on Twitter, and that community detection in the retweet network will likely yield the most influential communities. However, in the environmental domain, the community segregation is not as clear as in the political domain. We therefore characterize communities not only by their influential members, but also by their prevalent discussion topics and sentiment.

Sentiment analysis has been applied to Twitter in several domains [8], most notably for stock market predictions [9], and in political elections. There has been some controversy whether Twitter analysis can be used to predict the outcome of elections—Gayo-Avello gives a survey of various studies [10]. We have successfully applied Twitter sentiment analysis to monitor Slovenian presidential election in 2012 and Bulgarian parliamentary elections in 2013 [11]. Most of the other approaches are based on tweet volume or simple sentiment analysis by counting positive and negative sentiment words in tweets. In contrast, we apply supervised machine learning, the SVM classification in particular [12]. The training data comes either from manually annotated tweets (which are problem-specific and of high quality, but expensive in terms of resources needed), or from generic, smiley-based tweets [13] (which are of lower quality, but very extensive).

This paper is based on our preliminary work, presented in a workshop proceeding [14], and, in several aspects, extends the proposed methodology. First, the experiments capture 1 year of Twitter data and hence analyze twice the original amount of data. Second, the structural properties of most prominent communities discussing environmental topics are examined. Third, content filtering is enhanced by similarity calculation in a multi-dimensional vector space. Finally, a custom sentiment model, trained on manually labeled domain-specific tweets, is applied to produce better sentiment classification results.

The paper is organized as follows. In the "Methodology: discovering influential communities and their sentiment" section, we present the network and content analysis employed in our work. We describe the Twitter data acquisition and construction of the retweet network. We use a standard community detection algorithm and define the Twitter user and community influence measures. A standard text mining approach is used to identify topics discussed by the major communities. For sentiment analysis, we construct a binary SVM classifier with neutral zone, from three different sets of training data. The "Results and discussion" section describes the outcomes of the experiments. First, we analyze the structural properties of the most influential communities, in terms of their internal and external influence, and balance of the influence distribution. We identify categories of influential communities (e.g., environmental activists, news media, skeptics, celebrities) and the topics of their interests. Sentiment classification is applied to the tweets of different communities, and sentiment leaning of the communities towards different topics is analyzed. We highlight interesting findings and some unexpected results. We conclude with plans for future work.

Methodology: discovering influential communities and their sentiment

We have monitored Twitter for a period of the entire year 2014. We use the Twitter Search API and define a wide range of queries to select tweets related to environmental and energy topics (see see Table 6 in Appendix for the full list of queries). The collected environmental tweets are then used to construct a social network and identify influential users and communities, as well as their topics of interest and sentiment. The process of identifying community interests and their leanings consists of three steps. First, the network of users retweeting each other is constructed, and the densely connected communities are detected. Second, the content published by these communities is analyzed to reveal the communities' interests, and finally, sentiment analysis is performed to asses the sentiment leaning of the communities with respect to different topics of interest.

Network structure and influence measures

We explore which Twitter users share similar content on environmental topics. To model this phenomenon, we construct a retweet network, connecting users who are in a retweet relation, i.e., an undirected edge between two users indicates either one user retweeted the other or vice versa. The network is constructed from 30.5 million tweets about environmental topics, acquired between January 1, 2014 and December 31, 2014. The network consists of 3.7 million users (nodes) linked by 9.7 million retweet relations.

The largest part of the network consists of one large connected component of 3.4 million users, the rest are components of size smaller than 1000 users. In the largest component, we want to find groups of users that share similar views on environmental topics. If we assume that retweeting is a proxy of expressing agreement on the published content, the retweet network can be regarded as consisting of the connections between users who agree on a certain topic. Therefore, the problem translates into partitioning the network in the so-called communities. In the field of complex networks, the notion of "community" corresponds, loosely speaking, to a subset of nodes that are more densely connected among themselves than with the nodes outside the subset. Several definitions of community and methods to detect communities have been proposed in the literature (see [15] for a review).

We apply a standard community detection algorithm, the Louvain method [16], to our retweet network. The method partitions the network nodes in a way that maximizes the network's modularity. Modularity is a measure of community density in networks. It measures the fraction of edges falling within groups of a given network partitioning as compared to the expected fraction of edges in these groups, given a random distribution of links in the network [17]. Among the available detection algorithms in the optimization-based class, the Louvain method is one of the few methods that are suitable: (i) to analyze large networks with good scalability properties and (ii) to avoid ex-ante assumptions on their size [18].

Further, we propose an approach to identify the most influential users in the network, i.e., users whose content is apparently approved and shared the most. Let the retweet network be represented as a directed graph G, with edges $E(G)$. A directed edge $e_{u,v}$ from the user u to the user v indicates that contents of the user u have been retweeted by the user v. Let $w(e_{u,v})$ be the weight of the edge $e_{u,v}$ indicating the number of times that the user v retweeted the contents of the user u. Then *user influence* $I(u)$ is defined as

$$I(u) = \sum_{e_{u,v} \in E(G)} w(e_{u,v}) \tag{1}$$

The differences in the structure of the detected communities $C_1, \ldots, C_n$ are examined through the influence of the users of a particular community C_k. We address this by measuring the *intra and inter-community influence* of each community, as well as by measuring the distribution of influence among the community's users.

Community influence is defined as the cumulative influence of all its users,

$$I(C) = \sum_{u \in C} I(u) = \sum_{u \in C} \left(\sum_{e_{u,v} \in E(G)} w(e_{u,v}) \right) \tag{2}$$

It can be divided into the influence that the community users have within their own community and the influence they exert outside their community. Hence, we define *intra-community influence* I_{in} and *inter-community influence* I_{out} as:

$$I_{in}(C) = \sum_{u \in C} I_{in}(u) = \sum_{u \in C} \left(\sum_{\substack{e_{u,v} \in E(G) \\ v \in C}} w(e_{u,v}) \right) \tag{3}$$

$$I_{out}(C) = \sum_{u \in C} I_{out}(u) = \sum_{u \in C} \left(\sum_{\substack{e_{u,v} \in E(G) \\ v \notin C}} w(e_{u,v}) \right) \tag{4}$$

The ratio between these two measures I_{out}/I_{in} reveals the extent to which a community is influential outside its "borders" versus its internal content exchange.

Furthermore, to measure the distribution of user influence within a community, we use the *Herfindahl-Hirschman index* (HHI), commonly used in economics to measure the amount of competition among leading companies in an industry with respect to their market share [19]. When applied in the context of community structure, we look at the N leading users u_i, $i \in \{1, \ldots, N\}$, in a community C in terms of their normalized intra-community influence $r_i = I_{in}(u_i)/\sum_{j=1}^{N} I_{in}(u_j)$. Hence, the Herfindahl-Hirschman index is defined as

$$HHI(C) = \sum_{i=1}^{N} r_i^2 = \sum_{i=1}^{N} \left(\frac{I_{in}(u_i)}{\sum_{j=1}^{N} I_{in}(u_j)} \right)^2 \tag{5}$$

The squared sum of influence ratios ranges from $1/N$ to 1, where lower values indicate a dispersed and more balanced influence distribution, whereas higher values reflect the community influence being concentrated only on few strongly influential users.

Content identification and filtering

The retweet relation can be considered as the agreement between users on the published content. Hence the retweet network reveals which users support similar interests, without looking into the actual content. On the other hand, to identify the content and to see what are different groups of users talking about, we adopt a standard text mining approach as follows.

1. For each group of users g_i, $i \in \{1, \ldots, N\}$, create a document d_i that aggregates all the content which the users of the group g_i have published.

2. The vocabulary (i.e., the set of terms) used by groups $\{g_1, \ldots, g_N\}$ is obtained from the documents $\{d_1, \ldots, d_N\}$. Term frequency $TF_i(t)$ denotes the number of appearances of a term t in a document d_i.

3. For each term t from the vocabulary, *document frequency* $DF(t)$ is the number of documents in which t appears.

4. For each of the documents, $\{d_1, \ldots, d_N\}$ construct a bag of words (BoW) vector where each term value in the vector is the TFiDF value of the term t from the vocabulary:

$$TFiDF_i(t) = TF_i(t) \cdot \log \frac{N}{DF(t)} \tag{6}$$

Term frequency-inverse document frequency (TFiDF) is a standard and widely used measure of importance of a term t to a document in a collection of documents [20].

We use this adopted text mining approach to identify the terms that are the most distinctive and therefore the most characteristic for the content tweeted by different groups of users. More specifically, we use the detected retweet communities as the groups of users. Next, we employ the above procedure to summarize and represent the most characteristic topics in the content of each community. Such content identification and representation is done by displaying only the selected number of the highest *TFiDF* ranked terms from a BoW vector constructed for a selected community. In this way, we are able to get a readable and reliable overview of the specific interests and topics discussed in the observed communities.

On the other hand, for the purpose of identifying the leaning of different communities towards specific topics of interest, we have to retrieve the individual tweets forming a certain topic. We employ a filtering procedure based on document similarity, to obtain tweets that revolve around a specified topic (query). In this case, each tweet from the dataset is treated as an individual document and is transformed into a BoW vector. Hence, the filtering works as follows.

1. The vocabulary V of a specific domain is obtained from all unique tweets acquired for the targeted domain. From V the base of the document vector space is constructed by standard text preprocessing (stemming, stop-word removal, n-grams) resulting in terms $t_1, \ldots, t_n$.

2. For each tweet tw_i, $i \in \{1, \ldots, m\}$, from the dataset D, a BoW vector v_i of term frequencies $TF_i(t)$ for each term t in tw_i is constructed and normalized.

3. A BoW model of the examined domain can be represented by a matrix M with rows v_i for each $tw_i \in D$.

4. The dataset D is filtered according to a query that is transformed into a normalized BoW vector q.

5. Similarity between query q and tweets $tw_i \in D$ is calculated as $s = M \cdot q$:

$$
\begin{bmatrix} s_1 \\ \vdots \\ s_m \end{bmatrix} = \begin{bmatrix} m_{1,1} & \cdots & m_{1,n} \\ \vdots & & \vdots \\ m_{m,1} & \cdots & m_{m,n} \end{bmatrix} \cdot \begin{bmatrix} q_1 \\ \vdots \\ q_n \end{bmatrix} \tag{7}
$$

where s_i, $i \in \{1, \ldots, m\}$, is the cosine similarity[1] between the query vector q and v_i representing tweet tw_i, and $m_{i,j}$ is the (normalized) term frequency of term t_j in tweet tw_i.

Given a query q and the calculated similarity vector s, the filter returns tweets tw_i for the indices i where s_i is greater than a given threshold. Note that, since the number of terms (n) and especially the number of tweets (m) can be very large, in practice the computations are performed with sparse representations of vectors and matrices.

Sentiment analysis

Our goal is to measure the collective attitude of a Twitter community towards a certain topic. The first step is to measure the sentiment of each individual tweet posted by the community. To perform Twitter sentiment analysis, we construct a sentiment classifier from the training data. We employ the Support Vector Machine (SVM) algorithm [12], and in particular its SVM^{perf} [21–23] implementation. The SVM algorithm requires a labeled collection of instances to build a model. We have collected three labeled Twitter datasets which differ in terms of size, discussion topics, and labeling method. We have trained three corresponding sentiment models and compare their performance on the same testing set. The best sentiment classification model is then used in the rest of our analyses.

The first dataset consists of 1.6 million positively and negatively labeled tweets collected by the Stanford University [13][2]. The labeling of the tweets is based on the presence of positive (e.g., ":)") or negative (e.g., ":(") emoticons, which were then removed from the dataset for training. Although such approach does not provide the highest labeling quality, it is a reasonable and inexpensive substitute for manual tweet labeling [24]. The tweets in this dataset are general and not focused on any specific domain.

The second dataset consists of general English tweets too, but the tweet labels were obtained by manual annotation. In this dataset, there are 25,721 positive, 23,250 negative, and 37,951 neutral hand-labeled tweets.

The tweets in the third dataset are a uniformly sampled subset of our environmental tweets, therefore highly domain-specific. This dataset consists of 2,850 positive, 5,569 negative, and 11,439 neutral hand-labeled tweets, from January to December, 2014. We randomly choose 20 % of these tweets (preserving the labeling distribution of the whole dataset) as a test set, used for evaluating the trained sentiment models. The rest of the 80 % tweets from the domain-specific dataset were used for training the domain-specific sentiment model.

Sentiment models are built only from the positive and negative tweets. However, the classification covers three categories: positive, negative, and neutral as well. A tweet is classified as positive (negative) if its distance from the SVM hyperplane is higher than the average distance of positive (negative, respectively) training examples from the hyperplane. Otherwise, i.e., if it is too close to the hyperplane, it is classified as neutral. Similar approaches to adapting the binary SVM classifier to the three-class setting were already applied in our previous studies [24, 25].

Twitter messages are adequately preprocessed, using both standard and Twitter-specific techniques. Standard preprocessing [26] includes tokenization, stemming, unigram and bigram construction, removing terms which do not appear at least twice in the corpus, and construction of term frequency (TF) feature vectors.[3] Additionally, Twitter-specific preprocessing [8, 13, 24] transforms usernames, hashtags, and collapses repetitive letters.

We build three sentiment models (smiley-labeled general, hand-labeled general, and hand-labeled domain-specific) using the corresponding preprocessed positive and negative tweets, and tested their performance on the separate test set described above. In Table 1, we report the results in terms of macro-averaged error rate [27] and in terms of macro-averaged F-score of positive and negative classes [28]. We are particularly interested in the correct classification of the positive and negative tweets.

As can be seen from Table 1, the best performing sentiment model is the hand-labeled domain-specific one as it achieved the lowest error rate and the highest macro-averaged F-score on the test set. Note that this model is trained on only 6,735 tweets, while the other two models employed substantially more tweets (1.6 million for the smiley-labeled general model and 48,971 for the hand-labeled general model). Therefore, the results

Table 1 The evaluation results of smiley-labeled general, hand-labeled general, and hand-labeled domain-specific sentiment models on the test dataset in terms of the macro-averaged error rate and the macro-averaged F-score of positive and negative classes

Sentiment model	M error rate (%)	F_{avg}
Smiley-labeled general	61.3	0.20
Hand-labeled general	59.3	0.25
Hand-labeled domain-specific	52.9	0.39

indicate that the high-quality domain-specific tweets produce better sentiment models even if the number of such tweets is lower. For the rest of our study, we use the hand-labeled domain-specific sentiment model trained using the complete hand-labeled domain-specific dataset.

The sentiment of different communities regarding a specific topic is calculated as follows. First, for each community, the tweets posted by its users are selected. Second, the sentiment of each tweet is determined and weighted by its retweet count. Third, the weighted negative and positive sentiment of tweets is aggregated for each user and summed over all users in the community. Finally, the leaning of a community towards a specific topic is computed as the *polarity* of the aggregated weighted sentiment multiplied by the ratio of sentiment carrying tweets (*subjectivity*) of the respective community. The polarity and subjectivity measures are adapted from [29]. The pseudo-code for community sentiment computation is presented in Algorithm 1.

Algorithm 1 Computing community sentiment

Require: $\mathcal{C}$: community,

       T_S : sentiment annotated tweets,

       $\bar{D}_P$: avg. distance of positive training examples,

       $\bar{D}_N$: avg. distance of negative training examples

   function COMMUNITYSENTIMENT $(\mathcal{C}, T_S)$:

    $pos = 0$

    $neg = 0$

    $all = 0$

    for *user* in $\mathcal{C}$.*users* **do**

       userTweets $= T_S$.byUser(*user*)

       for *tw* in *userTweets* **do**

          if *tw.sentiment* $> \bar{D}_P$ **then**

             pos += *tw.retweetCount*

          else if *tw.sentiment* $< \bar{D}_N$ **then**

             neg += *tw.retweetCount*

          end if

          all += *tw.retweetCount*

       end for

    end for

    $polarity = \frac{pos-neg}{pos+neg}$

    $subjectivity = \frac{pos+neg}{all}$

    return *polarity* $\times$ *subjectivity*

   end function

Results and discussion

We present the results of the proposed methodology for identifying interest groups and their leaning towards different environmental topics, in terms of network and community structure, content categorization and identification, and sentiment analysis.

Network and community structure

We analyze a retweet network of 3.7 million users linked by 9.7 million retweet relations. In Fig. 1 we present the distribution of out-degree and influence I (as defined by Equation 1) for the nodes of the network. Community detection results in over 125,000 communities. Their size distribution is presented in Fig. 2. Notice that both plots are in *log–log* scale and therefore even only by eye inspection we can say that the distribution displays a fat tail in the sense that it deviates strongly to the right from a Gaussian distribution. This means that, in line with the empirical literature on social networks, nodes with very high degree and communities with a very large size occur with frequency much larger than in a Gaussian scenario.

We focus our analysis on communities of considerable size, which also produced a sufficient amount of tweets for meaningful content identification and sentiment analysis. This results in 12 communities, each with more than 50,000 users, and with at least 10,000 unique tweets.

The analysis in terms of community influence and its distribution among their users reveals significant structural differences among the largest communities. Results are presented in Table 2. The ratio between the inter- and intra-community influence, $I_{out}(C)$ and $I_{in}(C)$, shows that the majority of communities are greatly introverted, as their influence outside their "borders" presents less than a quarter of the impact they have. However, there are two communities ($k = 1$ and 4) that have almost a third of their influence outside the community, and one where its external influence is almost as high as its internal influence ($k = 5$).

The distribution of influence within communities, as measured by the Herfindahl-Hirshmann index (HHI), also shows interesting differences among communities. The lowest values of HHI are around 0.03, for communities $k = 6, 9, 10,$ and 11. Hence, these are the communities that have the lowest inequality in terms of I_{in} among their 50 most influential users. Whereas communities $k = 8$ and 12 have the highest inequality between their 50 most influential users. It is interesting to notice that community $k = 6$ with the lowest inequality is also the second most introverted. Other than that, we find no obvious relation between HHI and the relative inter-community influence.

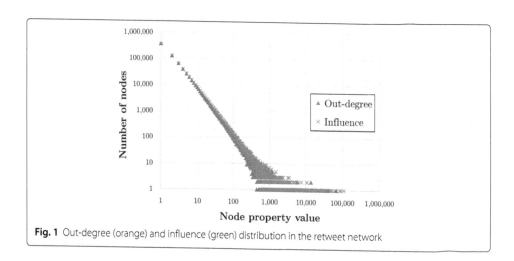

Fig. 1 Out-degree (orange) and influence (green) distribution in the retweet network

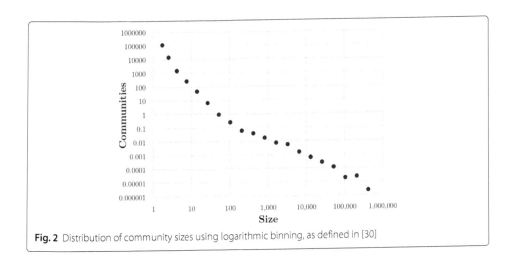

Fig. 2 Distribution of community sizes using logarithmic binning, as defined in [30]

In Fig. 3, we present the relation between the user influence, out-degree, and the number of unique tweets, for the top three most influential users of selected nine communities. The selection is explained in the subsequent section. The figure shows the magnitude of the top users in different communities and is consistent with the inequality measures by HHI. On the other hand, there is no obvious relation between the tweet volume and the influence of the users. It seems that higher out-degree is accompanied by higher influence, which can be seen also from Fig. 1.

Community content

A preliminary community categorization was performed by looking at the Twitter profiles of their most influential users and the contents of their tweets. We find that the communities could roughly be classified into six categories. Table 3 presents the community categories and examples of the most influential users in these categories.

The community categorization reveals that for our further investigations we can ignore certain categories of communities. First, in the "Humor" community, the presence of an actual leaning or sentiment towards a certain topic is for one questionable (every topic

Table 2 Structural properties of the 12 largest communities

k	Name	Users	Unique tweets	$I_{in}(C_k)$	$I_{out}(C_k)$	$\frac{I_{out}(C_k)}{I_{in}(C_k)}$	$HHI(C_k)$
1	Env 1	366,979	625,280	1,546,998	787,139	0.509	0.037
2	Env 2	324,518	561,659	2,189,373	796,861	0.364	0.034
3	News 1	275,172	325,867	1,160,347	385,355	0.332	0.035
4	Humor	272,780	12,971	330,897	150,148	0.454	0.065
5	News 2	254,159	44,587	363,539	307,039	0.845	0.036
6	Skeptic	160,257	236,618	983,672	132,509	0.135	0.029
7	India	96,158	32,981	311,754	37,849	0.121	0.045
8	Celebrity	92,434	13,480	174,105	36,414	0.209	0.158
9	News 3	91,446	95,415	274,704	91,323	0.332	0.032
10	Env 3	83,259	180,210	707,292	187,576	0.265	0.030
11	Other	65,363	13,697	115,709	41,309	0.357	0.031
12	Env 4	53,847	29,863	105,608	19,796	0.187	0.104

Community influence $I(C)$ is split into $I_{in}(C)$ and $I_{out}(C)$, intra- and inter-community influence, respectively. $HHI(C)$ is the Herfindahl-Hirshmann index of the intra-community influence

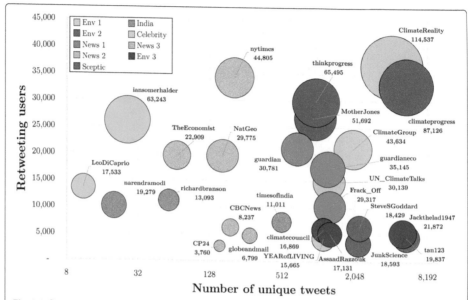

Fig. 3 Influence (bubble size), out-degree (number of retweeting users), and the number of unique tweets for the top three most influential users of the nine selected communities

can be made fun of using positive or negative words), and for two, it is hard to automatically identify the correct polarity due to frequent use of irony and sarcasm. Second, we also ignore a smaller community in the category "Other" that we are unable to strictly categorize.

One community from the "Environmental" category is also not included, because it contains numerous content duplicates as a result of marketing and spamming. The final selection includes three communities from the "Environmental" category (labeled as "Env 1", "Env 2", and "Env 3"), three from "News" ("News 1", "News 2", and "News 3"), the "Indian" community ("India"), one "Celebrities" community ("Celebrity"), and the "Skeptics" community ("Skeptic"). The network of these nine communities is outlined in Fig. 4.

Table 3 Community categories and their most influential users

Category	Count	Includes	Influential users
Environmental	4	Activists, organizations, green/eco news, and technology	ClimateReality, ClimateGroup, climateprogress, thinkprogress, Jackthelad1947, GreenrEnergy
News	3	News agencies, media	guardianeco, guardian, nytimes, NatGeo, TheEconomist, BBCWorld, CBCNews
Humor	1	Joke websites, commentators, comedians	emmkaff, StephenAtHome, TheTweetOfGod, neiltyson, michaelarria, pourmecoffee
Skeptics	1	Republicans, lobbyists	JunkScience, tan123, SteveSGoddard, hockeyschtick1, realDonaldTrump
Indian	1	Politics, news and business from India	narendramodi, richardbranson, timesofindia, MIB_India, EconomicTimes
Celebrities	1	Actors, musicians, athletes	iansomerhalder, LeoDiCaprio, YEARSofLIVING, JaredLeto
Other	1	Miscellaneous	-

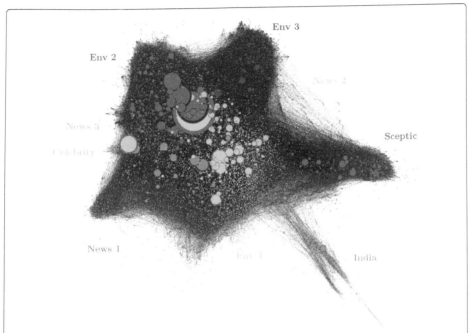

Fig. 4 Subgraph of the retweet network induced on the nine selected communities. Only users with influence larger than 100 retweets are displayed. The size of the nodes is proportional to the user influence and individual communities are distinguished by color

Each community is represented with its own color and the size of the nodes is proportional to the user's influence. The presented network layout shows a relatively clear segregation between the communities.

We analyze the content tweeted by a community in terms of (i) hashtags and (ii) plain text. Hashtags can represent entities in the tweet and/or user-inserted labels of a tweet, indicating the topic or broader context of the tweet. Content analysis in terms of hashtags, using the approach presented in section "Content identification and filtering", is therefore expected to show the characteristic entities and topics of interest in a selected community. On the other hand, plain text analysis is more appropriate for identification of actions, attitude, and phrases that are most distinctive for a particular community. The results of content analysis are presented in Table 4.

The most characteristic content of each community, as shown by the results in Table 4, reasonably distinguishes the communities of different categories. The hashtag content analysis supports the membership of the communities with the most influential users "ClimateReality" and "climateprogress" in the "Environmental" category, therefore from now on labeled by "Env 1" and "Env 2", respectively. Next two largest communities include topics present in the news in the United Kingdom and the United States of America, hence called "News 1" and "News 2", respectively. It reveals that the users retweeting "JunkScience" belong to the "Skeptic" community. Local topics from "India" are apparent from the hashtags of the next community. Similarly, the hashtags of the Ian Somerhalder Foundation (#isf) and their opinions point to the "Celebrity" community. Hashtag analysis of the last two communities shows interest in Canadian political and environmental issues, hence "News 3", and in environmental problems and political topics in Australia, therefore "Env 3".

Table 4 Characteristic content of the nine influential communities, selected on the basis of the largest number of unique tweets (in parenthesis are the most influential users)

Community	Users	Tweets	Content
Env 1 (ClimateReality)	366,979	625,280	#gridpowerstorage (0.49) #caribbeantech (0.20) #solars (0.19) #ag4dev (0.14) #jamaica (0.12) #idb (0.11) #energyefficiency (0.11) retw (0.18) global wind jobs: (0.14) global solar jobs: (0.11) green jobs: (0.09) lexinerus: retw (0.09) daily stories via (0.08) filed under: solar (0.07)
Env 2 (climateprogess)	324,518	561,659	#uniteblue (0.37) #p2 (0.28) #copolitics (0.26) #wiunion (0.16) #ofaction (0.14) #stoprush (0.14) #ctl (0.13) #libcrib (0.12) #coleg (0.11) without remorse please (0.12) dying plastic next. (0.11) next. watch share (0.11) companies poison water (0.09) stop now watch (0.09)
News 1 (guardianeco)	275,172	325,867	#olsx (0.34) #rhi (0.30) #bizitalk (0.26) #bartonmoss (0.24) #stopbrep (0.22) #udobiz (0.20) #besw14 (0.18) #gbhour (0.16) #ukair (0.15) 3 low (0.30) low 3 (0.21) average 2 low (0.16) pollution forecast tomorrow (0.14) moderate average (0.08) 40 % power 20 % (0.06)
News 2 (nytimes)	254,159	44,587	#la_chefs (0.44) #bos (0.43) #scistuchat (0.24) #lax (0.22) #ntrs (0.20) #washington (0.17) #sfo (0.15) #stockaction (0.15) #koreans (0.15) power personal branding (0.14) branding b2b lead (0.14) green chemistry pls (0.14) strange preferential treatment (0.11) japan privilege foreigners (0.11)
Skeptic (JunkScience)	160,257	236,618	#pjnet (0.84) #ccot (0.26) #cot (0.19) #climatescam (0.15) #teaparty (0.15) #sgp (0.11) #tlot (0.11) #nyhbt (0.10) #copolitics (0.09) man-made global-warming (0.14) conducts dangerous human (0.13) la dr. mengele (0.12) human experimentsa la (0.12) ibd obama's conducts (0.12)
India (narendramodi)	96,158	32,981	#invisiblekiller (0.37) #namo (0.26) #mufflerman (0.23) #insubcontinent (0.20) #aap (0.18) #upa (0.15) web-app share ur (0.16) resources hands aam (0.16) plz join reduce (0.14) air pollution. web-app (0.14) shri (0.12) ganga (0.10) kejriwal (0.09)
Celebrity (iansomerhalder)	92,434	13,480	#coalsucks (0.66) #isf (0.61) #beyondcoal (0.34) #nofrackla (0.19) #isfcommcrew (0.11) #yearsproject (0.08) #yearssolutions (0.03) warm idea solar (0.23) help recycle (0.20) solar powered energy (0.13) coal get heated (0.12) fan wind power (0.10) coalsucks (0.10)
News 3 (CBCNews)	91,446	95,415	#cdnpoli (0.81) #nbpoli (0.23) #bcpoli (0.23) #hamont (0.13) #onpoli (0.12) #nspoli (0.12) #yeg (0.11) #yql (0.09) #nofrackns (0.08) big top thought (0.16) maritime electric (0.16) alberta (0.13) share resources stories (0.08) energy efficiency job: (0.08) ceea (0.07) hydro one (0.07)
Env 3 (Jackthelad1947)	83,259	180,210	#nswpol (0.48) #csg (0.47) #auspol (0.47) #springst (0.22) #qldpol (0.20) #ret (0.16) #qanda (0.15) #insiders (0.14) #vicvotes (0.12) business news (0.37) local banks (0.37) energy via full (0.19) can finance renewable (0.14) lnp (0.13) ret (0.05) agl (0.05) full story business (0.04)

Community contents is characterized in terms of hashtags and plain text (with the respective *TFiDF* values in parenthesis)

On the other hand, the results of the plain text analysis mostly show more specific topics that are shared in the observed communities. The top terms or phrases (n-grams) in the "Env 1", "Env 2", "News 1", "News 2" and "Celebrity" communities, reflect their interest in the promotion of alternative, renewable, and environmentally friendly energy sources, in contrast to the controversial energy supply solution provided by fracking, as well as raise awareness of global pollution. The two most distinctive topics that surface from the content of the "Skeptic" community are "man-made global-warming" and "conducts dangerous human experiments". The former is related to the community's skepticism regarding human-caused global warming, and the latter is about an article published by the "Investor's Business Daily" newspaper [31] that criticizes an allegedly harmful experiment by the Environmental Protection Agency (EPA). The plain text content results for the communities "India", "News 3", and "Env 3" show less specific topics, with the main focus on the local political situation, or environmental and energy policies.

Community sentiment

Finally, we investigate the sentiment leaning of the most content-rich communities. In our dataset of over 30 million environmental tweets, there are almost 3.2 million unique tweets. We label them by the SVM sentiment model, described in the "Sentiment analysis" section, as *positive* (1), *neutral* (0), or *negative* (−1). Only 31 % of the unique tweets are labeled as subjective, i.e., non-neutral. Furthermore, among the sentiment-carrying tweets, there are 52 % of tweets with positive sentiment and 48 % with negative sentiment.

We analyze the sentiment leanings towards selected topics related to the environmental issues. The selection is based on three major groups of topics that are of interest to environmental policy makers: energy sources and energy generation, environmental side effects, and actions or initiatives for solving the environmental issues. We separate the first group into four topics: renewable or green energy sources, nuclear energy, fossil fuels, and fracking, as a separate controversial topic. The second group is represented by the broader topic of global warming and climate change, more general pollution and contamination, and its more specific variant about emissions of greenhouse gases (CO_2 and methane). The last group is separated into recycling and waste management, and environmental policies and initiatives.

The nine communities selected for investigation produce over two thirds of the unique tweets in our dataset. We use the approach presented in the "Content identification and filtering" section to filter these 2.1 million tweets by the nine topics defined above. Table 5 presents the queries used in the filtering process to describe a particular topic. The number of tweets filtered by topic for each community is shown in Fig. 5.

The sentiment of a community towards a selected topic is computed from the tweets on that topic, tweeted by that particular community, as proposed in the "Sentiment analysis" section, Algorithm 1. The results of the community sentiment analysis on different environmental topics are presented in Fig. 6. Community leaning towards a specific topic is computed as the difference between the community sentiment on this topic and the community's average sentiment in our dataset. In Figs. 5 and 6, the topics of interest are in descending order from left to right by their average sentiment over all the communities.

Table 5 Selected environmental topics and the associated queries for tweet filtering

Topic	Query
Green energy	green renewable sustainable sustainability solar wind photovoltaic biomass biofuel biofuels #green #cleanenergy #renewable #renewableenergy #sustainable #sustainability #solar #wind #solarpower #windpower #photovoltaic #biomass #biofuel #biofuels
Recycling	recycling reuse re-use "waste management" waste-management "carbon capture" carbon-capture "carbon storage" "co2 capture" "co2 storage" sequestration decarbonization decarbonisation #reuse #recycling #wastemanagement #CCS #carboncapture
Emissions	emission emissions carbon co2 "carbon dioxide" carbon-dioxide greenhouse greenhouse-gas ghg ch4 methane #emission #emissions #carbon #co2 #carbondioxide #greenhouse #greenhousegas #greenhousegases #ghg #ch4 #methane
Nuclear	nuclear #nuclear #nuclearenergy #nuclearpower #nuclearmatters
Policies	ipcc cop19 cop20 cop21 kyoto 2030 #ipcc #cop19 #cop20 #cop21 #kyoto #2030 #2030now
Fossil fuels	oil gas coal fossil #oil #gas #fossilfuel #coal #oilgas natgas #natgas
Climate change	"climate change" climate-change climate warming "global warming" global-warming #climatechange #climate-change #climate_change #globalwarming #global-warming #global_warming
Pollution	pollution contamination pollute contaminate spill #pollution #polluted #contamination #contaminated #spill #spills #oilspill #oilspills
Fracking	fracking frack shale shalegas aquifer #fracking #frack #shale #shalegas #aquifer #aquifers

The first interesting finding is that the sentiment analysis is in accordance to the commonly accepted attitude towards different environmental topics. All communities show positive leaning towards "green energy" and "recycling", and negative towards "fossil fuels", "climate change", "pollution", and "fracking", except for two outlier communities that we examine separately. Regarding "emissions", "nuclear energy", and "policies", the sentiment leanings are less unanimous, which is to some extent also expected. These results indicate that the domain-specific sentiment model produces reasonable results.

Observing individual communities, we find that most of them follow the same trend; however, there are two notable exceptions: the "Skeptic" and the "Celebrity" communities. The "Skeptic" community is very segregated from the rest (see Fig. 4), and its sentiment leanings show greatest deviations from the leaning of other communities (see Fig. 6). It is the only community having a positive sentiment leaning about the topics "fossil fuels" and "fracking", which is considerably different from all other communities. These results

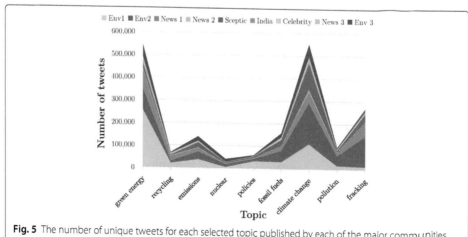

Fig. 5 The number of unique tweets for each selected topic published by each of the major communities

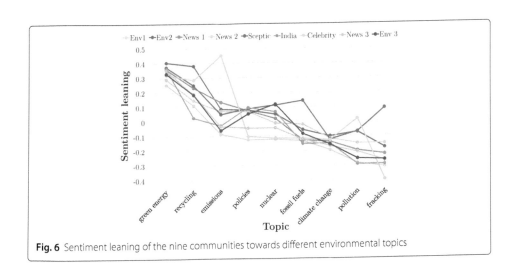

Fig. 6 Sentiment leaning of the nine communities towards different environmental topics

clearly indicate that the preferences of this community are diverging from the interests of the other communities.

The "Celebrity" community is dominated by "iansomerhalder", one of the most influential users overall (see Fig. 3). Despite the high influence, the community produces very low number of original tweets (less than 1 % of all the unique tweets, see Table 4). Its influence emerges from the large number of retweets, due to the large number of followers of "iansomerhalder". This hints at the possibility to engage high-profile celebrities, with the commitment to environmental issues, in promotion and spreading of influential contents.

This is exactly what can be observed for the topics "emissions" and "pollution". The extremely positive sentiment leaning towards these topics is predominantly (60 and 78 %, respectively) due to only three tweets by the two most influential users of the "Celebrity" community: "iansomerhalder" and "LeoDiCaprio". They are expressing their happiness and thankfulness regarding the "action to limit carbon pollution" and "cutting carbon pollution", which will "clean up our air and tackle climate disruption", as they put it. Hence, the distinctively positive leaning for the topics "emissions" and "pollution". On the other hand, the "Celebrity" community seems to be least in favor of "fracking".

Conclusions

The paper contributes to the research on complex networks in social media by combining a structural and content-based analysis of Twitter data. From structural properties of the retweet network, we identify influential users and communities. From the contents of their tweets, we characterize discussion topics and their sentiment. Sentiment of different communities shows perceivable differences in their leanings towards different topics. We have identified two communities that considerably diverge from the rest, "Skeptic" with the most different sentiment leanings on several topics, and "Celebrity" with a low number of original tweets, but highly influential, with the potential to spread interesting information.

Our previous research in sentiment analysis of Twitter data in politics and stock market suggests that different vocabularies are used in different domains and that high-quality expert labeling of domain-specific tweets yields better sentiment models. The comparison of the three sentiment models (smiley-based general, hand-labeled general, and hand-labeled domain specific) presented in this paper confirms our intuition: hand-labeled domain-specific model yields lower error rate and higher combination of precision and recall (F-score) than the other two models. However, more extensive evaluations are required to determine the amount of hand-labeled tweets needed to approach the "maximum" performance, e.g., the inter-annotator agreement.

Another line of future research is the construction of more sophisticated SVM classifiers. In the case of smiley-based training data, only positive and negative tweets were available, and a binary SVM classifier was extended with a neutral zone to allow for the three-class classification. However, in the case of hand-labeled tweets, there are three sets of training data available: positive, neutral, and negative tweets, so we are dealing with a multiclass problem. Further, we can assume that the classes are ordered (neutral is between the positive and negative), and therefore, we are faced with the problem of ordinal regression [32], instead of binary classification. In the future, we plan to exploit various extensions of an SVM to deal with the multiclass [33] and ordinal regression problems.

In this paper, we present a general methodology of combining a structural and content-based analysis of Twitter networks, and then apply it to 1 year of Twitter data about environmental topics. There are several plans for future work. On the one hand, we plan to study the temporal aspects of community formation and sentiment spreading. In addition to the retweet networks, we will also construct mention networks (which model mutual engagement of users in conversations). We will investigate various spreading models and study the differences in sentiment spreading at such multilayer (retweet and mention) networks.

We are also collecting Twitter data in several other interesting domains: stock market, EU commission and parliament members, and lobbying organizations. The application of the presented structural and content-based analysis to these new domains will result in complex 'Twitter' networks. On the other hand, networks between the same entities can also be constructed by other means, such as correlations between stock returns, national and party membership of politicians, vote similarity, and ownership between the companies. The research challenge for the future is the comparison between the Twitter induced and other types of networks, and the mutual interplay and property spreading between these multilayer networks.

Endnotes

[1]Cosine similarity is a measure of similarity between vectors **a** and **b**. It is calculated as the normalized dot product between vectors **a** and **b**: $\text{sim}(\mathbf{a}, \mathbf{b}) = \cos(\angle(\mathbf{a}, \mathbf{b})) = \frac{\mathbf{a} \cdot \mathbf{b}}{|\mathbf{a}| \cdot |\mathbf{b}|}$

[2]The dataset was obtained from "For Academics" section, at http://help.sentiment140.com/for-students.

[3]The approach to feature vector construction was implemented using the LATINO (Link Analysis and Text Mining Toolbox) software library, available at http://source.ijs.si/mgrcar/latino.

Appendix

Our dataset of over 30 million tweets on environmental topics was acquired using the Twitter Search API [34]. Table 6 shows the list of search queries used.

Table 6 Queries for the "Environmental dataset" acquisition from the Twitter Search API

("2030 framework") OR ("2c objective")	("energy transition")	("low carbon" (tech OR technology OR technologies))	(#ccs (climate OR eu))
("abatement cost")	("energy utilities")	("low carbon" economy)	(carbon capture storage))
("adaptation fund")	("environment friendly" OR "environmentally friendly")	("merit order")	(((cer OR cers) (kyoto OR co2 OR emission OR emissions)) OR "certified emission reduction")
("affordable energy")	("environmental footprint")	("micro cogeneration")	((cdm (climate OR co2 OR carbon))
("algal energy")	("environmental protection" OR "environment protection")	("natural resources")	("carbon development mechanism"))
("alternative energy" OR "alternative fuel")	("environmental regulation")	("non ets")	((emission reduction (unit OR units))
("arctic meltdown")	("environmental savings")	("oil spill")	((Kyoto OR CO2 OR warming) (ERU OR ERUs)))
("building stocks")	("ets reform")		((eu OR european OR unified) "power market" OR "electricity market")
("car sharing" OR "car share" OR carsharing OR carshare)	("expenditure of energy" OR "energy expenditure")		((ipcc (eu OR climate OR energy))
("carbon bubble")	("feed in tariff" OR "feed in tariffs")		(intergovernmental panel "climate change")
("carbon cap" (emission OR trade OR climate))	("fossil fuel" OR "fossil fuels")		((ipcc climate) assessment (impact OR report))
("carbon credits")	("fuel cost" OR "fuel costs")		((quota OR quotas) (renewable OR renewables))
("carbon dioxide" (emission OR emissions))	("fuel efficient" (car OR cars OR vehicle OR vehicles))		((reduce OR reducing) ("greenhouse gas" OR GHG) (emission OR emissions))
("carbon footprint")	("geo engineering" or "geoengineering")		((smart OR smarter) energy infrastructure)
("carbon leakage")	("geothermal energy" OR "thermal energy")		((vehicle ("zero emissions" OR "zero emission"))
("carbon lock in")	("global warming" OR globalwarming)		(zev (car OR vehicle)))
("carbon price")	("green cars")		((vsc (carbon OR climate)))
("carbon tax" OR "carbon taxes" OR "carbon taxation")	("green chemistry")		(verified carbon (standard OR standards)))
("clean energy")	("green economy")		(95g fleet)
("clean growth")	("green energy")		(actonclimate)
("clean tech")	("green growth")		(alternative energy sources)
("climate action" OR "action on climate" OR climateaction)	("green job" OR "green jobs" OR "greener jobs")		(anthropogenic "climate change")
("climate adaptation")	("green transportation" OR "green transport")		(biofuel OR biofuels)
("climate change")	("grid control" OR (control "power grid"))		(biomass)
("climate deal")	("heat insulation")		(carbon (credit OR credits) (trading OR auctioning))
("climate denier" OR "climate deniers")	("hydro power" OR hydropower)		(carbon energy intensity)
("climate finance")	("hydroelectric energy")		(chemtrail OR chemtrails)
("climate goal" OR "climate goals")	("icecap meltdown")		(cleantech (investment OR investments))
("climate mitigation")	("industry exemptions")		(climate energy (target OR targets))
("climate policy")	("intelligent networks")		(climate resilient economy)
("climate report" OR "report on climate")	("joint implementation")		(climate2015)
("climate sensitivity")	("kyoto protocol")		(climatechange)
("climate system")	("life cycle approach")		(co2)
("co2 neutral")	("light duty" vehicles)		(cop19 OR "cop 19" OR (cop warsaw))
("coal industry" OR "oil industry" OR "nuclear industry" OR "gas industry")	("low carbon")		(cop20 OR "cop 20" OR (cop peru))
("cohesion policy")			(cop21 OR "cop 21" OR (cop paris))
("district heating")			(cross border infrastructure)
("e bike" OR ebike)			(decarbonisation)
("e mobility" OR emobility)			(deforestation)
("eco design")			(demand side management)
("eco entrepreneurship")			(desertec)
("eco technologies")			(desertification)

Table 6 Queries for the "Environmental dataset" acquisition from the Twitter Search API

("effort sharing")
("electric motors" OR "electric motor")
("electricity costs" or "electricity costs")

("electricity mix")
("electricity storage" OR "energy storage")
("emission reduction" OR "emission reductions")
("emission trading" OR "emission trade")
("energy affordability")

("energy company" OR "energy companies")
("energy consumption")

("energy cost" OR "cost of energy")
("energy crisis" OR "crisis of energy")
("energy demand" OR "demand for energy")
("energy efficiency")
("energy efficient" (building OR buildings OR car OR cars OR home OR homes OR vehicle OR vehicles))
("energy efficient" (tech OR technology OR technologies))
("energy firm" OR "energy firms")
("energy future" OR "future of energy")
("energy generation" OR "electricity generation")

("energy independent" OR "energy independence")
("energy intensity")

("energy intensive" (industry OR sector OR business))
("energy market")
("energy mix")
("energy performance")
("energy policy")
("energy price" OR "energy prices")
("energy production")
("energy productivity")
("energy savings" OR "energy saving" OR "conserving energy" OR "energy conservation")
("energy sector")
("energy security")

("permanent set aside")
("polar meltdown")
("power blackout" OR "energy blackout" OR "electricity blackout")
("power plant" OR "coal plant" OR "gas plant")
("renewable energy" OR renewables")
("resource efficiency")
("sea level rise")
("shale gas" OR "unconventional gas" OR "unconventional hydrocarbons")
("smart grid" (energy OR electricity OR supply OR power))
("smarter city" OR "smart city" OR "smarter cities" OR "smart cities")
("solar panel" OR "solar panels")
("solar power" OR "solar energy")
("stranded assets" OR strandedassets)
("sustainable finance" OR "sustainable investment")
("sustainable manufacturing")
("tar sand" OR "oil sand")
("temp rise")
("transport sector")
("unburnable carbon" OR "unburnable coal")
("warming mitigation")
("waste management")
("wind farm")
("wind power" OR "wind energy")
("wind turbine" OR "wind turbines")
("zero emissions" OR "zero emission")
("combined heat power")
chp (climate OR energy OR electricity)))
(("emissions trading system") OR "eu ets")
(("energy efficiency directive")
(energy eed))
(("greenhouse gas" OR ghg) (emission OR emissions))
(("zero emissions" OR "zero emission" OR "low energy" house))

(eco best invest)
(emission allocation)
(emission cap)

(energy (price OR prices) (peak OR peaks))
(energy climate policy framework)
(energy efficiency (improvement OR improvements))
(energy efficiency policy)
(energy import dependency)

(energy supply security)
(energyaware OR "energy aware")

(environmentalist OR environmentalists)
(eu energy legislation)
(forestfinance)
(fossilfuel OR fossilfuels)
(fracking OR fracked)

(fukushima)
(global carbon (trading OR market))
(green climate (fund OR funds))
(greentech OR "green tech" OR "green technology" OR "green technologies")
(greenvc)
(model shift (climate OR CO2 OR environment OR carbon OR warming OR energy))
(pollution)
(primary energy consumption)
(recycling)
(renewableenergy)
(second generation (biofuel OR biofuels))
(single energy market)
(stopfracking)
(sustainability)
(sustainable2050)

(wholesale (energy OR electricity) (cost OR prices OR price))

("nuclear power" OR "solar power" OR "geothermal power" OR "thermal power" OR "electrical power" OR "electric power")
((industry OR sector OR bussines) specific (targets OR target) (energy OR climate OR EU OR emission OR emissions))
((offshore OR onshore) (climate OR CO2 OR environment OR carbon OR warming OR energy OR oil OR gas OR fracking OR wind))
(power (coal OR gas OR oil OR biomass OR diesel OR biogas OR photovoltaic OR thermoelectric OR hydrogen OR fuel OR climate OR emission OR emissions OR CO2 OR carbon OR electricity OR fusion OR fission OR generation OR turbine))

Competing interests
The authors declare that they have no competing interests.

Authors' contributions
BS and IM conceived and designed the experiments. BS and JS performed the experiments. BS, JS, IM, and SB analyzed the data and results and wrote the paper. All authors read and approved the final manuscript.

Acknowledgements
This work was supported in part by the European Commission under the FP7 projects SIMPOL (Financial Systems SIMulation and POLicy Modelling, grant no. 610704) and MULTIPLEX (Foundational Research on MULTIlevel comPLEX networks and systems, grant no. 317532), by the H2020 project DOLFINS (Distributed Global Financial Systems for Society, grant no. 640772), and by the Slovenian Research Agency programme Knowledge Technologies (grant no. P2-103). We thank Matjaž Juršič for his help on the construction of retweet networks, Petra Kralj Novak, Miha Grčar and Martin Žnidaršič for their help on sentiment models, their evaluation, and tweet preprocessing.

Author details
[1]Department of Knowledge Technologies, Jožef Stefan Institute, Ljubljana, Slovenia. [2]Department of Banking and Finance, University of Zurich, Zurich, Switzerland.

References
1. Dorsey, J, Williams, E, Stone, B, Glass, N, Twitter online social networking service. http://www.twitter.com/. Accessed: Feb 15, 2015
2. Cha, M, Haddadi, H, Benevenuto, F, Gummadi, PK: Measuring user influence in twitter: the million follower fallacy. ICWSM. **10**, 10–17 (2010)
3. Avnit, A: The million followers fallacy. Pravda Media Group, Tel Aviv, Israel (2009)
4. Suh, B, Hong, L, Pirolli, P, Chi, EH: Want to be retweeted? Large scale analytics on factors impacting retweet in twitter network. In: 2010 IEEE Second Intl. Conf. on Social Computing, pp. 177–184. IEEE, Piscataway, New Jersey, (2010)
5. Bakshy, E, Hofman, JM, Mason, WA, Watts, DJ: Everyone's an influencer: quantifying influence on twitter. In: Proc. Fourth ACM Intl. Conf. on Web Search and Data Mining, pp. 65–74. ACM, New York City, New York, (2011)
6. Conover, M, Ratkiewicz, J, Francisco, M, Gonçalves, B, Menczer, F, Flammini, A: Political polarization on twitter. In: Proc. Fifth Intl. Conf. on Weblogs and Social Media (ICWSM). AAAI, Palo Alto, California, (2011)
7. Conover, MD, Gonçalves, B, Ratkiewicz, J, Flammini, A, Menczer, F: Predicting the political alignment of twitter users. In: Privacy, Security, Risk and Trust, 2011 IEEE Third Intl. Conf. on Social Computing, pp. 192–199. IEEE, Piscataway, New Jersey, (2011)
8. Agarwal, A, Xie, B, Vovsha, I, Rambow, O, Passonneau, R: Sentiment analysis of twitter data. In: Proceedings of the Workshop on Languages in Social Media, pp. 30–38. Association for Computational Linguistics, Stroudsburg, PA, USA, (2011)
9. Bollen, J, Mao, H, Zeng, X: Twitter mood predicts the stock market. J. Comput. Sci. **2**(1), 1–8 (2011)
10. Gayo-Avello, D: A meta-analysis of state-of-the-art electoral prediction from twitter data. Soc. Sci. Comput. Rev. **31**(6), 649–679 (2013)
11. Smailović, J: Sentiment Analysis in Streams of Microblogging Posts. PhD thesis, Jožef Stefan International Postgraduate School, Ljubljana, Slovenia (2014)
12. Vapnik, VN: The Nature of Statistical Learning Theory. Springer, New York, NY, USA (1995)
13. Go, A, Bhayani, R, Huang, L. Twitter sentiment classification using distant supervision. CS224N Project Report, Stanford, 1–12 (2009)
14. Sluban, B, Smailović, J, Juršič, M, Mozetič, I, Battiston, S: Community sentiment on environmental topics in social networks. In: Proceeding of the Tenth International Conference on Signal-Image Technology & Internet-Based Systems, pp. 376–382. IEEE Computer Society, Washington, DC, USA, (2014)
15. Fortunato, S: Community detection in graphs. Phys. Rep. **486**, 75–174 (2010)
16. Blondel, VD, Guillaume, J-L, Lambiotte, R, Lefebvre, E: Fast unfolding of communities in large networks. J. Stat. Mech.: Theory Exp. **2008**(10), 10008 (2008)
17. Newman, MEJ: Modularity and community structure in networks. Proc. Natl. Acad. Sci. U. S. A. **103**(23), 8577–8582 (2006)
18. Lancichinetti, A, Fortunato, S: Community detection algorithms: a comparative analysis. Phys. Rev. E. **80**(5), 056117 (2009)
19. Werden, GJ: Using the Herfindahl–Hirschman index. In: Phlips, L (ed.) Applied Industrial Economics, pp. 368–374. Cambridge University Press, Cambridge, UK, (1998)
20. Feldman, R, Sanger, J: Text Mining Handbook: Advanced Approaches in Analyzing Unstructured Data. Cambridge University Press, New York, NY, USA (2006)
21. Joachims, T: A support vector method for multivariate performance measures. In: Proceedings of the 22nd International Conference on Machine Learning, pp. 377–384. ACM, New York City, New York, (2005)
22. Joachims, T: Training linear SVMs in linear time. In: Proceedings of the 12th ACM SIGKDD International Conference on Knowledge Discovery and Data Mining, pp. 217–226. ACM, New York City, New York, (2006)
23. Joachims, T, Yu, C-NJ: Sparse kernel SVMs via cutting-plane training. Mach. Learn. **76**(2-3), 179–193 (2009)
24. Smailović, J, Grčar, M, Lavrač, N, Žnidaršič, M: Stream-based active learning for sentiment analysis in the financial domain. Inf. Sci. **285**, 181–203 (2014)

25. Smailović, J, Grčar, M, Lavrač, N, Žnidaršič, M: Predictive sentiment analysis of tweets: A stock market application. In: Human-Computer Interaction and Knowledge Discovery in Complex, Unstructured, Big Data. Lecture Notes in Computer Science, pp. 77–88. Springer, Berlin Heidelberg, (2013)
26. Feldman, R, Sanger, J: Text Mining Handbook: Advanced Approaches in Analyzing Unstructured Data. Cambridge University Press, New York, NY, USA (2006)
27. Baccianella, S, Esuli, A, Sebastiani, F: Evaluation measures for ordinal regression. In: Intelligent Systems Design and Applications, 2009. ISDA'09. Ninth International Conference On, pp. 283–287. IEEE, Piscataway, New Jersey, (2009)
28. Kiritchenko, S, Zhu, X, Mohammad, SM: Sentiment analysis of short informal texts. J. Artif. Intell. Res. **50**, 723–762 (2014)
29. Zhang, W, Skiena, S: Trading strategies to exploit blog and news sentiment. In: Proc. Fourth Intl. AAAI Conf. on Weblogs and Social Media (ICWSM), pp. 375–378. AAAI, Palo Alto, California, (2010)
30. Newman, MEJ: Power laws, Pareto distributions and Zipf's law. Contemp. Phys. **46**(5), 323–351 (2005)
31. Obama's EPA Conducts Dangerous Human Experiments. Investors.com. http://news.investors.com/ibd-editorials/040414-696061-epa-conducts-pollution-experiments-on-humans.htm. Accessed: Sep 5, 2014
32. Cardoso, JS, Da Costa, JFP: Learning to classify ordinal data: the data replication method. J. Mach. Learn. Res. **8**, 1393–1429 (2007)
33. Crammer, K, Singer, Y: On the algorithmic implementation of multiclass kernel-based vector machines. J. Mach. Learn. Res. **2**, 265–292 (2002)
34. Twitter search API. Twitter, Inc. https://dev.twitter.com/rest/public/search. Accessed: Jan 1, 2014

Permissions

List of Contributors

Omid Atabati
Department of Economics, University of Calgary, 2500 University Drive NW, Calgary, AB T2N 1N4, Canada

Babak Farzad
Department of Mathematics, Brock University, 500 Glenridge Ave., St. Catharines, ON L2S 3A1, Canada

Vu H. Nguyen and Hien T. Nguyen
Faculty of Information Technology, Ton Duc Thang University, Ho Chi Minh City, Vietnam

Vaclav Snasel
Faculty of Electrical Engineering and Computer Science, VSB-Technical University of Ostrava, Ostrava, Czech Republic

Rundong Du
School of Mathematics, Georgia Institute of Technology, 686 Cherry Street, Atlanta, GA 30332-0160, USA

Da Kuang
Department of Mathematics, University of California, Los Angeles, 520 Portola Plaza, Los Angeles, CA 90095-1555, USA

Haesun Park
School of Computational Science and Engineering, Georgia Institute of Technology, 266 Ferst Drive, Atlanta, GA 30332-0765, USA

Barry Drake
School of Computational Science and Engineering, Georgia Institute of Technology, 266 Ferst Drive, Atlanta, GA 30332-0765, USA
Georgia Tech Research Institute, Georgia Institute of Technology, 250 14th Street, Atlanta, GA 30318, USA

Ashwin Bahulkar
Rensselaer Polytechnic Institute, 110 8th St., Troy, NY 12180, USA

Boleslaw K. Szymanski
Rensselaer Polytechnic Institute, 110 8th St., Troy, NY 12180, USA
Społeczna Akademia Nauk, Lodz, Poland

Kevin Chan
US Arm Research Laboratory, Adelphi, MD 20783, USA

Omar Lizardo
University of Notre Dame, Notre Dame, IN 46556, USA

Siman Zhang
College of Computer Science and Technology, Nanjing University of Aeronautics and Astronautics, Nanjing, China

Jiping Zheng
College of Computer Science and Technology, Nanjing University of Aeronautics and Astronautics, Nanjing, China
Collaborative Innovation Center of Novel Software Technology and Industrialization, Nanjing, China

Fernando Rosas
Centre of Complexity Science and Department of Mathematics, Imperial College London, Kensington, London SW72AZ, UK

Deniz Gündüz
Department of Electrical and Electronic Engineering, Imperial College London, Kensington, London SW72AZ, UK

Kwang-Cheng Chen
Department of Electrical Engineering, University of South Florida, 4202 E Fowler Ave, Tampa, FL 33620, USA

Weili Wu
College of Computer Science and Technology, Taiyuan University of Technology, Taiyuan 030024, China
Department of Computer Science, University of Texas at Dallas, 800 W. Campbell Rd, Richardson, TX 75080, USA

Xuming Zhai and Wen Xu
Department of Computer Science, University of Texas at Dallas, 800 W. Campbell Rd, Richardson, TX 75080, USA

Eleni Stai, Vasileios Karyotis and Symeon Papavassiliou
School of Electrical and Computer Engineering, National Technical University of Athens (NTUA), 15780 Zografou, Athens, Greece

Aleksandr Dorodnykh
Moscow Institute of Physics and Technology (SU), Moscow, Russia

Yana Kashinskaya
Moscow Institute of Physics and Technology (SU), Moscow, Russia
Skolkovo Institute of Science and Technology, Moscow, Russia

Akmal Artikov
Moscow Institute of Physics and Technology (SU), Moscow, Russia
Yandex, Moscow, Russia

Egor Samosvat
Yandex, Moscow, Russia

James Atwood and Don Towsley
School of Computer Science, University of Massachusetts Amherst, 01003, Amherst, MA, USA

Bruno Ribeiro
School of Computer Science, Carnegie Mellon University, 15213, Pittsburgh, PA, USA

Zaixin Lu, Lidan Fan, Weili Wu, Bhavani Thuraisingham and Kai Yang
Department of Computer Science, University of Texas at Dallas, 800 W. Campbell Road, Richardson, TX 75080, USA

Borut Sluban, Jasmina Smailović and Igor Mozetič
Department of Knowledge Technologies, Jožef Stefan Institute, Ljubljana, Slovenia

Stefano Battiston
Department of Banking and Finance, University of Zurich, Zurich, Switzerland

Index